Norming the Abnormal

Norming the Abnormal

*The Development and Function
of the Doctrine of Initial Evidence
in Classical Pentecostalism*

Aaron T. Friesen

⌒PICKWICK *Publications* • Eugene, Oregon

NORMING THE ABNORMAL
The Development and Function of the Doctrine of Initial Evidence in Classical Pentecostalism

Copyright © 2013 Aaron T. Friesen. All rights reserved. Except for brief quotations in critical publications or reviews, no part of this book may be reproduced in any manner without prior written permission from the publisher. Write: Permissions. Wipf and Stock Publishers, 199 W. 8th Ave., Suite 3, Eugene, OR 97401.

Pickwick Publications
An Imprint of Wipf and Stock Publishers
199 W. 8th Ave., Suite 3
Eugene, OR 97401

www.wipfandstock.com

ISBN 13: 978-1-62032-236-9

Cataloguing-in-Publication Data

Friesen, Aaron T.

Norming the abnormal : the development and function of the doctrine of initial evidence in classical Pentecostalism.

xxii + 298 p. ; 23 cm. —Includes bibliographical references.

ISBN 13: 978-1-62032-236-9

1. Glossolalia. 2. Baptism in the Holy Spirit. 3. Pentecostalism. 4. Language and languages—Religious aspects—Christianity. I. Title.

BT122.5 F853 2013

Manufactured in the U.S.A.

Dedicated to Heather,
my partner in life and ministry

Contents

Tables, Graphs, and Figures | viii
Foreword | xi
Acknowledgments | xv
Introduction | xix
Abbreviations | xxi

1. Pentecostal Definition and Speaking in Tongues | 1
2. Early Theological Approaches to the Evidence of Spirit Baptism | 40
3. The Emergence of a "Classical" Tradition in Pentecostalism | 83
4. Explications, Criticisms, and Derivatives of the Classical Pentecostal Tradition | 120
5. The Function of the Doctrine of Initial Evidence in the History of Classical Pentecostalism | 154
6. Spirit Baptism & Speaking in Tongues | 194
7. The Doctrine of Initial Evidence in the Future of Pentecostalism | 245

Appendix: Spirit Baptism Belief & Practice Survey | 273

Bibliography | 281

Tables, Graphs, and Figures

Tables

Table 6.01 *Gender of Sample* | 205
Table 6.02 *Age of Sample* | 206
Table 6.03 *Education of Sample* | 206
Table 6.04 *Percentage Decline and Growth of Minister's Congregations in Past Year* | 207
Table 6.05 *Average Congregational Weekend Attendance by Denomination* | 207
Table 6.06 *Frequency of Baptism in the Holy Spirit* | 208
Table 6.07 *Frequency of Speaking in Tongues When Baptized in the Holy Spirit* | 209
Table 6.08 *Age When Baptized in the Holy Spirit* | 209
Table 6.09 *Duration of Time Between Conversion and Baptism in the Holy Spirit* | 210
Table 6.10 *Frequency of Individual Experiences of Glossolalia in the Past Three Months* | 211
Table 6.11 *Frequency of Individual Experiences of Glossolalia in the Last Three Months by Denomination* | 212
Table 6.12 *Revelatory Experience (RevlExp) Scale* | 214
Table 6.13 *Prayer Language Experience (PrLangExp) Scale* | 214
Table 6.14 *Frequency of Speaking in Tongues Privately* | 215
Table 6.15 *Visible Manifestations Experience (VisbManExp) Scale* | 215

Tables, Graphs, and Figures

Table 6.16 One-way Analysis of Variance: Denomination by Charismatic Experience Scales | 216
Table 6.17 Agreement with "Finished-Work" Doctrine of Sanctification | 217
Table 6.18 General Results of Spirit Baptism | 218
Table 6.19 Practical Helps Item Scores | 218
Table 6.20 Practical Helps (BHSpractical) Scale | 219
Table 6.21 One-way Analysis of Variance: BHSpractical by Denomination | 220
Table 6.22 Multiple Comparisons of Means (Bonferroni): BHSpractical by Denomination | 220
Table 6.23 Agreement with Denominational Doctrinal Statements on Spirit Baptism | 222
Table 6.24 Holy Spirit Reception at Conversion & Water Baptism | 224
Table 6.25 Multiple Spirit Baptisms | 225
Table 6.26 Spirit Baptism Rigidity (BHSrigid) Scale | 226
Table 6.27 One-way Analysis of Variance: BHSrigid by Denomination | 227
Table 6.28 Multiple Comparisons of Means (Bonferroni): BHSrigid by Denomination | 227
Table 6.29 BHSrigid Scale Score by Experience of Evidential Tongues | 228
Table 6.30 BHSrigid Scale Score by Frequency of Speaking in Tongues Privately | 228
Table 6.31 Correlation Coefficients (r): Glossolalic Experience Adjectives | 229
Table 6.32 Correlation Coefficient Matrix (r): BHS Rigid + Practical Helps | 231
Table 6.33 Other Beliefs Associated with a Rigid Doctrine of Initial Evidence (BHSrigid) | 232
Table 6.34 One-way Analysis of Variance: BHSrigid by Age Group (Entire Sample) | 234
Table 6.35 One-way Analysis of Variance: BHSrigid by Age Group (Open Bible & Foursquare only) | 235
Table 6.36 BHSrigid Mean Values by Level of Degree (Open Bible & Foursquare only) | 237

Tables, Graphs, and Figures

Table 6.37   *Percentage Congregation Grew Last Year by Ministerial Charismatic Activity Level* | 239

Table 6.38   *Ministerial Charismatic Activity (CharAct) by Percentage Congregation Grew Last Year* | 239

Table 6.39   *BHSrigid Mean by Congregational Weekend Attendance (Open Bible & Foursquare only)* | 241

Graphs

Graph 6.1   *Mean Age vs. BHSrigid (Open Bible & Foursquare only)* | 236

Figures

Figure 6.1   *Spirit Baptism Belief & Practice Survey: Conceptual Model* | 195

Figure 6.2   *Antecedents to Three Classical Pentecostal "Finished-Work" Denominations: Assemblies of God (USA), The Foursquare Church and Open Bible Churches* | 201

Foreword

WHEN DURING THE FOURTH quinnquennium of the International Catholic-Pentecostal Dialogue David Barrett published research reporting that a mere 35 percent of Pentecostal church members have actually spoken in tongues, the following exchange took place:

"So," the Catholic team began, "you have told us that a Pentecostal is a person who has received the Baptism with the Holy Spirit."

"Yes," the Pentecostals replied.

"And the initial evidence of having received the Baptism with the Spirit is speaking in tongues."

"Yes," answered the Pentecostals.

"Well then," the Catholics queried, "are these 65 percent of the people in your churches who do not speak in tongues Pentecostal?"

It was a logical and good question.

Though in its earliest days there was certainly diversity within the burgeoning Pentecostal movement on the question of whether or not speaking in tongues constituted the initial, physical evidence of having received the Baptism with the Holy Spirit, by 1918 the Assemblies of God could assert that the doctrine constituted its "distinctive testimony."

The wider embrace of the doctrine was at first strengthened through the formation of the World Pentecostal Fellowship and The Pentecostal Fellowship of North America, both of whose statements of faith affirmed it.

But slowly things began to change.

For one thing, beginning in the late 1940s, Pentecostals began having more fellowship with Evangelicals, some of who eventually wrote influential books that called into question the biblical validity of the doctrine. Through the Charismatic Movement of the 1960s and 1970s and then later through the so-called "Third Wave" Pentecostals, such as John Wimber and the Vineyard Movement, classical Pentecostals began to meet believers who embraced the Baptism with the Holy Spirit but did not consider it to be a distinct work of grace subsequent to salvation and who may or may not have spoken in tongues.

By 1988 precise doctrinal formulations of Baptism with the Holy Spirit had diversified to the point where Henry Lederle's taxonomy could identify over twenty different ways of formulating the experience and doctrine! By the time of the publication of Margaret Poloma's 1989 study of the beliefs and practices concerning a variety of charismatic experiences in the Assemblies of God, USA it had become clear that there was significant conflict in classical Pentecostal churches between their stated belief and the actual practices in their churches, a conflict even more notable among younger adherents.

For denominational officials of classical Pentecostal churches this conflict and diversity of perspective represents a challenge to some of the traditional formulations of their respective churches and raises a question of how to respond. For Pentecostal pastors on the ground, like myself, who are attempting to negotiate the reality of peoples' increasingly busy schedules and limited grounding in particular sectarian doctrines in a decidedly post-denominational age, and who themselves have often run into significant biblical, theological, and pastoral problems with a rigid doctrine of evidential tongues, it raises questions of precisely how they can incorporate Baptism with the Holy Spirit and speaking in tongues into the evangelistic, instructional and liturgical life of their congregations.

What should we think about this? Is the doctrine of speaking in tongues as the initial physical evidence of having received the Baptism with the Holy Spirit important? Is it a non-negotiable core distinctive of Pentecostalism? Or can the biblical and historical experience of Spirit Baptism be thought about and expressed in different ways? Is it important for classical Pentecostal denominations to retain this doctrine? Or is it helpful for them to rethink it? And what might be some ramifications of either retaining or reconsidering it?

This demands some hefty conversation! But our discussions will be wiser and more helpful if we take time to consider such questions as how the doctrinal formulations of Spirit Baptism originally took place, how they were affected by developments over the past century of Pentecostal-Charismatic history and especially what functions those doctrines have performed in the life and ministry of classical Pentecostal churches. And here is where contributions such as Aaron Friesen's can help.

Foreword

After defining his terms and the limits and methodology of his research, Friesen charts the history of the doctrine of initial evidence, beginning with three representatives of the earliest period, Charles Parham, William Seymour, and Alexander Boddy. An explication of the emergence of the classical tradition of Pentecostalism in North America from 1910–40 is followed by a survey of the diverse developments of the period from 1940 to the present that began to criticize and question some of the classical Pentecostal formulations and practices.

At this point Friesen uses the categories of George Lindbeck and Alistair McGrath to explore the precise functions the doctrine of initial evidence has performed in the classical Pentecostal churches. Then, interacting with survey data obtained from three "finished-work" classical Pentecostal denominations—The Assemblies of God, (which he terms "Distinctive") the Open Bible Standard Churches ("Post-distinctive") and The Foursquare Church ("Non-distinctive"), Friesen asks whether the doctrine is still performing these functions today. He concludes with considerations for charting a course for the future that can be both faithful to the original Pentecostal movement and more consistent with the present experience of its members.

The precise location of Pentecostal origins will continue to be debated, as will the essential nature of its genius. In the meantime Pentecostal and Charismatic scholars, leaders and pastors must wrestle with how the fourfold gospel can be talked about and practiced in a new and global century. Friesen's contribution provides both knowledge and wisdom that can help us fulfill our desire to move forward in ways that are pleasing to the Lord and a true blessing to the peoples of the world.

Reverend Steve Overman
Eugene, Oregon, USA

Acknowledgments

THIS WORK COULD NEVER have been written without the help of many people and institutions along the way. It is truly humbling to realize how many people have supported this project in various ways. Although I am very grateful for the help I have received in the research and writing of this work, I am ultimately responsible for the contents. Any mistakes are my own.

First, I want to acknowledge those who inspired me to pursue this research project. I am a fifth generation Pentecostal. Even though I grew up attending a Pentecostal church, I didn't become interested in Pentecostalism as a movement until learning about my own family history. My great-grandmother's stories about the Welsh Revivals, my grandmother's experiences of visiting Angelus Temple as a little girl, my grandfather's accounts of "holy-roller" churches in the small farming communities of Southern California, and my parents' stories of worshipping as youth at Calvary Chapel in Costa Mesa, California, all introduced me to the depth and variety that exist in North American Pentecostalism. Their stories inspired me to look at my own heritage more closely.

As a graduate student at Fuller Theological Seminary, I took an independent study class from Dr. Cecil Robeck on Pentecostal history that changed me forever. It was Dr. Robeck who first exposed me to the whole field of Pentecostal studies and encouraged me to explore the wealth of historical documentation on Pentecostalism in the Fuller Seminary Archives.

Second, I want to acknowledge some of the many individuals who helped with the research and writing for this project. I want to thank my doctoral supervisor, Professor William Kay, for his encouragement and help in narrowing the scope of the project and his great insights into Pentecostal history. I am especially grateful for his extensive help in constructing the research survey and the presentation of the results in chapter six.

Acknowledgments

William has not only been a great supervisor, but a great friend in this process. I am also thankful to Dr. Andrew Davies for his insights and constructive criticisms on the historical portion of the dissertation.

I was very blessed to have Gary Matsdorf take time to be a proofreader and editor for this work in the final stages of writing.

I am indebted to all the librarians and archivists who have helped me in finding and documenting many of the sources in the historical portion of this dissertation: William Molenaar, Catherine McGee and Darren Rodgers at the Flower Pentecostal Heritage Center; Jan Hornshuh-Kent and Sharon Welker at the Open Bible Heritage Center and Open Bible National Office; Jorge Sandoval at the Foursquare Church Archives; Nancy Gower at the Fuller Theological Seminary Archives (David du Plessis, Society for Pentecostal Studies); Erica Rutland at the International Pentecostal Holiness Church Archives and Research Center; and David Garrard at the Donald Gee Pentecostal Research Center. I am especially grateful for the generous help from the Inter-Library Loan office at the Iowa State University Library that retrieved sources for me from all over the United States and even overseas with efficiency and accuracy.

I am very appreciative of those people who trusted me and worked with me to disseminate the research survey to ministers in their respective denomination: Sherri Doty, Gary Allen and George Wood in the Assemblies of God; Lisa Penberthy, Glen Burris and Beth Mead in the Foursquare Church; Mary Johnston and Jeff Farmer in Open Bible Churches. I am also grateful to the many members of Lifehouse Community Church in Des Moines who gave their feedback on the survey.

I am also grateful to Gavin Wakefield and Kim Alexander for allowing me early access to articles before publication.

Third, I want to acknowledge all those who helped me finish this project by encouraging and supporting me throughout this difficult season of life. My employers during this time have been gracious and understanding. Lifehouse Community Church and New Hope Christian College not only allowed me time away from other important duties to research and write, but also encouraged me along the way.

I am thankful for the encouragement, support and criticism I received from many friends in the Society for Pentecostal Studies.

I am very grateful to my friend and mentor, Paul Leavenworth, who not only arranged a workspace for me to write at the Open Bible National Office, but also pushed me and challenged me to keep going when I felt like quitting. I am also indebted to my parents and grandparents for their

Acknowledgments

support of this project financially and, more importantly, with their hearts. Their legitimate interest in this project, and their belief that this project was valuable and beneficial for the church, were a great encouragement to me through difficult times of research and writing.

Most of all, I am thankful for my wife, Heather. She has owned this project as much as I have. Through working, mothering, housekeeping, and countless other roles she has done whatever was needed for me to finish this project and still maintain a somewhat comfortable and normal life for our family. She has given me constant encouragement to "go write," even when she could have reasonably expected me to spend time with her and the boys. Throughout the entire process from start to finish, she has not only allowed me the freedom to go and write, but encouraged me that this was a valuable project and worth all the effort and sacrifice. She has been much more than an equal partner in this endeavor, and there is no way this work could have been finished without her love and support.

Introduction

GROWING UP, I KNEW I was a Pentecostal, but I never really knew what that meant until I was around non-Pentecostals.

In 2002, I began graduate studies at Fuller Theological Seminary in Pasadena, California. As a non-denominational seminary, Fuller attracted students from all kinds of traditions and cultures within Christendom. I remember one ecclesiology class where there was a Roman Catholic sitting in front of me, a Quaker on my left, a Methodist on my right, and a Presbyterian and Lutheran behind me. In this environment, one of the first questions you would ask to get to know somebody was, "What denomination are you from?" I remember when that question was first asked of me, I would answer, "Open Bible." I realized quickly that nobody at Fuller had ever heard of my small denomination, so I began to follow my answer with a comment about it being a small Pentecostal denomination. I was caught off-guard when a number of students responded to my claim of Pentecostal identity by asking something like, "Oh, so you believe that speaking in tongues is the evidence of the Baptism in the Holy Spirit?"

Of all the ways I could have categorized or defined my identity as a Pentecostal, this was one that I had never considered. I grew up in one of the flagship churches of the Open Bible denomination. During my undergraduate studies, I attended a large Foursquare Church. Despite this Pentecostal heritage, I could count the number of sermons I heard about speaking in tongues on one hand. Further, I could not remember hearing anything about tongues being an evidence of Spirit Baptism until my last year of Bible College in a class I took called Current Pentecostal Thought. Even then, it was mentioned as a side-note to the major events in Pentecostal history. Thus, when my classmates at Fuller assumed that one of my guiding tenets was a belief that speaking in tongues evidenced the Baptism in the Holy Spirit, I didn't know what to say.

Introduction

This loss for words generated questions that I would investigate and wrestle with throughout my time in seminary. Am I a Pentecostal? If I am a Pentecostal, what does that mean? What does it mean to be baptized in the Spirit? What, if anything, does speaking in tongues have to do with all of this? My search for answers to these questions eventually led to the research and study that has produced this present work. Many Pentecostals throughout the past century have asked these same questions, and they have answered them in many different ways. This work is an attempt to capture some of this richness and diversity within a fairly narrow circle: North American "finished-work" Pentecostalism.

Unfortunately, the above questions of Pentecostal identity and the relationship of Spirit Baptism to speaking in tongues have also led to heated arguments, factions, and exclusions. Pentecostals have often struggled to have fruitful conversations and debates amongst themselves about the meaning and significance of the narratives and experiences of the Holy Spirit that they hold in common. It is my hope that this work will contribute to better discussions through a deeper understanding of the history and collective experiences of Pentecostals and by highlighting the cultural-linguistic factors that contribute to the function and value of doctrine for a particular community.

Abbreviations

AG	Assemblies of God
ANOVA	Analysis of Variance
BHSpractical	Sprit Baptism Practical Helps Scale
BHSrigid	Spirit Baptism Rigidity Scale
F	F-Ratio Calculation
ICFG	International Church of the Foursquare Gospel
NS	Not Statistically Significant
OBC	Open Bible Churches
P	P-Value Probability
PFNA	Pentecostal Fellowship of North America
PrLangExp	Prayer Language Experience Scale
PWC	Pentecostal World Conference
R	Pearson's R Coefficient (Correlation)
RevlExp	Revelatory Experience Scale
SPS	Society for Pentecostal Studies
SPSS	Statistical Package for the Social Sciences
VisbManExp	Visible Manifestations Experience Scale
WCC	World Council of Churches
α	Cronbach's Alpha Coefficient (Scale Reliability)

1

Pentecostal Definition & Speaking in Tongues

Introduction

EARLY PENTECOSTAL PIONEERS ORIGINALLY envisioned their mission as one of sparking revival within existing church structures and denominations.[1] However, the rejection of the Pentecostal message by "most of organized Christendom" quickly caused early Pentecostals to adjust their goals.[2] Their ideal of awakening a spiritual renewal in what they perceived as frozen and lifeless religious institutions gave way to a practical need for some sort of formal organization for themselves.[3] As Pentecostal groups

---

1. Edith Blumhofer speaks of the "come-outist" urge of early Pentecostals to free themselves of formalism and creeds and emerge as a people whose only creed was the Bible, and only leader was the Holy Spirit. Blumhofer, "Restoration as Revival," 148–50. However, it was originally hoped that this vision for a breakdown of traditional church structures would see its fulfillment within existing churches as a way to forge unity between previously divided Christians. Thus, it is not incorrect to identify the seeds of ecumenism in early Pentecostalism as Cecil Robeck and others have done. Robeck, "Pentecostals and Christian Unity," 310. See also Hollenweger, "Crucial Issues for Pentecostals," 187–88.

2. It was the rejection of the Pentecostal message and those who claimed a Pentecostal experience by "most of organized Christendom" that caused early Pentecostals to form their own organizations and focus on a "spiritual" ecumenism that sought to apply the message of Pentecost non-selectively to all Christians. Kärkkäinen, "Anonymous Ecumenists?" 15–20; Robeck, "Taking Stock of Pentecostalism," 39–45.

3. Kärkkäinen, "Anonymous Ecumenists?" 18. The tension in early Pentecostalism between their logistical need for organizing structures and their disdain for formalism,

began to form—some more loosely than others—the need for a consensual self-definition naturally became important. Discussion concerning what exactly constituted the essentials of Pentecostalism commenced. In the Assemblies of God, the doctrine of initial evidence—that speaking in tongues is the initial evidence of a Christian's Baptism in the Holy Spirit—emerged as their "distinctive testimony."[4] Yet this doctrinal stance may not be the most accurate way to articulate the Pentecostal's "distinctive" contribution to the church either in North America or around the world.

Before 1990, historical research on Pentecostalism tended to focus on North America as the defining point of the worldwide movement based on various interpretations of the origins of Pentecostal distinctives.[5] However, recent studies of the origins of Pentecostal movements in other parts of the world have called into question the validity of a view of history that places North American Pentecostalism at the center of the worldwide movement.[6] Along with the question of Pentecostal origins, answers to the question of Pentecostal definition have also shifted. In recent years, many scholars have sought to look anew at the history of Pentecostalism

---

creeds and denominationalism can be seen in the December 1905 issue of Charles Parham's *Apostolic Faith* [Houston] in which a lengthy reprint of Parham's chapter on "Unity" from *Kol Kare Bomidbar* appears alongside an article condemning "popular churches," and another promoting the movement's headquarters and Bible college in Houston, Texas. Robeck has also identified such a tension in the early years of the General Council of the Assemblies of God who in 1914 argued against formal creeds, but published a "creed-like" statement of Fundamental Truths two years later. Robeck, "An Emerging Magisterium?" 217–18.

4. This is the doctrine formally delineated by the following statement, "The full consummation of the baptism of believers in the Holy Ghost is indicated by the initial physical sign of speaking with other tongues as the Spirit of God gives utterance." *Combined Minutes of the General Council of the Assemblies of God, 1914–1917*, 14. The doctrine was given status as their distinctive testimony two years later. *Minutes of the Sixth Annual Meeting of the General Council of the Assemblies of God, 1918*, 10.

5. For a doctrinal origin of the movement in North America beginning with Parham's doctrine of the "Bible Evidence," see Synan, *The Holiness-Pentecostal Movement in the United States*; Goff, *Fields White Unto Harvest*. See also Dayton, *Theological Roots of Pentecostalism*, 176. Dayton traces the theological antecedents of Pentecostal theology in the North American holiness movement, and affirms the doctrine of initial evidence as the *novum* of Pentecostalism. Hollenweger, in *The Pentecostals: The Charismatic Movement in the Churches*, and more recently in *Pentecostalism: Origins and Developments Worldwide*, also places the locus of Pentecostalism in North America, though not with Parham, but with Seymour, arguing for a "black oral root" of Pentecostalism.

6. Anderson, "Revising Pentecostal History," 147–73; Anderson, *An Introduction to Pentecostalism*, 170–76; Irwin, "Pentecostal Historiography and Global Christianity," 34–50; Wilson, "They Crossed the Red Sea Didn't They?" 85–115.

in order to identify that which is essentially Pentecostal. As a result, the eschatological, sociological, and pragmatic impulses of Pentecostalism have been brought to the fore in debates concerning the driving forces behind Pentecostalism. Studies of the origin and development of Pentecostal movements in non-Western countries have encouraged broader definition and application of the term "Pentecostal." Some scholars have even challenged the validity of *any* core Pentecostalism, instead proposing a range of "Pentecostalisms."[7] In an effort to define Pentecostalism in a way that encompasses the range of diversity present in Pentecostal groups around the world, global Pentecostal scholars have tended to move away from the traditionally accepted delineation of Pentecostals and non-Pentecostals along doctrinal lines. Seeing Pentecostalism as having a kind of amalgamation of doctrines with varying emphases, these scholars have upheld an experience of Spirit Baptism as an equally valid, perhaps more valid, way of defining a Pentecostal.[8] The growing trend in Pentecostal scholarship to define Pentecostals experientially rather than doctrinally has led to the initial evidence doctrine being removed from its place of primacy as *the* defining point of Pentecostalism.

As the doctrine of initial evidence has been increasingly questioned as "a shibboleth of orthodoxy" for Pentecostals,[9] the validity and necessity of such a rigid doctrinal formulation has also been questioned. Its positivistic dualistic slant toward irrefutable proof, its over-reliance on the Book of Acts, and its modernistic approach to the freedom of God's Spirit and

---

7. Robeck, "Making Sense of Pentecostalism," 18. Robeck similarly refers to Pentecostalism as a "Movement of movements." Robeck, Forward to *Asian and Pentecostal*, xi.

8. Allan Anderson has broadly defined the movement in this way: "In its simplest sense the term refers to ecstatic forms of Christianity defined in terms of special gifts given by the Holy Spirit." Anderson, "Revising Pentecostal History," 2. See also Anderson, "Introduction: World Pentecostalism," 19–20; Hollenweger, "From Azusa Street to the Toronto Phenomenon," 7. Robert Mapes Anderson proposed the defining of Pentecostalism along experiential rather than doctrinal lines, though he did so with a view toward Azusa Street as the rightful originating point of the movement. Anderson, *Vision of the Disinherited*, 4. Frank Macchia has noted that the doctrinal diversity in Pentecostalism highlighted by Hollenweger has caused many theologians to assume a separation of Pentecostal experience from Pentecostal doctrine which is not entirely accurate. Macchia, *Baptized in the Spirit: A Global Pentecostal Theology*, 49–57. Juan Sepulveda has argued for the necessity of a broader definition of the term "Pentecostal" that goes beyond "classical" definitions in North America and includes the experiences of Chilean Pentecostals whose self-understanding is centered on the Pentecost event of Acts 2. Juan Sepulveda, "Pentecostalism and the Chilean Experience," 133.

9. This is the phrase used by Jean-Daniel Plüss in "Azusa and Other Myths," 190.

Word have all been cited against the classical Pentecostal doctrine.[10] Many of these criticisms are not new. Pentecostals were challenged to defend the exegetical basis for their beliefs about Spirit Baptism and speaking in tongues from the beginning. However, these criticisms are now coming from Pentecostals—Pentecostals whose identity and self-definition are no longer intimately tied to the results of such a debate.

The move away from this doctrine as the "core" Pentecostal teaching in the academic world reflects what is happening in Pentecostal congregations. Empirical evidence suggests that there is an increasing gap between the beliefs of denominational leaders and pastors and the beliefs of lay people concerning the doctrine of initial evidence in "classical" Pentecostal churches. William Kay is responsible for obtaining many of these figures in Britain, and Margaret Poloma has gathered survey data corroborating this phenomenon in the United States.[11] In fact, Walter Hollenweger noticed a conflict between doctrine and practice among modern-day Pentecostals over two decades ago. He noted,

> Important Pentecostal churches (e.g. in Chile, Germany, Great Britain and other countries) disagree with the doctrine of "the initial physical sign" and believe that the baptism of the Holy Spirit is not always accompanied by this sign. In fact in many Pentecostal churches a great proportion of the members (and sometimes even some of the pastors) have never spoken in

---

10. Jean-Daniel Plüss argues that formalizing of the doctrine of initial evidence caused a change in perspective on speaking in tongues in Pentecostalism. Instead of being understood as a phenomenon of God's grace, it was understood as "basic empirical proof." According to Plüss, this change in perspective divorced the experience of speaking in tongues from its original context and caused an incorrect understanding of the purpose of the phenomenon to emerge in subsequent generations of Pentecostals. "Azusa and Other Myths," 190–91. Macchia recognizes that the works of Robert Menzies and Roger Stronstad nicely elucidate the distinct pneumatology of Luke over against Paul. However, he criticizes the ease with which they emphasize Luke's charismatic perspective without integrating it within context of Paul and the rest of the New Testament. Macchia, *Baptized in the Spirit*, 57–60. Clark Pinnock, despite validating the experience of glossolalia in the church as a way to express the inexpressible to God, argues against a doctrine that makes speaking in tongues normative. For Pinnock, this kind of doctrine places a human limitation on the freedom of the Spirit to teach and guide the church into new dimensions of truth. Clark Pinnock, *Flame of Love*, 172–73.

11. Poloma, *The Assemblies of God at the Crossroads*, 39–40. Kay has documented similar evidence of divergence between belief and practice in his study of British Pentecostals. Kay, *Pentecostals in Britain*, 72–81; "The 'Initial Evidence,'" 25–31. See also Holm, "A Paradigmatic Analysis of Authority within Pentecostalism," 26–41; Barratt, "Global Statistics," 291. For a recent independent survey of Pentecostals in America, see *Spirit and Power: A 10-Country Survey of Pentecostals*, 13–14.

tongues. How the Assemblies of God and other similar bodies are going to solve this conflict between their doctrine and their praxis is an open question.[12]

Pentecostal scholars have proposed many different solutions for dealing with this conflict. Some understand the weakness of classical Pentecostals to be in their defenses of their positions rather than in their positions themselves. As a result, they have written new expositions and canonically grounded treatises on the connection between speaking in tongues and Spirit Baptism that call for the reaffirmation of the classical Pentecostal doctrine of initial evidence in the face of increasing criticism from Charismatics, neo-Pentecostals and non-Pentecostals. They assert the normative character of the classical Pentecostal doctrine of initial evidence even though, in practice, some Pentecostals do not adhere to it.[13] Other theologians have understood the gap between doctrine and practice among Pentecostals as a call to broaden the theological base upon which Pentecostal doctrine is developed.[14] Finally, the last decade of Pentecostal scholarship has often wondered if a formal doctrinal change might be in order, and possibilities for reinterpreting or reformulating the doctrine of initial evidence have been explored.[15]

How are classical Pentecostals experiencing the conflict articulated by Hollenweger to decide between these proposed solutions? Certainly, such proposals raise some pressing questions that need to be answered. First, where did the doctrine come from? In order to assess the veracity of a particular doctrinal statement one must understand how the doctrine came into being and how it developed over time. Second, why is the doctrine important? In order to assess or assign value to a doctrine one needs to understand how the doctrine has functioned in community over time.

---

12. Hollenweger, "Pentecostal Research in Europe," 130–31.

13. Howard Ervin, Harold Hunter, Robert Menzies, and Roger Stronstad are four of the most widely referenced of these authors. In particular, the critical writings of James D. G. Dunn and Dale Bruner are addressed in their defenses of the doctrine. Also in view for Stronstad and Menzies are the criticisms of fellow Pentecostal, Gordon Fee. Ervin, *Conversion-Initiation and the Baptism in the Holy Spirit*; Hunter, *Spirit Baptism: A Pentecostal Alternative*; William Menzies and Robert Menzies, *Spirit and Power*; Stronstad, *The Charismatic Theology of St. Luke*; Dunn, *Baptism in the Holy Spirit*; Bruner, *A Theology of the Holy Spirit*.

14. Macchia, *Baptized in the Spirit*; Simon Chan, *Pentecostal Theology and the Christian Spiritual Tradition*; Yong, *The Spirit Poured Out on All Flesh*.

15. Macchia, "Groans Too Deep for Words," 149–73; Fee, "Baptism in the Holy Spirit: The Issue of Separability and Subsequence," 87–99; Hayford, *The Beauty of Spiritual Language*; Clifton, "The Spirit and Doctrinal Development," 5–23.

Third, what are the practical consequences of the doctrine? In order to judge whether a doctrine is operational or non-operational within a community one needs to explore how the doctrine presently works itself out in the beliefs and practices of the community. In the following chapters, each of these questions will be addressed. In order to set the stage for what follows, I will now undertake some preliminary discussion to: 1) Define the parameters of this project: classical Pentecostalism; 2) Survey significant research contributions in the field of study that will bear on the whole research project; and 3) Describe the chosen methodology for the current research project.

Defining Pentecostalism

A Latter-Rain Movement

Early on, Pentecostals collectively viewed their movement as that which would usher in the Second Coming of Christ by calling believers to be baptized in the Spirit. How exactly this baptism would prepare the way for Christ's return was debated. For some, this would be accomplished through an inward purifying work of the Spirit outwardly testified by speaking in tongues resulting in the emergence of a "spotless Bride." For others, the baptism served the more pragmatic purposes of identifying who was and who was not part of the Bride and calling others to join the Bride through the gift of foreign tongues on the mission field. The common denominator between these two views of Spirit Baptism is their understanding of the Pentecostal movement as a "Latter-Rain" movement.[16] In the early years of the movement, Pentecostals sought to define themselves as a missionary movement preparing the way for Christ's imminent return through the full gospel message. While speaking in tongues was a core element of the Pentecostal experience, Pentecostals sought to focus on Christ's calling out a group of overcomers as his Bride—a call which was signaled by one's reception of this heavenly gift of foreign languages. The Pentecostals' understanding of their movement being formed by God is evident in their providential understanding of Pentecostal history.

The rapid, seemingly unconnected growth and spread of Pentecostal experiences around the world made it easy for those involved in the

---

16. The term "Latter-Rain" was taken from the prophecy in Joel 2:23 (KJV) where God's Spirit would be poured out on all flesh immediately before the Lord's return. This was in contrast to the "former rain" that was understood to have been fulfilled in the outpouring of God's Spirit on the Day of Pentecost in Acts 2.

movement to believe that they were a part of something bigger and greater than themselves.[17] As early as 1907 reports from missionaries sent out around the world by the Azusa Street Mission made their way back to the United States confirming that the Spirit was being experienced with power and manifestations all around the world.[18] The testimony of missionaries led early Azusa reporter Frank Bartleman, along with many others who were intimately involved with the Los Angeles revival, to see the development of Pentecostalism worldwide as ripple effects of the Spirit having been poured out at Azusa Street.[19] Many early biographers of the Pentecostal movement perpetuated the views of Azusa Street participants by uncritically adopting their historical interpretations.[20] Other Pentecostal chroniclers like Stanley Frodsham, Donald Gee, and later, Carl Brumback believed that the Spirit was poured out spontaneously around the world marking the beginning of the "Latter-Rain" by which Christ would purify and prepare his Bride to usher in the Second Coming.[21] Until the 1950s, other than drawing a line of succession back to Azusa Street missionaries in some cases, Pentecostal historians viewed the chief cause of the spread of Pentecostalism globally as standing beyond history. This tendency to understand Pentecostal origins apart from its social or pre-Pentecostal

---

17. Edward Gitre has drawn attention to technological advances of the time (such as the railway) that actually connected people quite well during the Welsh Revival. Technology *annihilated* space and time and contributed to the feeling that the Spirit was *transcending* space and time. Even though the rapid growth and spread of early Pentecostalism seemed unconnected to many participants in the movement, this same phenomenon in North America may have contributed to the providential understanding of history held by many early Pentecostals. Gitre, "The 1904–05 Welsh Revival," 792–827.

18. Robeck, "The International Significance of Azusa Street," 2–3.

19. Bartleman, *How Pentecost Came to Los Angeles*, 89. For Bartleman's now famous designation of Azusa Street as the "American Jerusalem," see Bartleman, *Azusa Street*, 63. Bartleman is also quoted as saying, "Missionaries returned . . . to all parts of the world. They carried the Pentecostal message and power with them. Almost every country on the globe has been visited by them." Lawrence, *The Apostolic Faith Restored*, 75–76.

20. Creech, "Visions of Glory," 408.

21. Stanley Frodsham highlights the Pentecostal experience of people around the world without any connection to each other, and the independence of the Pentecostal movement from any one leader or people group. Frodsham, *With Signs Following*, 53, 105. Also, see Gee, *The Pentecostal Movement*, 29–30. Gee refers to the "truly spontaneous and simultaneous" Pentecostal revival in separated places where the only origin was a common hunger for "such a Revival produced in the hearts." Carl Brumback further promulgated this view in his history of the Assemblies of God in *Suddenly . . . from Heaven*, 48, 349.

religious context is what Augustus Cerillo has termed "the providential approach" to Pentecostal historiography.[22] An understanding of the movement as the work of the providential hand of God fit well within the framework of Latter-Rain eschatology. The Pentecostal movement was simply Christ's way of purifying his Bride for his imminent return.

Starting in the 1960s, Pentecostal historical analysis gradually shifted away from a providential understanding of history and sought to identify the roots of Pentecostalism in specific religious, cultural, social and economic aspects of the late nineteenth century. Still focusing on North America, historians looked to assign causes to aspects of Pentecostalism previously attributed to the sovereign hand of God.[23] Out of this emphasis on identifying the roots of Pentecostalism, many strands of Pentecostal historiography emerged into prominence, each with a different perspective on what constituted the defining characteristics of Pentecostals or the "core of Pentecostalism."

A Holiness Movement with a Common Theological Center

The Doctrine of Initial Evidence

In 1961, Klaude Kendrick, an ordained Assemblies of God educator and minister, wrote a history of the modern Pentecostal movement in which he detailed the roots of the Pentecostal movement as being located in the doctrine and practice of the nineteenth-century Wesleyan-Holiness movement. Further, he identified the doctrine of initial evidence as the single Pentecostal doctrine that distinguished the movement from the Holiness tradition from which it emerged. Consequently, Kendrick understood the first teacher of that doctrine, Charles Parham, as the rightful patriarch of modern Pentecostalism instead of William Seymour, his student.[24] Vinson Synan, in *The Holiness-Pentecostal Movement in the United States*, revised from his 1967 PhD dissertation for the University of Georgia, followed Kendrick by detailing the many connecting and overlapping features of the Pentecostal and Holiness movements. He too emphasized the Pentecostal Baptism in the Spirit along with the doctrine of initial evidence

---

22. Cerillo, "Interpretive Approaches," 31–36.

23. Cerillo, "The Beginnings of American Pentecostalism," 229; "Interpretive Approaches," 37.

24. Cerillo, "The Beginnings of American Pentecostalism," 230; Kendrick, *The Promise Fulfilled*, 38–64.

as the "third blessing" that defined the movement over against its parent, the Holiness movement, and grandparent, Methodism.[25] Synan's skill as a trained historian, particularly in assigning causes and meaning, has helped his history to hold a more lasting place in the broader context of Christian church historiography than many who came before him.

The observation of both Synan and Kendrick that the doctrine of initial evidence represents the singularly distinctive Pentecostal doctrine that cannot be naturally connected to the religious movements from which it emerged was welcomed by Pentecostals who advocated a providential understanding of history. It solidified in their minds that there were some unexplainable aspects of Pentecostal history that can only be attributed to God's sovereign hand, of which the origin of the doctrine of initial evidence was chief. The apparent emergence of this doctrine outside the influence of other denominations or traditions also presented firm footing for Pentecostal denominational leaders to stand in advocating the doctrine as the dividing line between Pentecostals and non-Pentecostals.

Naturally, being understood as the defining doctrine of Pentecostals, some historians began to understand the history of the doctrine of initial evidence as the history of Pentecostalism itself. The most avid proponent of this view has been James Goff. In his 1988 biography of Charles Fox Parham, *Fields White unto Harvest*, Goff chronicled what he called the origins of Pentecostalism. He argued, based on the scholarship of Synan, as well as Edith Waldvogel (later Edith Blumhofer),[26] that Pentecostalism has always been defined by its unique theology of Spirit Baptism evidenced by tongues. Goff detailed the origins of the Pentecostal doctrine with Charles Parham and revivals in Topeka, Kansas in 1901. Thus, Goff proclaimed Parham as the founder of the worldwide Pentecostal movement.[27] Goff was adamant in his position when he argued five years later, in answer to the question of how Pentecostalism should be defined, "The answer lies in the movement's uniqueness. What was new about its message? What became its identifying badge? What served as its chief point of departure from 19th-20th century orthodoxy? Clearly the answer to each is glossolalia interpreted as initial evidence and as an endtime sign." He further classified all arguments to the contrary as either theological problems or wishful thinking.[28]

25. Synan, *The Holiness-Pentecostal Tradition*, 106.
26. Waldvogel (Blumhofer), "The 'Overcoming Life,'" 181–97.
27. Introduction to Goff, *Fields White Unto Harvest*.
28. Goff, "Charles Parham and the Problem of History," 189.

Not many people take issue with Goff's statement that the Pentecostal movement should be defined by its uniqueness. However, among scholars there is widespread disagreement with Goff's narrowing the unique contribution of Pentecostalism to one single doctrine of initial evidence from one single person, Charles Parham. Parham's overt racism that grew more prevalent in his theology throughout his life, his understanding of all tongues as *xenolalia*, and his holding of an "unorthodox" doctrine of initial evidence at the end of his life have led many scholars to look elsewhere for "the father of Pentecostalism." Though many future scholars of Pentecostalism would not view the life of Charles Parham as being equal to the origins of Pentecostalism, Goff's biography has been widely taken as the authoritative history on the origins of the doctrine of initial evidence in Pentecostalism. Among Pentecostal denominational leaders, this stream of thought that defines Pentecostalism by its distinctive theological understanding of glossolalia as the evidence of Spirit Baptism is dominant. Typically, it has also been the level at which non-Pentecostal Protestant scholars have engaged Pentecostals in theological debate. However, in the last two decades, Pentecostal scholars have sought to define Pentecostalism more broadly.

The Four-Fold Gospel

In his 1987 book, *Theological Roots of Pentecostalism*, Donald Dayton examined the origins of Pentecostalism in the North American Holiness movement with a specific focus on historical theology. In an effort to trace the theological roots of Pentecostalism, Dayton deliberately avoided defining Pentecostals experientially by "bracketing the phenomenon of speaking in tongues."[29] Instead, he identified four popular Pentecostal themes as that which best represented the common core of Pentecostalism: Jesus as Savior, Baptizer in the Holy Spirit, Healer, and Coming King.[30] Dayton argued, "Tracing the development and interplay of these themes enables the historical and theological genesis of Pentecostalism to be understood, perhaps for the first time, at least in detail."[31] By focusing on the origin and

29. Dayton, *Theological Roots of Pentecostalism*, 173.

30. These four themes by no means originated with Dayton. In 1890, A. B. Simpson popularized a similar four-fold gospel where Jesus as "Sanctifier" instead of "Baptizer in the Holy Spirit" was the only difference. Robeck, "International Church of the Foursquare Gospel," 793–94. Aimee Simple McPherson founded the International Church of the Foursquare Gospel with this four-fold gospel as its foundational creed.

31. Dayton, *Theological Roots of Pentecostalism*, 28.

development of these themes in Pentecostalism, Dayton was able to place the movement into a theological and ecclesiastical context: the "Holiness currents and premillennial revivalists of the late nineteenth century," and to a lesser degree in the "Reformed revivalism and popular Evangelicalism" of the same era.[32] However, by bracketing the practice of speaking in tongues, Dayton steered away from a study of the theological roots of the Pentecostal doctrine of initial evidence.[33] In fact, using slightly nuanced language from Synan and Kendrick, Dayton identified the "experience of speaking in tongues as the evidence of having received the Baptism in the Holy Spirit" as a "phenomenon" which stood outside the natural developments of its theological and ecclesiastical contexts. By referring to the *experience* rather than the *doctrine* of initial evidence as "that which set Pentecostalism apart," Dayton avoided defining the origins of Pentecostalism by a single doctrine. Instead, he focused on a broad theological framework—in which a doctrine of evidence was the singularly unique doctrine—as that which created Pentecostalism.

Pre-Millennialism

Robert Mapes Anderson was the first historian from outside the Pentecostal tradition to examine the sociological and economic implications of Pentecostalism at a scholarly level. He located the *current* Pentecostal distinctive in its emphasis on the practice of speaking in tongues.[34] However, Anderson argued that the organizing component in the formative years of the Pentecostal movement was the imminent return of Christ and not speaking in tongues. He said that it was out of an expectation of "the immediate end" that an emphasis on speaking in tongues was inaugurated. He further postulated that it was only after the hope for Christ's imminent return began to fade that speaking in tongues began to be viewed as *the* Pentecostal distinctive.[35] Thus, at its foundational core, Anderson believed that the Pentecostal movement was most accurately described as a form of ecstatic-millenarianism. It was this form which Anderson said served the

32. Ibid., 176.

33. Though he does not ignore the origins of the doctrine completely, Dayton simplistically argues in less than two pages that the growing emphasis on evidences and testimony with regard to sanctification in Methodism led to asking the same questions with regard to Spirit Baptism. The evidence in Acts led to the obvious answer: speaking in tongues. Ibid., 176–77.

34. Anderson, *Vision of the Disinherited*, 4.

35. Ibid., 96–97.

function of providing the disinherited—the poor, outcasts, and excluded in American society—with a form of social deliverance.

Building on the millenarianism emphasis in Anderson's definition of Pentecostalism, D. William Faupel sought to reclaim the eschatological emphasis of early Pentecostals as the foundation upon which a Pentecostal ideology was built that included evangelism, divine healing and Spirit Baptism. For Faupel, the emphasis on Christ's imminent return provided a sense of unity in purpose and function around which a diverse community of people from many different races and backgrounds could dwell in harmony. It is the loss of this center-point in Pentecostal theology on which Faupel blames the breakdown of Pentecostal unity in the years following Azusa Street.[36]

The research of Faupel and Anderson has shown that since the 1920s, the notion of an imminent, pre-millennial return of Christ has slowly descended into the background of Pentecostal ideology. The major reason for this is obvious: Christ did not come back as quickly as was anticipated. Another reason, however, is that the imminent return of Christ was never adopted into a formal doctrinal statement as rigid as the doctrine of initial evidence. Thus, Christ's imminent return for a "spotless Bride" was not perceived as *the* defining doctrine of Pentecostalism, even though it was an integral part of Pentecostal ideology. It was understood instead as a carryover and adaptation from earlier streams of North American millenarian movements. Thus, in the minds of Pentecostals who joined the movement after the 1930s, the validity of this eschatological aspect of formative Pentecostal teaching could be contested without challenging the core of what it means to be a Pentecostal. For many of these Pentecostals, the doctrine of initial evidence was *the* doctrine that defined the movement.

A Global Movement with a Common Experience

Diversity Inherent in the Definition

The categories mentioned above represent different ways in which Pentecostal historical scholarship has sought to define Pentecostalism and answer the question, "What does it mean to be a Pentecostal?" With all of these categories, an organizing principle was imposed onto the past of a religious movement in order to form a common basis by which to define and mark out the boundaries of the movement. This method of historiography

---

36. Faupel, *The Everlasting Gospel*, 309.

is essential for understanding the general thrust of a Christian movement in church and society, and its general place in the structure, progression, and development of Christian theology. However, it must be recognized that any organizing principle will tend to minimize the complexities and diversity that are present in a movement of people. If any one organizing principle is given too strong a voice, the practical complexity that is present in any given historical context may be lost,[37] that is, unless diversity is located *in* the organizing principle. The move in historical scholarship to define Pentecostals experientially has done just that.[38]

Ecumenical Experience of the Spirit

Walter Hollenweger's work, *The Pentecostals*, published in 1972 as a condensed version of his ten-volume doctoral dissertation for the University of Zurich in which he devoted considerable attention to the spread of Pentecostalism in Africa, Latin America, Europe, and Asia was a landmark work in Pentecostal historiography. While Hollenweger organized his work around North America as the central place from which Pentecostalism spread, his work brought to the forefront the varied theological and sociological shades of Pentecostals on other continents. In 1997, Hollenweger wrote *Pentecostalism*, what he called a "thoroughly theological" work in contrast to his earlier book. More explicitly than in previous writing, Hollenweger identified the roots of global Pentecostalism in Azusa Street. Rather than grounding his argument in doctrinal origins, he elevated the "black oral root" of Pentecostalism in the African American tradition of its founding pastor, William Seymour, to the major cause of the rapid growth and acceptance of Pentecostalism around the world.[39] Countering the arguments of Goff, Hollenweger did not see Parham's doctrine of initial evidence as that which should define Pentecostalism or name its founder. Rather, he understood the question of defining Pentecostalism to be a theological question. In his view, the person of William

---

37. Everett Wilson is especially critical of a narrow organizing term being applied to Pentecostalism. Wilson, "They Crossed the Red Sea Didn't They?" 100.

38. Allan Anderson has followed Cecil Robeck in identifying diversity itself as a key feature in defining Pentecostalism. Anderson, "Diversity in the Definition," 40–41.

39. Hollenweger, *The Pentecostals*, xvii, 63; *Pentecostalism*, 18–24. In a more direct statement, Hollenweger calls William Seymour the "founder" of Pentecostalism. Hollenweger, "The Black Roots of Pentecostalism," 36. For a brief summary of the reasons for growth that Hollenweger attributes to the black oral root of Pentecostalism, see Hollenweger, "After Twenty Years' Research," 6.

Seymour, with his theological emphasis on the reconciling, ecumenical and barrier-transcending experience of the Spirit, stood at the core of what it meant to be Pentecostal, even if it was never fully adopted in Pentecostal churches. For Hollenweger, the religious experience of speaking in tongues following Spirit Baptism by itself does little to capture what it means to be Pentecostal in the New Testament sense of the word or in the sense in which it was taken at Azusa Street.

Global Experience of the Spirit

In the 1990s, Pentecostal historians working in the shadow of Hollenweger's emphasis on global Pentecostalism have identified an inappropriate bias in locating the origins of Pentecostalism in America. Historians of global Pentecostalism tend to treat each segment of Pentecostalism on its own terms and in its own context of development. They emphasize the fact that not all Pentecostal groups around the world have traceable origins to North America. In addition, this school of thought argues that groups that had a legitimate missiological connection to North America took on their own unique character once the movement began to expand indigenously.

The influence of global Pentecostalism on North American Pentecostal studies is significant. Because Pentecostals in other nations often do not hold to the doctrinal distinctives—subsequence and initial evidence—traditionally recognized in the "classical" Pentecostal denominations of North America, global Pentecostals are usually defined by their common experience of the Spirit. As a result of this broader definition, the delineation between Charismatics and Pentecostals that exists in North America often is not distinguished elsewhere in the world. Allan Anderson, a professor at the University of Birmingham, has been one of the chief proponents of a global history of Pentecostalism that takes seriously the developments of Pentecostalism in cultures and people groups independently of the Pentecostal revivals of North America.[40] Anderson defines Pentecostals thus, "Although the meaning of 'Pentecostal' is debated in this book and will continue to elude us for a long time, in its simplest sense the term refers to ecstatic forms of Christianity defined in terms of special gifts given by the Holy Spirit."[41] Elsewhere, Anderson argues, "'Pentecos-

---

40. Anderson, "Revising Pentecostal History," 147–73; *An Introduction to Pentecostalism*, 170–76.

41. Allan Anderson includes a brief but poignant examination of the terms "Pentecostal" and "Charismatic" as they relate to global Pentecostalism in *An Introduction*

talism' . . . includes all those movements and churches where the emphasis is on the *experience of the Spirit* and the *practice of spiritual gifts*."[42]

One would certainly have to agree that it would be difficult to call a person a Pentecostal if they did not fall within the broad limits that Anderson has suggested. However, one must ask the question: Is there more to being a Pentecostal than that? Can we be more specific? Is there a *particular* experience of the Spirit or a *particular* way of practicing spiritual gifts that should be considered normative for Pentecostals over against Charismatics? Some scholars have answered these questions by focusing on the Pentecostal's *experience* of glossolalia rather than their *doctrine* of glossolalia as that which sets them apart. While the doctrine of initial evidence is de-emphasized in global Pentecostal studies because of its rejection by many Pentecostals outside the United States, the experience of glossolalia is widely attested. Glossolalia has an appeal to global Pentecostals because of its ecumenically constructive trajectory. A rigid doctrine of initial evidence is understood as divisive, formulaic and constraining, whereas an experience of speaking in tongues is viewed as unifying, barrier-crossing, and empowering in the context of diversity.[43]

While recognizing the importance of experiences of glossolalia and other manifestations of the Holy Spirit in defining Pentecostals, Frank Macchia has made a solid case for Spirit Baptism as the common theological lens through which Pentecostals understand and interpret their varied experience.[44] Building on both the global emphasis on experience and Macchia's broad doctrinal focus on Spirit Baptism as the common interpretive framework for global Pentecostalism, this study will utilize the following working definition of Pentecostalism: a movement within Christianity that emphasizes Spirit Baptism as a distinct phase in the

to Pentecostalism, 9–15. Gary McGee has argued against the broadly inclusive definition of Anderson and others, advocating the use of North American definitions in the context of global Pentecostalism. McGee, "Pentecostal Missiology," 276–77.

42. Anderson, "Introduction: The Charismatic Face of Christianity in Asia," 2.

43. The Chilean Pentecostal movement in Latin America has been particularly opposed to a rigid doctrine of initial evidence. Sepulveda, "Future Perspectives for Latin American Pentecostalism," 190; "Born Again," 106. Finland has never formalized a strong doctrinal stance on the issue. Kärkkäinen, "The Pentecostal Movement in Finland," 110. Macchia is one of many recent theologians to emphasize the ecumenical nature of glossolalia. Macchia, "The Struggle for Global Witness," 16–18. For a thorough summary of the disagreement concerning evidential tongues in Germany and among the Elim Pentecostals in Britain, see Hudson, "Strange Words," 52–80.

44. Macchia, *Baptized in the Holy Spirit*, 19–60, esp. 33–38. Macchia's views are dealt with more fully later in this chapter.

Christian life by which a believer enters into a new depth of experience of the Holy Spirit characterized by the operation of various spiritual gifts, particularly speaking in tongues.

Classical Pentecostalism: Bad Historiography or Legitimate Distinction?

The tendency for historians of global Pentecostalism to define Pentecostals in terms of a broad category of Pentecostal experience or practice has led to the absence of a critical standard of orthodoxy by which to engage in a critique of Pentecostals according to a tradition. For some, the refusal to exalt any one group above another is cause for celebration as it allows for the maximum adaptability and flexibility of the movement. For others, particularly in North America, a definitive tradition is understood as absolutely necessary for the survival of the movement in a postmodern culture. The need for a foundation of criticism and evaluation has given rise to a view that delineates a tradition within the Pentecostal movement known as "classical Pentecostalism" as that which stands as the authoritative version of Pentecostalism in North America.[45]

Everett Wilson has argued strongly against the marking out of a classical tradition in Pentecostalism by which to measure and define orthodoxy. He identifies a complicating factor of Pentecostal historiography in the "lack of a distinguishable founder or inaugural event" from which the movement originated, and sees many problems in the methods of past historians of the Pentecostal movement.[46] Particularly disconcerting for Wilson is the tendency of Pentecostal historians to ignore the extremists, complexities, and diversity present in the movement's beginnings en route to an idealistic picture of unity and organization in the past for the sake of maintaining a predetermined standard of orthodoxy in the present.

While many of Wilson's criticisms are fully warranted, his methodology for dealing with the problem is less palpable. He says,

> By declaring the first (or any subsequent) generation of adherents a classical model of Pentecostalism, the historian detracts the reader from the real story of how a few believers with little

---

45. "Classical Pentecostalism" is a term originally put into use by the Roman Catholic ecumenist Kilian McDonnell to refer to the collective identity of Pentecostal groups that trace their origins to the first three decades of the twentieth century. See chapter 4 below.

46. Wilson, "They Crossed the Red Sea Didn't They?" 91.

apparent likelihood of achieving their goals made it across the Sea of Improbability. It is also futile to assume that the experience of the first set of Pentecostals provides a model for the future. In Pentecostalism every generation is the first generation.[47]

He goes on to argue that historians end up distorting the nature of the movement when they try to recapture the initial contexts of its infant stages for the sake of prescription rather than description. He identifies two problems with this type of history. When historians look to the roots of the movement to determine that which is truly Pentecostal they 1) run the risk of making the rather messy beginnings of Pentecostalism look "pristine," and 2) inevitably exalt one aspect—people group, belief set or ecclesiastical tradition—of the diverse beginnings of Pentecostalism ahead of others that are just as important in defining the movement. Wilson's criticism directly opposes the work of historians like D. William Faupel who argues, "To maintain its distinctive witness, the formative years of Pentecostalism must be perceived as the heart and not simply the infancy of the movement. That is, for Pentecostalism to remain a vital force into the twenty-first century, it must look to its origins as a source for theological and spiritual renewal."[48] In short, Wilson not only deems the search for a core Pentecostal definition an impossible task, he also deems *efforts* in that direction futile.

Wilson's position also stands in stark contrast to that of Cecil Robeck, professor of Church History and Ecumenics at Fuller Theological Seminary. While acknowledging the validity of much of Everett's criticisms, Robeck has maintained the value of looking at the roots of Pentecostalism as a standard by which to critique the movement. His position is clearly stated:

> What is emerging from recent studies is the realization that [the Charismatic movement] is not a single, unified, monolithic Movement; it is better understood as a "Movement of movements" that *share a core of common beliefs and common experiences*. . . . In a sense, it is a Movement very much at home in a "Post-Modern" setting while holding, in some cases quite strongly, to a variety of "Pre-Modern" and "Modern" worldviews.[49]

---

47. Ibid., 106.
48. Faupel, *The Everlasting Gospel*, 309.
49. Robeck, Forward to *Asian and Pentecostal*, xi. Italics mine.

In this statement, and in many other articles, Robeck acknowledges and appreciates the diversity within Pentecostalism but has not abandoned the idea of a common core upon which legitimate criticisms can be formed.[50] Robeck candidly admits that the search for a unique Pentecostal hermeneutic may never be successful, but he does not discount the benefits of critiquing the hermeneutics employed by Pentecostals on the basis of their collective history.[51] For Robeck, the diversity of the Pentecostal movement in America and worldwide "is something which can and should be celebrated, but it also holds the seeds for problems."[52] The problems are twofold: an attitude of indifference to divergent viewpoints on the one hand, and an attitude of competitiveness about the superiority of one's own viewpoints on the other.

In spite of these potential problems, Robeck has not discouraged the idea of a common historical root to which Pentecostals can turn as a standard against which to measure their current practices. As the authoritative scholar on the history of the Azusa Street Revival, Robeck has argued for the central place of Azusa Street in the early Pentecostals' own quest to define their movement both in North America and around the world. In reference to the debate whether to give credit to Parham or Seymour with the founding of the movement in North America, Robeck says, "While Parham may have contributed one or two items of significance to early Pentecostal self-understanding . . . it is clearly the thinking of William J. Seymour and the experience of Azusa Street which has played the more significant role in Pentecostal *and* Charismatic self-definition."[53] In another article Robeck argues for the centrality of the Azusa Street Revival in the spread of global Pentecostalism saying, "It must be said that from the perspective of those at the Mission in early 1907 they were clearly at the center of things as far as the international scene was concerned."[54] For Robeck, a common self-understanding held by early Pentecostals can best (though not perfectly) be described in terms of a common event: the Azusa Street Revival.[55]

---

50. Robeck has been particularly active in reminding Pentecostals that ecumenism and appreciation for diversity are at the core of Pentecostalism. Robeck, "Pentecostals and Ecumenism in a Pluralistic World," 338–62; "Pentecostals and the Apostolic Faith," 35–60.

51. Robeck, "Taking Stock of Pentecostalism," 60.

52. Ibid., 47.

53. Robeck, "Pentecostal Origins from a Global Perspective," 179.

54. Robeck, "The International Significance of Azusa Street," 2.

55. Robeck, "Pentecostal Origins from a Global Perspective," 170.

By locating the basis for criticism of members of a movement in their own understanding of the *events* and *experiences* at Azusa Street, Robeck has made room for the diversity and complexity of particular situations that Wilson sees missing from most Pentecostal historiography. Recognizing "the tendency to read all other Pentecostals in the same way we read ourselves,"[56] Robeck has tried to describe the early Pentecostal experience, particularly Azusa Street, in the most thorough and accurate way possible so that future Pentecostals might capture the intricacies and details of real events that cannot be gleamed through the examination of doctrinal statements or the handing down of a particular theological viewpoint.[57] Against a historiography that fails to take a contextual self-understanding seriously, Robeck says,

> We are not really helped if we attempt to assess our predecessors by today's standards. Nor are we fair to assign them motives which we believe they had without clear evidence from their own pens or mouths. They need to be viewed as people of their time in order for us to understand what it was that led them to take the positions which they took. They need to be judged objectively on the basis of how they lived up to the standards which they claimed for themselves.[58]

Although one might disagree with Robeck's focus on Azusa Street as that which best represents the roots of Pentecostalism, his advice is important for all historians of Pentecostalism to take seriously. It is by means of a thorough and accurate description of how Pentecostals originally understood and developed their own guiding principles that the historian is able to form a basis for constructive criticism of the movement and for engaging in ecumenical dialogue across denominational boundaries. It is precisely this kind of historical examination with regard to the origin and development of the doctrine of initial evidence in classical Pentecostalism that is needed to address the gap between their doctrine and practice that Pentecostals are experiencing in North America.

---

56. Robeck, "Taking Stock of Pentecostalism," 46.
57. Robeck, *The Azusa Street Mission & Revival*.
58. Robeck, "The Past," para. 9.

Background Literature

The Doctrine of Initial Evidence: Historical Theology

Gary McGee's 1993 edited volume, *Initial Evidence: Historical and Biblical Perspectives on the Pentecostal Doctrine of Spirit Baptism*, stands as the major scholarly work devoted to this topic. Within this volume only three chapters deal with the developments of this doctrine in the early Pentecostal movement. Two of these chapters deal with the theology of Charles Parham and William Seymour respectively, and one chapter, by Gary McGee, deals more broadly with early Pentecostal hermeneutics as a whole. In that chapter, McGee concluded, "From as early as 1906, [Pentecostals] failed to achieve consensus on the evidential nature of tongues. Hence, they also differed in their understanding of glossolalic manifestations in Acts."[59] He argued that those who focused on Pauline categories of thought tended not to see an indispensable connection between tongues and Spirit Baptism, while those who looked to the Book of Acts for their theology typically saw tongues as an essential part of a genuine experience of Spirit Baptism. Despite the observation of diverse opinions concerning the doctrine in the early years of the Pentecostal movement, McGee focused most of his discussion on popular defenses and expositions of the classic doctrine and did little to articulate the diversity other than to announce its existence (although McGee did so in some of his later writings).[60] Other writers of early Pentecostal history have also referred to the broad range of beliefs concerning the connection between tongues and Spirit Baptism among early Pentecostals.[61] However, historians have not articulated the actual range of opinions that existed in early Pentecostalism regarding this topic. Nor have historians described how such a controversial and debatable doctrine came to be established as a defining tenant of the movement in North America.

Douglas Jacobsen's chapter entitled, "Theology at the Boundaries of the Pentecostal Movement,"[62] provided a much-needed study on the theologies of those people whose ministries were intimately connected to the early growth of Pentecostalism but who were commonly recognized as

---

59. McGee, "Early Pentecostal Hermeneutics," 111.

60. McGee, "'Latter Rain' Falling in the East," 648–65; "The New World," 108–35; "The Calcutta Revival of 1907," 123–43.

61. Jacobsen, *Thinking in the Spirit*, 288–90; Anderson, *Vision of the Disinherited*, 4.

62. Jacobsen, *Thinking in the Spirit*, 286–352.

being unorthodox in their doctrine. However, Jacobsen's title may mark out a sharp "boundary" between orthodox and unorthodox Pentecostals where a spectrum is more appropriate. While many Pentecostal scholars have admitted the existence of diverse perspectives on Pentecostal doctrine and experience in the early years of the movement, documentation of the varied opinions among classical Pentecostals about the relationship of speaking in tongues to Spirit Baptism has yet to be compiled. Some scholars have identified variations of the doctrine of initial evidence within biographical articles and books on specific early Pentecostal leaders, but they have stopped short of assessing and explaining the relationship between the diversity of opinion that existed in the formative years of the movement and the establishment of a single doctrine of initial evidence as the defining doctrine for classical Pentecostals.[63]

The shift away from a view of the doctrine of initial evidence as the Pentecostals' "distinctive testimony" in the context of global Pentecostalism seems to have led to a decrease in writing on the topic from a historical perspective. Two issues of the *Asian Journal for Pentecostal Studies* in 1998 and 1999 were devoted to the doctrine of initial evidence, but few of the articles engaged in any historical study. One of the articles in the 1999 issue is a helpful bibliographical article on the subject of the initial evidence.[64] Of the 160 sources cited in the article, only about thirty constitute any kind of historical study, and most of these are brief articles focused on a narrow topic, and often the articles only indirectly refer to the doctrine of initial evidence. A survey of this bibliography clearly shows that the vast majority of study has been devoted to either defending or combating the validity of the doctrine on theological and hermeneutical grounds.

Recent historical scholarship concerning the theology of Charles Parham and William Seymour, the two most recognized patriarchs of American Pentecostalism, has helped to show that the doctrine of initial evidence developed independently of any one person.[65] In spite of the fact

63. Robeck, "William J. Seymour," 72–95; Goff, "The Theology of Charles Fox Parham," 57–71; Moon, "J. H. King on Initial Evidence," 261–86; Jacobsen, *Thinking in the Spirit*, 134–352; Robeck, "An Emerging Magisterium?" 171–211. Robeck specifically documents a gradual move in the Assemblies of God to suppress diverse beliefs and experiences of Spirit Baptism in order to maintain an appearance of unified doctrinal conformity.

64. Flokstra, "Sources for the Initial Evidence Discussion," 241–59.

65. For Seymour's relaxed view, see Robeck, "William J. Seymour," 72–95. For Parham's understanding of all genuine tongues as "Xenoglossa," see Goff, "The Theology of Charles Fox Parham," 57–71. For Parham's struggle with counterfeit manifestations of speaking in tongues, see Jacobsen, *Thinking in the Spirit*, 288–89.

that Parham and Seymour upheld "unorthodox" views of what constituted the evidence of Spirit Baptism in the later parts of their ministries, scholars have often assumed that early Pentecostal belief about the relationship of tongues to Spirit Baptism was mostly unified and in line with the famous Assemblies of God doctrinal statement of 1916. Until recently, pastoral concerns related to the doctrine of initial evidence were sidelined by historians as they traced the development of doctrinal statements in Pentecostalism. Unity in thought and practice was assumed to exist where diverse opinions and variety in application may have been more common.[66] The result was a simplistic, almost mythic, understanding of the establishment of a uniform doctrine of initial evidence in early Pentecostalism.[67]

Vinson Synan has written an article on the role the doctrine of initial evidence has played throughout the history of Pentecostalism. Among other things, Synan discusses the missiological influence of the doctrine in the early expansion of the Pentecostal movement.[68] Specifically, Synan makes a causal connection between a denomination "strongly" holding to the doctrine and missionary success after WWII. For support, Synan refers to the relatively slow growth of the Church of Christ (Holiness) and Christian Missionary Alliance denominations compared to the Church of God in Christ and the Assemblies of God respectively as models for what happens when Pentecostals "soften" or do away with the doctrine of initial evidence. For Synan, the function of the doctrine of initial evidence in Pentecostal denominations could be likened to other major denominational doctrines like "'eternal security' for Baptists, 'predestination of the elect' for Presbyterians, and 'Christian perfection' for Methodists."[69] Synan's conclusion is that "it is unthinkable that the Pentecostal movement could have developed as it did without the initial evidence position."[70] While Synan

---

66. The historical presence of diversity in theological belief and practice in the formative years of the Pentecostal movement is presented in the introduction to Jacobsen, *Thinking in the Spirit*, 1–15.

67. Here I use the word "mythic" to describe the story of the Bethel Bible School where the understanding of speaking in tongues as evidence of a Christian's Baptism in the Spirit is said to have originated. See Synan, *The Holiness-Pentecostal Tradition*, 90–92. I do not use the term as a description of a fictional or imagined story. Rather, "a traditional story, typically involving supernatural beings or forces, which embodies and provides an explanation, aetiology, or justification for something such as the early history of a society, a religious belief or ritual, or a natural phenomenon" as defined in the *Oxford English Dictionary*.

68. Synan, "The Role of Tongues as Initial Evidence," 67–82.

69. Ibid., 75.

70. Ibid., 82.

must be commended for highlighting the significant role the doctrine of initial evidence has played in Pentecostal history, his arguments and causal connections are too simplistic for prescribing the best course of action for Pentecostal denominations in the present. The doctrine has clearly played an important role in the definition and growth of the movement, but organizational, financial and other social factors also contributed to trends of growth or stagnancy in Pentecostal denominations. Further, Synan fails to consider the growth of Pentecostalism around the world where the doctrine of initial evidence has been softened, and the decline in recent years of classical Pentecostal denominations that have held fast to the doctrine. When it comes to church growth, it is not self-evident that what worked for Pentecostals in the past will work for them in the future.

In contrast to the benefits of the doctrine of initial evidence highlighted by Synan, Swiss Pentecostal Jean-Daniel Plüss argues that something important was lost when the doctrine of initial evidence replaced testimony as the primary explanation of early Pentecostal experience.[71] Plüss proposes that a reconsideration of the Azusa Street revival from a mythic point of view can recapture the heart of the experience that early Pentecostals conceptualized and intended to communicate in the doctrine of initial evidence.[72] The inevitable tension that groups face when they attempt to "routinize" and pass-on experiences through doctrinal statements is important for scholars of Pentecostalism to consider.[73] However, Plüss' proposal for dealing with the problem in Pentecostalism is reductionistic in that he argues that the formal doctrine of initial evidence emerged in 1916 as a result of the Pentecostals' need to clarify and "nail down" the theological meaning of their experience for non-Pentecostals and society at large.[74] In so doing, he ignores the early doctrinal expressions of initial evidence theory that were a part of the Pentecostal's vocabulary from as early as 1901. How are these early doctrinal statements related to the testimonies at Azusa Street? Why did so many early testimonies of Spirit

---

71. Plüss, "Azusa and Other Myths," 195.

72. Ibid., 199–200.

73. Margaret Poloma has done extensive research on the problems that revival movements such as the Toronto Blessing face when they attempt to institutionalize or routinize charismatic activity. Poloma, "The 'Toronto Blessing,'" 257–71.

74. Plüss, "Azusa and Other Myths," 190. Plüss used McGee's article, "Early Pentecostal Hermeneutics," as the historical basis for some of his critique. In that article, McGee stated that the earliest use of the term "initial evidence" that he could find in print was in the original 1916 Statement of Fundamental Truths by the Assemblies of God. In actuality, as McGee later recognized, the term was in print by at least 1908.

Baptism at Azusa Street look to doctrine not only for an explanation of experience but also for a prediction of experience? The historical relationship of the doctrine of initial evidence to the experience and testimony of early Pentecostals appears to be more dynamic than Plüss describes. Early doctrinal explanations of experience are inextricably linked with early Pentecostal testimonies. The two cannot be easily separated. The metaphorical meaning of glossolalia for the Pentecostal community that Plüss articulates, though valuable, misses something important if it is not connected to the propositional truth claims of the community. Thus, the development of Pentecostal doctrinal statements (explanations of experience) must be considered alongside the testimonies of Pentecostals (descriptions of experience) in order for the historian to fully grasp the heart of the Pentecostal movement.

The Doctrine of Initial Evidence: Practical Theology

In 1985, Hollenweger identified a conflict arising between the stated belief and praxis of Pentecostals regarding the doctrine of initial evidence.[75] In the last two decades, many theologians have corroborated the practical theological problem to which Hollenweger referred. However, little progress has been made toward a solution. Plüss has identified three helpful categories of response to this gap between theory and practice: dogmatic, programmatic, and redefinition.[76] For Pentecostals and Charismatics in traditions where a formal doctrine of evidential tongues has not been historically defended, the shift in emphasis from Pentecostal doctrines to Pentecostal experience has been easy to assimilate. However, in denominations that have historically supported a doctrine of initial evidence, the shift in recent Pentecostal studies away from classical Pentecostal doctrines has created an impasse between those who want to define Pentecostals by their historic doctrines (dogmatic), their past experiences (programmatic) or their current experience of the Spirit (redefinition).

Frank Macchia's decision to focus on the broader concept of Spirit Baptism rather than the doctrines of subsequence or initial evidence as that which is distinctly Pentecostal is a significant step beyond the impasse that Plüss has articulated. Macchia observes that the growing trend in Pentecostal theology of late has been to ignore Pentecostal distinctive doctrines in search of more ecumenically promising Pentecostal

---

75. Hollenweger, "Pentecostal Research in Europe," 130–31. See quote above.
76. Plüss, "Initial Evidence or Evident Initials?" 219.

perspectives.[77] Yet, Macchia rightly recognizes the serious need for Pentecostals to reflect theologically on Spirit Baptism and glossolalia in order for biblical and historical work on the doctrine of initial evidence to have any kind of practical significance.

Macchia argues for a "revisioning" of the doctrine of initial evidence so that its "gospel intention" may be rescued from the rigid, dogmatic approaches of the past so that it can possibly gain a hearing from non-Pentecostals and a place in the broader Christian credo.[78] In short, he argues that tongues is best understood as an integral symbol of the global, ecumenical and mission-oriented vision of Spirit Baptism that is present in the New Testament and in the early history of the Pentecostal movement. Macchia's work is an important step in the development of a robust Pentecostal theology, and it provides a welcome move away from the narrow treatments of Pentecostal theology that make fruitful ecumenical discussion difficult. Yet, Macchia's focus in systematic theology keeps his proposals mostly in the realm of theory. For example, when Macchia speaks of "The Marks of the Spirit-baptized Church," there is little discussion of how Pentecostal churches currently measure up to this challenge or have in the past.[79] Addressing what he sees as the "distinctive accents of Pentecostalism as a global movement," Macchia constructs a Pentecostal ecclesiology organized around the concept of Spirit Baptism.[80] Yet, Macchia's broad concept of Spirit Baptism incorporates such a variety of theologians and theological traditions that one wonders whether his proposal retains a distinctly Pentecostal voice over against non-Pentecostal ecclesiologies.

Macchia's basic proposal is that an ecumenical orientation toward others founded upon a common unifying experience of the Spirit that transcends worldly boundaries is the evidence of Spirit Baptism and that tongues move us in this direction. This may be a theologically accurate representation of the global Pentecostal experience, but it also raises some questions about how such a perspective would be received by the Pentecostal community, past and present. Would early Pentecostals understand speaking in tongues to be integral to such an ecumenical orientation? Do

---

77. Macchia, *Baptized in the Spirit*, 51.

78. Macchia specifically proposes a view of initial tongues as a "sign" rather than an "evidence" in "Groans Too Deep for Words," 172–73. This idea did not originate with Macchia. Plüss observes that European Pentecostals have always tended to speak about tongues as a "sign" or "gift" rather than as an "evidence" in "Initial Evidence or Evident Initials?" 218.

79. Macchia, *Baptized in the Spirit*, 204–41.

80. Ibid., 256.

Pentecostals today confirm their own experiences of Spirit Baptism in this way? These questions that stand outside the scope of Macchia's research build upon some more foundational questions: How have Pentecostals historically understood the relationship of speaking in tongues to Spirit Baptism? How does the doctrine of initial evidence currently function in the Pentecostal community? Without satisfactory answers to these questions, it remains to be seen how revisionary theological proposals such as Macchia's can gain a hearing and be put into practice by the Pentecostal community.

In practice, Pentecostal congregations tend to have their own feel, theological emphasis, and style of worship. Whether the uniqueness of Pentecostal worship is simply stylistic or is actually rooted in a unique Pentecostal theology is a question that needs to be addressed. John Christopher Thomas, in his 1998 Presidential Address to the Society for Pentecostal Studies, noted a tendency among Pentecostals to separate theology and ethics. He argued that this kind of theological work "misses the point completely" and that Pentecostal theology in the twenty-first century must be concerned not just with "orthodoxy (right doctrine), but orthopraxy (right practice) and orthopathy (right affections) as well."[81] Applying Thomas' advice to the present study, we may pose this question: Does the doctrine of initial evidence have any importance for the worship practices of Pentecostals in denominations that accept this doctrine? For denominations that hold to this doctrine as essential to their identity as Pentecostal, this is an extremely important question to answer.

Margaret Poloma and William Kay have engaged in comprehensive empirical studies of Pentecostal and Charismatic congregations in the United States and the United Kingdom respectively. Poloma's 1989 work, *The Assemblies of God at the Crossroads*, surveyed 1275 Assemblies of God congregants and 246 licensed Assemblies of God ministers. The survey gathered data about their belief and practice concerning a variety of charismatic experiences including glossolalia/Spirit Baptism, divine healing, and leadership. Based upon the results of the surveys, Poloma argued that even though charismatic experience was an integral part of the spiritual lives of Assemblies of God congregations and ministers, the denomination was facing "threats" associated with the institutionalization and routinization of charismatic activity.[82]

---

81. Thomas, "Pentecostal Theology in the Twenty-First Century," 8.
82. Poloma, *The Assemblies of God at the Crossroads*, 232–33.

Poloma has since updated her *Crossroads* work in a study with John Green published in 2010.[83] The study reported results from a 1999 survey of 447 Assemblies of God pastors and a survey of 1,827 congregants in twenty-one Assemblies of God churches. In the study, Poloma and Green documented a growing number of ministers and constituents who do not agree with the doctrine of initial evidence. This growth was especially noticeable among younger adherents. Poloma and Green also identified decreases in glossolalic activity both corporately and privately. Further, Poloma and Green argue it is glossolalic activity, as opposed to agreement with a doctrine of initial evidence, that is indicative of a depth of experience of God that results in Godly Love.

Mark Cartledge has also engaged in extensive empirical research on Pentecostals and Charismatics using both qualitative and quantitative methods. Cartledge's early work focused on the particular ecstatic experience of glossolalia. Cartledge researched glossolalia according to the five-stage empirical-theological cycle of Johannes van der Ven.[84] Using qualitative research in the form of participant observation in worship services, study of church documents and tapes, interviews, and quantitative analysis through a survey, Cartledge showed that glossolalia remains a central feature of Charismatic spirituality in the form of prayer language, and that in the context of worship it is most commonly associated with transcendence and intimacy while becoming a source of power in spiritual warfare.[85] Cartledge identified three factors that explain the attitudes Charismatics have toward glossolalia: prayer, charismatic socialization, and direct charismatic activity. Building on his research, Cartledge argued that glossolalia is a significant symbol of divine-human encounter that functions as a "Trinitarian sacrament of the Kingdom of God."[86] Cartledge's work on glossolalia is important for understanding why that particular charismatic manifestation is so important for Pentecostal-Charismatic spirituality. The study also raises some questions about how glossolalia might be understood and experienced differently for classical Pentecostals as compared to Charismatics. Do classical Pentecostals understand speaking in tongues differently so that it functions more significantly as a

---

83. Poloma and Green, *The Assemblies of God: Godly Love*. Of particular interest for this study is chapter 5: "Spirit Baptism and Spiritual Transformation."

84. Van der Ven's five stages are summarized by Cartledge as follows: 1) identification of the problem & goal, 2) induction, 3) deduction, 4) testing, and 5) evaluation. Cartledge, *Charismatic Glossolalia*, 14–16.

85. Cartledge, *Charismatic Glossolalia*, 172–76.

86. Ibid., 187.

symbol or "evidence" of Spirit Baptism? Cartledge specifically addressed the issue of evidential tongues in an extensive survey of over 600 individuals in twenty-nine Pentecostal and Charismatic congregations in Britain. He found that 58.5 percent of the respondents did not claim to speak in tongues when they were baptized in the Spirit.[87] One would expect that this number would be much higher in churches that subscribe to a rigid doctrine of initial evidence. If so, would their experience of evidential tongues correlate to a different understanding of the nature and purpose of glossolalia?

Methodology

Historical Theology

Descriptive History

Grant Wacker, professor of church history at Duke University, has identified pragmatism and primitivism as the two impulses that together contributed to the survival and success of the Pentecostal movement in North America. According to Wacker, one of these two impulses tends to assert itself more strongly depending on the sphere of study.[88] When it comes to matters of doctrinal defense and exposition, Wacker sees the Pentecostal's impulse toward primitivism as dominant.[89] According to Wacker, the primitive mindset of Pentecostals—a resolve to return to the original (and best) way of doing things through direct access to God's Spirit—overtly shows itself in their uncompromising defenses of doctrine and their dogmatic exposition of scripture. One might expect that the Pentecostal's voiced opposition to "denominationalism" and their desire to give authority to the freedom of the Spirit would have resulted in a greater acceptance of diversity when it came to the application and practice of their doctrinal stances. But, by and large this was not the case. Pentecostals frequently applied doctrines in practice as rigidly as they were presented on paper, and they would go against their pragmatic impulses toward friendship, unity and brotherly love when correct doctrine was at stake.[90]

---

87. Cartledge, *Practical Theology*, 223–24.
88. Wacker, *Heaven Below*, 11–14.
89. Ibid., 76–81.
90. Ibid., 79.

As evident as the primitive impulse was in early Pentecostal doctrine, it was also clearly influenced by the pragmatic impulses of North American culture at the turn of the century. Koo Dong Yun has argued, "The essence of the Pentecostal movement lies in its pragmatic method." Yun sees American pragmatism influencing *all* aspects of early Pentecostalism, particularly their doctrine of Spirit Baptism that looked to tongues as an empirically verifiable proof of the experience.[91] In a religious landscape that valued both a common sense approach to scripture and empirical proofs, the doctrine of initial evidence provided simplicity and clarity to a task that had been previously marked by complexity and ambiguity: marking out those who had been sanctified and baptized in the Holy Spirit. As Wacker puts it, "Holy Ghost baptism could not be heard, but tongues could."[92]

If both primitive and pragmatic impulses were present in the Pentecostal's approach to the doctrine of Spirit Baptism, controversy among Pentecostals often ensued along those same lines. The primitive impulse encouraged early Pentecostals to believe that all Christians ought to speak in tongues; the pragmatic impulse had to do deal with the fact that not all of them did. Wacker has observed a gap between the theory and practice of Pentecostals particularly in reference to speaking in tongues and the doctrine of initial evidence. The gap is most evident in the large number of lay people who never spoke in tongues despite affirming a commitment to Pentecostalism.[93] This gap can also be seen in leaders who accommodated a lack of tongues speakers among laity in their congregations with a more flexible application of a rigid doctrinal stance. Thus, if both the pragmatic and primitive impulses of early Pentecostals are to be accounted, the comparison of practices in relationship to belief statements is important for expounding the range of interpretation early Pentecostals actually accepted concerning the doctrine of initial evidence.

In his article about a possible "magisterium" emerging in the ranks of Assemblies of God leaders, Robeck uses the doctrine of initial evidence as a case in point.[94] Although the primary focus of Robeck's study is more recent historical revisionism, his documentation of the birth and maturation of the doctrine of initial evidence as the "distinctive testimony" of the Assemblies of God has implications for the use of sources in this present

---

91. Yun, *Baptism in the Holy Spirit*, 154.
92. Wacker, *Heaven Below*, 40.
93. Ibid., 41.
94. Robeck, "An Emerging Magisterium?" 171–211.

study. It is quite possible that the fear of being regarded as a "Pentecostal heretic" may have suppressed the views of some credentialed ministers in the Assemblies of God who had reservations about the doctrine of initial evidence. This would be particularly true when the doctrine of initial evidence was established among their denominational leaders as a matter of orthodoxy after F. F. Bosworth's resignation from the General Council in 1916. The possibility of suppression and censorship of diverse views on the relationship of tongues and Spirit Baptism, particularly in Assemblies of God periodicals after 1916, may be negotiated with the following two approaches. First, it is important for a history of the doctrine of initial evidence to carefully examine Pentecostal belief before 1916 when the presence of diversity may have been less likely to be suppressed knowingly or unknowingly by denominational entities. There were certainly denominational forces at work to gather and consolidate divergent beliefs among Pentecostal ministers before the Assemblies of God organization was formed in 1914. However, prior to the Assemblies of God, ministers had little to lose if they decided not to stay with an organized group and set out on their own as an itinerant preacher or traveling evangelist. Secondly, when examining sources after 1916, Pentecostal organizations outside the Assemblies of God must be represented and given a voice in the history of the doctrine's development in order to get a clear picture of what constituted the boundaries of Pentecostal thought during the early years of the movement.

This study will seek to implement these two strategies in the following three chapters. Chapter two will focus on three early proponents of the doctrine of initial evidence prior to 1910 that encapsulate the diversity present in early Pentecostal theology: Charles Parham, William Seymour, and Alexander Boddy. All three of these individuals approached Spirit Baptism and speaking in tongues differently, and they each had a significant influence on many individuals who came after them to form the first generation of Pentecostal denominations in the United States and Britain. Chapter 3 will detail the development of the classical Pentecostal tradition in North America that occurred between 1910 and WWII. First, the chapter will focus on the thought of William Durham who acted as a link between the first Pentecostal revivals in North America and the founding members of the Assemblies of God denomination. Second, the establishment of the doctrine of initial evidence in the Assemblies of God in 1916 (which has been detailed in many chapters and articles) will be summarized, along with the controversy that quickly ensued involving

F. F. Bosworth and responses by the denomination. Third, accounts of the formation of two other "finished-work" Pentecostal denominations, the International Church of the Foursquare Gospel and Open Bible Standard Churches, will be given with a detailed exposition of their unique approaches to the doctrine of initial evidence.

In addition to an articulation of the doctrinal diversity present in the early years of the Pentecostal movement with regard to the doctrine of initial evidence, the pastoral concerns, evangelistic strategies, and organizational methods that contributed to the establishment of the doctrine as the core tenet of classical Pentecostals in North America will be examined in chapter four. An overview of the doctrine's function in the Pentecostal community over time and the responses of the community to criticism from non-Pentecostals, Charismatics, and Third-Wavers will prove helpful in engaging the complicated pastoral and organizational issues now facing classical Pentecostal denominations regarding the doctrine. A thorough description of the doctrine's function in context, and the process by which Pentecostals came to their conclusions, should aid the development of proposals for the future of Pentecostalism that are thoroughly Pentecostal in force.

Evaluative History

In his foundational work on empirical theology, Johannes van der Ven argues that the praxis of the church can be reduced to "hermeneutic-communicative praxis," which he defines as, "The verbal and nonverbal interpretation of written and spoken texts and their verbal and nonverbal communication."[95] He describes the hermeneutic quality of praxis as "a dialogue of relationships"—a dialogue between the relationship of old texts to their contexts and the relationship of present-day texts to their contexts.[96] He further defends an empirical approach as the methodology that a study of present day texts and contexts demands. What about the relationship of old text to their contexts? Can the historian arrive at any kind of reliable assessment of hermeneutic-communicative praxis of Pentecostals in the past?

Grant Wacker has made the important, though obvious, observation that "hard data are impossible to come by" in the historical examination of how theory was put into practice concerning glossolalia in the early

95. Van der Ven, *Practical Theology*, 41.
96. Ibid., 46–48.

Pentecostal movement.⁹⁷ The theologian's inability to go back in history and gather empirical data concerning the belief and practice of Pentecostals means that historic generalizations and claims of normativity need to be deduced from qualitative observations rather than quantitative data.⁹⁸ Without the ability to support claims and arguments with empirical data, the move from historical description and understanding to explanation and identifying causes tends toward subjectivity. By way of introduction to his book, *Christian Martyrdom in Early Modern Europe*, Brad Gregory has drawn attention to the difference between "understanding others on their terms" and "explaining them according to modern or postmodern categories." He strongly argues that the historian's task lies strictly with the former. The imposition of current modern or postmodern assumptions on people and events of the past obscures the historian's ability to reconstruct the past. To avoid this pitfall, Gregory calls for "an approach that does justice to any and all evidence we might encounter, without distorting the convictions of any of its protagonists."⁹⁹

William Kay has also stressed the need for the dependence of historical interpretation upon its source. But he does not go as far as to discredit the value of interpretation and explanation in the examination of historical sources. He argues,

> It seems to me to be axiomatic that any historical account must be recognisable by its original participants. This axiom, like all axioms, cannot be proved, but if it is rejected, we assume that the interpretation of primary sources (i.e., those sources provided by participants) may legitimately be alien to the providers of primary sources. But the disjunction between source and interpretation is unacceptable because every source is inevitably a mixture of fact and value, of data and theory, of information and interpretation. Thus the failure to preserve some connection between source and interpretation is essentially a distortion of the source.¹⁰⁰

---

97. Wacker, *Heaven Below*, 41.

98. Kay is one scholar who has discussed the possibility of performing a multiple regression analysis of present-day empirical data at regular intervals in order to extrapolate back into the past. However, his proposal requires successive collections of data on a specific social construct over time. Insufficient data has been collected to apply his proposal to early Pentecostals' glossolalic practices. See Kay, "Three Generations On," 67–68.

99. Gregory, *Salvation at Stake*, 10–11.

100. Kay, "Three Generations On," 59.

In order to avoid this distortion, Kay proposes that history be written at two levels. In the first, a distance is maintained between the historian and the subject. This allows the subject to be understood on its own terms. The second level history is where the historian is allowed to speak "with the benefit of hindsight and perhaps with a greater understanding of the overall context of events."[101] The present study will seek to document the history of the Pentecostal doctrine at these two levels. Chapters 2–4 will operate at the first level, describing the origin and development of the doctrine of initial evidence from the late nineteenth century to the present. Chapter 5 will operate at the second level, evaluating the history of the doctrine of initial evidence based upon the various functions of the doctrine for the classical Pentecostal community.

Alister McGrath has provided a helpful breakdown of the significant functions of doctrine in the history of the Christian church: social demarcation, interpretation of experience, interpretation of narrative, and truth claiming.[102] It is my proposal that the doctrine of Spirit Baptism in classical, "finished-work" Pentecostal denominations has functioned in each of these four ways at different times in the history of the movement. It would be helpful to examine the history of the development of the doctrine of Spirit Baptism in the classical Pentecostal tradition within each of these four functional categories in order to discern appropriate doctrinal developments. In particular, such an analysis would move us toward answering the following questions: Are aspects of Pentecostal doctrine best understood as interpretations of an objective experience or narrative held by a majority of Pentecostals? How has doctrine defined Pentecostalism as a religious movement socially and culturally? What is the propositional-truth claim to which Pentecostals assent?

Answers to these questions would provide the grounds for making more effective proposals for doctrinal reform than those based solely on exegetical or systematic-theological concerns. It allows one to understand how a doctrine has (or has not) moved Pentecostals toward intellectual, moral, and religious conversion and thereby make a value judgment about the effectiveness of the doctrine for the Pentecostal community. These value judgments can, in turn, be helpful in evaluating the influence the doctrine of initial evidence has on the beliefs and practices of Pentecostals, and therefore, where the doctrine may need to hold its ground and where it may need to be reformed or even disbanded.

101. Ibid., 67.
102. McGrath, *The Genesis of Doctrine*, 35–80.

Practical-Empirical Theology

An Empirical Study of Classical Pentecostals

Practical theology has in view as its starting point the praxis of the church. That is, the church's *"theological and value laden actions, habits, and practices."*[103] Practical theology has as its goal the *right* praxis of the church. Thus, the discipline assumes some sort of transcendent set of eschatological principles guided by a metanarrative which may be called normative, and toward which the praxis of the church should move. However, the norms by which the church gauges *right* praxis are not entirely independent of the praxis it seeks to improve. In short, the process of moving theory into practice is inherently complex. Duncan Forrester has proposed a hermeneutic spiral as a way to explain the dynamic process by which theory and practice mutually inform each other and yet gradually "ascend toward higher levels of understanding and more appropriate and faithful practice through a constantly moving process of radical questioning."[104] The process of radical questioning begins with suspicions and concerns that arise from either the side of theory or practice. The church's metanarrative may suggest a starting point. A crisis situation or recurring problem that arises out of the praxis of the church may also be that which initiates the process.

The doctrine of initial evidence has recently been called into question on both sides. Exegetical concerns have caused Pentecostal ministers and denominational leaders to see the doctrine's theoretical basis as suspect. Recurring problems faced by Pentecostal pastors and denominational leaders in the implementation of the doctrine in their churches (i.e., hierarchies of spirituality, overemphasizing visible signs, fanaticism) have led them to distrust the practical usefulness of the doctrine. This theoretical and practical questioning that currently exists in Pentecostal congregations concerning the doctrine of initial evidence is the crisis situation with which this study seeks to engage.

Within the realm of practical theology, empirical theology offers an approach that may prove helpful for making sound judgments about

---

103. Here I use the definition proposed by Cartledge in Cartledge, *Practical Theology*, 17. Italics his. I use the word 'praxis' instead of 'practice' to emphasize the reflective nature of the practices examined in practical theology. The assumption of practical theological enquiry is that the praxis of the church embodies its theology.

104. Forrester, *Truthful Action*, 28–31.

the praxis of Pentecostals regarding the doctrine of Spirit Baptism. Hans-Günter Heimbrock has described empirical theology in this way:

> The overall task of empirical theology is to discover exact and empirically valid knowledge about religion, instead of relying purely on assumptions. The theological interest is to introduce a clarified knowledge about the realities of religious life into theological discourse. Combining the foundations and aims of Christian faith with empirical insight can then help the church to promote realistic perspectives, and perhaps better praxis, in accordance with basic theological values, like the kingdom of God.[105]

Within the present study, empirical knowledge concerning the presence or lack of connection between Spirit Baptism and speaking in tongues in the beliefs and practices of classical Pentecostal ministers should help lay the foundations for an accurate assessment of current Pentecostal praxis, and also point the way toward practices that are consistent with the normative theological values of Pentecostalism.

How does one determine the normative values of Pentecostals? In 2007, Earl Creps presented some preliminary results of an empirical research project called *Postmodern Pentecostals*. Interviews were conducted of thirty-one Pentecostals in their twenties or early thirties about their beliefs concerning Spirit Baptism, tongues and the doctrine of initial evidence.[106] Creps categorized the findings into three groups: loyalist, post-distinctive, and post-denominational. The loyalist category describes those Pentecostals who choose to identify themselves with the denomination of their parents and grandparents and confidently support traditional Pentecostal doctrines, including initial evidence. The post-distinctives are those Pentecostals less inclined than loyalists to define themselves on the basis of doctrine. Even if they agree with the doctrine of initial evidence, the post-distinctives refrain from promoting the doctrine in public while valuing forums for discussion and debate about the doctrine. The post-denominational group refers to those Pentecostals who affirm their allegiance to "Pentecostalism," but prefer not to align themselves with any formal denomination.

Creps' study is helpful for understanding the variety of perspectives about Pentecostal identity present among younger Pentecostals, and his categories are useful for organizing the empirical research in this present

---

105. Heimbrock, "From Data to Theory," 278.
106. Creps, "Postmodern Pentecostals?" 27–47.

study. Three corresponding types of denominations may be identified in "finished-work" Pentecostalism in relation to the doctrine of initial evidence: distinctive (those that have historically upheld the doctrine and continue to do so), post-distinctive (those that have historically upheld the doctrine but have recently softened their stance), and non-distinctive (those that have never codified a rigid doctrine of initial evidence in their doctrinal statements).[107] An empirical study of the beliefs and practices of ministers in each type of denomination will be conducted: Assemblies of God (Distinctive), Open Bible (Post-Distinctive), and Foursquare (Non-Distinctive). This study aims to identify the characteristics that classical Pentecostal ministers hold in common and the characteristics that are divergent between denominations with regard to Spirit Baptism. More broadly speaking, it will also help one to know how changes in a denomination's doctrine of Spirit Baptism may be expected to influence practices in the lives of Pentecostal ministers and their congregations.

Van der Ven has highlighted the explanatory benefit of an empirical approach to theology saying, "The use of empirical methodology can contribute to the development of explanatory concepts and theories within theology. In this way such concepts and theories become less contemplative and essayistic than if they are only the product of subjective associations and argumentations of individual theologians."[108] Claims of discontinuity between beliefs and practices within classical Pentecostalism have largely been based upon the subjective theories and emotions of individual theologians rather than observable facts. This is not to deny the trustworthiness of these subjective associations or to assert that empirical theology is entirely objective.[109] Rather, it simply points out the need for empirical studies to be done to test the theories advanced by individual theologians. It is the goal of this empirical study to gather observable data about classical Pentecostal beliefs and practices that will be useful in addressing the current crisis in North American Pentecostalism.

---

107. Kay has similarly argued that the core distinctive of the British Assemblies of God organization before 1939 was a belief in the doctrine of initial evidence and observes that the distinctive has remained unchanged throughout the twentieth century. Kay, "Assemblies of God," 51, 59.

108. Van der Ven, *Practical Theology*, 110.

109. Kay has argued convincingly that empirical theology need not be equated with reductionism that denies the reality of observable thoughts and emotions or positivism that claims that knowledge must be observable and quantifiable. Kay, "Empirical Theology," 172.

It may be surprising to some that this study would advocate the use of practical theology in the study of Pentecostalism. After all, the roots of the two traditions have different backgrounds, presuppositions and perspectives on God. However, Mark Cartledge's work has shown how the dialectic nature of practical theology works well within the framework of a Charismatic spirituality. Cartledge likens the process of Charismatic spirituality by which the Holy Spirit acts in a paradigm of search-encounter-transformation to the practical theological process. In other words, practical theology from a Charismatic perspective is concerned with the action of the Holy Spirit revealed and embodied in the practices of the church.[110] Similar to Cartledge's paradigm, Ray Anderson has developed a Christopraxis model for practical theology that seeks to discern the ongoing work of the resurrected Christ through Christ's present empowerment of ministry in the church by the Holy Spirit. According to Anderson's model, the event of Pentecost is at the very center of practical theology because it is through the Spirit's empowerment in the praxis of Christians that one is able to understand how Christ is calling his church to repentance and transformation.[111] Approached from a Charismatic perspective that assumes the ongoing ministry of the Christ through the Holy Spirit, empirical theology may lead to greater clarity and better understanding concerning the action and voice of the Holy Spirit in the Pentecostal community today.

Conclusion

The doctrine of "initial evidence"—that speaking in tongues is the initial evidence of a Christian's Baptism in the Holy Spirit—has been a defining doctrine for many classical Pentecostals over the past century. At the same time, theoretical and practical concerns have often caused Pentecostals to question the veracity of the doctrine. This tension has resulted in a loss of definition for many Pentecostals, and raises some important questions that need answers: How should classical Pentecostal churches think about this doctrine? How should it be preached? What is the purpose of such a doctrine? These questions are best answered by a critical examination of the origin and development of the doctrine of initial evidence and its present practice in the classical Pentecostal tradition. Effective proposals will not only account for the diversity of beliefs and practices concerning the

---

110. Cartledge, *Practical Theology*, 30.
111. Anderson, *The Shape of Practical Theology*, 37–39.

doctrine of initial evidence in history, but will also incorporate the beliefs and practices of classical Pentecostal congregations today.

The historical presence of diversity in thought and experience concerning the formulation of the formal Pentecostal doctrine of initial evidence demands a thorough examination of the pastoral concerns, evangelistic strategies, and organizational methods of early Pentecostal leaders as they relate to the formulation and application of the doctrine of initial evidence. Signs of an increasing disjuncture between the doctrinal stances and the beliefs and practices of current Pentecostal congregations in North America demands that comprehensive empirical studies be undertaken in order to articulate these beliefs and practices. Doing so will help form a concrete basis for a proposal that might otherwise risk being based on incorrect perceptions and feelings about the current situation in Pentecostal congregations.

This study will critically examine the origin and development of the doctrine of initial evidence in English speaking sources seeking answers not only to *how* the doctrine came about, but *why* it was received by ministers and instituted in the churches. First, a thorough description of the diversity of doctrines and practices of Pentecostals regarding evidential tongues in the formative years of the movement will be undertaken, organized around the thought of three early Pentecostal leaders and their respective organizations that are representative of this diversity. Second, the thought of William Durham and the process of establishment of the doctrine of initial evidence in the Assemblies of God, Foursquare and Open Bible will be examined, paying particular attention to marginalized individuals and groups. Third, this study will offer a thorough evaluation of the history of the doctrine with respect to the classical Pentecostal community in relation to Alister McGrath's four categories for understanding doctrine. Fourth, empirical studies will be undertaken to determine how classical Pentecostal ministers in distinctive, post-distinctive and non-distinctive denominations think about the doctrine of initial evidence within McGrath's four categories. Do they believe it? Have they experienced it? How do they practice it?

The findings will be consolidated and organized in order to identify some implications for the future of Pentecostalism in North America and make some proposals for how classical Pentecostal denominations and leaders should approach the doctrine of Spirit Baptism in relation to four key areas: mission, worship, denominational identity, and doctrine. Should the doctrine be kept as it stands in distinctive, post-distinctive and non-distinctive denominations? Should a particular formulation be considered orthodox? How should the doctrine of Spirit Baptism be taught and preached in churches? Should the doctrine define Pentecostals? The goal of this study is to move toward an understanding and corresponding practice of the doctrine of Spirit Baptism that is faithful to the history of the classical Pentecostal movement and consistent with the present experience of its members.

2

Early Theological Approaches to Spirit Baptism

(1900–1910)

Introduction

IN ORDER TO ATTEMPT to articulate the diverse perspectives present in the first decade of the Pentecostal movement regarding Spirit Baptism and its relationship to speaking in tongues, the thought of three individuals will be explored: Charles Parham, William Seymour, and Alexander Boddy. These three men by no means represent the entire range of thought that emerged on the subject at the beginning of the twentieth century. Yet, when taken together, their distinct approaches for dealing with Spirit Baptism and accompanying manifestations of tongues, and their answers to basic theological and ecclesiological questions regarding the new experience, provide the seminal components of early Pentecostal theology. Though Parham is commonly thought to be the founder of the classical Pentecostal doctrine of initial evidence, it is more accurate to say that he contributed the hermeneutic that later Pentecostals used to develop the doctrine. Charles Parham held a functional understanding of Spirit Baptism. The purposes for which he understood the Baptism in the Holy Spirit to be essential, sealing the Bride and worldwide evangelism, were pragmatically connected to the evidence of the experience: speaking in other tongues. In contrast to Parham, William Seymour, whose thought is difficult to distinguish from the thought of the mission he oversaw,[1] had a broader understanding of the benefits that Spirit Baptism held for the Christian life. In many cases, he blurred the lines between experiences of sanctification, "the anointing that abideth" and Spirit Baptism, believing that praise, love, unity, humility, inspired teaching, and holiness were all enabled or enhanced through Baptism in the Holy Spirit. Within this broader conception of Spirit Baptism, tongues began to be understood as a sign or symbol of the benefits available in Spirit Baptism rather than as a concrete representation of Spirit Baptism. In Britain, Alexander Boddy's approach to Spirit Baptism was thoroughly pastoral in nature. He placed primary emphasis on the practical needs of the worshipping community and constructed a theology of Spirit Baptism that addressed those needs. Upholding the need for all church people to enjoy the Pentecostal experience, Boddy adamantly opposed the formation of a separate Pentecostal church or denomination. Instead, he coordinated an annual convention and edited a monthly periodical in order to help a growing number of Pentecostals healthily integrate their experience into their own church contexts. Boddy allowed for a variety of perspectives and opinions about Spirit Baptism to be expressed through these avenues, and in so doing he promoted a Pentecostal theology that was flexible on many matters that his American contemporaries understood as Scriptural absolutes.

Charles Parham and the Apostolic Faith Movement

The Need for a "Bible Evidence"

The origins of the doctrine of initial evidence in North American Pentecostalism have almost exclusively been traced back to Charles Parham who founded the Apostolic Faith Movement in Topeka, Kansas in 1899.[2]

---

1. Douglas Jacobsen discusses this historiographical challenge in *Thinking in the Spirit*, 61.

2. Only Britain's Edward Irving and his followers in the Catholic Apostolic Church of the early nineteenth century pre-date Parham with a similar doctrine. Irving's understanding of tongues as the "standing sign" of a Christian's Baptism in the Spirit is remarkably similar to the initial evidence doctrine that would emerge out of the Assemblies of God in America in 1916. D. William Faupel has proposed a likely connection between Irving and John Alexander Dowie at the University of Edinburgh, which both attended. However, no textual evidence connecting the Irvingites to the Pentecostal movement of the twentieth century has yet been found. Dorries, "Edward Irving," 41–56; Purves, "The Interaction of Christology," 90; Faupel, "Theological Influences," 241–43.

Norming the Abnormal

The story of Agnes Ozman being baptized in the Holy Spirit and speaking in tongues at Parham's Bethel Bible School in early January 1901 is so famous in Pentecostal studies that it has taken on a mythic dimension as it has been passed along.[3] Due to its wide circulation (forty thousand in January 1908, according to the paper), the account in the Azusa paper would be repeatedly retold as the story of the movement's beginning in later Pentecostal papers and books.[4] Inherent in this story of Pentecostal beginnings is the search for an evidence—an irrefutable proof that one has been baptized in the Spirit. A fresh reading of the Book of Acts coupled with an outbreak of tongues speech left Parham and his students with a convincing answer: speaking in tongues was the Bible evidence of the Baptism in the Spirit. As inspiring as this story is to adherents of the Pentecostal faith, it is too simplistic to deduce from it Parham's distinctive approach to Spirit Baptism or his unique contribution to Pentecostalism. A thorough examination of Parham's theology of Spirit Baptism shows that Parham's understanding of the experience was adopted by later generations of Pentecostals only in word. Thus, Parham's contribution to Pentecostalism should be understood to reside at the level of hermeneutics, not doctrine.

Parham's understanding of tongues as the "Bible evidence" of a person's Baptism in the Holy Spirit was just one doctrine in a detailed theological system of ideas that stood independent of his contemporaries. Parham did not mind using doctrines from a variety of sources, and he had no problem taking some and leaving others as he saw fit. B. H. Irwin,

---

3. The account first appeared in print in Parham's book, *Kol Kare Bomidbar*, first published in 1902. Parham, *Kol Kare Bomidbar*, 32–34. This account would reappear again with slight revisions in an article entitled, "Pentecostal Baptism Restored," on the front page of the second issue of the Azusa Street newspaper. *Apostolic Faith* [Los Angeles] 1.2 (October 1906) 1. It also was relayed in issues of *Apostolic Faith* [Houston] edited by W. F. Carothers and later issues of *Apostolic Faith* [Baxter Springs] edited by Parham with more significant changes. The account in the Azusa Street newspaper appears to be paraphrased, and in many cases directly quoted from Parham's account in *Kol Kare Bomidbar*. However, there are some interesting additions to the story. There is reference to "continued prayer in the praying tower" that is absent from the original account. There is also reference to Parham's initial view of the outpouring on January third, his response, and his own experience of speaking in tongues on the same evening.

4. It appears that Agnes Ozman soon replaced Charles Parham as the central figure in the story. See W. F. Carothers, "History of Movement," and Agnes N. Ozman, "A Witness to First Scenes," *Apostolic Faith* [Houston] 2.2 (October 1908) 1–2. Carothers retells the story without any reference to Parham alongside a firsthand testimony by Ozman. See also Frodsham, *With Signs Following*, 9–17. Stanley Frodsham's early history fails to mention Parham in the story of the outpouring at Topeka and relies heavily on a personal testimony from Ozman for the details of the event.

A. B. Simpson, John Dowie, Dwight L. Moody, and Frank Sandford were just some of the people who contributed pieces to a theological puzzle that Parham would not complete until the beginning of the twentieth century.[5] Parham did not mind standing alone either if he felt he had strong scriptural support for his position. His perspective on speaking in tongues as the Bible evidence of a Christian's Baptism in the Holy Spirit was not the only doctrine that was unique. Leslie Callahan points out that "Parham modified characters, reorganized events, and interpreted the already difficult apocalyptic passages of the Old and New Testaments in ways that were singularly his own."[6] Parham also zealously defended his father-in-law's unpopular annihilationist perspective on hell—a view that significantly diminished his credibility in many of the Holiness circles in which he preached. Callahan rightly observes, "Throughout his life, Parham demonstrated a willingness to dispense with orthodoxy, even taking proud pleasure in his unorthodox conclusions."[7]

Parham left no room in his theological system for tolerance of disunity in the church. When Christians disagreed, it was because something was causing them to miss what the Holy Spirit was actually teaching. This, he argued, was denominationalism and ecclesiasticism itself. Parham truly believed that if people would simply study the Bible in a posture of humility and willingness to submit to God, everyone would agree.[8] This belief proved to be foundational for Parham and his students' new interpretation of the events of Pentecost in Acts 2, and the implications they would draw for the modern church context at the beginning of the twentieth century.

Parham was certainly not the first to look at the experience of the apostles in Acts 2 as something that should be repeated in the lives of modern Christians who are baptized in the Spirit. Benjamin H. Irwin and the Fire-Baptized Holiness Church believed that those who were genuinely fire-baptized would experience physical manifestations such as shouting, leaping, screaming, laughing, dancing, or shaking that represented the state of the apostles when they were supposed to be drunk.[9] James Goff claims that even though Parham showed support for Irwin's baptism

---

5. Goff, *Fields White Unto Harvest*, 50–61; Callahan, "Redeemed or Destroyed," 209–12.

6. Callahan, "Redeemed or Destroyed," 207.

7. Ibid., 224.

8. See Parham's chapter on "Unity" in *Kol Kare Bomidbar*, 61–68.

9. See Irwin's exposition of Acts 2 in "The Pentecostal Church," *Live Coals of Fire* 1.21 (June 1, 1900) 2–3. See also Martin Schrag, "The Spiritual Pilgrimage," 22–33.

of fire, "he never personally stressed the doctrine nor testified to having received it."[10] Yet, in March of 1899 Parham personally testified,

> When finally I discovered that there was a cleansing promised for the body as well as the soul, and that the Holy Ghost would not dwell in an unclean temple, and my body full of corruption and disease was unfit for the Holy Ghost and fire, I took The Promise in I Thess. 5:23, where he says he will sanctify us, spirit, soul, and BODY, and by repentance, humiliation, and fasting I neared Him, until "by the Faith of the Son of God" I was entirely cleansed, and, as Joel says, my blood was purged. What was the result? All know the result of pure blood. The Holy Ghost and fire, the real power of Pentecost, came in, and I have never had a pain or ache since, while hundreds have been healed in answer to the Pentecost prayer of the Holy Ghost through me.[11]

Though Parham did not use the term "baptism," he seemed to be testifying to his own experience of being baptized with the Holy Ghost and fire immediately following his experience of sanctification. He understood his own freedom from sickness and the effectiveness of his prayers for the healing of others to be the results of the experience. In the same issue of *The Apostolic Faith*, a woman testified to having received the Baptism of the Holy Ghost as a result of Parham's prayer and laying on of hands. The results in this case were a confirmation of calling and power to do His will in service.[12] Though physical manifestations are noticeably absent from either testimony, it seems that in 1899 Parham recognized with Irwin the need for the Pentecostal experience in Acts to be duplicated in the lives of believers, and he even saw himself as having received such an experience. Yet, it appears Parham was looking to other results besides the bodily manifestations championed by Irwin as evidence of the experience.

---

10. Goff, *Fields White Unto Harvest*, 55.

11. Charles F. Parham, "My Testimony," *Apostolic Faith* [Topeka] 1.3 (March 30, 1899) 6. Parham later called this experience "a touch of the fire," and said that a more full and definite experience of fire baptism came upon him a month after this initial experience. Charles F. Parham, "Crowning Gift from Heaven," *Apostolic Faith* [Topeka] 1.12 (June 7, 1899) 5.

12. J. A. Haskins, "Testimonies," *Apostolic Faith* [Topeka] 1.3 (March 30, 1899) 6–7.

Tongues as a Witness

By the end of 1900, Parham honed in on one particular evidence that he believed would settle all disagreements on the subject once and for all: *xenolalia*. Though they are not named, Parham seemingly had Irwin's Fire-Baptized church in mind when he criticized the hermeneutic of those who claimed shouting, leaping, and screaming to be the visible manifestations of the Spirit in imitation of the disciples in Acts 2. He offered speaking in tongues as an alternative evidence saying, "How much more reasonable it would be for modern Holy Ghost teachers to first receive a BIBLE EVIDENCE such as the disciples, instead of trying to get the world to take their word for it."[13] Speaking in tongues cut through all the difficulties inherent in subjective claims of spiritual maturity and functioned as an easily identifiable, objective criterion that had its basis in the experience of the apostles. With this newfound evidence came a new understanding of the two-fold blessing of Spirit Baptism.

For years, Parham had believed that the Baptism in the Holy Spirit accomplished two things in the life of a Christian: it "seal[ed] the Bride and bestow[ed] the gifts."[14] The experience of his students in January 1901 led him to narrow his understanding of Spirit Baptism. He still maintained that it sealed one as a member of the Bride of Christ to be raptured to heaven before the end-time tribulation. However, he now believed that a genuine experience of Spirit Baptism would give the recipient *one particular gift*: the gift of tongues. This gift, he argued, gave one power to witness at home[15] and in foreign lands in an unknown, unlearned language.

Douglas Jacobsen says that Parham believed the primary purpose of a Christian's Baptism in the Holy Spirit was to "dissolve away the normal human focus on one's own needs and comforts and to make one truly

---

13. Parham, *Kol Kare Bomidbar*, 27–28. Parham would later speak more strongly, "Argue away the tongues as the evidence of the Baptism as recorded in the second chapter of Acts, and you open the way to theological anarchy, and any evidence of the spirit's operation may be claimed. . . . You will throw us back into all the chaotic opinions of the past 25 years." Charles F. Parham, "Fanaticism," *Apostolic Faith* [Baxter Springs] (December 1910) 3.

14. This belief was included among Parham's printed statement of the central teachings of the movement in his *Apostolic Faith* [Topeka] periodical from March 1899 to April 1900.

15. Parham argued for the usefulness of speaking in tongues in one's own native country in conjunction with the gift of interpretation as proof that the message one preached had its origin in God, not humankind. He went as far as to claim, "This is truly the Acme of inspiration, prayed for every Sabbath and desired by all true ministers of God." Parham, *Kol Kare Bomidbar*, 31.

other oriented," and that this was the main feature of the Pentecostal experience alongside the "Bible evidence" of speaking in tongues that distinguished it from all other previous anointings.[16] However, Parham's identification of an outward orientation toward others as a distinguishing mark of Spirit Baptism seems to have been a later development in his theology.[17] From the first, Parham certainly recognized that according to Acts 2 the Baptism in the Holy Spirit was given as "power to make witness."[18] But, early on Parham understood that the gift of tongues was not only the manifest *presence* of an internalized orientation toward others, but it was *itself* the power to witness. For Parham, it was clear that the only tangible evidence that distinguished the disciples' post-Pentecost life from their pre-Pentecost life was the gift of tongues.[19]

This theological position led Parham to postulate that people like John Wesley, who was unanimously regarded as an "other-oriented" minister, had still not been baptized in the Holy Spirit.[20] Parham believed that the gift of speaking unknown languages would give missionaries immediate power to witness to people in foreign lands. He reasoned, "How much better it would be for our modern missionaries to obey the injunction of Jesus to tarry for the same power; instead of wasting thousands of dollars, and often their lives in the vain attempt to become conversant in almost impossible tongues which the Holy Ghost could freely speak."[21] Rather than being *initial* evidence, tongues, as Parham understood them, were the *only* evidence, and they constituted a proof that should be repeatedly

---

16. Jacobsen, *Thinking in the Spirit*, 48.

17. Though it is not directly traceable to Parham's pen, in 1912 Parham's *Apostolic Faith* proclaimed, "The meaning of Pentecost is to pour out. Brother, if you claim the second chapter of Acts experience and don't literally pour out your life for the salvation of others, you have not the real thing." Prior to 1912 any orientation toward others that Parham's Apostolic Faith organization connected to Spirit Baptism seems to have been particularly tied to speaking in tongues. *Apostolic Faith* [Baxter Springs] 1.7 (September 1912) 9.

18. Parham, *Kol Kare Bomidbar*, 28.

19. Ibid., 36. Parham would later nuance his language to distinguish between the *witness* of tongues and the *gift* of tongues. Parham, *The Everlasting Gospel*, 68; *Apostolic Faith* [Baxter Springs] 1.6 (August 1912) 6.

20. Parham, *Kol Kare Bomidbar*, 32.

21. Ibid., 28. Parham's reasoning was quite logical, and not unique to him. Mary Campbell, a follower of Edward Irving in Scotland, sought the gift of tongues to aid her in her proposed missionary endeavors to the heathen over 70 years before. Oliphant, *The Life of Edward Irving*, 379–80.

manifest throughout the life of a Spirit-baptized person.[22] Without speaking in tongues the purposes of Spirit Baptism, as Parham understood them, were impossible to accomplish.

In his chapter on Spirit Baptism in *Kol Kare Bomidbar*, Parham took issue with the "thousands of Christians" who professed sealing and the Baptism of the Holy Ghost, but for whom "the Bible evidence is lacking in their lives." He provided them a comprehensive list of mistaken evidences of Spirit Baptism: "mighty convictions, floods of joy, unctions, or anointings," "shouting, leaping, jumping, falling in trances," "inspiration, unction, and divine revelation," and "the anointing that abideth."[23] Parham believed that all of these blessings fell short of being a valid evidence of Spirit Baptism because the Bible was clear: "By careful study of Acts 1:8, we find that the power was to make them witnesses."[24] Parham argued that it was only by speaking in tongues that this witness could become a reality. There was, for Parham, a functional connection between the *purpose* of Spirit Baptism and the biblical *proof* that such an experience had taken place.

Though Parham never went as far as to say that speaking in tongues was equal to the Baptism in the Spirit, the close connection he made between tongues and the purpose of Spirit Baptism lent itself to this conclusion. In May 1906, William Faye Carothers, Parham's Texas State Director, wrote in Parham's *Apostolic Faith*, "The speaking in tongues is not merely the evidence of the baptism with the Holy Ghost, but it is the principle [sic] feature of the baptism. It is to cause us to speak with tongues that we are 'baptized' with the holy [sic] Ghost."[25] In language strikingly similar to Parham, Carothers argued that Baptism in the Holy Spirit is clearly presented in the Bible as "something different from being 'filled,' 'anointed' or otherwise influenced by the Spirit."[26] Carothers felt that a Christian in the process of being equipped for service may experience "the regenerating, sanctifying, anointing and witnessing power of the Spirit" prior to one's Baptism in the Spirit, and that "it only remains for the baptism to cause us

---

22. Parham's *Apostolic Faith* proclaimed, "When people yield to sin, error, false teaching or fanaticisms, they lose the real Seal and clear language." "The Sealing," *Apostolic Faith* [Baxter Springs] (December 1910) 8.

23. Parham, *Kol Kare Bomidbar*, 27–28.

24. Ibid., 28.

25. W. F. Carothers, "The Baptism with the Holy Ghost," *Apostolic Faith* [Baxter Springs] 1.9 (May 1906) 14.

26. Ibid., 14.

to speak in other languages" for the work to be complete.[27] Both Parham and Carothers saw a functional connection between the purpose of Spirit Baptism and its evidence: speaking in other languages. No other work of the Spirit in the life of a Christian could suffice as proof of the experience.

Tongues as a Seal

Edith Blumhofer has observed that even though both purposes for Spirit Baptism—sealing the Bride of Christ and inspiring foreign tongues for the purpose of world evangelism—fit nicely into Parham's eschatological framework, his actions clearly show that in practice he was more concerned with tongues as a seal.[28] Parham relentlessly promoted the Pentecostal message and championed the implications of the message for the foreign mission field. Yet, neither he nor his students did much to evangelize anyone beyond their own English-speaking country. Leslie Callahan further points out that although Parham repeatedly advocated an evangelistic mission to the heathen, he believed that it was a futile mission in terms of conversions. What it accomplished was an ushering in of the return of Christ on the basis of all nations having heard.[29]

Parham's focus on Spirit Baptism as a seal is also seen in his preoccupation with identifying and calling out those who were and were not genuinely baptized in the Spirit. Speaking spontaneously in a foreign language provided Parham a seemingly foolproof way to know that one was numbered among the upper echelon of all Christians: the Bride of Christ. Spirit Baptism, for Parham, was *not* about salvation, holiness, peace, inspiration to preach, ability to teach, feelings of joy, compassion, love, devotion, or giftedness. Spirit Baptism was about separating the called out from among the called out.[30] Within Parham's schema, speaking in

---

27. Ibid., 14–15.

28. Blumhofer notes the conspicuous lack of missionary zeal by the Apostolic Faith Movement and their preference for in-depth personal Bible study and prayer over the equipping and sending-out of missionaries. Blumhofer, *Restoring the Faith*, 52. See also Blumhofer, *The Assemblies of God*, 83–84.

29. Callahan, "Redeemed or Destoryed," 206.

30. Aimee Semple McPherson used this language to separate Spirit-baptized Christians from other Christians, or Foursquare Pentecostals from other Pentecostals. She said, "The Lord is calling a called-out, of a called-out, of a called-out people who will escape to the mountains (rise up into the heights of God)." Aimee Semple McPherson, "The Bride in Her Vail Types and Shadows," *Bridal Call* 2.10 (March 1919) 5. She reiterated this same language in Foursquare Convention notes claiming, "We of the Foursquare Gospel Movement are a called out of the called out!" *Yearbook*, 5.

tongues functioned as the dividing mark of separation between the Bride of Christ and all other Christians. Parham had a clear idea about what the Bride would look like, and he had no problem excluding people from this group. Parham believed that racial descent, physical health, intelligence, and persona were all variables of consequence in determining who would likely make up the Bride.[31] The quickness with which Parham invalidated the claims to Spirit Baptism by those at Azusa Street and elsewhere show just how eager Parham was to pronounce the supposed sealing of some to be null and void.[32]

An emerging distinction in the Apostolic Faith organization between the "sign" of tongues and the "gift" of tongues further increased Parham's emphasis on tongues as a seal and diminished the role of evidential tongues on the foreign mission field.[33] Carothers was the first to distinguish between the gift of tongues and the sign of tongues saying, "This ['baptism' or 'gift' of the Holy Ghost] is not to be confused with the gift of speaking in tongues. Many of us speak occasionally in the Pentecostal experience, who never develop the gift of readily and fluently speaking in tongues."[34] This distinction was retained by Parham's Apostolic Faith organization and stood out to them as the one point of doctrine that was different from that which Parham had first proclaimed.

> The only point wherein we differ from the first teaching regarding Pentecost is that neither the gift of tongues or any other of the nine gifts of the Spirit are the evidence of the baptism. If you have the gift of a tongue you can use it as you do your English, both in speaking and understanding it . . . Those who receive the baptism of the Holy Ghost can only speak as the Spirit gives utterance, while those who have the gift of tongues can use it at will and understand it.[35]

---

31. Callahan, "Redeemed or Destroyed," 211–12. See also Callahan, "A Sanctified Body," 5–12; Anderson, "The Dubious Legacy," 52–55.

32. "The Sealing," *Apostolic Faith* [Baxter Springs] (December 1910) 8.

33. *Apostolic Faith* [Baxter Springs] 1.6 (August 1912) 6. W. F. Carothers, "The Baptism with the Holy Ghost," *Apostolic Faith* [Baxter Springs] 1.9 (May 1906) 15.

34. W. F. Carothers, "The Baptism with the Holy Ghost," *Apostolic Faith* [Baxter Springs] 1.9 (May 1906) 15. See also Carothers, *The Baptism with the Holy Ghost*, 20.

35. *Apostolic Faith* [Baxter Springs] 1.6 (August 1912) 6. Parham differed from Carothers in his understanding that the gift of tongues might be given before or after an experience of Spirit Baptism. Parham's case in point was Sister Ellen Norton who received what Parham understood as the gift of the Italian language twenty-six years before her Baptism in the Spirit. Carothers held that the gift of speaking in tongues would never be given *prior* to one's Baptism in the Holy Spirit unlike the other eight

For Parham, this distinction solidified the passive nature of the experience of being baptized in the Spirit. It also placed more emphasis on the experience of Spirit Baptism as a seal than as a tool for evangelism. While spontaneous, inspired tongue-speech might be used in evangelization, the Baptism in the Holy Spirit was primarily God's way of separating out from among the entire company of believers, the relatively small Bride of Christ.[36]

Throughout his life, Parham remained consistent in his belief that an experience of sanctification was a perquisite to an experience of Spirit Baptism. Separating himself from many of his contemporaries in the Holiness tradition, Parham believed that Spirit Baptism had to do with sealing the Bride of Christ and equipping the Bride for worldwide evangelism rather than with effecting the inner transformation and bodily cleansing that was required to meet the Lord. For Parham, inner transformation came prior to one's Baptism in the Spirit. The Baptism was proof that one's inner transformation was complete, and that one was now being set apart as The Bride and sent out to witness for Christ in the world. In short, Spirit Baptism did not *make* a person clean; it was an experience reserved for people who were *already* clean.[37]

Spirit Baptism, Sanctification, and "the Anointing that Abideth"

Sanctification, for Parham, was a cleansing of the body as well as the soul. Thus, physical traits could indicate whether or not a person was sanctified. Parham believed a Christian could not expect to legitimately be baptized in the Holy Spirit without a proper cleansing of the body from disease and

---

gifts of the Holy Spirit. Carothers, *The Baptism with the Holy Ghost*, 20.

36. Parham's *Apostolic Faith* distinguished between the tongues that functioned as a seal, and those that should be sought for use in a foreign mission field: "Anyone going to a foreign field should seek the gift of the language of the country and should be able to use it and understand it when spoken by others, but those who have the Pentecostal sealing can only speak as the Spirit giveth utterance." "Baptism of the Holy Ghost," *Apostolic Faith* [Baxter Springs] 1.8 (October 1912) 9. Yet, this distinction between the sign and the gift of tongues did not sway Parham on his conviction that all valid cases of Spirit Baptism should be accompanied by tongues speech in a known foreign language and corroborated by a "disinterested foreigner." Charles F. Parham, "The Difference Between the Baptism of the Holy Ghost and the Anointing—Spooks," *Apostolic Faith* [Baxter Springs] 3.2 (February 1914) 9.

37. Parham criticized many later Pentecostals for their "denial of a well established tenet" in the holiness doctrine of sanctification. *Apostolic Faith* [Baxter Springs] (January 1912) 7.

sickness.[38] Taking things a step further, Parham understood the "fanaticism" that he repeatedly criticized at Azusa Street to be the result of "an unsanctified vessel" that allows the flesh to control the body. He believed that the supposed "epilepsy, fits, insanity, drunkenness, and abnormal passions" he found so offensive in other sectors of the Pentecostal movement could be avoided if people would be sanctified in their bodies, as well as in their minds and souls. Parham believed that sanctification of the body would lead to "decency and order . . . that appeals to people."[39] Apparently, Parham found many of the manifestations of the Spirit at Azusa Street to be "unseemly" and lacking in their ability to "command respect from all beholders."[40] This was cause enough for Parham to question whether the participants had experienced a full sanctification of mind, soul, and body.

In addition to sanctification and Spirit Baptism, Parham firmly believed that there was a third experience available to Christians that typically (but not always)[41] succeeded sanctification and preceded Spirit Baptism called the "anointing that abideth."[42] He explained, "Probably the greatest mistake has been of thinking 'the anointing that abideth,' (1 John 2:27), which the disciples received in the upper chamber where Christ breathed upon them, (John 20:22), the real baptism of the Holy Spirit."[43] Parham claimed that the "anointing that abideth" opened the door for a Christian to be taught by the Holy Spirit through the Scriptures and to have the

---

38. Parham, *Kol Kare Bomidbar*, chapter entitled, "Healing."

39. Charles F. Parham, "The Sources of Disease," *Apostolic Faith* [Baxter Springs] 1.6 (August 1912) 4.

40. Charles F. Parham, "Leadership," *Apostolic Faith* [Baxter Springs] 1.4 (June 1912) 9.

41. Parham observed, "The anointing of the Holy Spirit takes precedence to the Baptism of the Holy Spirit. When the vessel is cleansed and prepared as an instrument, then it needs something else. . . . The anointing of the Holy Spirit is sometimes given even before sanctification comes." Parham, *The Everlasting Gospel*, 17.

42. In an article devoted to their National Camp Meeting, a writer for *Apostolic Faith* described the "Word and Doctrine" taught at the meeting. "Conversion, with the spirit's witness; sanctification that keeps the spiritual life in the ascendancy; the Pentecostal Baptism *preceded by the annointing* [sic] *that abideth*, and evidenced by a clear language." W. M. Allison, "National Camp Meeting," *Apostolic Faith* [Baxter Springs] (December 1910) 6 (italics mine). Parham further included "The Anointing of the Holy Ghost" as a distinct phase in his "Chart of the Steps of Grace in Christian Life" in *Apostolic Faith* [Baxter Springs] (December 1910) 10; *Apostolic Faith* [Baxter Springs] 1.7 (September 1912) 16. Parham was not the first to use such terminology. Charles Finney used the term to refer to sanctification in Charles Finney, *Systematic Theology*, 481.

43. Parham, *Kol Kare Bomidbar*, 28.

Spirit's teaching flow through one's mouth to others, virtually bypassing the intellect.[44] "This anointing," Parham said, "is sufficient under all circumstances for needed inspiration when speaking in our tongue, but if you desire a personal Baptism of the Holy Ghost, the sealing power, escaping plagues, and putting you in a position to become part of the Body, the Bride or the Man-Child, seek the Holy Ghost."[45] Parham excluded divine revelation, inspiration, unction in the pulpit, conviction, and spiritual guidance from the benefits of Spirit Baptism. These were benefits that resulted from the "anointing that abideth," results that many Christians over the years had experienced and mistakenly assumed to be the Baptism in the Holy Spirit.[46] Thus, a preacher with the "anointing that abideth" was just as likely to preach an inspired sermon in English from his pulpit as one who had been baptized in the Holy Spirit.

Parham's Contribution to Pentecostalism

In a one-page appendix to his book, *Fields White Unto Harvest*, Goff acknowledges shifts in Pentecostal theology after Parham. He identifies "three theological planks" that Parham joined to form the first distinctly Pentecostal theology: "1) Tongue speech as the initial evidence of Holy Spirit Baptism, 2) Spirit-filled believers as the 'sealed' Bride of Christ, and 3) Xenoglossic tongues as the tool for a dramatic end-time revival."[47] Of these, Goff says that the first "plank" was the only one that survived in its original form. Though Goff has accurately identified the key elements of Parham's unique theological system, he does not sufficiently recognize the interdependence of the three planks in Parham's thought. He gives the impression that one plank could remain in place without the other two. This, however, is not the case. The theological link that Parham made between tongues as *xenolalia* and the purpose of Baptism in the Holy Spirit must be recognized. Goff concedes, "Most Pentecostals abandoned the specifics of the early vision," but without the "specifics" that Goff says were abandoned—tongues as *xenolalia* and tongues as a seal for the Bride of Christ—the "early vision" is really no vision at all.[48]

---

44. Parham, *Kol Kare Bomidbar*, 31; Parham, *The Everlasting Gospel*, 17.
45. Parham, *Kol Kare Bomidbar*, 31.
46. Ibid., 27–28, 30–31.
47. Goff, *Fields White Unto Harvest*, 173.
48. Goff, "The Theology of Charles Fox Parham," 69.

As the Pentecostal movement moved out from under Parham's control at Azusa Street, his views concerning both what it meant to be baptized in the Spirit and what constituted a genuine experience of speaking in tongues were not widely accepted. Thus, the first plank in Parham's theological system can be said to have survived in its original form only in *word*, not in *meaning*. In word, Parham held a very similar doctrine to the doctrine of initial evidence that firmly planted itself in the movement. However, what exactly Parham meant by the words is different from the meaning given to those words by the majority of Pentecostals after 1908. Rather than attribute the founding of the Pentecostal doctrine of initial evidence to Parham, it may be more appropriate to say that Parham inaugurated the application of a distinct hermeneutic to the Book of Acts. In short, he was the first to postulate that the experience of speaking in tongues by the first disciples in the Upper Room on the Day of Pentecost was meant to be repeated in the lives of modern Christians. Disagreement arose concerning the experience's content, purpose, and relationship to the rest of the Christian life, but all early Pentecostals agreed that Acts 2 was not just an example of the power of the Spirit available to Christians in a prior dispensation but a description of what Jesus Christ desired his church to experience in the present.

Parham's belief in tongues as a tool for evangelism was superseded by his focus on tongues as a seal of the Bride of Christ. Tongues functioned as a clear line of demarcation between those who were and were not part of the Bride. James Goff argues that Parham infused the Pentecostal movement with missionary zeal, but this appears to be far from the truth.[49] In contrast to the Azusa Street Mission in Los Angeles, which heralded the spreading fire of the Spirit around the globe, Parham never seemed to express a desire for "heathen" converted through the missionary efforts of Spirit-baptized Christians to be baptized in the Holy Spirit themselves. The purpose of Spirit Baptism was spreading the gospel to the ends of the earth quickly without having to waste time learning foreign languages. But more importantly for Parham, it ensured that those who were being *sent out* with this new gift would also be *caught up* with Christ in the rapture and escape the ensuing tribulation on earth. In the end, Parham was more interested in proclaiming who was excluded from the Bride than who was included. Such a mindset can hardly be described as "missionary zeal." Again, it was Parham's hermeneutic that, when taken up by later

---

49. Goff, *Fields White Unto Harvest*, 72–79, 164.

Pentecostals at Azusa Street, formed a basis for the movement's emphasis on foreign missions.

William Seymour and the Azusa Street Mission
A Broader Conception of Spirit Baptism

During the first six months of revivals at the Azusa Street Mission, William Seymour and the mission viewed their ministry in Los Angeles as an extension of Charles Parham's ministry in the Midwest and Texas. As a result, Parham's understanding of the Baptism of the Holy Spirit and the relationship of speaking in tongues to the Baptism was fully adopted by the first leaders at Azusa Street. The importance of speaking in a known foreign language as proof of the Pentecostal experience, and its value as an end-time seal and a tool for worldwide evangelism, were consistently upheld in the first two issues of their periodical, *The Apostolic Faith*. However, by December of 1906 the Azusa Street Mission no longer acknowledged Parham as its leader and made it clear that it desired to separate from him. In conjunction with this separation from Parham, a wider range of beliefs concerning the purpose, evidence and meaning of Spirit Baptism began to show itself in the writings and testimonies of Pentecostals at Azusa Street. With this broader understanding of what the Baptism in the Holy Spirit accomplished in the life of a Christian, came a more varied understanding of how speaking in tongues was related to the experience of Spirit Baptism.

When it came to the identifying marks of a genuinely Spirit-baptized Christian, Parham emphasized the ability to speak spontaneously in a foreign language that one had not previously learned. Though they always expected that tongues would accompany the Baptism in the Holy Spirit, Seymour and other contributors to the Azusa paper shifted their focus away from tongues to Christian character, virtues, and works of charity as that which validated a claim to have been filled with the Spirit. Cecil Robeck documents well the shift in Seymour's thought concerning the evidence of Spirit Baptism in the fall of 1907.[50] By the end of 1907, Seymour's periodical stated that the fruit of the Spirit manifested daily in a person's life was the real evidence of the Baptism in the Spirit.[51] Anger and gossip were specifically highlighted as traits that showed that a person

---

50. Robeck, "William J. Seymour," 81–82.

51. "Questions Answered," *Apostolic Faith* [Los Angeles] 1.11 (October-January 1908) 2.

was *not* baptized in the Spirit.[52] At that time, Seymour's *Apostolic Faith* continued to print the tenets they articulated in the first issue of the paper upholding a distinct difference between sanctification, "the anointing that abideth," and Baptism in the Holy Spirit.[53] However, statements made in testimonies and articles in the rest of the paper blurred and in some cases completely dissolved the lines between these three experiences.

Spirit Baptism and Sanctification

In the October-January 1908 issue of *The Apostolic Faith* the association of holy living with Spirit Baptism was made explicit:

> There is no difference in quality between the baptism with the Holy Ghost and sanctification. They are both holiness. Sanctification is the Lord-Jesus Christ crowned in your heart, and the baptism with the Holy Spirit is His power upon you. It is all holiness.[54]

Here, sanctification and Spirit Baptism were presented as two sides of the same coin: holiness. Others took many of the traits Parham associated with "the anointing that abideth" and attributed them to Spirit Baptism.

> The baptism of the Holy Ghost comes on the sanctified, cleansed life. After the vessel is cleansed and made holy, it is meet for the Master's use. . . . In seeking this baptism, if you realize that you are sanctified and cleansed by the Blood of Christ, and wait before Him for the outpouring of the Holy Spirit in thanksgiving and faith. He will come in and fill His temple from head to foot. This Holy Ghost is love, power, joy, blessing, wisdom and holiness. He will guide you and open the Scriptures to you.[55]

---

52. "To the Baptized Saints," *Apostolic Faith* [Los Angeles] 1.9 (June-September 1907) 2.

53. The first issue of *Apostolic Faith* [Los Angeles] proclaimed, "Too many have confused the grace of Sanctification with the enduement of Power, or the Baptism with the Holy Ghost; others have taken 'the anointing that abideth' for the Baptism, and failed to reach the glory and power of a true Pentecost." This statement continued to be printed as part of the teachings of the Apostolic Faith Movement until the paper ceased publication in May 1908.

54. "The Baptism with the Holy Ghost," *Apostolic Faith* [Los Angeles] 1.11 (October-January 1908) 4.

55. Ibid., 4.

In June 1907 an article identified sanctification with "the abiding anointing" and stated that if one did not have an abiding anointing one had a counterfeit sanctification. Other articles in the same issue spoke of the need to retain the anointing after one has received the Baptism in the Holy Spirit.[56] These and other examples show how the anticipated effects of Spirit Baptism gradually broadened at Azusa Street to encompass results that had been previously confined to phases of sanctification and "the anointing that abideth" in Parham's theological schema.

Like Parham, Seymour and the Azusa Street Mission clearly understood Spirit Baptism as an experience distinct from and subsequent to an experience of sanctification. They maintained,

> Sanctification is the second work of grace and the last work of grace. Sanctification is the act of God's free grace by which He makes us holy. . . . Sanctification is cleansing to make holy. . . . The Disciples were sanctified before the Day of Pentecost. . . . You know, that they could not receive the Spirit if they were not clean. Jesus cleansed and got all doubt out of His Church before He went back to glory. The Baptism in the Holy Ghost is the gift of power upon the sanctified life.[57]

The Azusa Street Mission consistently upheld a belief that the Holy Spirit only baptized sanctified Christians.[58] Their answer to the question, "Does a soul need the baptism with the Holy Ghost in order to live a pure and holy life?" drew a clear distinction between Spirit Baptism and sanctification: "No; sanctification makes us holy, Heb. 2:11. . . . The Holy Ghost does not cleanse anyone from sin. It is Jesus' shed Blood on Calvary. The Holy Ghost never died for our sins."[59]

Despite these doctrinal distinctions, a practical difference between sanctification and Spirit Baptism is not always easily discernible in the

---

56. "Christ Abides in Sanctification," *Apostolic Faith* [Los Angeles] 1.9 (June 1907) 2. Another article proclaimed, "Every sanctified person has the abiding anointing in their soul." *Apostolic Faith* [Los Angeles] 1.6 (February-March 1906) 1.

57. "The Apostolic Faith Movement," *Apostolic Faith* [Los Angeles] 1.1 (September 1906) 2. Parham later used these same doctrinal statements as the basis for an expanded discussion of his own views on sanctification. Parham, *The Everlasting Gospel*, 10–16. But despite their use of the same language, the two groups clearly parted ways in their application of these stated values in their own ministries.

58. Douglas Jacobsen goes as far as to say that the mission's understanding that Christian life progresses in the three distinct steps—justification, sanctification and Spirit Baptism—was their "central message." Jacobsen, *Thinking in the Spirit*, 70.

59. "Questions Answered," *Apostolic Faith* [Los Angeles] 1.9 (June-September 1907) 2.

mission's writings. One woman testified to an external witness to her sanctification,

> Besides this witness of the Spirit, was the witness of the fruits; for under whatever provocation, there is no uprising, for there is nothing to rise up. Glory to Jesus. When sanctified, I was filled with such glory that I felt sure it must be the baptism, which did not come for three weeks.[60]

Yet, the results of her subsequent Baptism in the Spirit were not all that different in quality than the "fruits" of her sanctification: "To sum it up, the baptism of the Spirit means to me what I never dreamed it could this side of Heaven: victory, glory in my soul, perfect peace, rest, liberty, nearness to Christ, deadness to this old world, and power in witnessing."[61] In other testimonies, Spirit Baptism is presented as a continuation of the work begun in sanctification. Two statements from the September 1907 issue of *The Apostolic Faith* show how, in the minds of at least some at the Azusa Street Mission, Spirit Baptism was not qualitatively different from sanctification as much as quantitatively. "In sanctification the unction of the Holy Ghost comes on you in speaking, but the baptism is power through your whole body day and night." Another noted, "When a man or woman gets the baptism with the Holy Ghost, they are filled with continual light. It is a greater light than when you were sanctified. It is the full blessing of Christ."[62]

When seeking the Baptism in the Holy Spirit, the mission encouraged people to seek holiness rather than manifestations or signs.[63] At times, Seymour's own descriptions of the results of the Baptism in the Holy Spirit are indistinguishable from the results of sanctification to which many Holiness people of the day testified. Seymour saw "the real Bible evidence" of Spirit Baptism in "Divine love" and "the fruits of the Spirit" alongside the destruction of the works of the flesh.[64] Robeck convincingly argues that this and other statements show Seymour "clearly broadened

---

60. Antoinette Moomau, "China Missionary Receives Pentecost," *Apostolic Faith* [Los Angeles] 1.11 (October-January 1908) 3.

61. Ibid., 3.

62. "Pentecostal Notes," *Apostolic Faith* [Los Angeles] 1.10 (September 1907) 3.

63. "The Baptism with the Holy Ghost," *Apostolic Faith* [Los Angeles] 1.11 (October-January 1908) 4.

64. "Questions Answered," *Apostolic Faith* [Los Angeles] 1.11 (October-January 1907) 2.

his understanding of Spirit Baptism to include an ethical dimension."[65] Seymour later would make a connection between Spirit Baptism and purity of doctrine with regard to the mission's stance on annihilationism, a stance meant to indirectly call into question the validity of Parham's Spirit Baptism.

> We don't believe in the doctrine of Annihiation [sic] of the wicked. That is the reason why we could not stand for tongues being the evidence of the Baptism in the Holy Ghost and fire. If tongues was the evidence of the gift of the Holy Spirit, then men and women that have received the gift of tongues could not believed [sic] contrary to the teachings of the Holy Spirit.[66]

The boundaries between sanctification and Spirit Baptism became less refined as the mission came to believe that a Spirit-baptized person might "lose their Pentecost."[67] They felt the need in later issues of *The Apostolic Faith* to emphasize the need for Spirit-baptized people to live out the Word of God "with perfect obedience" in order to maintain their anointing.[68] In a column entitled, "To the Baptized Saints," the call to maintain one's anointing after receiving the Pentecostal Baptism was repeatedly given. The article opened with an admonition, "It is one thing to receive the baptism and another thing to keep the anointing." The article went on to give precedence to the fruit of the Spirit over tongues as evidence of Spirit Baptism. "Your life must measure with the fruit of the Spirit. If you get angry, or speak evil, or backbite, I care not how many tongues you may have, you have not the Baptism with the Holy Spirit. You have lost your salvation." The article concluded by addressing the danger of losing the Spirit of Jesus and even the gifts themselves.[69]

---

65. Robeck, "William J. Seymour," 81.

66. Seymour, *The Doctrines and Discipline*, 52.

67. In the article, "Questions Answered," the question is asked, "Can a person lose the Pentecost and be restored?" The answer: "Yes; if they have not sinned willfully." *Apostolic Faith* [Los Angeles] 1.11 (October-January 1907) 2

68. "Questions Answered," *Apostolic Faith* [Los Angeles] 1.11 (October-January 1907) 2.

69. "To the Baptized Saints," *Apostolic Faith* [Los Angeles] 1.9 (June-September 1907) 2.

Spirit Baptism and "the Anointing that Abideth"

Not only were some of the benefits of sanctification difficult to distinguish from the benefits of Spirit Baptism at the Azusa Street Mission, the phase between sanctification and Spirit Baptism that Parham understood as "the anointing that abideth" became so fully absorbed in their understanding of Spirit Baptism and sanctification that it remained as a distinct experience only in theory. Seymour's periodical printed many articles referring to the benefits of the Spirit's work as teacher and guide in personal Bible study, and in witnessing that came upon believers when they were baptized in the Spirit. One article proclaimed, "The baptism of the Holy Spirit is power and understanding of the Word and the glory of God upon your life. . . . The man that hears you speak a message right from the throne falls down and seeks God and gets up to report that God is in you of a truth."[70] In an article that asked and answered various questions about Spirit Baptism, the question was raised, "Do we need to study the Bible as much after receiving the Holy Ghost?" The mission answered that reading the Bible was essential even after receiving the Spirit as a safeguard against fanaticism, misappropriation of the Word, and pride. The Spirit did not bypass Scripture in its teaching, but spoke through Scripture messages that Spirit-baptized Christians were uniquely qualified to hear and receive.[71] Seymour would later write, "Some one will ask: How do you know when you will get the Holy Ghost? He, the spirit of truth, will guide you into all truth. St. John 16:13. The gift of the Holy Ghost is more than speaking in tongues. He is wisdom, power, truth, holiness. He is a person that teaches us truth."[72]

At other points, Seymour used the term "abiding" to describe the Baptism in the Holy Spirit. "The greatest evidence of the Holy Spirit abiding in the believer is what Jesus Christ promised he would do. Jesus promised he would teach us all things, and bring all things to your remembrance, whatsoever I have said unto you, so he means what he says

---

70. *Apostolic Faith* [Los Angeles] 2.13 (May 1908) 2.

71. "Questions Answered," *Apostolic Faith* [Los Angeles] 1.11 (October-January 1907) 2. In another issue of *The Apostolic Faith* the following observation was printed: "There was a time when we were fed upon theological chips, shavings, and wind, but now the long, long night is past. We are feeding upon the Word which is revealed by the Holy Ghost—the whole Word and nothing but the Word." *Apostolic Faith* [Los Angeles] 1.7 (April 1907) 3.

72. Seymour, *The Doctrines and Discipline*, 51.

... John 14:17–26. Also John 16:7–15."[73] For most Pentecostals, the Azusa Street revival would mark an end to a belief in an experience other than sanctification and Spirit Baptism by which the Spirit imparted a lasting anointing to the believer.[74] The experience and subsequent results of "the anointing that abideth" that Parham expounded came to be seen as part of sanctification and Spirit Baptism for the majority of later Pentecostals.

The Changing Role of Tongues

As aspects that had previously been relegated to sanctification and "the anointing that abideth" began to be attributed to Spirit Baptism, the evidence of Spirit Baptism broadened as well. The inclusion of praise, ethics, holiness, and insight into Scripture into the realm possible results of Spirit Baptism dissolved much of the logical connection between the purpose of and proof of Spirit Baptism that Parham made. There had been a concrete correlation between speaking in tongues and the purposes of Spirit Baptism that Parham articulated.[75] At the Azusa Street Mission, a more symbolic correlation emerged alongside their more inclusive understanding of the results of Spirit Baptism. The ability to speak in tongues began to be understood as an avenue of praise to God that symbolized the heavenly praise that would soon be instituted in the rapture.[76] One article made it clear that tongues were simply an outward symbol of an inward submission to God,

> A person may not speak in tongues for a week after the baptism, but as soon as he gets to praying or praising God in the liberty of the Spirit, the tongues will follow. Tongues are not salvation. It is

---

73. Ibid., 93.

74. Even beyond Azusa Street, Pentecostal leaders were attributing illumination in reading Scripture and inspiration from the pulpit to their Baptism in the Holy Spirit. Testifying to his own Spirit Baptism in early 1907, J. H. King described the results, "Soon the Word began to be opened to me in a new way, and it seemed as if I had a different Bible . . . during all the remaining months of that year I preached with such inspiration and power as I have never before experienced." Underwood, *Christ—God's Love Gift*, 13; quoted in Alexander, "Boundless Love Divine," 17.

75. Parham's periodical articulated four purposes of Spirit Baptism that were functionally connected to an individual speaking in known foreign languages: 1) a "sign of a believer," 2) a "sign to unbelievers," 3) "power to witness," and 4) "the sealing power." "Baptism of the Holy Ghost," *Apostolic Faith* [Baxter Springs] 1.8 (October 1912) 8–9.

76. "The Heavenly Anthem," *Apostolic Faith* [Los Angeles] 1.5 (January 1907) 3. See also, Frank Bartleman, "Letter from Los Angeles," *Triumphs of Faith* 26.12 (December 1906) 251–52, printed in Robeck, "CH 547–847 Syllabus," 55–56.

a gift that God throws in with the baptism with the Holy Spirit. People do not have to travail and agonize for the baptism, for when our work ceases, then God comes. We cease from our own works, which is the very type of the millennium.[77]

Kim Alexander has drawn attention to the presence of a number of early testimonies and sermons in *The Apostolic Faith*, even from Seymour himself, that likened being baptized in the Holy Spirit to being married to Jesus. Not only did they describe Spirit Baptism as a sealing of the Bride, but also an experience that inaugurated an intimate connection with Christ that produced feelings and emotions of love and affection not unlike those between a husband and wife.[78]

The idea of tongues as a private prayer language also began to emerge in *The Apostolic Faith* as a symbol of a direct communion with God reminiscent of Parham's notion of "the anointing that abideth":

> Those who speak in tongues seem to live in another world. The experience they have entered into corresponds exactly with that which is described in the 10th chapter of Acts. The tongues they speak in do not seem to be intended as a means of communication between themselves and others, as on the Day of Pentecost, but corresponds more closely with that described in the 14th of I. Corinthians, 2nd verse, and seems to be a means of communication between the soul and God.[79]

Speaking in tongues was increasingly seen as an experience that in different ways symbolized the many varied blessings and benefits of Spirit Baptism testified to by people at Azusa Street. By 1909, a sermon by Wesley Myland was published in the *Latter Rain Evangel* that specifically talked about the benefit of speaking in tongues for the soul as they enabled one to praise and magnify God in spirit, soul, and body.[80]

Gary McGee sees a greater continuity in the ideas concerning speaking in tongues held by early Pentecostals between 1901 and 1908 than

---

77. "Questions Answered," *Apostolic Faith* [Los Angeles] 1.11 (October-January 1907) 2.

78. Alexander, "Boundless Love Divine," 14.

79. The Christian Missionary Alliance, "The Promise of the Father and Speaking with Tongues in Chicago," *Apostolic Faith* [Los Angeles] 1.9 (June-September 1907) 3. McGee has documented a similar change in focus from the use of tongues for public preaching to tongues as private prayer by A. H. Garr, an Azusa missionary to India, in early 1907. McGee, "'Latter Rain' Falling in the East," 659–60.

80. Wesley Myland, "The Yielded Life: An Exposition of the 29th Psalm," *The Latter Rain Evangel* 1.4 (January 1909) 3–5.

what has been presented above.[81] In particular, McGee argues that the notion of speaking in tongues as prayer and worship was present from the very beginning of the movement alongside the understanding of tongues as languages for preaching on the mission field.[82] However, the significant pieces of evidence that McGee has used to defend his position do not date any earlier than August 1905 in connection with the revivals that were taking place in Orchard and Houston, Texas, under the leadership of Parham and Carothers.[83] McGee cited Parham's own testimony that commensurate with his experience of Spirit Baptism in 1901 he "began to *worship* God in the Swedish tongue." However, the testimony that McGee cited was a version not published by Parham until 1926.[84] The earliest surviving testimony of Parham's Baptism says that upon being baptized in the Spirit, he began "*preaching* the Word in another language," and that he continued to "*preach* in different languages" all around the United States.[85] The evidence seems to suggest that up until 1905, Pentecostals understood that the primary reasons for speaking in tongues were sealing the Bride of Christ and preaching on the mission field. W. F. Carothers, who directed the *Apostolic Faith* ministry in Texas, appears to be the first Pentecostal to champion tongues as primarily a means of communion with God through prayer and worship in 1906.[86]

In the same breath that Pentecostals at Azusa Street began to include more reasons for the importance of the manifestation of tongues in conjunction with the Baptism in the Holy Spirit, they began to exclude others. In particular, a distinction between the *evidence* or *sign* of tongues, which would manifest itself in an experience of Spirit Baptism, and the *gift* of tongues, which would be used on the mission field as a means of communicating with people in their native tongue, diminished the importance of tongues for foreign missions. The gift and sign of tongues were distinguished by the degree to which the intellect was involved in the speaking

81. McGee, "The New World," 108–35.

82. Ibid., 109–10.

83. In August 1905, Parham's *Apostolic Faith* reported on the revivals in Orchard and Houston, saying that Spirit Baptism was enabling recipients to "speak in languages they know not of, and when the language is interpreted or known it is always in *praise* or *supplication* to God." "Revivals at Orchard and Houston, Texas," *Apostolic Faith* [Melrose] 1.3 (August 1905) 11.

84. *Apostolic Faith* [Baxter Springs] 2.7 (July 1926) 2–3.

85. *Apostolic Faith* [Los Angeles] 1.2 (October 1906) 1. Italics mine.

86. W. F. Carothers, "The Baptism with the Holy Ghost," *Apostolic Faith* [Baxter Springs] 1.9 (May 1906) 15–16; Carothers, *The Baptism with the Holy Ghost*, 20–21.

process. The sign of tongues was considered to be inspired speech that came spontaneously and passively. The gift of tongues was understood as the sudden ability to intellectually understand, speak, and comprehend a foreign language.[87] As more Pentecostals recognized this distinction, an authentic experience of Spirit Baptism began to replace the gift of tongues as that which was essential for Spirit-empowered missionary endeavors.

Robeck observes, "Any nuance between tongues as the evidence of Baptism with the Spirit and the 'gift of tongues' eluded the secular press just as it did most early Apostolic Faith people."[88] This is probably an accurate assessment since most testimonies in *The Apostolic Faith* refer to their initial experience of tongues as a "gift." However, this nuance in language proved to be an important distinction for at least some who had difficulty seeing tongues as a uniform evidence for all Spirit-baptized Christians in the face of Paul's implicit admonition that the gift of tongues is for *some* and not *all* in 1 Cor 12:27–30. In March 1907, it was reported in *The Apostolic Faith* that the *Live Coals* paper published in Royston, Georgia dramatically changed their position on speaking in tongues as evidence of Spirit Baptism. Previously, they had been "stoutly opposed to and rejected" that tongues would always accompany a genuine experience of Spirit Baptism. Those responsible for the *Live Coals* paper (J. H. King was editor) understood a distinction between tongues as evidence and tongues as a gift as essential for maintaining a doctrine of evidential tongues. They had previously felt this distinction to be a "fanatical proposition." Now they felt such a distinction was appropriate, and this led them to adopt a belief that tongues would *always* accompany a genuine experience of Spirit Baptism. Further, the *Live Coals* paper claimed they would censor all articles and testimonies that did not line-up with such a doctrine.[89] The inclusion of

87. W. F. Carothers, "The Baptism with the Holy Ghost," *Apostolic Faith* [Baxter Springs] 1.9 (May 1906) 15; Carothers, *The Baptism with the Holy Ghost*, 20; G. F. Taylor, *The Spirit and the Bride* (Dunn, NC: n.p., 1907), 63. Belief in the gift of tongues as a tool for evangelizing the world was present even in non-Pentecostal denominations of the time. "Seeking Pentecost," *Gospel Trumpet* (December 28, 1906) 2–3, printed in Robeck, "CH 547–847 Syllabus," 96–98. In this article protesting the Pentecostal emphasis that all people should speak in tongues, the story is told of a man who lived in an area surrounded by people from Holland. In answer to prayer, he was reportedly given the gift of reading and translating the "Holland language."

88. Robeck, "William J. Seymour," 76.

89. "Transformed by the Holy Ghost," *Apostolic Faith* [Los Angeles] 1.6 (February-March 1907) 5. In the February 13, 1907 issue of *Live Coals* an article was printed in which 1 Cor 12:27–30 was used as a defense against a rigid evidential tongues stance saying, "To some He surely 'divides' the gift of tongues, but not to all." J. Hudson Ballard, "Spiritual Gifts with Special Reference to the Gift of Tongues," *Live Coals*

this article in *The Apostolic Faith* shows that the mission clearly believed the distinction was appropriate.[90]

Spreading the Fire

The break with Parham's theology of Spirit Baptism that occurred at Azusa Street is most easily seen in the differences between the two organizations' approaches to foreign missions. As stated above, even though Parham's Apostolic Faith organization championed the benefits of Spirit Baptism and speaking in tongues for the foreign mission field, Parham sent few people overseas. Theologically, Parham understood the benefits of Spirit Baptism for the foreign mission field to be a practical linguistic aid for evangelizing (not necessarily converting) as many people as possible. He does not appear to have been concerned that those on the mission field also be baptized in the Spirit. In contrast, even a cursory reading of the Azusa Street periodical shows the mission's passion that the Pentecostal Baptism be spread to the converts of overseas missionaries.[91] The revival under the leadership of Pandita Ramabai at the Mukti Mission near Pune, India is a case in point.

News of the revival in India appeared in the third issue of *Apostolic Faith*. The article celebrated the fact that spiritual gifts, including tongues, were being poured out on the natives demonstrating that "all have a place in the present revival" and that "[God] is no respecter of persons."[92] In September 1907, a report from Albert and Lilian Garr who had been sent out as missionaries to India from Azusa Street was printed. It proclaimed that "300 native girls" were among those who had received the Spirit.[93] The Garrs were among those that left Azusa Street for foreign mission fields with confidence that they had been given the ability to speak spontaneously in the language of the natives.[94] However, they were clearly con-

---

[Royston] 5.6 (February 13, 1907) 2–3.

90. Other articles in *The Apostolic Faith* made a distinction between the sign and gift of tongues. Mrs. James Hebden, "This is the Power of the Holy Ghost," *Apostolic Faith* [Los Angeles] 1.6 (February-March 1907) 4; The Christian Missionary Alliance, "The Promise of the Father and Speaking with Tongues in Chicago," *Apostolic Faith* [Los Angeles] 1.9 (June-September 1907) 3.

91. Anderson, *Spreading Fires*, 50–57.

92. "Pentecost in India," *Apostolic Faith* [Los Angeles] 1.3 (November 1906) 1.

93. "The Work in India," *Apostolic Faith* [Los Angeles] 1.9 (June-September 1907) 1.

94. McGee, "'Latter Rain' Falling in the East," 660–61.

vinced that the Pentecostal Baptism was more than just a blessing received by mature Christians for the purpose of foreign mission work. It was a blessing of spiritual renewal and power that all Christians were given the privilege of enjoying. That was the message of the Azusa Street Mission when it heralded the "Beginning of World Wide Revival." The mission believed that revival was a result of the distinctly Pentecostal message and experience that brought unity among believers as it made its way around the world.[95]

Seymour's Contribution to Pentecostalism

Though Seymour and the Azusa Street Mission initially saw Parham as their leader, their separation from him as an organization also triggered a separation from his theology. Soon, a broader understanding of both the purpose and proof of Spirit Baptism began to emerge. This change is particularly noticeable in their testimonies and personal accounts of Spirit Baptism at home and abroad. The boundary lines between sanctification, "the anointing that abideth," and Spirit Baptism became blurry, and the benefits of Spirit Baptism focused on praise, love, unity, humility, teaching, and holiness, in addition to the sealing power and evangelistic tool that Parham championed. This broader understanding of Spirit Baptism caused speaking in tongues to be viewed more broadly as well. In many cases, tongues were seen as a sign or symbol of the benefits obtained in Spirit Baptism instead of as a concrete representation.

The varied and diverse testimonies regarding Spirit Baptism in *The Apostolic Faith* show how highly valued individual experiences were in forming their collective theology. Seymour and other leaders at the Azusa Street Mission devoted most of their energy to directing people toward an authentic experience of Pentecost in the present rather than speculating about the future or reveling in the past. Their emphasis upon an intimate experience with God broke down barriers between people groups that were often divided in the church; black and white, male and female, rich and poor were all welcomed to take part in the Pentecostal experience. While Parham could not reconcile fanaticism, racial mingling, and uncontrollable demonstrations with his understanding of a genuine move of God's Spirit, Seymour could not reconcile a lack of charity and goodwill toward others with what he understood as the results of Spirit Baptism. Instead

---

95. "Beginning of World Wide Revival," *Apostolic Faith* [Los Angeles] 1.5 (January 1907) 1.

of seeing Spirit Baptism as a functional blessing given to people strictly in order to delineate those who were sealed and equipped, Seymour valued Spirit Baptism as a firsthand experience of God. The details of that experience could be as varied as God himself. But one thing was certain: divine love and unity were always present when God was experienced.

Alexander Boddy and the British Pentecostal Movement

Pentecost for Everyone

The Whitsun Sunderland Conventions held in the summers from 1908 to 1914 at All Saints Church in Monkwearmouth, Sunderland, and overseen by vicar Alexander Boddy, significantly influenced the shape and direction of the early Pentecostal movement in Britain. These conferences were organized, publicized and chaired by Boddy in order to facilitate the mutual exhortation and spiritual growth of those throughout the British Isles and Western Europe who "have received their 'Pentecost,' or who are seeking it."[96] Current and future Pentecostal leaders from around the world came to visit and sometimes speak at the conferences including: Smith Wigglesworth, Gerritt Polman, Arthur Booth-Clibborn, T. B. Barratt, Johnathan Paul, Carrie Judd Montgomery, Cecil Polhill, George Jeffereys, William Hutchinson, J. H. King, Frank Bartleman, and Stanley Frodsham.[97] From these conferences the British Pentecostal movement derived a more unified understanding of Pentecostal doctrine and experience, and also gained a level of credibility and credence that had been lacking among the British public.[98] Through these yearly conferences and his monthly periodical, *Confidence*, Boddy had a powerful influence on the direction and shape of Pentecostalism in Britain,[99] and it was because of his leadership that the movement progressed and developed very differently than American Pentecostalism both organizationally and doctrinally during the first two decades of the twentieth century.

Richard Quebedeaux has recognized that the transition from a "nondenominational movement to a distinct form of (non-moderated)

---

96. *Confidence*, 1.2 (May 1908) 2; "The Whitsuntide Conference," *Confidence* 1.3 (June 1908) 4–11.

97. Wakefield, *Alexander Boddy*, 119–21.

98. Kay, "Sunderland's Legacy," 2. For specific influences of Sunderland on belief and practice concerning vocal charismatic gifts (tongues, interpretation, and prophecy) in British Pentecostalism, see Kay, *Pentecostals in Britain*, 55–69.

99. Gee, *Wind and Flame*, 37.

denominational sectarianism" that occurred rapidly among Pentecostals in the United States took much longer in Great Britain.[100] He argues that the transition took longer because the established national church in Great Britain discouraged the formation of new denominations in contrast to the United States that had no national church and for which there was no "evil connotation" associated with the idea of religious sectarianism. Quebedeaux further suggests that within this context, Alexander Boddy's intent to remain within the national church was heavily influenced by the loss of money and respectability that would have accompanied any priest who left the Anglican Church.[101] In contrast, Tim Walsh has argued that the context in which the British Pentecostal movement emerged mirrored "the fissiparous nature of the American Holiness movement." He has shown that the Pentecostal movement did not find ready acceptance in Britain. Rather, the first years of the Pentecostal outpouring in Britain were marked by a "climate of criticism" that quickly led to the formulation of Pentecostal credos.[102] In that context, Walsh argues that Boddy "manifestly risked his reputation" in his candid support of the Pentecostal experience.[103] This was certainly the case from Boddy's own point of view. In the same breath that Boddy championed the Pentecostal blessing as "Inter-national and Inter-denominational," he called for commitment in the face of harsh criticism saying, "We were spoken against, written against, shut out and banned, but we have continued to this day, and do not intend to go back."[104] The Sunderland conventions and the groups associated with the meetings quickly became objects of respect or disdain in British public opinion. Few held a neutral position regarding the new movement. By far the most controversial element of the British Pentecostal movement was a focus on speaking in tongues, particularly when understood as a sign that one had been baptized in the Holy Spirit.[105] By the time the first issue of

100. Quebedeaux, "Charismatic Renewal," 71.

101. Ibid., 74–75.

102. Walsh, "Living With Signs and Wonders," 419.

103. Ibid., 416.

104. A. A. Boddy, "Speaking in Tongues: What Is It?" *Confidence* 3.5 (May 1910) 103–4.

105. The initial criticisms levied against the "Tongues Movement" at Sunderland through the Pentecostal League of Prayer periodical, *Tongues of Fire*, were primarily concerned with disorderly or unseemly conduct and teaching the universality of the gift of tongues and its necessity as evidence of Spirit Baptism. Reader Harris, "Editorials: The Gift of Tongues," *Tongues of Fire* 17 (March 1907) 6; Reader Harris, "The Gift of Tongues, *Tongues of Fire* 17 (November 1907) 1–2; Reader Harris, "Editorials: The Gift of Tongues; Two Very Grave Errors," *Tongues of Fire* 17 (November 1907) 6;

Confidence was printed in 1908, it seems that many believed the risks of the Pentecostal Baptism outweighed its benefits. T. B. Barratt wrote,

> It is really sad to think that numbers are being prevented in England and elsewhere from seeking the Baptism of Fire because of their terror for counterfeits. This proves satisfactorily to my mind that the way in which some or the leaders of Christian thought in Great Britain have been dealing with the matter has not been a wise one.[106]

Though Anglicanism in England at the close of the nineteenth century was diverse in form and relatively open to theological inquiry, the issue of speaking in tongues proved divisive.[107] On the one hand, a growing respect for scholarship and academic inquiry among many Anglican churches of the High Church tradition was difficult to reconcile with the seemingly anti-intellectual phenomenon of tongues-speech.[108] On the other hand, a strict reliance on Scripture as the final authority for church doctrine and practice upheld by more conservative Anglicans was not receptive to a theology that appeared to give equal Scripture-like authority to tongues and interpretation.[109] As the leader of a movement that soon was being defined by the controversial "tongues" experience that it advocated,[110] Boddy could have easily worked to galvanize supporters and

---

Oswald Chambers, "Tongues and Testing," *Tongues of Fire* 18 (January 1908) 3; Reader Harris, "Review of 1907," *Tongues of Fire* 18 (January 1908) 7; Reader Harris, "Editorials: The Beginning of Error," *Tongues of Fire* 18 (February 1908) 6.

106. T. B. Barratt, "An Important Letter from Pastor Barratt," *Confidence* 1.1 (April 1908, special supplement) 2.

107. In reference to the manifestation of tongues, Boddy noted, "Nothing has been more attacked: we find that the great Enemy hates this Apostolic sign and would fain forbid us to speak in Tongues." A. A. Boddy, "Tongues: The Pentecostal Sign," *Confidence* 3.11 (November 1910) 260.

108. Evidence for this can be seen in the early Pentecostal movement's almost exclusive appeal to the uneducated class in Britain. Cecil Polhill, the leader of the Pentecostal Missionary Union and educated at Jesus College, Cambridge and Boddy, educated at University College, Durham, were exceptional. Hocken, "Cecil H. Polhill,"137; Wakefield, *Alexander Boddy*, 20–27.

109. As conservative Anglicans, both Boddy and Polhill were critical and skeptical of the use of tongues as a means of daily guidance as promoted by William Hutchinson and the Apostolic Faith Church. Peter Hocken, "Cecil H. Polhill," 129–30; A. A. Boddy, "The Pentecostal Baptism: Counsel to Leaders and Others," *Confidence* 4.1 (January 1911) 6; W. F. Carothers, "The Gift of Interpretation: Is it Intended to be a Means of Guidance?" *Confidence* 3.11 (November 1910) 255–57.

110. By November 1907, the Pentecostal League of Prayer's periodical, *Tongues of Fire*, referred to the group repeatedly as the "Tongues Movement." "Editorials,"

antagonists of the movement based on their views concerning speaking in tongues and its connection to Spirit Baptism. Instead, Boddy's firm belief that Pentecost was for everyone, and his heart for revival to spread throughout England, compelled him to remain flexible and generous as he sought to develop a healthy theology of Pentecost.

A Practical Theology of Spirit Baptism

Edith Blumhofer has rightly observed, "In Britain, although the doctrinal issues [raised by Pentecostalism] seemed potentially more troublesome, they were less divisive in the first decade."[111] She credits this phenomenon to Boddy's stature as a well-respected leader with a "long and effective pastoral ministry" functioning within the context of Anglican and Keswick ecumenical traditions.[112] To be sure, Boddy's reputation among young religious leaders bolstered the extent of his influence across Britain. However, it was not only the relative openness of Boddy's context but also his uniquely pastoral approach to Pentecostal theology that allowed early Pentecostalism in Britain to be perceived as a "movement with validity for all confessions."[113] I have argued above that the Pentecostal rejection of Parham was not simply a rejection of his person, but a rejection of his theology. In the same vein, British Pentecostals were attracted to Boddy not just because of his stature and vision, but also because his theology was palatable. Boddy's tolerance and proclivity to bridge divides were not traits representative of Anglican priests of the time as much as they were distinctive aspects of his own style and theology, which made him uniquely effective when dealing with conflict in the church.[114] Compared with American Pentecostalism, "early British Pentecostalism was," as Blumhofer says, "from its emergence, both less sectarian and less prone to insist on doctrinal and methodological uniformity."[115] Yet, the diverse religious backgrounds of European Pentecostals were only a secondary cause of this. It was primarily Boddy's pastoral abilities and skills in practical theological reasoning that enabled him to unite and retain the early British Pentecostal movement within existing church structures, and it is

---

Tongues of Fire 17 (November 1907) 6.
   111. Blumhofer, "Alexander Boddy," 35.
   112. Ibid., 35.
   113. Ibid., 34.
   114. Manwaring, *From Controversy to Co-existence*, 6.
   115. Blumhofer, "Alexander Boddy," 34.

probable that they would have easily been divided under the leadership of another.

Boddy located his theology of Spirit Baptism within a version of the five-fold gospel that was popular among the first generation of Pentecostals that emerged out of the Holiness movement in America: Jesus Christ as Savior, Sanctifier, Baptizer in the Holy Spirit, Healer, and Coming King.[116] However, Boddy's gospel was informed by no less than three ecclesiastical traditions. Being educated at Durham, Boddy was grounded in Anglican theology and ecclesiology. Yet, Boddy's devotion to the Church of England was tempered by a deep desire for a spiritual awakening and renewal in the national church, a desire that began to be met through nonconformist Wesleyan and Keswick traditions. Thanks to the receptivity of Bishop Moule, Boddy brought the focus on personal holiness and spiritual renewal he experienced at the Keswick conventions into his All Saints Church. Not fully satisfied, Boddy sought and found further renewal in the revivals of Wales. As a priest in the Church of England, Boddy embraced Anglican ecclesiology, upholding an appreciation for diversity and freedom within the limits of Scripture, maintaining an emphasis on the sacraments of water baptism and holy communion, and promoting an egalitarian view of women in ministry.[117] Boddy added to his Anglican ecclesiology a Higher Life spirituality, believing in the need for individuals to have a personal encounter with God through the Holy Spirit leading to the removal of sin and increasing personal holiness. These core beliefs of Boddy are evident throughout the issues of *Confidence*.

As a pastor, the religious community's spiritual, physical, and social wellbeing were of primary importance to Boddy as he developed a working theology of Pentecostal experience. Gavin Wakefield notes, "Boddy was primarily a pastor who desired to help people encounter God through

---

116. Cartledge, "Early Pentecostal Theology"; Dayton, *Theological Roots of Pentecostalism*, 21. From April 1911 *Confidence* printed the following doctrinal commitment, "'Confidence' advocates an unlimited Salvation for Spirit, Soul, and Body; the Honouring of the Precious Blood: Identification with Christ in Death and Resurrection, etc.; Regeneration, Sanctification; The Baptism of the Holy Ghost; the Soon-Coming of the Lord in the air (1 Thess. iv., 14); Divine Healing and Health (Acts iv., 13) . . ."

117. When it comes to women in leadership, Boddy edited out a section of Carothers' article in *The Latter Rain Evangel* that referred to the inappropriateness of women teaching. See W. F. Carothers, "The Gift of Interpretation," *Confidence* 3.11 (November, 1910) 255; "The Gift of Interpretation," *Latter Rain Evangel* October 3.1 (October 1910) 7.

Christ in the power of the Holy Spirit."[118] Boddy realized that God's encounter with the individual was often unique and unpatterned. Unlike Parham or Seymour in the United States, Boddy took extra care to maintain flexibility in applying the experience of individuals to the community as a whole. Boddy's theology of Spirit Baptism resisted classification, encouraging lay people to integrate their new understanding of the Spirit with their existing theology. Wakefield has shown that it was his "powerful combination of spiritual openness and pastoral realism" that set Boddy apart.[119] These traits are obvious in Boddy's theology of Spirit Baptism.

In his essay, *The Pentecostal Baptism: Counsel to Leaders and Others*,[120] Boddy addressed many practical theological issues arising in the new movement that had "for some time . . . been learning by experience."[121] Rather than constructing a simple set of dogmatic creedal statements concerning Spirit Baptism, Boddy offered practical advice and wisdom on how the Pentecostal experience should be dealt with in the churches. Though he used Scripture to support many of his points, Boddy's ecclesiology provided the basis for most of his arguments. Boddy presented specific guidelines for speaking in tongues and prophesying in large gatherings. He cautioned against what he understood as the unwise practices of prefacing an interpretation of tongues with "the Lord says," acknowledging that some people unconsciously exert their own will in place of God's. Boddy also encouraged seekers to have patience in the process of seeking the Pentecostal blessing, and he asked people to refrain from pushing the Pentecostal blessing on seekers. Finally, Boddy addressed those Pentecostals who believed they could discern a call to a foreign mission field based on their specific gift of tongues. Based on the fact that he had not received a single letter from a missionary abroad confirming their miraculous ability to speak fluently in a foreign language, Boddy suggested to anyone who thought they had received such a gift that they have it verified. Apparent throughout this essay are Boddy's attempts to be humble and generous

---

118. Wakefield, *Alexander Boddy*, 156.

119. Ibid., 105.

120. A second edition of this essay, with two additional sections ("Calls to Foreign Service" and "As to Darkness, etc."), is retained in the Mattersey Hall archives in Mattersey, England. Internal evidence suggests that the first edition of the essay was written in 1908. A more widely available copy of the second edition with a few editorial changes is printed in A. A. Boddy, "The Pentecostal Baptism: Counsel to Leaders and Others," *Confidence* 4.1 (January 1911) 5–8.

121. A. A. Boddy, "The Pentecostal Baptism: Counsel to Leaders and Others," *Confidence* 4.1 (January 1911) 5.

toward those with whom he disagreed, and his strong desire to err on the side inclusion rather than exclusion. Boddy encouraged Pentecostals to unite regardless of their religious background. "The Lord is granting the Pentecostal Baptism to members of many different 'Churches,' and to those who have 'Missions,' etc. Let us unite when it is possible. In love to the Lord Jesus we are one; in other things we may not agree, but let there be mutual toleration and great love among Pentecostal brethren."[122] Addressing opposition and false accusations facing the movement, Boddy went as far as to encourage his readers to "be willing to learn even through harsh criticisms" and to remember the Proverb, "Let him that thinketh he standeth take heed lest he fall."[123]

Sanctification

Unlike the Pentecostal League of Prayer, the Holiness group led by Reader Harris of which he was a member for at least six years, Boddy defined Spirit Baptism and sanctification as two separate experiences.[124] Early in 1909, Boddy clearly articulated his belief in "three steps" for the Christian life: justification, sanctification, and the Baptism of the Holy Spirit.[125] In an article entitled, "The Holy Ghost For Us," Boddy expounded on the work of the Holy Spirit in justification and sanctification. He explained that by trusting in redemption and by the work of the Holy Sprit, the "Family of God consists of those who have accepted a new nature from above . . . [they] become partakers of the *Divine* Nature." He went on to proclaim that the Spirit brings "constant victory" over the ever-present temptations of Satan. Not only focusing on sin, Boddy taught that "Christ's finished work on the Cross" amounted to a healing of "both body and soul." Boddy summarized the goal of sanctification as follows, "The work of the Holy Spirit after our new birth is ever to make Christ very real to us, and to

---

122. Ibid., 8.

123. Ibid., 7.

124. The Pentecostal League of Prayer equated Spirit Baptism and sanctification. One article addressed the error of seeking a third blessing instead of a fresh anointing. "Baptism means cleansing. Anointing is taken from the Old Testament custom of pouring oil upon one who was set apart for some special work or service. . . . Jesus was anointed by the Holy Spirit at Jordan. He was not baptized with the Spirit, for he had no sin to be cleansed away." "Baptism and Anointing," *Tongues of Fire* 15 (March 1905) 2.

125. A. A. Boddy, "Tongues as a Sign," *Confidence* 2.2 (1909) 33.

show us the possibilities there are in Him for us, and to communicate the power of His Life."[126]

Though he used the phrase "finished-work" in expounding his view of sanctification, it appears that Boddy personally maintained a belief in sanctification as a definite second work of grace subsequent to conversion over against the "finished-work" doctrine of Durham.[127] Despite his own personal beliefs and experiences, Boddy was convinced that churches should not be divided over different doctrines of sanctification. He called for Pentecostal churches to "refrain from condemning one another in the matter of the question known on the one hand as 'The Second Work of Grace' and on the other as 'The Finished Work of Christ.'" Instead, he encouraged "each one to be fully persuaded in his own mind."[128] The timing of sanctification in the Christian life was an issue about which Boddy had an opinion, but which he refused to elevate to the status of dogma. Rather than worry about *when* people were sanctified, Boddy focused his energy on *why* such an experience was needed. He left it to the individual's conscience to determine when this was achieved.

Boddy consistently advocated a distinct experience separate from justification and sanctification called the Baptism of the Holy Spirit. Yet, as with sanctification, Boddy allowed for a wide range of beliefs about the timing and results of the experience. In November 1911, Boddy printed a sermon by Herr Beyerhaus of Berlin that argued, "A chief reason why so many Christians do not understand the work of the Spirit of Pentecost, is that they believe this Spirit can not come on a person who is not fully sanctified." Beyerhaus proposed that the Spirit could baptize a young Christian and act as an entrance point "into the High School of highest spirituality" that takes one from "penitent sinner" to "the likeness of Christ."[129] This seems to be consistent with the London Declaration, which Boddy and twenty-seven other Pentecostal leaders signed in December 1909, which concluded, "It also should be clearly understood that the Baptism of the Holy Ghost is the 'Gate' into, and not the 'Goal' of a true and full Christian

---

126. A. A. Boddy, "The Holy Ghost For Us," *Confidence* 5.1 (January 1912): 11, 19–21. A portion of this article appears in April 1910 with the endnote "From 'The Holy Ghost for us.'" Thus, the full article printed in 1912 may have been authored in tract or essay form in 1910. "He Comes to Abide," *Confidence* 3.4 (April 1910) 96.

127. Cartledge, "The Early Pentecostal Theology," 8.

128. A. A. Boddy, "In Southern California," *Confidence* 5.11 (November 1912) 246.

129. Friedrich Beyerhaus, "The Baptism in the Holy Ghost," *Confidence* 4.11 (November 1911) 253.

Life."[130] For Boddy and many other leaders in the British Pentecostal movement, Spirit Baptism was not the culmination of a life devoted and separated to God, but it was a means of getting there. Boddy admitted that, early on, he might not have sufficiently recognized the dangers of gifts such as tongues being given to unsanctified people. However, he refused to let the possibility of abuse stifle his strong desire to see as many people as possible awakened and revitalized through Spirit Baptism.[131]

Spirit Baptism: The Gateway to a Full Christian Life

Boddy broadly understood Spirit Baptism to be the start of an intimate relationship with Jesus Christ that would empower one's Christian ministry and witness in a unique way.[132] Thus he believed the results of Spirit Baptism to be many and varied. In language similar to that used by Parham to talk about "the anointing that abideth," Boddy spoke of Spirit Baptism as that moment in time when the Holy Spirit takes full possession of the individual.[133] Speaking in tongues was important in Boddy's theology as a seal because it showed in a tangible way that God was, in fact, now controlling the actions of the person. Boddy recognized five results of this possession by the Holy Spirit:

1. Wondrous joy that the Spirit has thus sealed the believer unto the day of redemption. It is something very real.
2. An increase in the believer's personal love of the Lord Jesus.
3. A new interest in the Word of God. The Bible becomes very precious and its messages very real.
4. A love to the souls for whom Christ has died and a desire to bring them to Him.
5. The soon coming of the Lord is now often laid upon the believer's heart.[134]

Interestingly, none of these results were functionally connected to speaking in tongues. In fact, Boddy cautioned those who would make a pragmatic

130. "A London Declaration," *Confidence* 2.12 (December 1909) 287.

131. A. A. Boddy, "Speaking in Tongues: What is it?" *Confidence* 3.5 (May 1910) 104.

132. White, "Pentecost with Signs," 12–15.

133. A. A. Boddy, "Speaking in Tongues: What is it?" *Confidence* 3.5 (May 1910) 99.

134. Ibid., 100.

connection between speaking in tongues and foreign missions, citing the absence of any biblical example. Though opinionated, Boddy graciously left room for interpretation other than his own on the subject saying, "We are not always correct in our attempted diagnosis of the workings of the Holy Spirit. Let us be careful not to grieve Him by condemnation and by criticisms of what we cannot understand."[135]

Boddy recognized one of the results of Spirit Baptism to be the sealing of the believer for the day of redemption. This language is similar to Parham's belief that Spirit Baptism sealed the Bride of Christ. However, unlike Parham and many other early Pentecostals, it appears that Boddy never understood this sealing as a marking out of those who would be raptured when Christ returned. Mary Boddy wrote at length about preparing oneself for Jesus' soon return and the rapture of the saints. Yet, she did not mention speaking in tongues or Spirit Baptism as a means of attaining this experience.[136] Neil Hudson accurately states that Mary Boddy understood Spirit Baptism as "preparation of the Pentecostals for the rapture."[137] But it is significant that she understood the preparation as a way to begin to experience some of the joy of heaven on earth, and not as the point of entry into an exclusive group of Christians who would be raptured.

Speaking in Tongues: Normative But Not Definitive

Boddy was always concerned that tongues should not become the defining feature of the Pentecostal's experience. In the first issue of *Confidence*, Boddy printed a short article emphasizing the Christian's need for a "real Baptism of Love" ahead of anything else.[138] In May 1909, an article in the form of questions and answers affirmed that alongside the sign of tongues, those baptized in the Holy Spirit receive a "new love for the Lord Jesus and His will."[139] Five months later, Mary Boddy stated her belief that tongues

135. Ibid., 101.
136. M. Boddy, "The Coming Rapture," *Confidence* 4.7 (July 1910) 153–55. Another article suggested that tongues would be used during the rapture, but not exclusively by those who had been baptized in the Spirit on earth. Instead, tongues were said to act as a common expression of joy from the saints toward Christ in which all the redeemed would participate. The article argued that there was no reason to wait for the rapture to speak in tongues when such a blessing could be experienced today. "Tongues in the Air," *Confidence* 4.9 (September 1910) 204.
137. Hudson, "Strange Words," 66.
138. "After 'Pentecost'—Love," *Confidence* 1.1 (April 1908) 16.
139. "The Baptism of the Holy Ghost with the Sign of Tongues," *Confidence* 2.5

would always accompany a genuine experience of Spirit Baptism, but she added that she could not affirm that tongues alone should be relied on as proof of the experience. She argued, "Merely speaking in Tongues is not necessarily a convincing sign that a person has got God in them."[140] By May 1910, Boddy felt the need to redirect the focus of his readers from tongues, which he understood simply as a "confirmatory token," to the experience of Spirit Baptism. Unlike Carothers and Parham, who understood speaking in tongues as the main reason for Spirit Baptism, Boddy minimized the interconnectedness of the two saying, "To me personally the chief thing is not the Speaking in Tongues, but the Baptism of the Holy Ghost, of which it is a sign."[141] In November 1910, Boddy sought to clarify his beliefs about the evidence of Spirit Baptism. In agreement with his wife's statement a year earlier, Boddy was forthright in his "personal conviction" that *both* tongues *and* "Divine Love" would need to be present before one could be certain that a person had been baptized in the Spirit. He drew a distinction between tongues as the "Pentecostal sign" and love as the "evidence of continuance." As with other issues that could have been divisive, Boddy made it clear that he was only stating his personal beliefs on the matter. Possibly showing his aversion to write about such a controversial issue, Boddy added as a parenthetical note that he wrote on the subject only because he had received so many letters about it.[142]

Boddy's practical approach to Spirit Baptism is most easily seen in his dealing with the controversial issue of speaking in tongues and its place in the church. Boddy boldly recognized the role his own experience played in forming his understanding of Spirit Baptism and tongues. He testified to his experience of being baptized in the Spirit and unapologetically used it as a basis for his beliefs concerning the Baptism in the Holy Spirit.

> The personal testimony I must give is this. I asked the Lord to give me "Tongues" as a sign of my Baptism of (or in) the Holy Ghost. He answered my prayer fully, and has greatly blessed me ever since and enlarged my opportunities for helping others beyond all possible thought. . . . If it was all wrong then one would expect to be left by God, and one's work for Him would

---

(May 1909) 122.

140. M. Boddy, "The Real Baptism of the Holy Ghost," *Confidence* 2.11 (November 1909) 260–61.

141. A. A. Boddy, "Speaking in Tongues: What is it?" *Confidence* 3.5 (May 1910) 102.

142. A. A. Boddy, "Tongues: The Pentecostal Sign," *Confidence* 3.11 (November 1910) 260–61.

Early Theological Approaches to Spirit Baptism

ere this have withered; but, on the contrary, life after life has been glorified and filled with love of Jesus, and become a centre of blessing. Therefore *for me* Pentecost means the Baptism of the Holy Ghost and the sign of "Tongues."[143]

Yet, Boddy did not view his own personal experience of being baptized in the Spirit as a sufficient basis upon which a *rule* about Spirit Baptism should be built. Boddy's experience certainly weighed heavily in his own beliefs concerning the relationship of tongues to Spirit Baptism. However, Boddy was careful to make room for experiences of Spirit Baptism by other people that were different than his own saying, "I dare not lay down any rule for others. I can only say this is the way the Lord has led me."[144]

Boddy's ability to draw a line between what was "for him" and what was "for all" set him apart from his North American contemporaries. Boddy did not take his particular experience of the Spirit and use it as a guide for a universal interpretation and application of Scripture on the subject. Boddy certainly believed that any sound theology would be rooted in Scripture, but he made allowance for differences of interpretation in matters that the Bible did not make absolutely clear. Boddy called his readers to "keep as near as possible to what we see in the Scriptures when seeking the Baptism of the Holy Ghost," but added that in the same way God makes allowance for honest mistakes, they should make allowance for those "who seem to act somewhat differently in detail."[145]

T. B. Barratt, under whose leadership Boddy was baptized in the Spirit in Norway, believed that tongues were the normal sign of the Baptism. But, like Boddy, Barratt did not understand it as imperative.

> The Baptism is HIM; the Tongues are the Sign of His presence. It is the flag waving over the Palace, telling that He is at home. If not the Flag of the Tongues, then the Blood Red Flag of Love or the White Flag of Purity. But the special flag for these days is the Tongues. The Tongues will as a rule come with the Holy Ghost's

---

143. A. A. Boddy, "A Personal Testimony," *Confidence* 2.2 (February 1909) 33. Italics mine. This statement is consistent with the question and answer given by Boddy in the first issue of *Confidence*, "One is often asked, 'Do you think anyone can have had the Baptism of the Holy Ghost and not have the Sign of Tongues?' I cannot judge another, but *for me*, 'Pentecost means the Baptism of the Holy Ghost with the evidence of Tongues.'" A. A. Boddy, "'Tongues' as a Seal of 'Pentecost,'" *Confidence* 1.1 (April 1908) 18. Italics mine.

144. A. A. Boddy, "A Personal Testimony," *Confidence* 2.2 (February 1909) 33.

145. A. A. Boddy, "'Tongues' as a Seal of 'Pentecost,'" *Confidence* 1.1 (April 1908) 18.

power. Yet for some reason or other there are cases where they have not immediately come, or come at all.[146]

In an article expressing various perspectives in the Pentecostal movement regarding baptism, the Lord's Supper, and tongues, Barratt was more explicit about the reasons why a Spirit-baptized person might not speak in tongues. "Some believe that *all* may speak in tongues on receiving a *full* Pentecost, but that many have clearly received a mighty baptism of the Holy Ghost without doing so. The tongues may have been kept back by *will-force* from fear, distrust, unwillingness, ignorance, or unbelief."[147] In fact, Barratt dated his own Baptism in the Spirit over a month before he first spoke in tongues.[148] Barratt's openness on the timing of tongues, an openness affirmed by his correspondence with Azusa Street,[149] almost certainly helped Boddy to be comfortable in dating his own experience of Spirit Baptism nine months before he spoke in tongues.[150]

146. "The Pentecostal Conference in Germany," *Confidence* 2.2 (Feb 1909) 35.

147. T. B. Barratt, "An Urgent Plea for Charity and Unity," *Confidence* 4.2 (February 1911) 31. Barratt later seems to have taken care to use the term "full Pentecost" when he referred to an experience of Spirit Baptism accompanied by speaking in tongues. He would not deny that a person could receive a lesser baptism by the Holy Spirit, anointing, or "foretaste of Pentecost" without speaking in tongues. He simply believed that a "full Pentecost" was, by definition, accompanied by speaking in tongues as on the Day of Pentecost. Barratt, *The Baptism of the Holy Ghost*, 9, 18, 32.

148. Barratt dated his Baptism in the Holy Spirit on October 7, 1906. He did not speak in tongues until the early morning hours of November 16th. He understood this later experience as a sealing of his earlier baptism of fire believing that "doubt and the thought of the strangeness in the experience was always in the way." T. B. Barratt, "The Seal of My Pentecost," *Living Truths* 6.12 (December 1906) 736; "Baptized in New York," *Apostolic Faith* [Los Angeles] 1.4 (December 1906) 3.

149. Interestingly, Barratt received a letter from G. A. Cook of the Azusa Street Mission during the month between his baptism and first experience of tongues that affirmed the validity of his early Baptism in the Holy Spirit, but which also encouraged him, "While we are getting a Bible experience we may as well go all the way with Jesus and measure up in every particular." Cook also explained that many people who claim an anointing without tongues as "their Pentecost" only have a limited power. David Bundy, "Spiritual Advice to a Shaker,"164.

150. Boddy testified, "I asked those who had received the Holy Spirit with the sign of the Tongues to lay hands on me for a Baptism of the Holy Ghost. The Blessed Holy Spirit came upon me just then, filling me with love, joy and peace. This inflow of the blessed Holy Spirit occurred March 5, 1907, but not until Dec. 2nd, nine months later, did the Lord give me the sign of the tongues." "Pentecost in Sunderland," *Latter Rain Evangel* 1.5 (February 1909) 10. Tim Walsh states that Boddy did not receive his Baptism until December 2nd, the day he first spoke in tongues. However, the quote cited above suggests that Boddy did not view the day he "received the sign and gift of 'Tongues'" as the day of his Baptism in the Holy Spirit. Walsh, "Living With Signs and

While both Barratt and Boddy expected that tongues would be an integral part of a Christian's Baptism in the Spirit, they both were cautious about denying the validity of an experience solely because tongues were not present. If an individual had the witness of the Spirit in their heart that they had indeed received the Baptism, they believed the experience ought to be affirmed whether or not there was a manifestation of tongues.[151] Boddy advised Pentecostals not to refer to their unique experience as "Pentecost," which could mean different things to different people. Yet, Boddy was quick to add, "While we dare not say that no one else has received the Holy Presence in their hearts, we are very grateful to Him for the Tongues, given as at Caesarea, Ephesus, Corinth, and Jerusalem. For He has made no difference between us and them at the beginning."[152]

In 1911, widespread disagreement over the relationship of tongues to Spirit Baptism caused it to be a major topic of discussion at the yearly Whitsuntide Convention. Boddy, Dutch pastor Gerrit Polman and his wife, and German pastors Jonathan Paul and Wilhelm Friemel all gave addresses on "The Place of Tongues in the Pentecostal Movement." While all of the speakers upheld the importance of speaking in tongues in conjunction with Spirit Baptism, all were willing to allow for the possibility that a person could be baptized in the Holy Spirit and not immediately speak in tongues.[153] Though the issue was clearly becoming increasingly divisive, Boddy refused to unite the movement around a single stance. Boddy believed that doing so would mark the beginning of a new Pentecostal "organization" and the end of a Pentecostal "movement" that functioned effectively within existing church structures.[154] Boddy's commitment to

---

Wonders," 416; "Sunderland: A Joyful Gathering," *Confidence* 1.9 (December 1908) 7–8. Despite Barratt's status as "apostle of the Pentecostal Movement in Europe" and Boddy's indebtedness to Barratt for his own introduction the Pentecostal experience, Gavin Wakefield notes that there was a reciprocal relationship between Barratt and Boddy in which each was allowed to correct the other. Wakefield, *The First Pentecostal Anglican*, 12.

151. Barratt seems less flexible concerning the timing of tongues a decade later when he attacked F. F. Bosworth's assertion that "not all may receive tongues the moment they are baptized in the Holy Ghost." T. B. Barratt, *The Baptism of the Holy Ghost*, 19, 24. At this time he also appears to have recanted his belief that individuals may receive the full power of Pentecost accompanied by the gift of tongues but might repress the gift so as to not actually speak in tongues. Bundy, "An Early Pentecostal Theological Treatise."

152. A. A. Boddy, *The Pentecostal Baptism*, 3.

153. "The Place of Tongues in the Pentecostal Movement," *Confidence* 4.8 (August 1911) 176–79, 182.

154. A. A. Boddy, "Where We Stand," *Confidence* 4.8 (August 1911) 180.

uphold and appreciate diverse experiences of the Spirit is further seen in the revisions to the Pentecostal Missionary Union's teachings on the relationship of tongues to Spirit Baptism that he and Polhill advocated. "The Council express their unanimous opinion that all who are baptised in the Holy Spirit may speak in tongues as the Spirit giveth utterance, but the recipients should give clear proof of their life and 'magnify God' Acts 10:46."[155] The careful phrasing again shows how Boddy refused to make a hard and fast doctrinal rule out of what he understood to be a normal pattern.

Boddy's Contribution to Pentecostalism

Boddy evidently did not see it as his primary objective to develop a Pentecostal theology. Noticeably few in *Confidence* are articles defending the validity of the Pentecostal experience or explanation about how Pentecostal ideas might be understood within the broader context of Anglican or Holiness thought. Boddy was more interested in advising those who already assumed its validity on how to appropriately seek the experience and, once received, healthily integrate their newfound experience into private and corporate worship in their own church contexts. Therein lies Boddy's most important contribution to early Pentecostal theology. He firmly believed that the Pentecostal blessing of Spirit Baptism was "International and Inter-denominational," and he consistently maintained the conviction: "When we Church people receive the Baptism we become better Church people."[156] Thus, Boddy devoted his energy and resources to exhort and advise a diverse constituency of believers in Spirit Baptism concerning the benefits of the experience for their unique context through his *Confidence* periodical and annual Sunderland Conventions. Indeed, Kay is correct in arguing that it was "the reasonable and balanced" approach to "potentially explosive issues" that took place at Sunderland and in the pages of *Confidence* that enabled the British Pentecostal movement to deal with their new experience in a healthy manner.[157]

In an effort not to isolate anyone from the Pentecostal experience, Boddy refused to make his own beliefs about the relationship of Spirit Baptism to speaking in tongues a matter of orthodoxy. Instead, Boddy

---

155. Hocken, "Cecil H. Polhill," 133–34.

156. A. A. Boddy, "Speaking in Tongues: What is it?" *Confidence* 3.5 (May 1910) 104.

157. Kay, *Inside Story*, 38.

repeatedly made a distinction between aspects of his experience and theology of Spirit Baptism that were his own, and those that ought to be applied universally. Instead of spiritual gifts, Boddy chose to focus on a greater love for Jesus, a passion for lost souls, insight into Scripture, and a sense of Jesus' soon return as the results of the Pentecostal experience. Boddy led the way in promoting a view that tongues were a gateway into the Pentecostal experience, and not the primary feature of the benefits of Spirit Baptism for the Christian life. This allowed the new movement's conception of Spirit Baptism to be easily integrated into the Christian spirituality advocated by established theological traditions in Britain. The new movement was not developing a new concept of spirituality. It was drawing attention to a new experience with biblical precedent that often inaugurated the spiritual experience for which many in Britain already longed.

Conclusion

Charles Parham and the now famous glossolalic experience of his students in Topeka, Kansas, at the turn of the twentieth century inaugurated a new way for Holiness people to interpret the Book of Acts. Not only was the Apostles' Baptism in the Holy Spirit on the Day of Pentecost understood as an experience that should be repeated in the lives of believers, but Parham called for specific attention to be given to the manifestation of tongues as the "Bible evidence" that such an experience had occurred. Most Pentecostals would come to reject Parham's beliefs about the purposes of Spirit Baptism and speaking in tongues and the relationship of those experiences to the rest of the Christian life. Yet, Parham's interpretation of Scripture, that saw the repeatable pattern of tongues speech connected to Spirit Baptism in Acts as applicable to the lives of present day Christians, provided the hermeneutical foundation upon which the Pentecostal movement would be formed.

William Seymour took Parham's unique doctrine of Spirit Baptism with him to Los Angeles. However, as many people under Seymour's leadership sought for and received "their Pentecost" at the Azusa Street Mission, their understanding of the experience began to differ quite markedly from Parham's. The sharp distinctions between sanctification, "the anointing that abideth," and Spirit Baptism that Parham maintained dissolved and the expected results of the experiences began to overlap. The enhancement or enablement of holiness, divine love, joy, preaching, scriptural insight, and intimacy with God, came to be understood as normal results of Spirit Baptism. With this broader conception of Spirit Baptism came a more symbolic correlation between the results of Spirit Baptism and speaking in tongues. Where Parham championed the practical benefits of Spirit Baptism for foreign evangelistic efforts, the Azusa Street Mission actively participated in the sending out of Spirit-baptized missionaries all around the world.

In Britain, Alexander Boddy's approach to Spirit Baptism was primarily pastoral. While emphasizing the distinctiveness and importance of the Pentecostal experience of Spirit Baptism through the organization of the annual Sunderland Conventions and the editing of *Confidence*, Boddy worked hard to promote the experience within the context of worship. Boddy strove to bring unity among Pentecostal people in Britain without forming a separate organization or creed that opposed existing church structures. Though strongly opinionated, Boddy respected and appreciated fellow Pentecostals that arrived at different conclusions than his own. In the development of his theology of Spirit Baptism, Boddy was careful to maintain a sharp distinction between his own theology and the theological absolutes to which every Christian should be called to adhere.

3

The Emergence of a "Classical" Tradition in Pentecostalism

(1910–1940)

Introduction

BOTH SEYMOUR AND BODDY moved away from the rigid functional connection between speaking in tongues and Spirit Baptism that Parham advocated. Although they both personally expected that tongues would eventually manifest themselves in the life of a Spirit-baptized Christian, they allowed for diverse expressions and viewpoints regarding the proofs for and purposes of Spirit Baptism among those in their ministerial care. This appreciation for diversity gradually gave rise to feelings of disunity among Pentecostals in the United States and Britain with regard to their core identity as members of a new movement in Christianity. As criticism from outsiders mounted on both sides of the Atlantic, particularly regarding speaking in tongues, Pentecostals naturally sought to provide a more cohesive and well-defined identity for themselves within Christianity.

William Durham's simplified approach to Spirit Baptism and its relationship to tongues and sanctification formed an appealing theological foundation for many Pentecostals to rest their case. Not without criticism and controversy, Durham's views would be adopted by the Assemblies of God and other subsequent denominations that would emerge from the Assemblies. F. F. Bosworth, a member of the Assemblies of God's first

Executive Presbytery, was particularly critical of Article 6 in their Statement of Fundamental Truths, which held that speaking in tongues was "the initial evidence" of a Christian's Baptism in the Holy Spirit. His criticisms led, in part, to the Assemblies of God's decision to single out the doctrine as the "distinctive testimony" of the Pentecostal movement and disavow any credentialed minister who would attack the doctrine as an error.

A far cry from Boddy's work in Britain, the move by the Assemblies of God to reign in diversity regarding the connection of tongues to Spirit Baptism signaled the rise of a "classical" Pentecostal tradition in the United States. Pentecostal individuals and groups that would advocate a less than rigid stance on initial evidence, such as Foursquare and Open Bible, would later risk being ostracized from the movement altogether.

William H. Durham

Durham's "Finished-Work" Doctrine

Gary McGee has written one of the few articles about the early Pentecostal hermeneutics that supported the development of the doctrine of "initial evidence."[1] The article is quite right to focus on the accounts of Spirit Baptism in the Book of Acts as the focal point upon which most early Pentecostal hermeneutics were based. However, a noticeable void in McGee's article is his failure to mention William Durham. Durham's approach to Spirit Baptism is significant in the study of early Pentecostal hermeneutics because he simplified two theological issues that were steadily growing more complex and less refined: 1) the role of sanctification in relationship to conversion and Spirit Baptism, and 2) the evidence of Spirit Baptism. Durham was certainly not the only Pentecostal of his era that was dogmatic and inflexible on issues of faith and practice. What set him apart from others was that his dogmatic, clear-cut approach to the phases of the Christian life was rooted in a simple reading of Scripture that was appealing to most of the members of Pentecostal churches in the United States.

Sanctification and Conversion

William Durham is most famous in Pentecostal historiography for his "finished-work" doctrine of sanctification. His belief was that there was only one definite work of grace in a person's life: conversion. He proclaimed,

1. McGee, "Early Pentecostal Hermenutics."

The Emergence of a "Classical" Tradition in Pentecostalism

"The moment a sinner accepts Jesus Christ, he is saved; just as saved as he will ever be."[2] Against the idea that justification took away all "outward sins and uncleanness" and left the heart "full of sin and corruption," Durham argued, "God in conversion brings a man into Christ and makes him holy by washing away all his sins, inward and outward and giving him a new, clean heart, thus making a new creature of him."[3] Durham believed that it was the non-Christian's sinful state of unbelief and "not the actual sins or crimes a man commits that makes him a sinner and causes him to be lost."[4] Thus, conversion entailed a cleansing of the heart to its pre-fall state of purity.

For Durham, the Wesleyan understanding of sanctification as a second work of grace was the result of people who had not taken their initial conversion as seriously as they should have. He observed, "People are saved, and the glory and power of God fills their souls, but they grow careless and lose the joy of their salvation, and often get into darkness and confusion.... They need to be sanctified, but *reclamation* would be a much better name for it."[5] For Durham, those who claimed to have experienced new grace to overcome sin and walk in holiness had only reclaimed the grace they had received by faith in conversion but had failed to utilize. Durham's argument was that the sanctified state that people sought was really no different than the state they were in when they were first converted. The problem was that people failed to walk faithfully in that state of grace. According to Durham, there was a need for many people in the church to *reclaim* that old grace, but it was not *scriptural* to say that all Christians needed to *obtain* a new grace.

The fact that "process sanctification" was not advocated by Durham himself, but by those who came after him and misapplied the "finished-work" terminology to their understanding of sanctification as a process, is nicely presented by Thomas Farkas. Farkas rightly argues that Durham's "finished-work" doctrine of sanctification does not fit well into either Wesleyan, Keswick, or Reformed understandings of the doctrine. Rather, Durham's doctrine is somewhat of a "hybrid" of these traditions.[6]

---

2. W. H. Durham, "The Two Great Experiences or Gifts," *Pentecostal Testimony* 1.8 (1911) 5.

3. W. H. Durham, "Some Other Phases of Sanctification," *Pentecostal Testimony* 2.2 (1912) 8.

4. W. H. Durham, "The Two Great Experiences or Gifts," *Pentecostal Testimony* 1.8 (1911) 5.

5. W. H. Durham, "Sanctification," *Pentecostal Testimony* 1.8 (1911) 2.

6. Farkas, "William H. Durham," 256.

Farkas proposes that the most appropriate label to apply to the theological dynamic present in Durham's "finished-work" doctrine is "single work perfectionism" in accordance with Wesley's understanding of perfection. Admitting that they do not agree on the timing or terminology of the "single work," Farkas holds that Wesley and Durham both theologically agree concerning what takes place in sanctification. Farkas points out that there are passages in Durham's periodical that *appear* to directly contradict the label, but he argues that in the end they do nothing to contradict Durham's "denial of any lingering proclivity to sin." Thus, it can still be appropriately labeled perfectionism.[7]

Yet, in his quest to apply an existing category to Durham's thought, Farkas has taken those passages that agree with Wesley and given them precedent over those passages that appear to contradict the idea of sanctification as "single work perfectionism." Sin after one's conversion seems to be virtually assumed in the following statement by Durham.

> "If, through our weakness, we get from under the precious Blood, one or even more times, after conversion, it is necessary for us to humble ourselves before God and get back; but we can only approach Him, as at the first, through the precious Blood of Christ, as one who has sinned, and not as a justified person. As stated above, *most Christians have had to come several times*."[8]

For Durham, the root of sin was destroyed in conversion so that it was *theologically possible* for a person to live without sin after conversion. However, it was *practically improbable* that they actually would without being baptized in the Spirit. The Christian was no longer destined to sin, but like Adam, he could choose to succumb to temptation and sin. Durham believed,

> As long as we live in this world we are in our humanity, and that instead of God's destroying our human nature, He expects us to control it. In other words, after cleansing us and filling us with the Spirit, he expects us to so yield ourselves to the Holy Spirit continually, that He will have full control of all our faculties.[9]

---

7. Ibid., 261–64.

8. W. H. Durham, "The Second Work of Grace People Answered," *Pentecostal Testimony* 1.8 (1911) 8. Italics mine.

9. W. H. Durham, "Some Other Phases of Sanctification," *Pentecostal Testimony* 2.2 (1912) 10.

In contrast to Durham, Wesley understood sanctification as the culminating event in a gradual mortification of sin and renewal in the image of God whereby a person no longer knowingly commits sin.[10] Whereas Wesley understood the eradication of inbred sin in sanctification to apply to relatively few Christians as evidenced by their obvious failure to keep from sinning, Durham applied this eradication to all Christians. In short, sometimes Durham sounds exactly like a Wesleyan in his view of sanctification as an instantaneous or crisis event. At other times, he sounds nothing like a Wesleyan in his view of the sanctified life as one in which "carnality," fleshly motives and jealousy can still exist.[11] Durham consistently maintained three points that are difficult to mesh into one cohesive doctrine of sanctification. First, he wanted to say that in conversion the "root of sin" or "Adamic nature" is destroyed and that one's heart is made clean. Second, he wanted to affirm that there is a continual need for spiritual growth in a Christian's life up until the point at which he dies or is raptured. Third, Durham wanted to say that Spirit Baptism is essential if a Christian is going to keep from falling back into sin and away from the salvation he first experienced in conversion. The most important factors for Durham in advocating these points were his own experience and a simple reading of Scripture.

Sanctification and Spirit Baptism

Durham believed that Spirit Baptism was synonymous with the entrance of the Spirit into the Christian's life. In his reading of Scripture, terms like "filled with the Spirit," "baptized in the Spirit," "received the gift of Holy Spirit," "sealed with the Spirit," and "anointed with the Spirit" all referred to the same post-conversion experience.[12] Durham criticized the biblical support for "those who believe that it is one thing to receive the Holy Spirit, and another thing to be baptized in the Holy Spirit."[13] Durham believed that the Spirit was present *with* a Christian even before his Baptism

---

10. Wesley, "A Plain Account," 401–5.

11. W. H. Durham, "The Second Work of Grace People Answered," *Pentecostal Testimony* 1.8 (1911) 8–9.

12. W. H. Durham, "Sealed with the Spirit," *Pentecostal Testimony* 1 (1909) 12.

13. Reprinted from a lost issue of *Pentecostal Testimony* in William H. Durham, "What is the Evidence of the Baptism of the Holy Ghose[sic]?" *Apostolic Faith* [Fort Worth] 7.2 (May 1911) 3. This entire section was removed when the article was reprinted by the Assemblies of God in *The Pentecostal Evangel* 1912 (December 31, 1950) 11–12.

in the Spirit bearing witness to his conversion, teaching him "when he pleases God and when he does not," and "influencing and leading him on."[14] Yet, Durham believed that much greater blessings of the Spirit were reserved for those who were baptized in the Spirit. In fact, Durham boldly proclaimed, "No one can have the same power with God who has not received the gift of the Holy Ghost than those have who have received Him."[15] According to Durham, it was Spirit Baptism that gave the minister an "inward revelation of Christ which is necessary to successfully preach Him."[16] Even more, it was through Spirit Baptism that Christians came under the full control of the Spirit, and were empowered through the Spirit's gifts to restore the spiritual strength and vitality that the church had lost over the years.[17]

For Durham, speaking in tongues was a matter of significant importance for the Christian because it was only by speaking in tongues that one could enjoy the Spirit-filled life.[18] Durham was forthright in the pastoral implications of his adamant position regarding tongues as the evidence of Spirit Baptism. He reasoned,

> If speaking in new tongues evidences the baptism in the Holy Spirit, then only those who have spoken in tongues have any just claim to the experience. If it is not necessary for a person to speak in tongues at the time he is baptized in the Holy Spirit, it is an awful mistake to teach it as the evidence, as in that case the teaching will reflect upon the experiences of all who have received the gift of the Holy Ghost, but who have not spoken in tongues.[19]

For Durham, the implications of the Pentecostal doctrine were not to be smoothed over or softened in any way because the stakes were too high: the abiding and empowering presence of the Holy Spirit in the life of the Christian. Charges of arrogance and superiority did not deter Durham

---

14. W. H. Durham, "False Doctrines," *Pentecostal Testimony* 2.2 (1912) 7.

15. W. H. Durham, "What is the Evidence of the Baptism of the Holy Ghose[sic]?" *Apostolic Faith* [Fort Worth] 7.2 (May 1911) 3.

16. W. H. Durham, "A Word to Ministers, from a Minister," *Pentecostal Testimony* 1 (1909) 10.

17. W. H. Durham, "The Great Crisis Number Two," *Pentecostal Testimony* 1.5 (July 1910) 4.

18. W. H. Durham, "The Great Need of the Hour," *Pentecostal Testimony* 2.1 (1911) 10.

19. W. H. Durham, "What is the Evidence of the Baptism of the Holy Ghose[sic]?" *Apostolic Faith* [Forth Worth] 7.2 (May 1911) 2.

from calling out those who were baptized in the Spirit and those who were not. He fully acknowledged the difficulty it caused some Christians to hear others' claims to having attained a higher level of spirituality because they had spoken in tongues.[20] Yet, he never allowed this pastoral problem to influence him toward a more relaxed position on the subject. Nor did the possibility of offending some cause him to soften his language. Durham was unapologetically harsh and blunt with his theology, particularly the doctrine of evidential tongues. Yet, Durham's refusal to compromise his belief in tongues as the evidence of Spirit Baptism was exactly what attracted people to his position. Like his doctrine of sanctification, his rigid stance on evidential tongues simplified matters and it was rooted in a straightforward reading of Scripture.

In 1979, Allen Clayton wrote an article for *Pneuma* in which he sought to relocate Durham's place in Pentecostal historiography.[21] Instead of focusing on Durham's "finished-work" doctrine of sanctification as his most significant contribution to the Pentecostal movement, Clayton argued that his doctrine was simply a manifestation of a "growing Jesus-piety" among non-Wesleyan Pentecostals. Clayton rightly identified a common Christocentric leaning in Durham's opposition to the Wesleyan understanding of sanctification and the later opposition to the Trinitarian understanding of the Godhead by oneness Pentecostals. However, he took the evidence farther than it should go when he argued that the dispute over sanctification was only a "battleground" for the war between Spirit-centered and Christ-centered Pentecostals. It is no surprise that many Pentecostals who would later become leaders in the Jesus-only and Oneness movement accepted Durham's doctrine of sanctification and reiterated his arguments against the Wesleyan view of sanctification. However, their actions should not be made the central issue as Clayton suggests. Rather than "a rising tide of Jesus-piety," the Pentecostal's desire to follow the example of the Christians in the Book of Acts seems be the chief cause of the Pentecostal attack on the Wesleyan understanding of sanctification.[22]

---

20. In his own testimony, Durham spoke of the distastefulness in being told that he had not received the Holy Ghost in spite of the fact that he had been experiencing the Spirit's guidance and witness for years. W. H. Durham, "Personal Testimony of Pastor Durham," *Pentecostal Testimony* 1 (1909) 6. In another article, Durham talked about how it "grated on" him to hear people teach the doctrine before he had spoken in tongues. W. H. Durham, "What is the Evidence of the Baptism of the Holy Ghose[sic]?" *Apostolic Faith* [Fort Worth] 7.2 (May 1911) 3.

21. Clayton, "The Significance of William H. Durham," 27–42.

22. Ibid., 41.

Durham's own testimony states that the event that triggered his own disbelief in the idea of sanctification as a second definite work of grace was "the time the Spirit of God called my attention to the fact that there is not even one Scripture that teaches that sanctification is a second work of grace."[23] In fact, Durham staunchly denied the tenets of the Jesus-only movement, and upheld a classic doctrine of the Trinity based on Scripture.[24] The issue of the timing and naming of the experiences of Christians in the Book of Acts favors considerably in most of Durham's expositions of the "finished-work" doctrine. In defense of his understanding of the Christian life he wrote,

> The moment a man believes on Jesus Christ he is made a new creature. He passes out of death—the natural state of all men—into life, and life is actually imparted unto him. This makes him a candidate for water baptism, which is the only thing required of him between conversion and the baptism in the Holy Spirit. *This is the continual order of things in the Acts of the Apostles.*[25]

It was a rereading of Acts 2 as the pattern that Christians should experience today that formed the basis for Durham's belief that speaking in tongues would accompany a genuine experience of Spirit Baptism.[26] It is natural that this fresh look at Acts 2 along with the other instances of Spirit Baptism in Acts would raise the question, "Why isn't an immediate experience of sanctification ever mentioned?" Durham's answer to that question was simple: "There is none to refer to."[27]

Durham was convinced that the vast majority of criticism that the doctrine of tongues as the evidence of Spirit Baptism received was the result of those who were unwilling "to honestly confess that they have

---

23. W. H. Durham, "Sanctification," *Pentecostal Testimony* 1.8 (1911) 1.

24. Addressing a number of doctrines he considered to be false, Durham stated, "Another doctrine which we believe should be classed as false, is the teaching that converts should be baptized in the name of Jesus only. In Matt. 28:19 Jesus, after His resurrection, gives His instructions to His Disciples just before leaving them, and He said, 'Baptizing them into the Name of the Father and of the Son and of the Holy Spirit.' Nothing could be plainer. To our mind there is no conflict between this plain command and those passages in Acts." W. H. Durham, "False Doctrines," *Pentecostal Testimony* 2.2 (1912) 7.

25. W. H. Durham, "The Two Great Experiences or Gifts," *Pentecostal Testimony* 1.8 (1911) 5. Italics mine.

26. Jacobsen, *Thinking in the Spirit*, 138.

27. W. H. Durham, "The Two Great Experiences or Gifts," *Pentecostal Testimony* 1.8 (1911) 5.

not received the Holy Ghost and then take the attitude of seekers."²⁸ He believed that the logical and biblical arguments for the doctrine were so strong that opposition had to be the result of irrational prejudices against the doctrine because "it says to them, in so many words, that they have not the baptism."²⁹ Durham was harshly critical of those who were "soothing the consciences of the really convicted, telling them they could have the Holy Ghost and not speak in tongues."³⁰ He believed that such advice only enabled Christians to settle for an empty experience with no real results. As surely as Durham believed that the Bible supported the doctrine of evidential tongues, Durham believed that a belief in sanctification as a second, definite work of grace was a case of placing personal experience and tradition ahead of Scripture as the basis for establishing a point of doctrine. He called all Christians to "leave their experience with God, and line their teaching up with the Word of God."³¹

From Complexity to Simplicity

D. William Faupel has rightly noted the importance of the Acts accounts in Durham's change of view regarding the Wesleyan doctrine of sanctification.³² Faupel argues that the specific "kind of experience he had at Azusa" was responsible for bringing about the theological crisis in which he adjusted his entire theological system to bring it in line with the Acts of the Apostles. In short, Faupel argues that it was Durham's experience of Spirit Baptism in which "Christ became alive for Him[sic] in a totally new way" that caused Durham's change in belief and then led him to reexamine Scripture to find support for his experience.³³ Faupel also concludes that Durham's new theological position regarding sanctification gained such a broad acceptance among Pentecostals because it offered many who had

---

28. W. H. Durham, "What is the Evidence of the Baptism of the Holy Ghose[sic]?" *Apostolic Faith* [Forth Worth] 7.2 (May 1911) 3.

29. W. H. Durham, "Speaking in Tongues is the Evidence of the Baptism in the Holy Spirit," *Pentecostal Testimony* 2.2 (1912) 11.

30. W. H. Durham, "An Open Letter to My Brother Ministers In and Out of the Pentecostal Movement: A Strong Appeal," *Pentecostal Testimony* 1.8 (1911) 12.

31. W. H. Durham, "The Second Work of Grace People Answered," *Pentecostal Testimony* 1.8 (1911) 7.

32. Faupel goes as far as to say, "Rooting his experience in conformity with the Acts of the Apostles, [Durham] took a stance that made this book the paradigm for Pentecostal faith and practice." Faupel, "William H. Durham," 93.

33. Ibid., 92.

a similar experience a "lens" through which to view the Scriptures that meshed with their experience.[34]

Whether Durham's experience caused him to reinterpret Scripture or his reading of Scripture caused him to view his past experience differently is difficult to say. In one testimony, Durham said it was a deep conviction of sin "through the Bible and the Spirit moving" upon him that led to his conversion.[35] In a more detailed testimony in his own periodical three years later, Durham attributed more influence to the Bible saying, "God, by His Spirit, began to convict me of sin and this time through the reading of the Word and not by attending revival meetings."[36] Concerning his Baptism in the Spirit, in his earlier testimony he said it was the experience of those around him compared with his own that led him to seek the Baptism.[37] In his later testimony he admitted, "There was a conscious shortage in my own experience and I could never make it compare favorably with the teaching of the Acts of the Apostles."[38] It seems to be the case that Durham's determination to be baptized in the Spirit with tongues was at least as much dependent on the experience of people around him as it was on a desire to emulate the Book of Acts accounts. Nevertheless, Durham looked back on his experience as one that was brought about by his sincere desire to be in line with the Word of God, and it was this line of reasoning—experience submitted to and interpreted by a straightforward reading of Scripture—that formed the basis of his theology of sanctification as well as Spirit Baptism.

Durham's stance on sanctification lent itself to Christians who preferred an uncomplicated message that they could easily apply in their own pursuit of holiness. Theologians of the day may have understood Durham's thought regarding sanctification as complex and difficult to articulate. Pentecostal churchgoers of the day understood it as straightforward and gloriously simple. Durham's "finished-work" doctrine of holiness took away any doubts or questions concerning exactly when a Christian might claim sanctification. Thus, the doctrine held an important implication for

34. Ibid., 93.

35. W. H. Durham, "A Chicago Evangelist's Pentecost," *Apostolic Faith* [Los Angeles] 1.6 (February-March 1907) 4.

36. W. H. Durham, "Personal Testimony of Pastor Durham," *Pentecostal Testimony* 1 (1909) 6.

37. W. H. Durham, "A Chicago Evangelist's Pentecost," *Apostolic Faith* [Los Angeles] 1.6 (February-March 1907) 4.

38. W. H. Durham, "Personal Testimony of Pastor Durham," *Pentecostal Testimony* 1 (1909) 6.

those who were seeking their personal Baptism in the Holy Spirit: *Spirit Baptism was immediately available to new Christians.* There was no intermediate step. While there were some people who had been converted, sanctified, and baptized in the Spirit in a single trip to the altar under the leadership of Seymour, the second step of sanctification was still considered an essential element in the process. Prior to Durham's "finished-work" doctrine, Spirit Baptism was understood as an experience that one was led into through sanctification. This intermediate step complicated matters because there were no objective criteria by which one could determine whether it had been experienced or not. Durham's doctrine removed this ambiguity and reduced the Christian life to two essential experiences: conversion and Spirit Baptism, both of which he believed could be objectively shown to have occurred or not.

It is important to remember that Durham was not a theologian speaking to theologians. He was a minister speaking to other ministers, as the title of one of his articles proclaimed.[39] In the context in which Durham lived, taught, and preached, it is doubtful that very many of his readers would have struggled to make sense of the nuances and complexity present in his doctrine of sanctification. Instead, his listeners would be prone to reduce his ideas to theological or doctrinal "sound-bites." Shortly after Durham's untimely death in 1912, E. N. Bell wrote of him, "He was and is yet much misunderstood. No man among us believed more firmly than he in Bible Holiness nor insisted more strongly that without holiness no man could see the Lord, holding it as God's only standard for all believers; yet some thought he did not believe in holiness at all."[40] Durham certainly did his best to piece together his theology into some kind of cohesive system that could withstand criticism, but the majority of people who listened to Durham's teachings would have been attracted to its straightforward biblical basis and the way in which it simplified and defined experiences that had previously been complex and ambiguous: sanctification and Spirit Baptism.

---

39. W. H. Durham, "A Word to Ministers, from a Minister," *Pentecostal Testimony* 1 (1909) 10–12.

40. E. N. Bell, "Editor's Word About Bro. Durham," *Word and Witness* 8.6 (August 20, 1912) 3.

Norming the Abnormal

Durham and the Assemblies of God

Robin Johnston notes that at the time of Durham's death, "No single leader had the scope of his influence."[41] Durham's simplified understanding of the Pentecostal experience gained a hearing across the United States through his *Pentecostal Testimony* periodical that circulated over fifty thousand copies of the second issue in 1909.[42] However, Durham not only influenced the theological horizons of the early Pentecostal movement through the wide circulation of his periodical, but also through his relationships with key individuals in the North American Pentecostal movement both in Chicago and Los Angeles.[43] One of these individuals was Eudorus N. Bell. Bell received his initial Pentecostal experience of Spirit Baptism in July 1908 after seeking it for eleven months at Durham's North Avenue Mission.[44] Bell's testimony of his Baptism in the Holy Spirit at Durham's Full Gospel Mission church in Chicago first appeared in print in Durham's *Pentecostal Testimony*.[45] In 1909, Bell and Howard A. Goss took over the leadership of the "Apostolic Faith Movement" from W. F. Carothers, a group that had been started by Parham in Orchard, Texas in April 1906 but quickly severed connection with him following his arrest on charges of sodomy.[46] Soon, Bell began to offer his voice to Pentecostals around the country by taking over the editing of the group's periodical, *The Apostolic Faith*, in 1910, which would later become *Word and Witness*.[47] Durham's

---

41. Johnston, "Howard A. Goss," 61.

42. Durham printed 25,000 copies each of issue numbers 1, 3 and 4, and 51, 900 of issue number 2 in the first year of publication for his *Pentecostal Testimony*. W. H. Durham, "Criticisms Answered," *Pentecostal Testimony* 1.5 (July 1910) 11. By the time of Durham's death in 1912, the paper estimated the total number of issues printed at 382,000. By comparison, *Apostolic Faith* from the Azusa Street Mission boasted a circulation of 40,000 by the end of 1907. *Apostolic Faith* [Los Angeles] 1.12 (January 1908) 2. *Confidence* in England, edited by A. A. Boddy, had a circulation of about 5,000 by the end of its second year of publication. " A. A. Boddy, "The Third Volume of 'Confidence,'" *Confidence* 3.1 (January 1910) 12.

43. For a thorough biography of Durham's interaction with key Pentecostal leaders, see Blumhofer, "William H. Durham," 123–42.

44. Goss, *The Winds of God*, 122–23.

45. E. N. Bell, "Testimony of a Baptist Pastor," *Pentecostal Testimony* 1 (1909) 8.

46. Synan, *The Pentecostal-Holiness Tradition*, 153; Goff, "Apostolic Faith," 326–27.

47. Bell's *Apostolic Faith* was not an independent periodical started by Bell as is sometimes assumed (Synan, *The Pentecostal-Holiness Tradition*, 153). The two surviving issues of *Apostolic Faith* [Fort Worth] with Bell as editor that have survived are dated 1911 and are printed as volume 7 of the periodical. In fact, Bell's publication

influence upon Bell is evident in the May 1911 issue of *Apostolic Faith* that reprinted one of Durham's articles in his periodical, *Pentecostal Testimony*, entitled, "What is the Evidence of the Baptism of the Holy Ghost?" and gave notice of a trip by Bell to Los Angeles to minister alongside Durham.[48] The strong relationship between Bell and Durham is further seen in Bell's printing of a letter announcing the death of Durham, and an editorial response upholding Durham's personal integrity and strong commitment to "establish the truth about the Pentecostal Baptism with the Spirit in all the earth."[49]

It was largely through the influence of E. N. Bell, the first general chairman of the Assemblies of God, that Durham's theological perspectives on the relationship of tongues and sanctification to Spirit Baptism soon came to be understood as normative positions for a majority of Pentecostals in the United States. Bell had enormous influence on the character and shape of the General Council of the Assemblies of God in its first decade of existence. He made the first call to "all Pentecostal or Apostolic Faith Assemblies" to organize in the spring of 1914 at Hot Springs, Arkansas.[50] He acted as chairman in 1914 and again from 1920-23, and as secretary from 1919-20. He also was a member of the Executive Presbytery and a member of the Committee on Resolutions from 1915-20. Perhaps most importantly, he served as editor of the primary means of communication between the General Council and its ministers: *Word and Witness* (1912-15) and *Pentecostal Evangel* (1917-19). Through these avenues of influence, Durham's views on Spirit Baptism and sanctification—views

---

was a continuation of the periodical by the same name started by Parham in 1905 and continued by Carothers out of Houston, Texas. Bell would later merge his periodical with Mac Pinson's *Word and Witness* in 1911, a periodical that would ultimately become the voice of the newly formed Assemblies of God. Goss, *The Winds of God*, 122. Johnston, "Howard A. Goss," 116. I am indebted to the late Gary McGee for an email exchange in 2008 to help me sort out some of the connections between Bell and Carothers' organization in Texas.

48. W. H. Durham, "What is the Evidence of the Baptism of the Holy Ghose[sic]?" *Apostolic Faith* [Fort Worth] 7.2 (May 1911) 2-3. Durham's influence on later Pentecostal defenses of the doctrine of initial evidence can be seen in the reprints of the same article by Bell as editor of the Assemblies of God periodical in *Christian Evangel* 250-251 (August 10, 1918) 2-3, and by Aimee Semple McPherson in *Bridal Call* 3.3 (August 1919) 6-9.

49. E. N. Bell, "Brother Durham Fallen Asleep," *Word and Witness* 8.6 (August 20, 1912) 3.

50. "General Convention of Pentecostal Saints and Churches of God in Christ," *Word and Witness* 10.1 (January 20, 1914) 4.

that Bell apparently accepted and then later nuanced—came to be well established among Assemblies of God ministers as a point of unity.[51]

Showing his agreement with Durham's doctrine of Spirit Baptism, in 1912 Bell reprinted, unedited, a lengthy article by Durham in which he expounded his doctrine of evidential tongues.[52] As times changed, Bell sought to clarify theological issues related to Spirit Baptism that Durham had failed to address. Against those who would limit the work of the Spirit to those that were baptized in the Spirit with the evidence of speaking in tongues, Bell argued that the Spirit was active among all Christians and manifest in the fruit of "a clean heart, faith, joy, obedience, prayer, love, and unity." He went on to explain that none of those fruit were a result of speaking in tongues.[53] At the same time, Bell explained that it was "abnormal" for a young Christian not to speak in tongues. He proposed, "Every child of God ought, from the first moment of faith, to see Christ is made unto him sanctification, to be at once baptized in water, then be filled with the Spirit and be talking in tongues in less than three days from the time he received Christ as Savior."[54] An article written by Bell in 1911 made explicit two "phases of sanctification" that only seem to be implied in some of Durham's later articles.[55] Bell proposed, "There are two phases of sanctification. One is the instantaneous, the other the gradual."[56] The instantaneous phase of sanctification, Bell argued, was characterized by subtraction or emptying, while the gradual was concerned with addition or filling. The first phase was an instantaneous, definite work of grace that occurs at conversion, cleansing the heart and preparing the way for the Holy Spirit. Bell encouraged people who attained to this phase not to stop

---

51. Howard Goss recounts that in the summer of 1910, Durham was invited to speak at a camp meeting in Malvern, Arkansas that he and E. N. Bell were responsible for organizing. At the camp they debated the "Finished Work of Calvary" vs. "Second Work of Grace" and Goss became convinced of Durham's teaching. By the following summer, in Goss' view, "The whole movement in the Central States had swung in line with the 'Finished work' teaching, the other issue having faded out." Goss, *The Winds of God*, 126–27, 135–36.

52. W. H. Durham, "What is the Evidence of the Baptism of the Holy Ghose[sic]?" *Apostolic Faith* [Fort Worth] 7.2 (May 1911) 2–3.

53. E. N. Bell, "The New Birth and the Baptism with the Spirit," *Word and Witness* 9.11 (November, 1913) 2.

54. E. N. Bell, "Second Blessing," *Word and Witness* 9.12 (December 1913) 2.

55. These two aspects of sanctification are most noticeable in W. H. Durham, "Some Other Phases of Sanctification," *Pentecostal Testimony* 2.2 (1912) 7–9.

56. E. N. Bell, "Sanctify Through the Truth," *Apostolic Faith* [Fort Worth] 7.1 (February 1911) 2.

their pursuit of holiness. He called Christians to move beyond the cleansing from sin that "every babe in Christ can and should have," and "be filled with every holy virtue, every divine grace, all the fruits of the Spirit." This was the second, gradual phase of sanctification, and Bell believed, as did Durham, that a key part of this second phase was being baptized or filled with the Holy Spirit.[57] Two weeks after the first meeting of the General Council of the Assemblies of God in Hot Springs, Bell used space in his periodical to explain what was meant by the "finished-work" doctrine. He referred to Durham as the main proponent of the doctrine emerging among Pentecostals, and, clearly in favor of the doctrine, remarked that there was a growing unity on the subject.[58] The conference at Hot Springs must have been some indication to Bell that Durham's doctrine was finding a wide acceptance among Pentecostals. Some, however, had taken Durham's doctrine further than he had ever anticipated.

The Assemblies of God: A Distinctive Testimony?

Oneness Pentecostalism Emerges

In the spring of 1913, a camp meeting was held on some acreage in Arroyo Seco, California just north of Los Angeles. The meeting, originally intended to be led by Maria Woodworth-Etter, featured a variety of speakers including R. E. McAlister who preached a message on the correct water baptismal formula being in Jesus' name only.[59] Although response to McAlister's proposal was mixed at the camp meeting, by the time the "Call to Hot Springs" was made by Bell in early 1914 the "new issue" had become a full-fledged movement on the West Coast through the preaching of Frank Ewart and Glenn Cook.[60] In April 1914, the same month that the meeting in Hot Springs would form the largest Pentecostal denomination in America, Ewart and Cook re-baptized each other in Jesus' name, and each soon began traveling around the country and promoting the new doctrine.

---

57. Bell's two processes of sanctification are expounded upon more comprehensively in Bell, *Questions and Answers*, 19–21.

58. E. N. Bell, "Editorials: the Finished Work," *Word and Witness* 10.4 (April 1914) 2.

59. Johnston, "Howard A. Goss," 62–65, 126–27.

60. Reed, "Origins and Development," 103–4.

By the following summer the controversy had influenced ministers in the young Assemblies of God denomination enough that Bell felt the need to publicly address the "sad new issue" in *Word and Witness*. In the article, Bell respectfully, but systematically, denounced the teaching of those who would deny the validity of water baptism in the Trinitarian formula as a so-called "revelation" without explicit support from Scripture or the history of the Christian church.[61] If Bell's denouncement of oneness doctrine helped to stabilize the Assemblies of God on the new issue, Bell's actions over the next few months had the opposite effect. Bell apparently had second thoughts about his original baptism and in the summer of 1915 he was re-baptized in Jesus' name in Jackson, Tennessee along with sixty-six other ministers of the Assemblies of God.[62] Soon after, Bell admitted that he made a mistake in being re-baptized and by October 1915 an article was printed in *Word and Witness* urging ministers not to be re-baptized and to allow for variation in the baptismal formula.[63] That same month, the third General Council of the Assemblies of God convened in St. Louis. At the meeting, the new issue was debated and the conference sided with the Trinitarians and called for ministers not to encourage re-baptism from the pulpit, but to only allow it for individuals where their original baptism was considered by the candidate not to be "Christian baptism."[64] The issue, however, would not die and the following year the Assemblies of God had no choice but to take a definite side on the issue.

Statement of Fundamental Truths

Two years after their first meeting, propelled by a desire to rein in the promotion and dissemination of anti-Trinitarian teaching among their ranks, the General Council of the Assemblies of God agreed on a statement of seventeen "fundamental truths" as a basis for unity in the new

61. E. N. Bell, "The Sad New Issue," *Word and Witness* 12.6 (June 1915) 2–3.

62. Thomas Fudge argues that Bell's re-baptism should not be understood as a "conversion" to the "new issue" movement. Rather, Bell's re-baptism was a response to "a long-held personal question about his original baptism." Fudge shows that there is no textual evidence to support that Bell ever was swayed to agree with the unique theological positions of the "new issue." Fudge, "Did E. N. Bell Convert?" 129.

63. E. N. Bell, "There is Safety in Counsel," *Word and Witness* 12.10 (October 1915) 1.

64. *Minutes of the General Council of the Assemblies of God in the United States of America, Canada and Foreign Lands held at Turner Hall, St. Louis, Mo. October 1–10th, 1915,* 5.

organization. In Articles 4–8, Durham's influence is evident. Article 4 addressed salvation, with an "inward evidence" of the "witness of the Spirit," and "outward evidence" of "righteousness, true holiness . . . the fruits of the Spirit . . . and brotherly love." Article 5 proposed, "All believers are entitled to, and should ardently expect, and earnestly seek the promise of the Father, the baptism in the Holy Ghost and fire, according to the command of our Lord Jesus Christ." Article 6 explained that Spirit Baptism was "indicated by the initial sign of speaking in tongues" and that the experience was "distinct from and subsequent to the experience of the new birth." Finally, Article 7 stated that "entire sanctification" was "the will of God for all believers" and "pursued by walking in obedience to God's Word."[65] With these four articles, Durham's conception of the Christian life secured a place of primacy in the Pentecostal movement, but not without disagreement.[66]

The Bosworth Controversy

During the next two years following the General Council's authoring of the first "Statement of Fundamental Truths," Fred Francis Bosworth became increasingly critical of Article 6, eventually resigning his credentials from the Assemblies of God in 1918 over the matter. A sermon by F. F. Bosworth given at Stone's Church in Chicago on November 21, 1915 seems to present Bosworth's position as one in agreement with the initial evidence doctrine adopted by the Assemblies of God in 1916. He stated,

> I have learned both from the Bible and also from nine years continual observation during revivals, that if people will sufficiently yield and obey when the Spirit is poured upon them, it is their privilege to receive the Holy Ghost, "AS AT THE BEGINNING," when on the Day of Pentecost. There are five points mentioned in the account that analyzes the experience of Cornelius and his household, in receiving the baptism, and while many fall short

---

65. *Minutes of the General Council of the Assemblies of God in the United States of America, Canada and Foreign Lands held at Bethel Chapel, St. Louis, Mo. October 1–7th, 1916*, 10–11.

66. Other Pentecostal denominations preceded the Assemblies of God in their inclusion of a doctrine of "initial evidence" in their statement of beliefs, but the Assemblies of God was the first major Pentecostal organization to adopt Durham's view of sanctification as official. *Constitution and General Rules of the Fire Baptized Holiness Church 1908*, 2–3; *Constitution and General Rules of the Pentecostal Holiness Church 1911*, 3.

of this by not sufficiently yielding and obeying when the Spirit is poured upon them, it is the privilege of everyone to have an experience that can be described by the same five points that described this outpouring in the tenth chapter of Acts. The five points are these: first, "the Spirit was POURED OUT;" second, "the Holy Ghost *fell on them*;" third, they "spake with tongues and magnified God"; fourth, Peter says "they received the Holy Ghost," and fifth, in Acts 11:16 Peter calls it "the baptism with the Holy Ghost."[67]

While Bosworth allowed for the possibility that these five points may not immediately accompany all experiences of Spirit Baptism, he was clear that the evidence of speaking in tongues was *available* to all. Two years later, Bosworth had formed quite a different opinion,

After eleven years in the work on Pentecostal lines, during which it has been my pleasure to see thousands receive the precious baptism in the Holy Spirit, I am absolutely certain that many who receive the most powerful baptism for service do not receive the manifestation of speaking in tongues.[68]

Stating his position even more strongly, Bosworth's letter of July 24, 1918 to Executive Presbyter John W. Welch resigning his credentials stated, "If I had a thousand souls, I would not be afraid to risk them all on the truth of my position that some may receive the *fullest* baptism in the Spirit without receiving the Gift of tongues."[69] Here, Bosworth did not even allow for a Baptism without tongues to be referred to as "incomplete" or "partial."

What was it that caused this change in Bosworth's beliefs? The main criticism that Bosworth levied against the doctrine in his "Open Letter to the Saints and Ministers of the Pentecostal Movement" was that it necessitated a problematic distinction between the gift of tongues referred to in 1 Corinthians 12 and the evidence of tongues referred to in the Book of Acts. The changes made to Article 6 by the General Council in 1917 addressed exactly this point. In addition to adding the word "physical," the Council added a statement that the experience was "distinct from the gift of tongues." These changes were approved by the Council with "only

---

67. F. F. Bosworth, "The Promise of the Father: Rain the Remedy for a Spiritual Death," *Latter Rain Evangel* (February 1916) 4.

68. Bosworth, *Do All Speak with Tongues?* 4.

69. Bosworth, "Letter of Resignation." Italics mine. Here, as in other places, Bosworth made it clear that he did not draw a distinction between "evidential tongues" and the "gift of tongues."

three or four dissenting votes."⁷⁰ It seems likely that Bosworth was one of the dissenting voices. If so, it is probable that the Council's decision to go ahead with the changes in spite of the objections caused Bosworth to be more vocal in his opposition to the doctrine during the following year.

Bosworth's resignation in July 1918 evidently sparked a desire in Assemblies of God leadership to work toward unity by clarifying the doctrine and establishing its biblical basis and place of primacy in Pentecostal tradition. An article by Durham that answered the question, "What is the Evidence of the Baptism of the Holy Ghost?" was reprinted in the *Christian Evangel* the following month with an interesting editorial exclusion. Perhaps in a desire to project a sense of Pentecostal unity on the subject, the editor chose to remove the following statement in reference to the doctrine of tongues as necessary evidence of Spirit Baptism: "It has also resulted in more Pentecostal preachers and people's compromising the truth, than any other one point of doctrine."⁷¹ Two weeks later, an article was printed by Executive Presbyter D. W. Kerr in which he reiterated the doctrine as the organization's "distinctive testimony," and also stated the Council's assumption that all ministers would submit any point of contention they had with the Fundamental Truths to them for review and action. Perhaps anticipating the debate with Bosworth that would ensue a few weeks later, Kerr also argued that nothing outside the Bible, whether personal experiences, personal observations, or any other "outside evidence pro or con," be used in defense of any doctrine, particularly the doctrine of evidential tongues.⁷² In the same issue, E. N. Bell wrote an article in which he addressed possible misreadings of Article 6 that made it more rigid than was intended. He said that the article did not claim that tongues were the *only* evidence of Spirit Baptism, but that there were "many other corroborating evidences." He also reminded readers that not just any tongues were considered an evidence of Spirit Baptism, but only tongues "as the Spirit of God gives the utterance."⁷³

---

70. *Minutes of the General Council of the Assemblies of God in the United States of America, Canada, and Foreign Lands held at Bethel Chapel, St. Louis, Mo. Sept 9th to 14th, 1917*, 21.

71. W. H. Durham, "What is the Evidence of the Baptism of the Holy Ghost?" *Christian Evangel* 250–251 (August 10, 1918) 2. Compare with W. H. Durham, "What is the Evidence of the Baptism of the Holy Ghose[sic]?" *Apostolic Faith* [Fort Worth] 7.2 (May 1911) 2.

72. D. W. Kerr. "Paul's Interpretation of the Baptism in Holy Spirit," *Christian Evangel* 252–253 (August 24, 1918) 6.

73. E. N. Bell, "A Correction," *Christian Evangel* 252–53 (August 24, 1918) 7.

At the General Council's meeting in September 1918, room was given to debate Article 6. Though he had already resigned his credentials, Bosworth was invited to attend. In what the *Minutes* deemed an "animated discussion" with "the utmost enthusiasm," Bosworth and at least eight Council members spoke to the issue. In the end, Bosworth quietly admitted defeat to the Council's arguments in defense of the doctrine. Though they were not enough to persuade him to change his own mind on the issue, it was clear to him that unity in the organization was best achieved by his departure.[74] One of the results of the debate was the approval, the very next day, of another addition to Article 6 to further clarify the distinction between the "gift" and "sign" of tongues added the previous year. The addition read, "The speaking in tongues in this instance is the same in essence as the gift of tongues . . . but different in purpose and use."[75] No doubt, this clarification was the General Council's response (probably led by W. F. Carothers) to the arguments against the doctrine given by Bosworth.[76]

A Distinctive Testimony

Another result of the debate was an affirmation of the doctrine by the Council as "our distinctive testimony," and a statement that it was "inconsistent and unscriptural" for a credentialed minister to attack the doctrine as an error.[77] Bosworth's criticisms of Article 6 were unique in that they could not be easily dismissed. Six years earlier, Durham had contended that most critics of the doctrine of evidential tongues were motivated by a hatred for a doctrine that concluded that they were not baptized in the Spirit. He further observed, "Whenever they cease in any place to teach

---

74. Stanley Frodsham, "The 1918 General Council," *Christian Evangel* 256–57 (October 5, 1918) 3.

75. *Minutes from the Sixth Annual Meeting of the General Council of the Assemblies of God*, 10.

76. Robeck proposes that Carothers, who was the first to make a distinction between the sign and gift, played a leading role in the Council's decision to add the statement. Robeck, "An Emerging Magisterium?" 229. Carothers first made the case for the distinction in W. F. Carothers, "The Baptism with the Holy Ghost," *Apostolic Faith* [Baxter Springs] 1.9 (May 1906) 15. See also W. F. Carothers, *The Baptism with the Holy Ghost*, 20.

77. *Minutes of the Sixth Annual Meeting of the General Council of the Assemblies of God*, 7–8.

that the tongues are the evidence, the power of God lifts."[78] Neither of these arguments could be made against Bosworth. His own experience of Spirit Baptism included the manifestation of tongues.

More importantly, Bosworth was well respected by Pentecostals all around the country. As a band director at Dowie's Zion City, Bosworth was baptized in the Spirit at a meeting there led by Charles Parham. He was the founding pastor of a prominent Pentecostal church in Dallas, Texas. He was also notably used by God to heal many people in his revival meetings. His exemplary reputation in the Pentecostal community is shown by his being installed as one of sixteen members of the Assemblies of God's first Executive Presbytery. The fact that criticism of the defining doctrine of the movement was coming from one of its most respected members was troubling for the Council, and they wished it not to happen again. Referring to the doctrine of evidential tongues, Durham wrote in 1911, "The work has never suffered from the effects of the opposition of those who stood on the outside of the movement. . . . It has suffered from the effects of those who claim to be Pentecostal people, and at the same time deny this great distinguishing truth of the movement."[79] In many ways, this statement captured the sentiment of many in the General Council five years later when criticism of Article 6 of the Fundamental Truths began to emerge from within their ranks led by Bosworth. More significant than the doctrinal changes to Article 6 that were instigated by Bosworth's criticisms—for the vast majority of changes were simply clarifying the beliefs that most in the group already held—was the raising of the stakes for all who wished to follow Bosworth's lead. With the affirmation of Article 6 as the "distinctive testimony" of Pentecostals, the Assemblies of God drew a line in the sand between Pentecostals and non-Pentecostals. In the future, they would not hesitate to designate an individual as being on one side or the other solely on the basis of their agreement or disagreement with the statement.

Later Developments in the Assemblies of God

The controversy over Article 6 at the General Council meetings in 1917 and 1918 led to the printing of many subsequent articles in Assemblies of

---

78. W. H. Durham, "Speaking in Tongues is the Evidence of the Baptism in the Holy Spirit," *Pentecostal Testimony* 2.3 (1912) 12.

79. W. H. Durham, "Speaking in Tongues is the Evidence of the Baptism in the Holy Spirit," *Pentecostal Testimony* 2.2 (May 1912) 9.

God periodicals defending the doctrine, and providing explanation and elaboration on certain controversial points. D. W. Kerr, who led the arguments against Bosworth's position at the 1918 meeting, wrote an article specifically addressing Paul's question in 1 Corinthians 12, "Do All Speak with Tongues?" In it, Kerr proposed two distinct uses of tongues. The "sign" of tongues was a "Godward" use of tongues where one "rises above the natural into the realm of the supernatural in adoring and worshiping God." In contrast, Kerr argued that the gift of tongues was a "manward aspect of the use of tongues" used solely for the benefit of believers.[80] Up until this time, a distinction between the sign and gift of tongues had been based on the degree to which the intellect was involved in speaking.

In later articles, Kerr not only defended the biblical basis for the doctrine of evidential tongues, but also set out to show that the apostles held the same doctrine. He addressed the five manifestations of the Spirit promised by Christ in Mark 16:7, and argued that in Acts, tongues was the sign "selected from the great mass of supernatural manifestations . . . and elevated to a position in which it was regarded by the apostles and writers of the new Testament as the evidence, the initial physical evidence, of the fullness of the Spirit."[81] Kerr further argued that the inability of other Christian traditions to see this fact was reason enough not to "work together with those who oppose or reject this Pentecostal truth." Further distancing himself from outsiders, Kerr proposed that those who "have no experimental knowledge" of the doctrine had no right to give input on the matter.[82]

The formal appeal to the doctrine of initial evidence as the "distinctive testimony" by the Assemblies of God was short lived. In 1925, a revised statement about the distinctive testimony was recommended by the Executive Presbytery, but the proposed revision was never accepted. A five-person committee was commissioned go through all the resolutions and adopt only what they believed were essential for the organization. As a result of their proposal, the statement on the distinctive testimony was taken out altogether in 1927.[83] Yet, the doctrine had already served

80. D. W. Kerr, "Do All Speak in Tongues?" *Christian Evangel* 270–71 (January 11, 1919) 7.

81. D. W. Kerr, "The Bible Evidence of the Baptism with the Holy Ghost," *The Pentecostal Evangel* 509 (August 11, 1923) 2.

82. D. W. Kerr, "The Basis for Our Distinctive Testimony," *Pentecostal Evangel* 460–61 (September 2, 1922) 4.

83. For the proposed revision, see *The Interpretation of the Constitutional Agreements*, 18. For the decision to table the recommendations of the Executive Presbytery

its purpose in bringing conformity on the doctrine among Assemblies of God ministers and establishing the doctrine as the defining tenet of Pentecostals in America.

The 1930s–1940s in the Assemblies of God was a period characterized by a shift in how Pentecostals approached matters of doctrine. Douglas Jacobsen argues that the era may be best described as an era of "Pentecostal Scholasticism." Jacobsen observes that while many new organizations follow an era of creativity with one of consolidation, the Pentecostal scholastics were unique in that they tended not to emphasize the distinctive tenets of the movement. Rather, they "sought to temper the more radical claims of the movement's varied 'founders' and to reframe the distinctive beliefs of Pentecostals in the light of their compatibility with and place in the longer, larger, and broader 'catholic' Christian tradition. The resultant theology was surprisingly moderate in tone and content."[84] Thus, in comparison with the decade prior, there were few articles or books written on the subject of initial evidence.

One of the few writers on the subject of initial evidence in this era was Donald Gee. Gee passionately defended the importance of the doctrine of initial evidence and speaking in tongues, but in doing so, Gee was careful to frame his arguments in such a way as to not put down other Christians outside the Pentecostal tradition. In fact, most of Gee's articles were written to address pastoral concerns he had for his fellow Pentecostals rather than challenging the errors of non-Pentecostals. In 1932, Gee addressed the controversial subject of "disappointing" baptisms head on, providing some practical steps for Pentecostals to follow to "rekindle" the flame of Pentecost in their lives.[85] In 1937, Gee wrote an article in which he defended the doctrine on the traditional grounds of a precedent in the Book of Acts, but he also provided a pastoral reason of why tongues and not other gifts of the Spirit could be the initial evidence. "For an immediate evidence at the beginning some simple manifestation is palpably required that needs no space of time to allow opportunity for growth and no special

---

and appoint a committee to review the minutes and compile the essential resolutions, see *Combined Minutes of the General Council of the Assemblies of God in the United States of America and Foreign Lands, 1914-1925*, 64, 69. For the final report of the committee, see *Final Report of Revision Committee*, 3–29. The five people on the committee were: J. Narver Gortner, E. S. Williams, A. G. Ward, S. A. Jamieson, and F. M. Boyd.

84. Jacobsen, "Knowing the Doctrines," 91.

85. Donald Gee, "Disappointing Baptisms," *Latter Rain Evangel* 25.3 (December 1932) 15.

circumstances to give opportunity for exercise." Gee argued that the only gift that could meet these criteria was the gift of speaking in tongues.[86] In 1941, Gee wrote about the need for Pentecostals to endure and persevere in their Pentecostal experience saying, "It is a grand thing for those who have had the Baptism in the Holy Ghost to renew their vows."[87] The printing of these articles by Gee, a leader in the British Assemblies of God, in American Assemblies of God Periodicals demonstrates the shift in focus of the Assemblies of God in the United States from emphasizing the beginning of the Pentecostal life to explaining how the Pentecostal experience, once received, should influence the rest of the Christian's life.[88]

Foursquare and Open Bible: A Not So Distinctive Testimony?

Foursquare

The early heritage of the International Church of the Foursquare Gospel cannot be separated from the life of Aimee Semple McPherson. In a real sense, her beliefs and practices were the beliefs and practices of the denomination in the beginning, and developments in her own life and thought directly affected the denomination. As founder and lifetime president, every decision of the denomination up until 1942 started and stopped with her words of approval or dissatisfaction. Thus, a study of the early doctrine of Foursquare is a study of the developments of "Sister Aimee's" beliefs and practices herself.

Alongside Bell and Kerr, another person the Assemblies of God called on in the wake of the Bosworth controversy to defend their distinctive testimony was a newly credentialed female evangelist, Aimee Semple McPherson. For almost a year and a half between 1908 and 1910, Aimee and her husband Robert Semple studied, traveled, and worked alongside

---

86. Donald Gee, "Why Tongues?" *Pentecostal Evangel* 1213 (August 7, 1937) 2.

87. Donald Gee, "More Than Conquerors," *Pentecostal Evangel* 1401 (March 15, 1941) 3.

88. There were still articles that focused on the beginning of the Spirit-filled life during this era, but the shift in emphasis from entering to living the Pentecostal life is clear. Donald Gee, "How to Receive the Baptism with the Holy Spirit," *Pentecostal Evangel* 1418 (July 12, 1941) 6; Arthur Graves, "How to Receive the Baptism in the Holy Ghost," *Pentecostal Evangel* 1473 (August 1, 1942) 2–3; Stanley Frodsham, "Have Ye Received the Holy Ghost Since Ye Believed?" *Pentecostal Evangel* 1568 (May 27, 1944) 1–5.

William Durham of the North Avenue Mission in Chicago. During that time, Aimee and Robert occasionally accompanied Durham on his travels to camp meetings and conventions around the United States and in Canada. Aimee discovered and developed her gift of interpretation of tongues while with Durham, and often publicly delivered interpretations in their meetings.[89] It is difficult to know exactly how much, if any, of Aimee's doctrinal stances can be attributed to her contact with Durham. Aimee held to the same "finished-work" doctrine of sanctification that Durham adamantly proclaimed in Los Angeles, Chicago, and wherever else he preached. However, it was not until after he had separated ways with the Semples early in 1910 that he began to preach the doctrine.[90]

Aimee also advocated the doctrine of evidential tongues that Durham espoused. Even before her association with the Assemblies of God, Aimee supported a rigid doctrine of evidential tongues. The second issue of the *Bridal Call* periodical she and her second husband, Harold McPherson, edited provided the following statement,

> The baptism of the Holy Ghost is received today in exactly the same way as in the Bible days when the hundred and twenty were all filled with the Holy Ghost and spake with other tongues as the Spirit gave them utterance (Acts 2:4). His incoming today is still accompanied by the same sign that so greatly astonished the Jews, in Acts 10:44–46.[91]

In an article printed a few months later in the Christian Worker's Union periodical, *Word and Work*, Aimee left no room for irregular baptisms. Regarding the roughly ten thousand people she had seen baptized in the Spirit, she stated, "Without any exception, all had the same Bible evidence, as recorded in the Word of God."[92] Aimee also made a distinction between

---

89. Durham printed at least one of these messages in his periodical. Mrs. R. J. Semple, "A Prophetic Message," *Pentecostal Testimony* 1.1 (July 1910) 12.

90. The Semples separated from Durham for their mission work in January 1910. It was not until after the death of his daughter Bessie that same year that Durham began to preach on the "Finished-work of Calvary." Jacobsen, *Thinking in the Spirit*, 139; Blumhofer, "William H. Durham," 135.

91. Harold S. McPherson, "What We Believe and Teach," *Bridal Call* 1.2 (July 1917) 4.

92. Aimee Semple McPherson, "Questions and Answers Concerning the Baptism of the Holy Ghost," *Word and Work* 39 (September 8, 1917) 488. For other pre-1919 articles by Aimee that defend a rigid doctrine of evidential tongues, see Aimee Simple McPherson, "The Work of the Holy Spirit," *Bridal Call* 1.3 (August 1917) 1–2; "Covet Earnestly Spiritual Gifts," *Word and Work* 39 (October 13, 1917) 568–70; "Acts Two, Four," *Bridal Call* 1.10 (March 1918) 11–12; "Has God Changed His Patterns?" *Bridal*

the sign of tongues and tongues "as the Spirit gives utterance." She believed that the two were different in the way one's will or volition was involved in the speaking process. She argued, "All who receive the baptism of the Holy Ghost speak in tongues involuntarily as the Spirit gives utterance. Not all, in fact few, receive the gift of tongues. We have met some, however, who could speak at will to foreigners in their own language telling them of Jesus."[93]

When the opportunity arose for Aimee to be credentialed with the Assemblies of God in 1919, she apparently could adopt and support their Statement of Fundamental Truths with ease. Her unwavering stance on the issue of tongues as the evidence of Spirit Baptism was printed in *The Pentecostal Evangel* in November 1919.[94] It provided an exhaustive list of what she perceived as "unscriptural evidences" of Spirit Baptism. The list included, among other things, joy, power to overcome, power to pray, power to preach, a conscious walk with God, an anointing of the Spirit, gifts of the Spirit, prophecy, the gift of tongues, healing, and miracles. She went on to defend the Assemblies of God position, "Thousands are receiving the Baptism with the Spirit, and all who receive Him today speak with other tongues, just as did the early believers in Bible days. All who are receiving have a definite knowledge of the day, place, and hour when He came in to abide." There were reasons, however, for Aimee's affiliation with the Assemblies of God to be short lived. Aimee returned her credential papers to the Assemblies of God on January 5, 1922. According to Robeck, it was the issue of the property rights to Angelus Temple—then in the process of being built—that was the primary reason for the separation.[95]

Call 1.12 (May 1918) 10–11.

93. Aimee Semple McPherson, "Questions and Answers Concerning the Baptism of the Holy Ghost," *Word and Work* 39 (September 8, 1917) 487.

94. Aimee Semple McPherson, "What is the Evidence of the Baptism of the Holy Ghost?" *Pentecostal Evangel* 312–13 (November 1, 1919) 6. McPherson was ordained as an evangelist with the Assemblies of God in April 1919. Blumhofer, *Aimee Semple McPherson*, 144.

95. Robeck, "International Church of the Foursquare Gospel," 793. It is also probable that her recent divorce from Harold McPherson, which directly violated the recommendations of the General Council on "Marriage and Divorce," would have been a cause for concern if she had continued her ministry with the Assemblies of God. Her limited status within the Assemblies of God as a female "evangelist" and not "as an Elder with authority" may have also contributed to her desire to separate from the organization. The General Council, "General Council Special," *Word and Witness* 10.5 (May 20, 1914) 1.

In 1921, Aimee had already established the four-fold gospel—Jesus as Savior, Healer, Baptizer in the Holy Spirit, and Coming King—as the primary message of her *Bridal Call* periodical, but she began to promote the message more strongly after her separation from the Assemblies of God in 1922.[96] In 1923, Aimee composed the Foursquare Declaration of Faith and added "Foursquare" to the name of her monthly periodical. Although she did not express any disagreement with the Assemblies of God doctrines during her time with the organization, when the Assemblies of God Fundamental Truths are compared side-by-side with the Foursquare Declaration of Faith composed by Aimee, there are some notable differences between the two.

Unlike the Statement of Fundamental Truths of the Assemblies of God, the Foursquare Declaration of Faith does not contain a clear doctrine of initial evidence. The closest thing to an initial evidence doctrine in the Foursquare statement is the following:

> The believer may have every reason to expect His incoming to be after the same manner as that in which He came upon Jew and Gentile alike in Bible days and as recorded in the Word, that it may be truly said of us as of the house of Cornelius: The Holy Ghost fell on them as on us at the beginning.[97]

In fact, after 1920, it is difficult to find any printed statement by Aimee that is comparable to the Assemblies of God doctrine of evidential tongues in specificity or rigidity. Raymond Cox has argued that Aimee "consistently and emphatically" emphasized speaking in tongues as the initial physical evidence of the Baptism with the Holy Spirit in all three of her periodicals.[98] But Cox cites little support for his position. That Aimee still believed in the doctrine is clearly implied in her many statements advocating the importance of a biblical evidence that identifies the specific time and place of one's Baptism in the Spirit.[99] However, she refused to make an explicit creed-like

---

96. McPherson cited a personal prophetic vision as the source of this four-fold gospel message during crusade meetings in Oakland, California in July of 1922. Blumhofer, *Aimee Semple McPherson*, 191–92. However, her reference to this same four-fold message in her own periodical in June 1921 and another by a contributing author the following month shows that these themes were already active in her ministry a year earlier. *Bridal Call* 5.1 (June 1921) 1; John Quincy Adams, "A Baptist's View on the Dallas Campaign," *Bridal Call* 5.2 (July 1921) 16.

97. McPherson, *Declaration of Faith*, 17.

98. Cox, "Was Amy Semple McPherson Pentecostal?" 1–2.

99. For some articles that indicate that Aimee continued to hold a doctrine of evidential tongues, see Aimee Semple McPherson, "Tongues of Flame," *Bridal Call*

statement on the issue. If Aimee continued to espouse a doctrine of evidential tongues throughout her lifetime, she certainly refrained from referring to such a doctrine as "the distinctive testimony" of Pentecostals.

In fact, Edith Blumhofer suggests that Aimee had little interest in defining her denomination as Pentecostal saying,

> The issues that came into focus in the course of the emergence of denominations in classical Pentecostalism reshaped in critical ways the practical meaning of *being* Pentecostal. Denominations such as the Assemblies of God insisted that ministers subscribe to the view that tongues speech uniformly evidence Spirit Baptism. But that point simply did not matter to Sister, who—at least after 1919—refused to be diverted by such discussions; they became unimportant in her scheme of things. She shifted her focus from the spiritual gifts that Pentecostals coveted (and she also cherished) to the simple statement that Christ was still the same. . . . She preached "Bible Christianity," and everything else followed.[100]

Like Boddy in Britain, "Rather than separate from the nation's historic denominations, [Sister Aimee] hoped to reform them from the inside out."[101] She separated herself from her American Pentecostal contemporaries, not in her doctrine, but in her refusal to impose every point of her doctrine on her followers without flexibility.[102] Her purposeful exclusion of a strict "initial evidence" doctrine from the Foursquare Declaration of Faith is just one example of how she was not willing to reduce the essence of the Pentecostal message to one particular doctrine. After 1920, Aimee seems to have understood the doctrine of tongues as the initial evidence of Spirit Baptism as an important doctrine, but one that certainly did not capture the "distinctive testimony" of Pentecostals.

In the 1920s and 1930s, Aimee shifted the focus of many of her sermons and teachings from defending the Pentecostal experience to

---

Foursquare 7.12 (May 1924) 8–9; "The Upper Room," *Bridal Call Foursquare* 12.5 (May 1928) 13–14, 31–32; "What We Teach Concerning the Baptism of the Holy Spirit," *Bridal Call Foursquare* 15.2 (February 1931): 5–8, 28–29. For a more expanded discussion, see McPherson, *The Holy Spirit*, 135–84.

100. Blumhofer, *Everybody's Sister*, 214.

101. Sutton, *Aimee Semple McPherson*, 43.

102. Aimee's decision to distinguish between doctrinal essentials and non-essentials in terms of fellowship allowed her to champion her message as "undenominational," and it made her a forerunner in Pentecostalism's gradual alignment with Evangelicalism that would take place over the next fifty years. Barfoot, *Aimee Semple McPherson*, 384.

engaging the fundamentalist-modernist controversies in America.[103] Yet, the Baptism in the Holy Spirit was still an important part of her message. It represented the feature that distinguished the true church from the cold, backslidden world. Aimee located debate on the Pentecostal experience in the context of a larger debate between the old-time religion of the Bible and Modernism. A sermon by Aimee given at Angelus Temple in April 1925 addressed those who did not support tongues as evidence arguing that the only criteria for Spirit Baptism was faith. She believed that such an argument was just a façade for the modernist ideology that would promote the receiving of the Holy Spirit "by theory," and argued, "There is no '20th Century way' of receiving the Holy Spirit."[104] In 1933, Aimee presented the position of the apostles as one in favor of tongues as evidence of Spirit Baptism, but did so again with an eye to challenge the prevailing culture: "These are days of coldness and of perplexity: days of atheism and unbelief: days of modernism, higher criticism and pantheism.... The Baptism of the Holy Spirit is needed today as never before!"[105] In September 1936, Aimee systematically responded to a lecture given by Dr. Norman Harrison entitled, "Why I Am Not a Pentecostal, Why I Am Not Seeking the Baptism and Do Not Talk in Tongues." In her response, Aimee described Spirit Baptism as the power of God "to get people saved," and tongues as a sign that this power was present in the individual and the community. Against "talking to the Lord in a quiet communion," Aimee challenged, "Friend, this is the quietest world we will ever live in. We are going to have lots of shouting in Heaven.... Better get used to the noise here."[106]

While Aimee maintained a personal belief that tongues was the definitive evidence of Spirit Baptism, she focused in on a broader conception of Spirit Baptism—a conception that included empowerment for social issues, evangelism, and holiness—as that which represented the Pentecostal's distinctive testimony. In 1934, afraid that some young ministers had begun to shy away from preaching on the topic of Spirit Baptism, Aimee wrote, "If you let down and compromise of [sic] the Baptism of the Holy

---

103. Sutton, "Between the Refrigerator," 179–80.

104. Aimee Semple McPherson, "The Holy Spirit in Old Testament Types and Shadows and New Testament Power," *Bridal Call Foursquare* 9.1 (June 1925) 26–27. McPherson reiterated the difference between receiving the Spirit "by faith" and "by theory" in *The Holy Spirit*, 179.

105. Aimee Semple McPherson, "Pentecostal Pattern Persists," *Bridal Call Foursquare* 17.5 (October 1933) 16–17.

106. Aimee Semple McPherson, "Sister Answers Dr. Harrison," *Foursquare Crusader* 3.13 (September 23, 1936) 3, 6.

Spirit, the one great essential which makes us different than all the others, we are doomed before we see another year."[107] For Aimee, it was not tongues but Spirit Baptism that represented the Pentecostal's unique experience that made them different from all other groups in Christendom.

A doctrine that is distinctly Foursquare is Aimee doctrine of moderation. In a religious climate that often looked on spiritual excesses as a sign of spiritual power, Aimee advocated a position that said the Christian life should be sober, thoughtful, balanced, forgiving and zealous, while refraining from extremes, fanaticism, unseemly manifestations, backbiting, and murmuring.[108] Aimee acted on this belief well before 1927 and the founding of the Foursquare denomination. In 1921, she reportedly withheld some extreme manifestations of the Spirit from a revival service in Wichita. Based on this, and her receiving a license to preach from a Baptist church in San Jose shortly after withdrawing her credentials from the Assemblies of God, *The Pentecostal Evangel*, the official Assemblies of God periodical, published a brief article entitled "Is Mrs. McPherson Pentecostal?" In this article, the General Council office accused Aimee of rapidly loosing "Pentecostal power" in her meetings and straying from the "full Pentecostal faith."[109]

In her defense, Aimee wrote a response in her own *Bridal Call* periodical with an article under the same title. In this article, Aimee called the report "hasty and unproven . . . silly and unjust . . . pitiful!"[110] She also expressed her own vision to walk a narrow line between being Spirit-filled on one side and exhibiting Christian virtues such as piety, humility, sanity, and sobriety on the other, a line which most denominations tended to walk on one side or the other. She defended her Pentecostalism by saying,

> We stand for, believe, preach and rejoice in the power of the Holy Spirit, Third Person of the Trinity, blessed Paraclete sent from the Father, and for all that happened in the second chapter of the Acts of the Apostles. . . . For fourteen years we have believed in, preached and seen outpoured this blessed and glorious power of the Holy Spirit, just as He came to the waiting hearts on the memorable day of Pentecost. But we have never

---

107. Aimee Semple McPherson, "Forward Foursquare!" *Bridal Call Foursquare* 18.8 (January 1934) 17.

108. McPherson, *The Foursquare Gospel*, 162–63.

109. The General Council Office, "Is Mrs. McPherson Pentecostal?" *Pentecostal Evangel* 448–49 (June 10, 1922) 9.

110. Aimee Semple McPherson, "Is Mrs. McPherson Pentecostal? Yes or No?" *Bridal Call* 6.5 (October 1922) 10.

been convinced that God meant any small company to organize "Pentecost" or put a corner on it.[111]

This statement is as remarkable for what it did *not* say as for what it did. Aimee refused to engage in arguments over doctrines such as "initial evidence" or specific regulations concerning what was and was not truly "Pentecostal." Aimee's position of moderation allowed for the Pentecostal power to be spread throughout all churches and denominations, not just to churches labeled as Pentecostal. She felt that Pentecostal churches had been given plenty of time to carry the message of the Holy Spirit to other churches, but had never succeeded in preaching it without causing disruption. Thus, as Matthew Sutton has observed, Aimee "downplayed the controversial elements of the [Pentecostal] movement and instead took a moderate position that facilitated broad alliances."[112] This decision allowed her ministry to be well-received by many non-Pentecostal churches and leaders who were troubled by Pentecostal "Holy Rollers," but it also distanced her from Pentecostal insiders that understood public manifestations of tongues as an essential aspect of Pentecostal ethos.[113]

Aimee's moderation stance could be described as one of the first moves toward a "seeker-sensitive" Pentecostal worship service. She instituted a program where an "Upper Room" was designated for those who desired to tarry for the Baptism of the Holy Spirit before attending the larger public worship gathering. She explained, "The Upper Room is the power house. . . . The Church and the field constitute the great harvest land, and the Spirit-filled are winners of souls therein; quiet, moderate, efficient, spiritual workers."[114] This practical distinction between the context in which Pentecostals received their power and the context in which they used their power in service to others was a creative response to an issue that Pentecostal ministers were all forced to address: how best to accommodate the needs of seekers without quenching the Holy Spirit.

Open Bible

Less than a year after her Baptism in the Holy Spirit at Azusa Street, Florence Crawford left Los Angeles for Portland, Oregon. In early 1907,

---

111. Ibid., 11.
112. Sutton, *Aimee Semple McPherson*, 43.
113. Barfoot, *Aimee Semple McPherson*, 216–17.
114. McPherson, *The Holy Spirit*, 199–200.

Crawford held revival services in Portland, and the meetings led to the formation of the Apostolic Faith Mission. After traveling around the Pacific Northwest for the better part of 1907 looking for an appropriate location, Crawford decided to permanently settle in Portland. Originally conceived as an extension of Seymour's mission in Los Angeles, Crawford's mission soon severed a formal connection with Seymour. Yet, when she began to publish her own paper in 1908, Crawford used the same title, *The Apostolic Faith*, and the same mailing list that was used by Seymour at Azusa Street. Crawford, and the new organization she oversaw, followed a strict holiness standard of conduct. Strongly opposed to Durham's "finished-work" doctrine, the Apostolic Faith Mission maintained a belief in sanctification as a second, definite work of grace that was a necessary prerequisite to receiving the Baptism in the Holy Spirit. In addition to a relentless call for her followers to remain separate from the world, Crawford was strongly opposed to denominational organizations. In July 1913, an evangelist from Crawford's Apostolic Faith Mission named Fred Hornshuh began to hold revival services in Eugene, Oregon. Out of these initial meetings a mission was established in Eugene that grew rapidly. Soon, ministers in Eugene began to feel that their association with Crawford's organization in Portland hindered their ministry more than it helped. The separatist ideology of the Apostolic Faith organization, and the harsh enforcement of regulations on affiliated ministers in Portland, were their primary points of disagreement. In 1919, the Eugene-based group officially separated from affiliation with Crawford's mission and formed the Bible Standard Mission. Over the next fifteen years, the newly formed organization flourished on the West Coast.[115]

The early issues of Bible Standard's periodical featured a section entitled "Fundamental Teachings of the Bible Standard Missions." This statement covered many doctrines not covered in the original doctrinal statement of the Azusa Street Mission, but for the doctrines that were listed in the Azusa paper, Bible Standard retained much of the same language. The doctrine of Spirit Baptism was particularly close in wording.

Apostolic Faith (1906)

The Baptism with the Holy Ghost is a gift of power upon the sanctified life; so, when we get it we have the same evidence as

---

115. Mitchell, *Heritage & Horizons*, 21–52.

the Disciples received on the Day of Pentecost (Acts 2:3, 4), in speaking in new tongues.[116]

Bible Standard (1920)

The Baptism of the Holy Ghost is the gift of power upon the sanctified life. When we *receive* it we have the same *sign or Bible* evidence as the disciples *had* on the day of Pentecost speaking with [new] tongues *as the Spirit gives utterance.*[117]

In 1922, *Bible Standard* printed a new statement of "Fundamental Teachings" that was their own. Consistent with their desire to be more inclusive than the Apostolic Faith organization from which they separated, the new statement was more concise and less specific than their previous one. The doctrinal statement on "Baptism" read as follows: "We believe in the Baptism of the Holy Spirit, which is the gift of power upon a pure life. The baptism is received as on the day of Pentecost Acts 2:4."[118] Noticeably absent from the statement was any reference to "evidence" or "tongues." After 1923, doctrinal statements by the Bible Standard organization became even less specific with a simple "bullet point" list of core tenets and Scripture references with no accompanying explanations. Clearly, the young organization valued brevity and simplicity when it came to doctrinal statements. In his history of the Open Bible Standard Churches, Fred Hornshuh highlighted tolerance as one of the original values of Bible Standard:

Are We Right or Wrong?

Spiritual maturity is never attained in this world in its entirety. But we must grow in grace and knowledge. Possibly no two people interpret every Scripture identically alike. Yet we must be of one mind (II Cor. 13:11); also be tolerant and not dogmatic. Divine love will solve the problem. In honor preferring one another.[119]

---

116. *Apostolic Faith* [Los Angeles] 1.1 (September 1906) 2.

117. *Bible Standard* 1.5 (November 1920) 2. Words in italics were added or replaced prior wording. Words in brackets were removed.

118. *Bible Standard* 3.2 (n.d. [Jan 1922?]) 2.

119. Fred Hornshuh, *Historical Sketches*, 17.

In August 1928, Hornshuh's *Bible Standard* periodical merged with Orville Benham's *Overcomer*.[120] Benham was a traveling evangelist with a successful healing ministry and a talented composer and musician of gospel music. He had previously worked with F. F. Bosworth's revival campaigns before he set out on his own. He held successful revival meetings in Eugene in 1924 and 1925 that contributed to the rapid growth of Bible Standard in Eugene during that time and the need to construct the three thousand seat Lighthouse Temple.[121] In an article announcing the decision to merge the two periodicals under the name *The Overcomer* as "The Official Organ of the Bible Standard Interdenominational Evangelistic Association," Fred Hornshuh asked the rhetorical question, "What could be more all-inclusive?"[122] The new periodical refrained from any official statement of beliefs and as a collection of the "world's greatest Christian writers" gave the following mission statement: "We seek to encourage *Scriptural Unity* by co-operating with all the people of God, but fellowshipping the blood-washed *everywhere* and by *keeping aloof* from the spirit of sectarianism."[123]

Although they did not have a specific doctrinal statement in their periodical, *Overcomer* printed articles that promoted the integral connection between speaking in tongues and Spirit Baptism. One writer, a Bible Standard pastor in Lodi, California, opposed using the word "evidence" in reference to speaking in tongues. He preferred to call it "the ACCOMPANYING SIGN in every case" and argued that the only reliable evidence was "the SPIRIT FILLED LIFE."[124] If Bible Standard's refusal to print extended doctrinal statements raised questions about their stance on the doctrine of initial evidence, the periodical answered them with their clearest statement in support of the doctrine in 1933: "Our attention has been called forcibly to the fact there is being preached the notion that not all who are baptized in the Holy Spirit speak with other tongues. Bible Standard stands flatfootedly for the teaching that the Baptism in the Holy Spirit is according to the pattern in Acts 2:4."[125]

In 1929, John R. Richey, a graduate of L.I.F.E Bible College in Los Angeles in 1928, became the director of the Iowa-Minnesota division

---

120. Mitchell, *Heritage & Horizons*, 81.

121. Ibid., 61–69.

122. Fred Hornshuh, "A Great Step Forward," *Bible Standard* 9.8 (August 1928) 4.

123. *Overcomer* 9.10 (October 1928) 2.

124. Donald Fee, "The Supreme Purpose of the Baptism in the Holy Spirit," *Overcomer* 11.11 (November 1930) 4. Italics in original.

125. "Rightly Dividing the Word," *Overcomer* 14.7 (December 1933) 9.

The Emergence of a "Classical" Tradition in Pentecostalism

of the International Church of the Foursquare Gospel. The organization grew rapidly under his leadership, and Des Moines became a center for Foursquare in the Midwest.[126] In August 1932, thirty-two ministers, representing the Iowa-Minnesota division, voted to withdraw from the Foursquare Church. "'Certain widespread publicity' and policies" were given as the main reasons for the separation. Proposed changes to the Foursquare bylaws governing local church property ownership and Aimee Semple McPherson's recent marriage to David Hutton were likely the issues that most disturbed the Midwest group. A new organization was formed under the name, "Open Bible Evangelistic Association."[127]

The new organization arranged the publication of their own periodical, *Open Bible Messenger*. The first issue confirmed the organization's desire to continue to promote the teachings of the Foursquare organization that they left. An article written by Louise Richey, the woman who first suggested the "Open Bible" name, summarized the teachings of the new organization and included a graphic that had been used to describe the Foursquare message many times, along with the following statement:

> "The message of the open Bible?" What is it? . . . What is this message? It is the Lord Jesus Christ as the Saviour for the sin-sick soul; it is the Lord Jesus Christ as the Healer of the sick body; it is the Lord Jesus Christ as the Baptizer of the Holy Ghost upon the consecrated believer; it is the Lord Jesus Christ as the Coming King for His Church. That is God's message through His crucified Son to the whole wide world.[128]

On July 25, 1935, Bible Standard and the Open Bible Evangelistic Association joined together to form a new organization called the Open Bible Standard Evangelistic Association. At the time of their joining, they agreed that they would adopt the Articles of Faith, Constitution, and By-Laws of the Open Bible Evangelistic Association.[129] An article in the *Open Bible Messenger* called their respective doctrinal statements almost identical.[130]

---

126. Mitchell, *Heritage & Horizons*, 130–43.

127. Ibid., 145–47.

128. Louise Richey, "The Message of the Open Bible," *Open Bible Messenger* 1.1 (November 1932) 13; Mitchell, *Heritage & Horizons*, 147.

129. *Minutes of the Executive Committee, National Convention and Board of Directors, 1932–1945*, 17. Open Bible Standard Evangelistic Association became officially known as Open Bible Standard Church on July 6th, 1940. On the same page, a motion was given and passed to add a statement to the articles of faith concerning the organization's views on war. Ibid., 160.

130. "Bible Standard-Open Bible Unite," *Open Bible Messenger* 3.9 (August 1935) 1

Bible Standard, with their roots in Crawford's Apostolic Faith organization, that staunchly supported entire sanctification as a definite work for grace subsequent to salvation, originally held to a "finished-work" doctrine of sanctification.[131] Yet, over time this conviction appears to have waned. In 1926, the Bible Standard organization still claimed that after regeneration there was a "consecration and surrender that brings perfect love," but called such an experience "a matter of walking in the light" rather than a one-time event.[132] Fred Horshuh remembered the following,

> The Bible Standard group encountered many who measured up to the Scriptural teaching of holiness, yet could not designate the moment they were sanctified. Thus, Biblical terms such as holiness, heart, purity, and wholly sanctified were used. The great question is not where or when one received the experience, but that the life measures up to the Bible standard of holy living.[133]

The ease with which the new organization adopted a "finished-work" statement of faith suggests that sanctification was not a point of contention among the leadership in 1935. This decision marked the Foursquare stream of the new movement as the prevailing voice in matters of doctrine. In fact, the Articles of Faith of Open Bible Standard Churches followed the same outline as the Foursquare Statement of Faith. Though they are not identical, the wording of the sections on Baptism of the Holy Spirit, Spirit-Filled Life, Gifts and Fruits of the Spirit, and Moderation are strikingly similar. As with Foursquare, the Open Bible Articles of Faith refrained from any dogmatic statement on evidential tongues saying, "Every believer has the right to expect His incoming to be after the same manner as recorded by the Word of God in Bible Days."[134] This statement would remain unchanged in Open Bible until 1958.

Conclusion

Through the influence of E. N. Bell and others, William Durham's "finished-work" doctrine became established in the Assemblies of God

---

131. "Fundamental Teachings: Taught and Practiced in Bible Standard Missions," *Bible Standard* 3.2 (n.d. [Jan 1922?]) 2; "What Christians Need in this Twentieth Century: The Baptism of the Holy Ghost—An Experience Subsequent to Sanctification," *Bible Standard* 4.1 (n.d. [Jan. 1923?]) 1.

132. "The Gospel Pathway," *Bible Standard* 7.1 (n.d. [Feb 1926?]) 11.

133. Hornshuh, *Historical Sketches*, 11.

134. *Policies and Principles of the Open Bible Standard Churches* (1940), 45.

denomination. In addition, Durham's dogmatic stance on initial evidence was also a part of the denomination's first Statement of Fundamental Truths in 1916. Two years later the doctrine was marked out as the "distinctive testimony" of Pentecostals, without which the Pentecostal had no point of distinction from other groups in Christendom. The "finished-work" doctrine coupled with a dogmatic stance on initial evidence simplified and clarified areas of complexity and ambiguity in defining those who were sanctified and Spirit-baptized.

Despite these benefits, some Pentecostal ministers struggled with the doctrine. While Pentecostal ministers were unanimously convinced of the veracity of speaking in tongues and believed that such an experience was integral to an authentic experience of Spirit Baptism, they were not in agreement about how such an experience should be formalized in a doctrinal statement. In spite of disagreement, the Assemblies of God became convinced that ministers who compromised on the doctrine of initial evidence were rejecting the core component of the Pentecostal faith and they made it clear that those ministers would have no part in their fellowship.

Other Pentecostal "finished-work" denominations, such as Foursquare and Open Bible, chose to nuance the Assemblies of God's initial evidence doctrine in favor of doctrinal statements that were more flexible and open to interpretation. Although the leaders in these denominations clearly believed that tongues would normally accompany an experience of Spirit Baptism, they were not comfortable formalizing this belief in a statement or propagating such a statement as their distinctive tenet. With a desire to be "interdenominational" ministries, Open Bible and Foursquare maintained a belief in the four-fold gospel as that which defined their respective organizations.

Even though Pentecostal denominations did not articulate the relationship in the same way, the link between speaking in tongues and Spirit Baptism that Pentecostals advocated began to be established as the defining characteristic of Pentecostals during this time period. As the divide between Pentecostal and non-Pentecostal shifted from experience to doctrine, the line that was somewhat blurred up until the 1920s became more and more defined and focused. This allowed Pentecostals to have a more unified voice in communication to non-Pentecostals, but it also pigeonholed Pentecostal ministers in their expression of Pentecostal truths, causing the doctrine of initial evidence to be given *the* place of primacy in defining Pentecostals in North America.

4

Explications, Criticisms, and Derivatives of the Classical Pentecostal Tradition

(1940—Present)

Introduction

THE INTERIM BETWEEN WWI and WWII was a time in which Pentecostals saw their influence move from the fringes of the church to mainstream Christianity in the United States. It was also a time of rapid expansion and growth of Pentecostalism on the foreign mission field. The result of this growth in popularity and adherents was that a classical Pentecostal tradition became established as distinct voice in Christendom by the end of WWII. A natural result of the establishment of a classical Pentecostal tradition was the formation of groups that would work to uphold the sanctity of the tradition. The World Pentecostal Conference and Pentecost Fellowship of North America helped Pentecostals to move beyond doctrinal disagreements with each other to promote a common bond of fellowship centered on a distinctive Pentecostal experience. If the movement of Pentecostals toward engagement with each other as a tradition was natural, their move to engage outsiders to Pentecostalism was painful, but necessary if a Pentecostal revival was ever going to reach the whole church. Through their involvement with the World Council of Churches, encouraged by Donald Gee and led by David Du Plessis, Pentecostals were challenged to consider the Spirit's presence at work among non-Pentecostals. In addition, they were convinced that the spread of their unique testimony, a testimony encapsulated in the doctrine of initial evidence, was what was necessary for a world-wide revival in the church. At the same time that Pentecostals were concerned with promoting their unique message among other churches, their association with the National Association of Evangelicals helped to show that there were far more commonalities than differences between Evangelicals and Pentecostals.

The Charismatic movement in the historic churches, which began around 1960, brought unique organizational and doctrinal challenges to the classical Pentecostal tradition. Those with Charismatic experiences in mainline churches were initially greeted with disdain from their denominational leaders causing them to look to Pentecostals for theological and ecclesial guidance in such matters. As the Charismatic movement became more widespread among both traditional Protestants as well as Catholics, most of the historic churches came to accept and embrace Charismatic experiences, though some rejected the Pentecostals' doctrines and explanations. The relationship of Spirit Baptism to prayer, Christian initiation, and spectacular gifts was understood differently by Charismatics and Pentecostals, and each group sought to defend their distinct perspective against the other. In their debates, Pentecostals and Roman Catholics recognized that many of their disagreements were the result of misunderstanding their respective theological traditions. As a result, a Roman Catholic-Pentecostal dialogue was officially established to facilitate the exchange of resources and mutual understanding between the two groups. The debates between Pentecostals and mainline Protestants and Charismatics encouraged Pentecostals to improve their capacity to engage in academic theology at the highest level. Through the meetings of the Society for Pentecostal Studies and journals like *Pneuma*, *EPTA Bulletin* and the *Journal of Pentecostal Theology*, Pentecostal scholars interpreted, defended, promoted, challenged and qualified the distinctive tenets of classical Pentecostalism. More recently, Pentecostal scholars like Frank Macchia, Simon Chan, and Amos Yong worked to counter the notion that Pentecostalism is simply Evangelicalism *plus tongues*. By deconstructing the theological components of Pentecostal experience, they were able to demonstrate that classical Pentecostalism is a tradition with a unique theological orientation that should complement and inform other Christian traditions.

Upholding the Tradition: Associations and Ecumenism

Pentecostal Associations

In the years following WWII, many Pentecostal groups in the United States and Europe desired to meet together for the purpose of mutual encouragement, dialogue, sharing resources, and coordinating missionary efforts. The gathering of these groups helped to represent a unified voice among Pentecostals to the rest of Western Christendom. Two of these gatherings were the triennial meetings of the World Pentecostal Conference (WPC) inaugurated at Zurich, Switzerland in 1947[1] and the annual meetings of the Pentecostal Fellowship of North America (PFNA) formed at Des Moines, Iowa in 1948.[2] In the first meeting of the WPC, Donald Gee, a leader in British Pentecostalism,[3] was assigned the task of editing a quarterly periodical on behalf of the organization called *Pentecost*. Nearly all of the seventy-seven issues of *Pentecost* that Gee edited between 1948 and 1966 included an editorial on the back page of the cover where he freely addressed what he felt were the most pressing issues for Pentecostals.[4] Already well respected in Pentecostal circles in Europe and North America, Gee's writings in *Pentecost* and later books gained an appreciative hearing by those outside the Pentecostal movement. Shortly after his death in 1966, Kilian McDonnell would refer to him as "undoubtedly the most articulate leader Pentecostalism has produced so far."[5]

As editor of *Pentecost*, one of the first issues that Gee was compelled to address was that of Pentecostal identity. Gee believed that reducing Pentecostalism to its core components was important, not only for building constructive relationships among Pentecostals, but also for fostering healthy dialogue with those outside Pentecostalism, particularly in the growing ecumenical movement.[6] When deciding what was essential and what was peripheral, Gee consistently upheld the classical doctrine of initial evidence to

1. Robeck, "Pentecostal World Conference," 971–74.

2. Warner, "Pentecostal Fellowship of North America," 968–69.

3. For Gee's influence on the Pentecostal movement in Britain, see Bundy, "Donald Gee," 662–63; Bundy, "Donald Gee: The Pentecostal Leader," 9–11; Kay, "Donald Gee," 133–53.

4. Kay, "Donald Gee," 145.

5. McDonnell, "Holy Spirit and Pentecostalism," 201.

6. Donald Gee, "Zurich: Review of Reviews," *Pentecost* 1 (September 1947) 1–2; Donald Gee, "Amsterdam and Pentecost," *Pentecost* 6 (December 1948) back cover; Donald Gee, "Possible Pentecostal Unity," *Pentecost* 13 (September 1950) back cover; Donald Gee, "Pentecost Re-Valued," *Pentecost* 28 (June 1954) back cover.

be an essential element of Pentecostal identity. Through his earlier writings in *Redemption Tidings* and elsewhere, Gee had been an ardent supporter of the initial evidence position of the Assemblies of God in Britain and upheld the doctrine as the distinctive testimony of Pentecostals. In *Pentecost*, Gee maintained that position and argued that compromise of the initial evidence doctrine would hinder revival and take away the distinctive contribution of Pentecostals for the worldwide church.[7]

The 1955 WPC conference in Stockholm, Sweden, had the theme "A Reevaluation of the Pentecostal Movement." In his address to the conference, Gee said that there was one aspect of Pentecostalism that certainly did not need to be reevaluated: "The value speaking with tongues as the initial evidence." He argued that it was this unique teaching that made Pentecostalism "a definitely separate entity" within Christendom. He further elaborated that the doctrine was the one point upon which the Pentecostal movement spoke unanimously, and which testified to the common experience of Pentecostals.[8] Yet, in contrast to Kerr's writing a decade earlier, Gee believed that loyalty to the distinctive Pentecostal testimony did not necessitate discountenance toward the larger church.[9] Instead of condemning non-Pentecostals, he strove to validate the work of Christ in non-Pentecostal denominations while advocating for the value of the unique voice that Pentecostalism contributed to the choir of voices in Christendom.

Pentecostal Ecumenism

In 1948, a year after the first WPC meeting in Zurich, the World Council of Churches (WCC) was formed in Amsterdam. A gathering of some 147 churches from forty-four countries,[10] the WCC was organized for the pur-

---

7. Donald Gee, "Do 'Tongues' Matter?" *Pentecost* 45 (September 1958) back cover; Donald Gee, "I Believe in the Holy Ghost," *Pentecost* 44 (June 1958) back cover; Donald Gee, "'Tongues' and Truth," *Pentecost* 25 (September 1953) back cover; Donald Gee, "The Initial Evidence," *Pentecost* 17 (September 1951) back cover.

8. Donald Gee, "Speaking with Tongues and Prophesying," *Pentecostal Evangel* 2193 (May 20, 1956) 6.

9. Donald Gee, *Redemption Tidings* 10.13 (July 1934) 10. In 1922, Kerr wrote, "That is why we can't work together with those who oppose or reject this Pentecostal truth. They might invite us to come and labor with them, but you know it would not work. Some have tried and failed. You cannot mix Pentecost with denominationalism." D. W. Kerr, "The Basis for Our Distinctive Testimony," *Pentecostal Evangel* 460–61 (September 2, 1922) 4.

10. Hooft, *The Genesis and Formation*, 63.

pose of meeting every seven years to promote Christian unity by crossing denominational lines and building bridges between the churches.[11] While many Pentecostals looked down on such a gathering as a prelude to apostasy, Gee was forthright in his support of ecumenical organizations and optimistic that the WCC might help to lead churches closer to "the truth as it is in Jesus."[12] Though he never attended a WCC assembly himself, Gee encouraged others to do so. He commented judiciously on the first WCC meeting in *Pentecost*. Following the Second Assembly at Evanston in 1952, Gee was more openly supportive of the WCC and critical of those who condemned such an organization. He also published guest editorials that cast the WCC in a favorable light written by his friend and fellow Assemblies of God minister, David Du Plessis.[13] In 1960, Gee and Du Plessis attended the WCC's Commission on Faith and Order in St. Andrews, Scotland, in preparation of the Third Assembly to be held in New Delhi the following year, for which they both received an invitation. Gee's positive editorial remarks in *Pentecost* on the experience were not welcomed by Thomas Zimmerman, president of the National Association of Evangelicals and General Superintendent of the Assemblies of God in North America. Under pressure from Zimmerman and others, Gee reluctantly declined the WCC's invitation to the Third Assembly.[14] Du Plessis, on the other hand, attended the WCC assembly at New Delhi, and by September the following year he was stripped of his status as an ordained minister of the Assemblies of God for "problems surrounding his continued involvement with the National and World Councils of Churches."[15]

While taking a posture of openness toward the WCC that was opposed by "Pentecostal Fundamentalist die-hards," Gee made it clear that neither he nor Du Plessis had any "intention or desire to compromise [the

---

11. Robeck and Sandidge, "World Council of Churches," 1213-17.

12. Donald Gee, "Contact is Not Compromise," *Pentecost* 53 (September-November 1960) back cover.

13. David Du Plessis, "The World Council of Churches," *Pentecost* 30 (December 1954) 10-11; David Du Plessis, "Are We Going Back to the Churches?" *Pentecost* 34 (December 1955) back cover.

14. In his address to the WPC in Jerusalem in 1961, Zimmerman called the intention of some Pentecostal churches in Chile and Yugoslavia to join the WCC a decision that compromised basic Pentecostal beliefs. In no ambiguous terms, he added, "No individual has been authorized by the General Council of the Assemblies of God to speak in favor of, or to support, the Ecumenical Movement." Thomas Zimmerman, "Twentieth-Century Pentecost," *Pentecostal Evangel* 2465 (August 6, 1961) 3.

15. Robeck, "Assemblies of God and Ecumenical Cooperation," 146.

Pentecostals'] distinctive testimony."[16] Though Du Plessis was determined to be actively involved in the ecumenical movement and encouraged others to do so against the wishes of Assemblies of God leadership, he was equally determined to see that Pentecostals did not compromise their belief that speaking in tongues accompanied a genuine experience of Spirit Baptism.[17] Du Plessis tended to use slightly different language than Gee, speaking of tongues as "the immediate consequence" or "confirmation" rather than the "initial evidence" of Baptism in the Holy Spirit.[18] He believed that it was possible for everyone who confessed Jesus as Lord to be baptized in the Spirit saying,

> All Churches—Roman Catholic, Protestant and Pentecostal—acknowledge that JESUS CHRIST is head of the church. So, in every church the people that worship there can BECOME CHILDREN OF GOD by drinking the living water that Jesus gives, and be BAPTIZED in the Spirit by Jesus.[19]

His ecumenical outlook also led him to focus on the importance of spreading Pentecostal experience rather than Pentecostal doctrine. When comparing the modern Pentecostal revival to other revivals in the history of Christianity, Du Plessis argued,

> The Pentecostal revival of this century is different. . . . There has been no new emphasis on any special doctrine. Rather, the emphasis is upon an experience. . . . The Pentecostal revival today is merely a restoration of a personal experience of a life-changing salvation followed by the receiving of the Baptism into the Holy Spirit with the evidence or confirmation of the initial manifestation of speaking in unknown tongues, which in turn is usually followed by experiences of power to cast out devils, heal the sick and miracles.[20]

---

16. Private correspondence to David Du Plessis from Donald Gee dated 17 December 1955. The letter is held in the David Du Plessis Archive at Fuller Theological Seminary. Parts of the letter are quoted in Hollenweger, "Two Extraordinary Ecumenists," 395.

17. Robeck, "Assemblies of God and Ecumenical Cooperation," 143–46.

18. David Du Plessis, "Jesus is the Baptizer," *Message of the Open Bible* 54 (February 1971) 5; Du Plessis, " 'Born Of' and 'Baptized In' the Holy Spirit," 10; Spittler, "David du Plessis," 592.

19. Du Plessis, " 'Born Of' and 'Baptized In' the Holy Spirit," 10.

20. Du Plessis, "Golden Jubilees," 194.

Yet, in private, Du Plessis was critical of Leonhard Steiner, a Swiss Pentecostal who upheld the validity of Pentecostal experience but spoke out against the classical Pentecostal doctrine of Spirit Baptism.[21] Thus, even though his ecumenical energies were primarily focused on increasing openness to the Pentecostal experience rather than assent to Pentecostal doctrine, Du Plessis felt it was important for Pentecostals not to compromise their distinctive doctrines.

Doctrinal Conformity

Despite a desire by many who attended the first meeting of the WPC in 1947 to form a fellowship of Pentecostal groups from around the world, the conference was never able to form a basis for fellowship upon which all attendees could agree.[22] Swedish Pentecostals, in particular, made an agreement on polity impossible to achieve because of their strong opposition to organization beyond the local church.[23] In contrast, the PFNA established a basis for organization with relative ease. In 1948, representatives from the Assemblies of God, the International Church of the Foursquare Gospel, Open Bible Standard Churches, and Church of God, Cleveland were appointed to draft a statement of faith. They responded by simply adopting the statement of faith of the National Association of Evangelicals (NAE) with an added paragraph concerning Pentecostal doctrine.[24] It read, "We believe that the full gospel includes holiness of heart and life, healing for the body and the Baptism in the Holy Spirit

---

21. Leonard Steiner of Basel was the chairman of the first Pentecostal World Conference at Zurich. In a private correspondence to Donald Gee dated 8 March 1961, Du Plessis said that he was "deeply disturbed" by Steiner's view on the Baptism in the Holy Spirit, and he felt "that brethren who hold those views can no longer be considered TRULY PENTECOSTAL." The letter is held in the David Du Plessis Archive at Fuller Theological Seminary. For more on Steiner's view on Spirit Baptism, see Hollenweger, *The Pentecostals*, 335.

22. Robeck, "Pentecostal World Conference," 972.

23. Kay, "Donald Gee," 145.

24. The NAE was formed in 1942. With seven Pentecostal groups involved in the formation of the NAE in order to promote unity among Evangelicals, the new organization sparked interest among member Pentecostals to form a similar association for themselves. Following the 1948 meeting of the NAE in Chicago, twenty-four Pentecostal leaders met to formally discuss the formation of such a group. Less than six months later, the first meeting of the PFNA took place in Des Moines, Iowa. Warner, "Pentecostal Fellowship of North America," 968; Robeck, "National Association of Evangelicals," 922–25.

with the initial evidence of speaking in other tongues as the Spirit gives utterance."[25] Nobody involved in the formation of the PFNA doctrinal statement could have foreseen the far-reaching impact of the document. The statement defined Pentecostalism in North America as a whole and identified the doctrine of initial evidence as that which singularly defined themselves over against other Evangelical bodies.

By their statement, the doctrine of initial evidence that was singled out as the "distinctive testimony" of those affiliated with the Assemblies of God came to be established as the "distinctive testimony" of Pentecostals as a whole in North America. It also represented the establishment of that which would later be known as the defining doctrine of *classical* Pentecostalism. Thirty-two years later the PFNA doctrinal statement still stood out as "the only agreed upon statement of faith in the entire Pentecostal world" when the Society for Pentecostal Studies adopted it as their own.[26] When the Full Gospel Business Men's Fellowship International (FGBMFI) formed in 1953, the para-church organization also based their official statement of beliefs on the PFNA doctrinal statement.[27] Though the fellowship held doctrines consistent with classical Pentecostal denominations, they were more closely associated with independent healing evangelists of the day such as Oral Roberts, Tommy Hicks, and William Branham. In fact, the FGBMFI chapters and periodical became the platform for healing evangelists to communicate with a unified voice. As the Charismatic movement made its way through mainline churches, the FGBMFI would become a place of refuge for those who had Pentecostal experiences but were leery of joining Pentecostal congregations.[28]

For Pentecostals in the United States and Britain, the roughly fifteen years between the end of WWII and the beginning of the Charismatic movement was a period in which Pentecostals upheld the uniqueness of their tradition while they searched for common bonds of fellowship with Christian bodies inside and outside the Pentecostal tradition. The "distinctive testimony" of Pentecostals that the Assemblies of God established in 1920—speaking in tongues as the initial evidence of the Baptism in the Holy Spirit—came to be understood as the common doctrinal point around which Pentecostals could organize themselves as a separate

    25. *Minutes of the Constitutional Convention of the Pentecostal Fellowship of North America*, Des Moines, Iowa, October 26–28, 1948, 2.
    26. Synan, "Fifteen Years," 3.
    27. Synan, *Under His Banner*, 53; "Doctrinal Statement," *Full Gospel Men's Voice* 1.1 (February 1953) back cover.
    28. Synan, *Under His Banner*, 87–89.

tradition within Christendom. The doctrine also gave veracity to their position that the Pentecostal experience of Spirit Baptism was unique in relation to experiences of the same name in other Christian traditions. During this time, Pentecostal experience went hand-in-hand with Pentecostal doctrine. Each validated the other, so that Pentecostals were understood as the gatekeepers to the experience.

Although both Open Bible Standard Churches and the International Church of the Foursquare Gospel became charter members of the PFNA, neither denomination had a doctrine of initial evidence in their own statement of belief. As a result, the threat of being perceived as compromising the Pentecostal message was clearly a concern for both denominations during this time. In 1949, a year after joining the PFNA, Foursquare published a series of Sunday school lessons based on the Foursquare Declaration of Faith prepared by Nathaniel Van Cleve. In lesson nine on "The Baptism with the Holy Spirit," the author of the lesson was clearly concerned that a decline in interest on the topic of Spirit Baptism would lead to an identity crisis for the denomination. "If we ever disappoint the hopes of our founder and become reticent on this great truth of the Baptism in the Holy Spirit, our separate denominational existence will no longer be justified."[29] In 1960, Guy P. Duffield wrote the last article in a series of publications on "The Pentecostal Baptism with the Holy Spirit." Duffield gave no room for questioning the denomination's stance on the doctrine saying, "We believe that speaking with other tongues is the *initial* evidence of the Baptism with the Holy Spirit. There may be many other evidences to be sure, but this is the one great initial evidence."[30] In 1975, Foursquare formalized earlier statements advocating the organization's support of the doctrine of initial evidence at their 52nd Annual Convention. They made the following official statement on the Evidence of the Baptism in the Holy Spirit: "On the basis of Scriptural precedent, and guided by our original Foursquare teaching, we affirm that the initial physical evidence of the Baptism in the Holy Spirit is that of speaking in other tongues."[31]

At the 1956 meeting of the Board of Directors of Open Bible Standard Churches, it was recommended by the publication committee as a prerequisite to the preparation of training materials in Open Bible doctrine and beliefs that "the Board clarify certain points of doctrine in the

---

29. Van Cleave, *Foursquare Sunday School*, 72.

30. Duffield, "The Pentecostal Baptism," 14.

31. "Organizational Statements," *Foursquare World Advance* 11.7 (April 1975) 3. This statement, although seemingly official, did not constitute an official change to the Foursquare Declaration of Faith.

Open Bible Articles of Faith where there is divergence of opinion, namely, rapture, tongues, and eternal security." As a result, the following sentence was added to the Articles of Faith on the Baptism of the Holy Spirit: "The initial evidence of this experience is the speaking in other tongues as the Spirit gives utterance."[32] This change in doctrine almost certainly paved the way for the possibility of a merger between the Assemblies of God and Open Bible Standard Churches three years later. In late 1958, a meeting in Toronto, Canada with officials from Foursquare and Open Bible was arranged by officials in the Assemblies of God. This meeting led to a discussion between Open Bible and the Assemblies of God about a possible amalgamation between the two organizations, and eventuated in the Assemblies of God extending of a formal invitation to Open Bible to join their organization. A special meeting of the Board of Directors of Open Bible was called on February 4, 1959, in Des Moines. After "several hours of discussion" the invitation was formally rejected.[33] For the next forty-seven years, Open Bible's statement on Spirit Baptism remained unchanged.

Challenging the Tradition: The Charismatic Movement

The New Pentecostals

The term "classical Pentecostalism" did not become popular in Pentecostal scholarship until the mid-1970s. According to Cecil Robeck, Kilian McDonnell, the Benedictine scholar of the Catholic Charismatic movement, coined the term.[34] McDonnell first published the term in 1968 alongside the term "neo-Pentecostal" to distinguish between Pentecostals with roots in the formal or "classical" Pentecostal denominations that were formed in the first three decades of the twentieth century, and Pentecostals that emerged in the historic churches (Episcopal, Presbyterian, Lutheran and Catholic) from around 1955.[35] Russell Spittler has accurately observed,

---

32. "Minutes of the 24th Annual Meeting of the General Board of Directors of Open Bible Standard Churches, Inc.," in *Minutes of the Executive Committee, National Convention and Board of Directors, 1956–1957*, 1943, 1967; R. Bryant Mitchell, "General Conference Business," *Message of the Open Bible* (July-August 1956) 17.

33. "Special Called Meeting of the General Board of Directors in Des Moines, IA, February 4–6 1959," in *Minutes of the Executive Committee, National Convention and Board of Directors, 1958–1960*, 2226.

34. Robeck, "Kilian McDonnell," 853.

35. McDonnell, "Holy Spirit and Pentecostalism," 198–204.

"Somewhere in the early 70s it became clear that the classical Pentecostal churches and the charismatic movement are two different forces."[36] McDonnell's term became popular among scholars of Pentecostalism as more and more people from the historical churches had what they deemed to be Pentecostal experiences while exhibiting marked differences from old-line Pentecostals structurally, sociologically and theologically.[37] Though they are clearly different, there is not a single characteristic that can be universally applied to Charismatics (or neo-Pentecostals) over against classical Pentecostals.[38] Often the difference between the two is a matter of degrees rather than absolutes.

In 1983, Richard Quebedeaux said that neo-Pentecostalism was at its inception and still remains a "transdenominational" movement.[39] Looking back on the last twenty-five years, it might be more appropriate to say that Charismatics are multi-denominational in origin rather than trans-denominational in trajectory. Classical Pentecostalism originated in a church environment where, for the most part, those who experienced Spirit Baptism accompanied by speaking in tongues were quickly ostracized from their congregations in the historic denominations. Though some Charismatics still faced adverse reactions from church leaders and their fellow members, many found their experience well accepted by their congregations within the historic denominations so that they could integrate Pentecostal beliefs, values, and practices into their respective traditions.[40] Thus, what distinguishes the Charismatic movement from

36. Spittler, preface to *Perspectives on the New Pentecostalism*, 8.

37. By 1972, the term "classical Pentecostal" was being used by many contributors to the Second Annual Meeting of the Society of Pentecostal Studies. These papers have been edited and preserved in Spittler, *Perspectives on the New Pentecostalism*. In 1976, Richard Quebedeaux used the term "classical Pentecostalism" as a formal classification of Pentecostals that did not belong to the neo-Pentecostal movement. Quebedeaux, *The New Charismatics*.

38. The terms "neo-Pentecostal" and "Charismatic" are here used interchangeably as is often the case. Lederle, *Treasures New and Old*, 41; Quebedeaux, *The New Charsmatics II*, 3; Jones, *The Charismatic Movement: A Guide to the Study of Neo-Pentecostalism*. More recently, the terms "neo-Charismatic" and "neo-Pentecostal" have been used to broadly describe those "independent, postdenominational, non-denominational, or indigenous groups or organizations" that embrace Pentecostal experience but have no connection to classical Pentecostal denominations or mainline churches. Introduction to *The New International Dictionary of Pentecostal and Charismatic Movements*, xx.

39. Quebedeaux, *The New Charismatics II*, 4.

40. Spittler argues that the increased openness to Charismatic experience in the historic churches was due to approximately fifty years of "ecumenical friendliness and

classical Pentecostalism is not its philosophical opposition to denominationalism—the first generation of Pentecostals was equally wary of forming denominational creeds and structures—but the relative openness of the existing ecclesiastical structures to receive and validate charismatic experiences. Thus, Henry Lederle rightly argues that the only unambiguous distinction between the two forces of classical Pentecostalism and the Charismatic movement is in their historical roots.[41]

Though they are most clearly defined by their roots in the historic denominations, the Charismatic movement can also be identified by the distinct theological positions that came to be associated with the group over time. As Catholics, Eastern Orthodox, Presbyterians, Episcopalians, Lutherans and others in the historic denominations increasingly had experiences of Spirit Baptism consistent with those attested to by classical Pentecostals, leaders in the historic denominations attempted to integrate the experience into their respective theological frameworks. Some allowed the Pentecostals to interpret it for them; others recognized some positive aspects of Pentecostal theology on the subject, but offered their own critique as well. The fact that Charismatics were people who affirmed and in many cases participated in the Pentecostal experience of Spirit Baptism caused Pentecostals to take their criticisms seriously. Broadly speaking, the criticisms levied against classical Pentecostal theology by Charismatics set the agenda for Pentecostal theology in the 60s and 70s. The new ways in which old Pentecostal experiences were evaluated, defined, explained, and prescribed for the church by theologians in the historic churches forced Pentecostal scholars to develop a more robust Pentecostal theology. At the same time the Charismatic movement was emerging on the scene, classical Pentecostals were questioning the validity of their distinctive doctrine, much to the alarm of denominational officials.[42]

---

globe-shrinking forces" that made "intolerance a fashionable vice." Spittler, "Are Pentecostals and Charismatics Fundamentalists?" 105. In contrast, Quebedeaux says that it was the "upper-middle-class origins in the white community" that allowed for a much quicker acceptance of neo-Pentecostalism in the historic churches. Quebedeaux, *The New Charismatics II*, 4.

41. Lederle, *Treasures New and Old*, 43.
42. Menzies, "The Challenges of Organization," 115–18.

Doctrinal Challenges

Prayer Language

Walter Hollenweger has observed that most of the Protestants involved in the early part of the Charismatic movement uncritically adopted a Pentecostal theological orientation. He argues that it was not until the movement reached the Roman Catholic Church that classical Pentecostal tenets were forcefully challenged.[43] Broadly speaking, Hollenweger's assessment is correct. However, even early on in the Charismatic movement, one can detect a distinctly different emphasis, and in some cases a different theology, than that held by classical Pentecostals. The Charismatic emphasis on personal prayer language is one example. Dennis Bennett, who many consider a founding father of the Charismatic movement, was an Anglican rector in Van Nuys, California, who was baptized in the Spirit in 1959. Forced to resign his post, Bennett became vicar of a small Episcopal church in Seattle, Washington.[44] Over the next decade, his church was at the center of the Charismatic movement as it made its way into all the major Protestant denominations. Bennett clearly replaced most of his Anglican pneumatology with classical Pentecostal doctrine. He was adamant that the Book of Acts represented the New Testament pattern for being baptized in the Holy Spirit, which should be duplicated in the lives of Christians today. He was also unwavering in his belief that speaking in tongues always "comes with the package" when one is baptized in the Holy Spirit.[45]

However, there are some slight differences in Bennett's understanding of tongues than what was expounded by many classical Pentecostals. Bennett argued that speaking in tongues, even evidential tongues, did not occur involuntarily, but required a decision on the part of the recipient to speak out in faith. He encouraged seekers to speak out in faith regardless of how they felt. Even though their initial vocalization might not be legitimate tongues, Bennett believed that real tongues would soon follow such an act of faith.[46] Bennett also believed that the tongues that accompanied Spirit Baptism were synonymous with one's private prayer language, and he believed that all Spirit-baptized Christians maintained this ability to

---

43. Hollenweger, *The Pentecostals*, 15–17; Hollenweger, "After Twenty Years' Research on Pentecostalism," 7–9.
44. Christenson, "Dennis Joseph and Rita Bennett," 369–70.
45. Bennett and Bennett, *The Holy Spirit and You*, 64–65.
46. Ibid., 70–71.

speak in tongues privately to God. Bennett understood the gift of tongues to be tongues inspired for the purpose of declaration in the public assembly, and he held that this public gift was only given to some Spirit-baptized Christians.[47]

Classical Pentecostals were not unified on these issues. In 1952, the Assemblies of God reprinted an article written by W. T. Gaston in 1923 arguing that evidential tongues were a matter of the human vessel being entirely controlled by God and not by the mind. Gaston further understood the gift of tongues as a gift that resides with *some* after their initial experience of Spirit Baptism that might be used privately for the edification of one's self or publicly for the edification of a group.[48] In short, Gaston believed that a private prayer language was not given to all that received the Baptism in the Holy Spirit. Gaston's arguments were reiterated in *Pentecostal Evangel* by W. S. Smith in 1964 and Ernest Williams, the former General Superintendent of the Assemblies of God, in 1965.[49]

While these views represented a common Pentecostal position, others agreed with Bennett. In November 1964, an article written by Open Bible minister Frank W. Smith was reprinted in the *Pentecostal Evangel* that advocated the value of tongues as an individual prayer language and means of spiritual worship for *all* Spirit-baptized Christians.[50] This article was made into a tract and distributed by Gospel Publishing House. That same year, an article was printed by Evangelist Arthur Berg that also argued that *all* Spirit-baptized believers could speak in tongues privately for the purpose of self-edification, and that the gift of tongues was only given to some for the purpose of public-edification.[51] More explicitly, the article answered the specific question, "How do you explain the question Paul asked, 'Do all speak with tongues?' (1 Corinthians 12:30)." The answer was given,

47. Ibid., 71, 84–86.

48. W. T. Gaston, "The 'Sign' and the 'Gift' of Tongues," *Pentecostal Evangel* 1986 (June 1, 1952) 5, reprinted with slight changes from W. T. Gaston, "The Sign and the Gift of Tongues," *Pentecostal Evangel* 513 (September 8, 1923) 7–8.

49. W. S. Smith, "Speaking with Tongues: The Gift and the Sign," *Pentecostal Evangel* 2622 (August 9, 1964) 7. Ernest S. Williams, "Speaking with Other Tongues: The Sign and the Gift," *Pentecostal Evangel* 2690 (November 28, 1965) 2–3.

50. Frank W. Smith, "What Value Tongues? Some Answers to a Question Being Asked by Many," *Pentecostal Evangel* 2636 (November 15, 1964) 5–7, reprinted from Frank W. Smith, "A Question of Value: What Value Tongues?" *Message of the Open Bible* 45 (June 1963) 4–5.

51. Arthur Berg, "The Twofold Purpose of Speaking with Tongues," *Pentecostal Evangel* 2614 (June 14, 1964) 20–21.

> From the context, it is evident Paul was speaking of the gift of tongues, not the sign of tongues. We may expect all to speak with tongues as a sign that they have been filled with the Spirit, but we should not expect all to exercise the gift of tongues in the church.... One must read the entire chapter (1 Corinthians 12) to understand that the *gift* of tongues, and the *gift* of the interpretation of tongues, are among the gifts that operate in the assembly of believers. Paul was not writing about the personal use of tongues here, either as a sign of the Baptism or as an exercise in private devotions.[52]

What seems to be the case is that during the 1960s a shift began to occur among some classical Pentecostals from a view that understood a personal prayer language as a gift given only to some Spirit-baptized saints to an understanding that a prayer language was given to all when they were baptized in the Holy Sprit. As late as 1977, Kilian McDonnell still characterized the Pentecostals' belief as follows:

> Tongues is either considered as the initial sign of the baptism or is considered as a gift of the Spirit which may be exercised subsequent to baptism, and possibly frequently. It is possible that a person will speak in tongues when he or she received the baptism but never again in his or her life.[53]

Yet, it appears that this view was becoming less popular during this time. The view that a prayer language was available to all Spirit-baptized Christians would finally become the official position of the Assemblies of God in 1981.[54] Despite this change in doctrine, Assemblies of God leaders were still struggling with the fact that many of the members spoke in

---

52. "Speaking with Other Tongues," *Pentecostal Evangel* 2807 (April 26, 1964) 10.

53. McDonnell, "The Function of Tongues," 27.

54. For Assemblies of God articles assuming the view that every Spirit-baptized Christian has the privilege of praying in tongues privately, see Leland Keys, "What is the Value of Tongues After You Are Baptized in the Holy Spirit?" *Pentecostal Evangel* 3129 (April 28, 1974) 4–5; Robert Cunningham, "Why Speak With Other Tongues?" *Pentecostal Evangel* 3271 (January 16, 1977) 14–15; Forrest Smith, "I Wish That You All Spoke in Tongues," *Pentecostal Evangel* 3328 (February 19, 1978) 5. The official statement on the initial evidence approved by the General Council in 1981 read, "All believers at the time of the Baptism in the Spirit begin speaking with tongues and may continue on in personal prayer or personal edification. All, however, are not the instruments through which the Holy Spirit manifests himself through tongues and interpretation in the congregation." The General Council of the Assemblies of God, *The Initial Physical Evidence*, 11–12.

tongues only once in their life.⁵⁵ The official Assemblies of God Position was updated in 2000 to read,

> Though not all Spirit-filled believers are given the gift of tongues which through interpretation edifies the church congregation (1 Corinthians 12:30), they all have the privilege of praying in the Spirit, especially at times when the human intellect does not know how to pray. Likewise, every Spirit-filled believer can and should expect to be used in supernatural ways in some, though not all, of the gifts of the Spirit.⁵⁶

This change in doctrine is important because it shifted the focus from tongues as evidence of Spirit Baptism to Spirit Baptism as the inauguration of a means to intimacy and closeness to God through a private prayer language, a focus emphasized by the Charismatic movement.⁵⁷ It seems likely that the Charismatic emphasis on a personal prayer language as a consequence of Spirit Baptism that emerged during this period moved classical Pentecostals to reconsider their views on the subject. By 1968, the Pentecostal emphasis on prayer language was strong enough that Kilian McDonnell, in one of his early articles on the Pentecostal movement, focused on personal prayer language as the primary benefit of glossolalia for the Pentecostal. He understood that it was "only by glossolalia as a prayer gift" that speaking in tongues functioned to "glorify Christ and to build up the community." He identified a deep prayer life, a great love of prayer, joy in praying, a strong desire to praise and glorify God in prayer, and prayer as a means for personal transformation as common characteristics of those who come into the Pentecostal experience.⁵⁸ In fact, McDonnell argued that the Pentecostal's dynamic prayer life was so attractive to

---

55. Hunter, "Aspects of Initial Evidence Dogma," 200.

56. *The Baptism in the Holy Spirit: The Initial Experience and Continuing Evidences of the Spirit-Filled Life*, 6.

57. In 1963, Bishop Pike of the Episcopal Church, USA appointed a "Study Commission on Glossolalia" to report on the status of glossolalia in the Church. The report specifically recognized that "sign-tongues" were to be used as a means of private prayer over against the gift of tongues that was given solely for use in public to convey a message from God. When the Commission offered recommendations for use of glossolalia in the Church, they were fully supportive of the use of sign-tongues and a private prayer language, but hesitant to give a green light to the use of the gift of tongues in public gatherings. McDonnell, *Presence, Power, and Praise*, 1:76–77. Other mainline churches responded similarly, such as the Lutheran Church in America. McDonnell, *Presence, Power, and Praise*, 1:555.

58. McDonnell, "Holy Spirit and Pentecostalism," 199.

neo-Pentecostals "that one might be led to think of Pentecostalism simply as a prayer movement."[59]

Ordo Salutis

The classic Pentecostal stance on the position of Spirit Baptism in the order of salvation as a "second blessing" subsequent to conversion-initiation has been one that has defined the tradition alongside its stance on speaking in tongues as initial evidence.[60] In defense of this view, the Baptism experiences recorded in the Book of Acts are of primary importance. The experience of the apostles on the Day of Pentecost predicted by Jesus in 1:5 and 1:8 and fulfilled in 2:4 are considered to be normative for all Christians who are filled with the Holy Spirit. Based on the delay between the death of Christ and the outpouring of the Spirit on the Day of Pentecost, classical Pentecostal hermeneutics understand that the apostles experienced Baptism in the Spirit fifty days after their conversion-initiation. Viewing this as the normative example for all other experiences of Spirit Baptism, "conversion and the regenerating action of the Holy Spirit" are said to be prerequisites for receiving the Baptism in the Holy Spirit.[61] According to the classical Pentecostal view, the length of time between conversion and Spirit Baptism may vary depending on the circumstances. In the case of the Samaritans in Acts 8, it was an indefinite period of time; in the case of Paul it was the three days between his Damascus road "conversion" and his baptism at the hand of Ananias; and in the case of Cornelius it was "in close proximity to each other."[62] Thus, while Baptism in the Holy Spirit ought to be a normal part of initiation into Christian community, it exists as an entirely different and separate event from Christian conversion.[63]

Though the Pentecostal uses the term "Baptism in the Spirit" to refer to this post-conversion experience, the key verses in the Book of Acts that Pentecostals use to defend their view (1:8, 2:4, 2:38, 8:17, 9:17, 10:44, 15:8, 19:6) never use the verb βαπτίζω to refer to anything that the Spirit is doing. Rather, terms like ἐπέρχομαι (1:8), πίμπλημι (2:4, 9:17), λαμβάνω (2:38, 8:17), ἐπιπίπτω (10:44), δίδομι (15:8) and ἔρχομαι (19:6) are used to describe the Spirit's action. The Pentecostal may be justified in calling these

59. Ibid., 204.
60. Sepulveda, "Born Again," 104.
61. Ervin, *Conversion-Initiation*, 53.
62. Ibid., 53.
63. Kärkkäinen, *Spiritus Ubi Vult Spirat*, 188.

instances a *Baptism* in the Spirit based on an implicit correlation between 1:5 and 2:4. Yet, their use of a term that has traditionally stood for initiation and conversion throughout centuries of Christian history made their doctrine more controversial. As the Charismatic movement made its way into the historic churches, many adopted the Pentecostal conception of *ordo salutis* in order to accommodate their experience. This trend among Charismatics eventuated in some detailed challenges by non-Charismatic Protestant and Catholic theologians.

In 1970, F. Dale Bruner and James D. G. Dunn each published a work that systematically assessed and challenged the key Pentecostal doctrines of subsequence and initial evidence.[64] Dunn's work focused more on the doctrine of subsequence rather than initial evidence. Bruner engaged both doctrines thoroughly in his rebuttals to the new challenges of Pentecostal experience. Dunn's main contention was that Spirit Baptism in the New Testament represents the principle act of initiation into the Christian community, and that it is intimately tied to the saving faith of a person and not exclusively to water baptism. His view challenged the Pentecostal belief that a person may be a Christian without having been baptized in the Spirit. Dunn's view was also distinct from the Sacramentalist who believes that the Spirit is intimately tied to water baptism, and understands that which takes place in the physical immersion into water as the principle act of initiation into the church. For Dunn, Acts 2:38 represents most clearly the pattern of conversion-initiation to be practiced by future followers of Christ.[65] In this "complex of conversion-initiation" faith, water baptism, and Baptism in the Spirit are intimately connected to becoming a Christian. According to Dunn, the New Testament witness shows that faith is the unifying element between Spirit Baptism and water baptism. Water baptism neither guarantees faith nor the Spirit, but saving faith should be followed by both the *rite* of water baptism and the initiating experience of Spirit Baptism (though not necessarily in that order as in the case of Cornelius). Therefore, water baptism "is neither to be equated or confused with Spirit-baptism nor to be given the most prominent part in that complex event."[66] Bruner's conclusions, drawn from his analysis of the key passages in Acts, were similar to Dunn's, though he more closely connected

---

64. Dunn, *Baptism in the Holy Spirit*; Bruner, *A Theology of the Holy Spirit*. These two works represented a coming of age for Pentecostal theology. Up until this point, no scholars of the caliber of Dunn or Bruner had taken the Pentecostals' claims seriously enough to engage them in-depth on their own terms.

65. Dunn, *Baptism in the Holy Spirit*, 91ff.

66. Ibid., 4.

water baptism to Spirit Baptism. He argued, "The unambiguous result of faith-baptism into *Christ* is that the Holy Spirit is given . . . 'the Baptism in the Holy Spirit' is simply Christian baptism."[67] While upholding the biblical viability of future fillings of the Spirit as the privilege of all Christians, Bruner repudiated the Pentecostal notion that such a filling is a "burden obtained through a program of conditions."[68]

Many Protestant denominations took up the work of Bruner and Dunn as representative of their position against the Pentecostal doctrine of subsequence. They believed that it was inappropriate to subordinate the new life experienced through the Spirit in conversion to a work that was yet to be realized. Upholding the Spirit's work in conversion as the power to cleanse, renew, and transform the sinner into the saved, they felt that Pentecostal theology tended to understand this power as a "light-duty" work of the Holy Spirit. The result being that the presence of Christ in their own life and in the lives of their congregation, a presence causing them to conform into his image, was reduced to a half-presence.[69] These concerns are nicely captured in the following statement by the Presbyterian Church in Canada.

> Sometimes neo-Pentecostal teaching is in danger of losing sight of the all-sufficiency of Jesus. This happens when Christians are called upon to move into a life-in-the-Spirit *beyond* redemption; to enter into a new dimension of communion with God; to receive a "second blessing" after having received Christ into their lives, to strive for new heights, to expect a further dramatic act of God in the so-called "Baptism in the Spirit."[70]

When the Charismatic movement arrived in the Roman Catholic Church in 1967, Roman Catholic theologians did not imitate Protestants by "taking over the whole Pentecostal vocabulary, exegesis and doctrine simply because the experience has validity."[71] Rather, Charismatic experience was validated and interpreted within the framework of the Roman Catholic tradition. Classical Pentecostal doctrine was separated from Pentecostal experience. Among the doctrines of classical Pentecostals, the doctrine of subsequence received the most criticism from Roman Catholic scholars. In 1975, Donald Gelpi recognized, "The most serious doctrinal

67. Bruner, *A Theology of the Holy Spirit*, 213.
68. Ibid., 214.
69. Dunn, "Born Again," 111.
70. McDonnell, *Presence, Power, and Praise*, 1:62.
71. McDonnell, "Holy Spirit and Pentecostalism," 204.

differences dividing Catholic Charismatic and Protestant Pentecostals lie in the area of sacramental theology."[72] At first, the Pentecostal objections to the Charismatic Catholic understanding of Spirit Baptism were no different than evangelical objections to sacramental theology as a whole.[73] However, the Roman Catholic/Pentecostal Dialogue that was formally established in 1972 caused Pentecostals to nuance and narrow their particular criticisms. During the first two quinquennia (1972–82), the topics covered were varied and the relationship of Christian initiation to Spirit Baptism was repeatedly discussed during this time.[74] The fifth quinquennium (1998–2003) focused specifically on the relationship of Spirit Baptism to Christian initiation.

Charismatic Catholics, while affirming the Pentecostal experience, preferred not to call it "the Baptism in the Holy Spirit." Instead, they chose to describe it as "a bringing to awareness and a new actuality of the graces of initiation already received,"[75] that is those graces received in the sacraments of Christian initiation.[76] Charismatic Catholics wanted to say that in the Pentecostal experience, "the power of the Holy Spirit given in Christian initiation, but hitherto unexperienced, becomes a matter of personal conscious experience."[77] For the Catholic, the sacrament of baptism is necessary for salvation as its two main results are "purification from sins and new birth in the Holy Spirit."[78] Part of the results for those who receive the grace of justification received in water baptism is "giving them the power to live and act under the prompting of the Holy Spirit through the gifts of the Holy Spirit."[79] This doctrine obviously places water baptism at the very core of the conversion experience; it is what causes Christ's death for all

---

72. Gelpi, "Ecumenical Problems and Possibilities," 180.

73. Joseph R. Flower, "The Charismatic Movement: Some Problem Areas and Solutions," *The Pentecostal Evangel* 3051 (October 29, 1972) 10–13; Donald Gee, "Two Baptisms" *Pentecostal Evangel* 2986 (August 1, 1971) 2–3; F. B. Meyer, "Seven Reasons for the Believer's Baptism," *Pentecostal Evangel* 2933 (July 26, 1970) 22–23.

74. Jerry Sandidge called the subject of water baptism the most important subject discussed in the entire first quinquennium. Jerry Sandidge, *Roman Catholic/ Pentecostal Dialogue*, 1:90.

75. McDonnell and Montague, *Christian Initiation*, 84.

76. The Roman Catholic Church understands the whole process of Christian initiation in terms of three sacraments that "incorporate human beings into the church and its life and thus into the fullness of being a Christian, namely, baptism, confirmation, and Eucharist." Koch, "Sacraments of Initiation,"634–36.

77. McDonnell, "Statement of the Theological Basis," 617.

78. Koch, "Sacraments of Initiation," 634–36.

79. *Catechism*, 1257–66.

to be appropriated in one's own life. While water baptism communicates results, the sacrament of confirmation as separate from water baptism does so more fully. Concerning the sacrament of confirmation, the Catholic Catechism says, "By the sacrament of Confirmation, [the baptized] are more perfectly bound to the Church and are enriched with a special strength of the Holy Spirit. Hence they are, as true witnesses of Christ, more strictly obliged to spread and defend the faith by word and deed."[80] Confirmation involves the same kinds of results that baptism brings, but it brings with them a greater sense of obligation to the Church, and to Christ. As for the Spirit, it is said to be at work in the entire process, but with almost identical language as that used by the Pentecostals, the effects of the sacrament of confirmation are described as "the full outpouring of the Holy Spirit as once granted to the apostles on the day of Pentecost."[81] Thus, Charismatic Catholics would say that the Baptism in the Holy Spirit and the sacraments of initiation have the same "theological locus."[82]

Despite the similarities in language, French Catholic scholar Michel Quesnel argues that confirmation cannot be accurately compared to the Pentecostal understanding of Spirit Baptism. He warns that the traditional placement of the sacrament of confirmation alongside the sacrament of water baptism as an essential element in the Catholic program of initiation makes it a theoretical distinction more than an actual difference that is reflected in the life of the recipient.[83] In other words, the sacrament of confirmation is still objectively determined by the Church rather than by the subjective free choice of the individual. Rather than focus on the sacraments of initiation as representative of Pentecostal experience, Charismatic Catholics draw attention to the notion in their tradition that the subsequent faith of the individual being baptized in water is absolutely essential for the effects of the baptism to be realized.[84] Adults cannot become Christians "by proxy" on the basis of their parents' faith. Rather, they must each say "yes" to their baptism as an infant. It is in the subjective expectancy and awareness of the benefits of one's past initiation as a Christian that

---

80. *Catechism*, 1285. See also *Catechism*, 1309.

81. *Catechism*, 1302.

82. McDonnell and Bittlinger, *The Baptism in the Holy Spirit*, 33.

83. Quesnel, "Discerning Who Builds the Church," 116–17. For more on how the effects of the sacraments of baptism and confirmation are traditionally not meant to be separated from each other in the Roman Catholic Church, see Serra, "Baptism and Confirmation," 63–71.

84. For a summary of the thinking of the Sacramentalist on this point, see Cullmann, *Baptism in the New Testament*, 36ff.

Charismatic Catholics see a place for the Pentecostal experience of Spirit Baptism in their Sacramental theology.[85] The Pentecostal experience, then, is not the inauguration of new possibilities in the Spirit, but a coming to grips with the reality of the Spirit's activity already present. This emerging consciousness of the graces received in the sacraments of initiation may occur gradually or abruptly. Whether or not this has taken place is strictly determined by the individual, and therefore totally subjective.

The criticisms of the Pentecostal doctrine of subsequence raised by Catholics and Protestants have significant implications for how Charismatics within these traditions understand the relationship of tongues to Spirit Baptism. According to both the sacramentalist and non-sacramentalist conceptions of Spirit Baptism, charismatic activity is not considered an indispensable part of being baptized in the Holy Spirit. Rather, charismatic activity is one of many possible signs of the presence and power of the Holy Spirit that all Christians possess. Thus, both Protestants and Catholics have fundamental problems with the gift of tongues being given a place of primacy in validating an experience of Spirit Baptism. According to Kilian McDonnell, if Catholic Charismatics favor speaking in tongues above other charisms, it is only because of the benefits tongues holds for their personal prayer life. The act of praying in tongues is significant as an authentic experience of God that bears witness to the reality of one's initiation into the Church. As such, tongues may help to bring awareness of the graces of initiation, but other charisms and other experiences of God's presence independent of charisms may do this just as well.[86]

Spectacular Gifts

The predictable result of Protestant and Catholic arguments against tongues as an evidence of Spirit Baptism is that tongues were not considered by Charismatics as the *gateway* into a full life in the Spirit as much as a natural, though by no means normative, *outworking* of a full life in the Spirit. For many in the historic denominations, the Charismatic movement represented a resurgence, renewal, or revival of the spectacular gifts of the Spirit that had been neglected throughout much of the history of the church. Charismatic spirituality expanded people's expectations with

---

85. McDonnell and Bittlinger, *The Baptism in the Holy Spirit*, 45–47; McDonnell, "Statement of the Theological Basis," 617; McDonnell, "Classical Pentecostal/Roman Catholic Dialogue," 254.

86. McDonnell, "Statement of the Theological Basis," 616.

regard to what the Spirit had to offer. According to Kilian McDonnell, "[Pentecostals] demonstrated by a living witness that tongues, prophecy, and healing are not extraordinary gifts but belong to the daily life of the ordinary congregation."[87]

The importance of adopting an attitude of expectancy with regard to charismatic gifts was expressed by many in the historic Protestant denominations in their formal responses to the Charismatic movement. The Presbyterian Church in Canada wrote that the primary contribution of the Pentecostal movement was to urge the church to "renew her awareness and desire for the gifts of the Spirit," to "recognize the freedom of the Spirit to bestow his gifts according to His will," and to "be open to an acknowledgement of the full spectrum of the gifts of the Spirit."[88] In response to the Charismatic movement among Lutherans, The American Lutheran Church, the Lutheran Church Missouri Synod and the Lutheran Church in America all encouraged their ministers and congregations to recognize the validity of spectacular gifts of the Spirit for today, while cautioning that such gifts not be moved to the center.[89] The Presbyterian Church in the United States wrote that such extraordinary manifestations of the Spirit as prophecy and speaking in tongues were possible manifestations of the Spirit that ought to be allowed and affirmed, but added that such manifestations were exceptional.[90]

The above examples show how for many Protestants and Catholics, the appropriate response to the Pentecostal movement was understood not as an acceptance of Pentecostal theology but an adoption of the Pentecostal attitude—an attitude characterized by an expectancy and openness toward the spectacular gifts of the Spirit. The result was that what classical Pentecostals had understood as the evidence or consequence of the Pentecostal experience came to be seen as the experience itself. Thus, Henry Lederle concludes that the central contribution of the Charismatic movement for Christianity was not Spirit Baptism itself but the acknowledgment and actualization of the dimension of the Spirit manifest in charismatic activity.[91] Within this framework, "The difference between a committed Christian, without a Pentecostal experience, and one with such an experience is generally that of an expanded openness and expectancy

---

87. McDonnell, "The Function of Tongues," 29.
88. McDonnell, *Presence, Power, and Praise*, 1:67.
89. Ibid., 1:346, 1:562.
90. Ibid., 1:315.
91. Lederle, *Treasures New and Old*, 216.

in the latter with regard to the Holy Spirit and his gifts."[92] Henry Lederle, representing the Charismatic position on the relationship between glossolalia and Spirit Baptism, says that Charismatics tend to reject a rigid doctrine of initial evidence not only on the basis of inconclusive Scriptural support, but also because life in the Spirit is guaranteed "based on a single empirical event." For Charismatics, this empirical proof of "the ongoing experience of Christ's power and presence" inevitably leads to triumphalism and elitism. He argues that the classical doctrine of initial evidence places too much emphasis on the packaging of the Pentecostal gifts, and not enough emphasis on the gift itself. Thus, Lederle calls for "a critical reinterpretation and reappropriation" of the doctrine in the same vein as past reinterpretations in church history (papal infallibility, water baptism, and double predestination) that have opened the door to fruitful ecumenical dialogue.[93]

Through the influence of the Charismatic movement, most of the historic churches came to officially accept the benefits of spectacular gifts for individuals and congregations in theory. In practice, however, the emphasis was overwhelmingly placed upon the benefits for the individual. The possibility of abuse and the divergence of opinions about charismatic gifts caused the public usage of tongues, interpretation, prophecy, and prayers for healing to be relegated to specific prayer groups and Bible studies or neglected altogether in many mainline churches. This fact was countered by the emergence of what has been called the Third Wave movement. The term was coined by C. Peter Wagner in 1983 while a professor at Fuller Theological Seminary to refer to a growing group of Christians sympathetic to the Pentecostal and Charismatic experience, but distinct in focus and trajectory.[94] In contrast to the Charismatic movement that tended to emphasize the importance of individual spiritual experience ahead of corporate manifestations, the Third Wave movement upheld ministry to others under the power of the Spirit with accompanying signs and wonders as essential for the health and growth of the church.

The Third Wave movement was philosophically committed to "avoid divisiveness at any cost," and to promote power encounters with the Holy Spirit within the structural and worship guidelines of one's own

---

92. Lee, "Pneumatological Ecclesiology," 175–76.

93. Lederle, "Initial Evidence," 131–41.

94. For an interview with Wagner on his views, and early usage of the term "third wave," see Wagner, "A Third Wave?" 1–5.

congregation.[95] In practice, however, the distinct spiritual phenomena associated with Third Wavers (i.e., demonization, territorial spirits, cosmic battle ideology, and personal prophecy) and a desire by many to freely actualize prophetic gifts in a congregational setting resulted in the establishment of new denominations and independent congregations under the guise of "neo-Charismatic." The Vineyard Fellowship,[96] the Toronto Blessing,[97] and the Kansas City Prophets[98] were some of the groups that came to be identified as part of the Third Wave movement. Diverse and fluid in their doctrinal convictions, the Third Wave movement looked even less favorably on classical Pentecostal doctrine than did many Charismatics. Not only did they reject the distinctive Pentecostal doctrines of subsequence and initial evidence, they rejected altogether the idea of a separate experience of Spirit Baptism by which spiritual gifts are imparted to the believer.[99] Thus, Margaret Poloma identified Third-Wavers as "congregations made up of evangelicals who eschew the label 'charismatic' but who engage in charismatic ritual."[100] Theologically, Third-Wavers attempted

---

95. Wagner, "Third Wave," 1141.

96. The Association of Vineyard Churches was established by John Wimber in 1986. Wimber first assumed leadership of a fledgling Vineyard movement of eight congregations in 1982. He gained widespread recognition for his course "Signs and Wonders (MC510)" at Fuller Theological Seminary that he taught from 1981 to 1985 and subsequently taught in seminars around the world. In 1997, the Vineyard had 400 churches in the United States and almost 200 churches abroad. Miller, *Reinventing American Protestantism*, 46–51; Coggins and Hiebert, "The Man, the Message and the Movement," 15–22.

97. The Toronto Blessing was a term first applied by the British press to the distinct and controversial spiritual manifestations experienced at Toronto's Airport Vineyard Church. Along with speaking in tongues and being "slain in the Spirit," common manifestations included deep weeping, laughter, dancing, "spiritual drunkenness," shaking, jerking, rolling and barking/roaring. The revival in Toronto became a catalyst for similar revivals in London, Pensacola, and elsewhere. Poloma, *Main Street Mystics*, 67; Poloma, "Toronto Blessing," 1149–52.

98. The Kansas City Prophets refers to a group of six congregations that joined the Vineyard Fellowship in 1989. The group believed that God desires all of the five-fold ministries (Ephesians 4) to function in the life of the church. In particular, the movement emphasized the restoration of the offices of prophet and apostle. Some important leaders in the group were Bob Jones, Paul Cain, John-Paul Jackson, Jim Goll, Mike Bickle and Jack Deere. Römer, *The Toronto Blessing*, 24–27; Gohr, "Kansas City Prophets," 816–17.

99. Breshears, "Encountering the Vineyard," 1–2; Wagner, "Healing Without Hassle," 115.

100. Poloma, "The Toronto Blessing," 259.

to chart a middle-ground between Evangelicalism and Pentecostalism.[101] However, their embrace of spectacular gifts of prophecy as authoritative among church leaders and in the context of the public worship services caused them to be more controversial among Evangelicals than classical Pentecostals for what seemed to be a compromise of the Evangelical commitment to *sola scriptura*.[102]

Redefining the Tradition: Pentecostal Scholarship

In 1970, the Society for Pentecostal Studies (SPS) was formed at the Pentecostal World Conference (PWC)[103] in Dallas, Texas by a group of classical Pentecostal scholars wishing to gather for the purpose of sharing research and study of the Pentecostal movement. The society had 108 charter members that were committed to "offer Pentecostal scholarship in all academic disciplines as a spiritual service to the Kingdom of God."[104] The group adopted the statement of faith of the PFNA as their own and made it necessary for "full members" to subscribe to this statement. The statements concerning the Godhead and the evidence of Spirit Baptism excluded oneness Pentecostals and many Charismatics from full membership right from the start. At the twelfth Meeting of the Society at Fuller Theological Seminary in 1982, upon the recommendation of Harold Hunter, the PFNA statement of faith was replaced with the broader statement of purpose agreed upon by the PWC. The new statement made the "things most assuredly agreed among us" the basis for full membership rather than assent to distinctively classical Pentecostal doctrines.[105] Though those who could not agree with classical Pentecostal doctrine were never barred from membership in SPS, the broader statement of faith led to increased

---

101. Wagner, "Healing Without Hassle," 114; Nathan and Wilson, *Empowered Evangelicals*, 9–12.

102. Smedes, *Ministry and the Miraculous*, 40–49; Wacker, "Wimber and Wonders," 16–19; Sarles, "An Appraisal of the Signs and Wonders Movement," 57–82; Beverley, *Holy Laughter*, 149–60.

103. The World Pentecostal Conference was officially recognized as the Pentecostal World Conference after 1961. Robeck, "Pentecostal World Conference," 971.

104. "Dr. Vinson Synan Elected Secretary for Society of Pentecostal Studies," *Pentecostal Holiness Advocate* 54.18 (January 2, 1971) 15; "Pentecostal World Conference," *Message of the Open Bible* 53.12 (December 1970) 16, 18–19.

105. *Minutes of the Annual Business Meeting for the Society for Pentecostal Studies, Pasadena, California, November 20, 1982*. Copy of minutes held in the SPS Archives at Fuller Theological Seminary. See also Synan, "Fifteen Years of the Society for Pentecostal Studies," 7.

membership among neo-Charismatics, Protestant and Roman Catholic Charismatics, oneness Penetecostals, Wesleyans, and Episcopalians.[106]

Since its inception, SPS meetings have consistently been a venue in which Pentecostals could discuss, assess, and even challenge the traditional tenets of Pentecostal faith. Gordon Fee, the most widely respected New Testament scholar from the Pentecostal tradition, was the first to take advantage of this atmosphere to argue against the validity of the "cherished Pentecostal interpretations" of subsequence and initial evidence in relation to Spirit Baptism.[107] Upholding the "dynamic, empowering presence" of the Spirit in an experience of Spirit Baptism as that which is truly "essential to Pentecostalism," Fee argued that a *rigid* doctrine of either subsequence or initial evidence—one that prescribes either as obligatory for all Christians—could not be upheld by a proper exegesis of the New Testament.[108] "A charismatic dimension was a normal phenomenon in the reception of the Spirit," according to Fee, but an argument that speaking in tongues is "the only valid sign" of Spirit Baptism could not be proven by the relevant passages in Acts. He suggested a move from "You Must" speak in tongues to "Why Not."[109] In other words, tongues are not an essential evidence of Spirit Baptism, but all who are baptized in the Spirit should expect to speak in tongues.

Fee's papers sparked a dialogue between himself and other SPS members, notably Roger Stronstad and Robert Menzies, which would continue for decades. Far from agreeing that Fee maintained that which was essential to Pentecostalism, both Stronstad and Menzies believed that Fee's hermeneutics cast doubt on "the possibility of a Pentecostal theology" altogether.[110] In 1984, Stronstad published *The Charismatic Theology of*

---

106. Hunter, "Aspects of Initial Evidence Dogma," 199.

107. Fee's arguments were presented in two papers: Fee, "Hermeneutics and Historical Precedent" and "Baptism in the Holy Spirit: The Issue of Separability and Subsequence." Both of these papers were published again with minor revisions and a postscript by Fee in *Gospel and Spirit: Issues in New Testament Hermeneutics*.

108. Fee, "Baptism in the Holy Spirit," 91.

109. Fee, "Hermeneutics and Historical Precedent," 131–32. The main issue for Fee was how historical precedent (repeatable patterns in history) should be used in formulating doctrine. His argument was that historical precedent in the New Testament could be used to defend what is "normal" or expected for most Christians but not what is "normative" or essential for all Christians. Fee clarifies his understanding of the terms "norm," "normal" and "normative" in *Gospel and Spirit*, 101–3.

110. Menzies, "The Essence of Pentecostalism," 6; Stronstad, "The Biblical Precedent," 3, 9. Stronstad asserted, "Pentecostal theology is the product of a hermeneutic which affirms that normative beliefs and practices may properly be derived from

St. Luke, in which he challenged James Dunn's contention that the gift of the Holy Spirit was the "focal point" of Luke's conception of conversion-initiation.[111] He argued that the impartation of the gift of prophecy and other charisms was the central purpose of Spirit Baptism for Luke, and that scholars tended to miss this point because they wrongly imposed Pauline categories of thought on Luke. Stronstad extended his arguments to rebut Fee's criticisms of Pentecostal hermeneutics four years later.[112] In response to the publication of Fee's two earlier articles in *Gospel and Spirit* in 1991, Stronstad directly challenged Fee's arguments against historical precedent at SPS in 1992 with a paper entitled, "The Biblical Precedent for Historical Precedent." He argued that Pentecostal theologians had a biblical basis for establishing normative beliefs and practices from historical narratives on the basis of historical precedent, and called for Fee to "abandon his counterproductive opposition" to such hermeneutics.[113] Robert Menzies' criticisms of Fee are along the same lines as Stronstad's, based on the understanding that "Luke's pneumatology is *different* from—although *complimentary* to—that of Paul." Menzies suggested that when Luke's pneumatology is taken seriously on its own terms it becomes clear that Luke conceived of the gift of the Spirit in prophetic rather than salvific terms. According to Menzies, a distinction between conversion and Spirit Baptism would be the logical outgrowth of this distinctly Lukan pneumatology.[114] The dialogue sparked by Fee was significant for Pentecostal scholarship in at least three ways. First, Fee's papers showed academia that Pentecostals were committed to be proactive in their pursuit of theological

---

historical narrative on the basis of historical precedent." Interestingly, Stronstad would conclude the opposite a year later saying, "It is also time to abandon the debate about issues of historical precedent, which, in the final analysis, is pointless because Pentecostal theology, as I have illustrated, is *not* primarily derived from historical narrative on the basis of historical precedent" (italics mine). Stronstad, "Pentecostal Hermeneutics," 215.

111. Stronstad, *The Charismatic Theology of St. Luke*, 64; Dunn, *Baptism in the Holy Spirit*, 226.

112. Stronstad, "Trends in Pentecostal Hermeneutics," 1–12; Stronstad, "The Hermeneutics of Lucan Historiography," 5–17. These papers were first given as a series of lectures at Assemblies of God Theological Seminary.

113. Stronstad, "The Biblical Precedent," 9.

114. Menzies, *Empowered for Witness*, 233–43. For a more recent Pentecostal response to Dunn (and Fee) concerning the timing and purpose of Spirit Baptism in Luke-Acts see Atkinson, *Baptism in the Spirit*. Atkinson argues that the diversity of voices in the New Testament requires a fluid and flexible understanding of how the Spirit works in conversion and post-conversion. Within this flexibility, Atkinson says, the Pentecostal view ought to be considered the most faithful reading of Luke-Acts.

excellence even if it meant critiquing themselves about issues fundamental to their identity. Second, the conversation that ensued showed that Pentecostals had the intellectual fortitude to engage in theological dialogue with scholars at the highest level. Third, the proposal of Stronstad and Menzies that Paul and Luke held different pneumatologies showed that Pentecostal scholars were capable of and willing to split with the Fundamentalist approaches to Scripture in pursuit of a robust Pentecostal theology.

Consistent with their desire to reach beyond classical Pentecostal denominations, SPS elected a Charismatic Presbyterian, Rodman Williams, as President in 1985. In his presidential address, Williams decided to "try his hand" at writing a much needed Pentecostal theology. Just one year after Fee had presented his SPS paper criticizing much of the hermeneutics that classical Pentecostals employed to defend their distinctive doctrines of subsequence and initial evidence, Williams would make the case for the validity of both. Williams challenged the issues Fee and Dunn had with the Pentecostal doctrine of subsequence, arguing that both Luke and the epistles assumed that one could be a Christian without receiving the gift of the Holy Spirit.[115] Williams argued that reception of the gift of the Holy Spirit was characterized by "transcendent praise" in the form of speaking in unknown tongues. He further observed that this was the common testimony of the Book of Acts and participants in the modern renewal movement around the world.[116] In his discussion on "the phenomenon of tongues" in his 3 volume *Renewal Theology* that he completed in 1992, Williams argued that in all the cases where tongues is mentioned or strongly implied in Acts (Jerusalem, Ephesus, Caesarea and Samaria) they either functioned as "*the* evidence" or "*initial evidence*." Thus, "Speaking in tongues," Williams concluded, "was the primary evidence of the people's receiving the Holy Spirit."[117] The fact that Williams, a self-proclaimed Charismatic, defended classical Pentecostal doctrinal stances in the face of the criticisms of Fee, a self-proclaimed Pentecostal, illustrates the breakdown of a clear division between Pentecostals and Charismatics along doctrinal lines that began to occur during this time.

Like Williams, Frank Macchia, a Pentecostal theologian who received his ThD from the University of Basel, worked at constructing a theology of tongues where tongues was understood not just as an experience "tacked on or worked into" a non-Pentecostal theology, but as a vital mode of

---

115. Williams, "Presidential Address: A Pentecostal Theology," A25–A35.
116. Ibid., A9–A15.
117. Williams, *Renewal Theology*, 2:211–12.

expressing theological truths fundamental to the Christian faith. Following a line of thought similar to Williams' notion of tongues as transcendent praise, Macchia developed an understanding of tongues as a kind of eschatological theophany—a symbol of the mystery of God that helps give expression to inherent tensions in the otherness and closeness of God and the now and not yet of God's kingdom on earth.[118] Thus, tongues do not function as an escape from the world to the glory of heaven but as a symbolic manifestation of God's glorious kingdom in a fallen world. In later articles, Macchia expanded this concept to propose a sacramental understanding of tongues as "the audible medium for realizing the presence of God to empower and heal."[119] In this sense, tongues act as the sacramental sign of an experience of the Spirit initiated and given freely by God for the purpose of empowerment and witness. Reconsidering the classical doctrine of initial evidence in this light, Macchia argued that it may be more accurate to refer to tongues as an objective "sign" of the spiritual reality that Spirit Baptism symbolizes rather than as empirically verifiable "evidence."[120]

Macchia's reconsideration of the classical Pentecostal doctrine of tongues was only the beginning of his contribution to Pentecostal theology. In his 2006 book, *Baptized in the Spirit: A Global Pentecostal Theology*, Macchia astutely recognizes, "It [has become] increasingly difficult to publish a book on Spirit Baptism as subsequent to conversion and necessarily evidenced by tongues without appearing provincial in one's theology and completely off the mark in terms of what is really ecumenically significant about global Pentecostalism."[121] Thus, Macchia undertook to reconsider Spirit Baptism with the hope that the diverse experiences of the Spirit among Pentecostals around the world could be incorporated into a distinctly Pentecostal theology. In order to develop a systematic theology of Spirit Baptism that incorporates all the New Testament voices, Macchia expanded the boundaries of the classic Pentecostal understanding of Spirit Baptism beyond simply an experience subsequent to conversion and evidenced by glossolalia for the purpose of empowered witness. By taking the biblical metaphor of Spirit Baptism—which he summarizes as a baptism in divine love—and placing it in the broader theological con-

---

118. Macchia, "Sighs Too Deep for Words," 47–73.

119. Macchia, "Tongues as a Sign," 63.

120. Macchia, "Groans Too Deep for Words," 172–73; Macchia, "Tongues as a Sign," 66, 68.

121. Macchia, *Baptized in the Spirit*, 50.

text of "inauguration and fulfillment of the Kingdom of God," Macchia was able to integrate Lukan and Pauline understandings of Spirit Baptism into a single theology that includes both "incorporative and experiential dimensions."[122] According to Macchia, Spirit Baptism is both the divine act that forms God's creation into His "dwelling place" and the human experience of God's presence through which the church participates in building the Kingdom of God on earth.[123]

Within this broader conception of Spirit Baptism, tongues are symbolic of Christians being so abundantly filled with God's love that they are able to transcend their own human limitations as they reach out in sacrificial love to others. Macchia contends that Christians can expect such a sign based upon the biblical witness. But, as the free act of a sovereign God whereby he brings about his kingdom on earth, it cannot degenerate into an incontrovertible rule or law. God is free to act as he wills.[124] The result of Macchia's work on glossolalia and Spirit Baptism was an apology for the connection between the two that was not based on the recognition of a normative pattern in the Book of Acts, but rooted in the history of Christian theology. This move away from traditional Pentecostal hermeneutics opened the door for the classical doctrine of initial evidence to be reformulated in an ecumenically sensitive manner that would avoid the harshest criticisms from scholars both within and outside of Pentecostalism.

Simon Chan is another Pentecostal theologian who has defended the validity of the classical Pentecostal doctrine of initial evidence without basing his argument on the establishment of a precedent in the Book of Acts.[125] In doing so, Chan is particularly concerned that any proposal to reinterpret or reformulate Pentecostal doctrine should uphold the integrity of Pentecostal experience. Chan finds historical basis for his proposal in his understanding that the doctrine of "initial physical evidence" was originally developed in order to capture a depth of personal intimacy with God that early Pentecostals experienced.[126] Based on this view of Pentecostal history, Chan proposes that it is only within the context of intimacy with God that the doctrine of initial evidence makes sense.[127] Focusing on evidential tongues in contrast to the gift of tongues for public proclama-

---

122. Ibid., 63.
123. Ibid., 84–88.
124. Ibid., 281.
125. Chan, "The Language Game of Glossolalia," 80–95.
126. I have argued for a different view in chapters 2 and 3.
127. Chan, "The Language Game of Glossolalia," 85.

tion and private prayer, Chan calls such an experience a response whereby all or part of one's "ordinary rational processes" are suspended and the Spirit assumes entire control. Chan argues, by way of analogy, that in the same way that tears are related to sadness, tongues are a "highly personalized kind of idiolect" that may designate a uniquely intimate relationship with God—a relationship in which one is entirely controlled by the Spirit—in a way that nothing else could.[128] Chan's conclusion is that the Pentecostal community needs a new (deeper) understanding of the early Pentecostals' experience of Spirit Baptism that resulted in the formulation of the doctrine of initial evidence (e.g., an overwhelming theophany that results in a spontaneous outburst of verbal utterances controlled solely by the Spirit of God), rather than a revision of the doctrine based on current (shallow) understandings of Spirit Baptism. Thus, Chan's work challenged Pentecostal scholars to focus their attention on the nature and purpose of Spirit Baptism rather than on the wording of a specific doctrine.

In order to gain a deeper understanding of the purpose and use of glossolalia for the Pentecostal community, Amos Yong has explored the "truth value" of tongues in light of the theory of religious symbols expounded by R. C. Neville in his *The Truth of Broken Symbols*.[129] Rather than defend the truth of glossolalia on the basis of its linguistic validity with respect to known or unknown languages, Yong argues that the truth of glossolalia is found in its "symbolic function," or to use Neville's language, "the carryover of value from the object into the interpreters' experience by means of signs."[130] For Neville, the truth of a religious symbol is found in its ability to lead the individual to conform to the religious object by encountering it devotionally, practically, and theologically.[131] Applying Neville's idea to the Pentecostal, Yong argues that glossolalia is true in so far as it brings about a conformity to the divine reality in the individual and community through three overlapping and interweaving stages he calls *innocence, growth*, and *adept*. In *innocence*, the glossolalist longs for and experiences the otherness of God in Spirit Baptism that unleashes the majesty and glory of the divine freedom into the life of the speaker. In *growth*, the glossolalist experiences divine empowerment to effectively bear witness to the gospel of Christ to fellow believers and non-believers through improved and inspired verbal and communicative abilities. In

128. Ibid., 87–90.
129. Yong, "Tongues of Fire," 39–65.
130. Ibid., 43–44.
131. Ibid., 49.

adept, the glossolalist experiences a more intimate communion with the divine unity by which the worshipper is connected to God resulting in a will conformed to Christ's, and the worshipping community is connected to each other resulting in an expression of the eschatological unity of the Body of Christ.[132]

These three stages of glossolalic transformation are parallel to the soteriological, charismatic and eschatological functions of Spirit Baptism that Yong expounds in *The Spirit Poured Out on All Flesh*. Yong argues that Baptism in the Holy Spirit carries a soteriological function as well as a charismatic function in the life of the believer. The soteriological function, however, is more than Christian initiation, but a multidimensional salvation directed toward the individual, family, church, society, world and future.[133] Thus, tongues not only symbolize the Spirit's work in Christian initiation or charismatic empowerment for witness, they are a sign of all that the Spirit does to bring about God's creative and restorative purposes on earth.[134] Yong's work gives theological and biblical backing to the classical Pentecostal's claim to a normative connection between speaking in tongues and Spirit Baptism. At the same time, his work also suggests that such a connection is never meant to be commemorative of a moment in the past as much as inauguration and celebration of a moment in the future. In this regard, a doctrine of initial evidence should be continually appropriated throughout the lifetime of a Pentecostal.

Though many Pentecostals initially perceived the challenges to their distinctive doctrines raised by academic theology as a threat to the veracity of the classical Pentecostal tradition, the results of scholarly inquiry into the fundamental workings of Pentecostal experience that have occurred over the last quarter century has only bolstered the theological strength of the tradition. Scholars have found a place for Pentecostal experience at the highest levels of academic theology in Pentecostal and non-Pentecostal circles. At the same time, scholars have been increasingly skeptical of the value of the classical doctrine of initial evidence for the Pentecostal community. While Pentecostal scholars continue to affirm the inherent

---

132. Ibid., 50–62.

133. Yong, *The Spirit Poured Out on All Flesh*, 88–106.

134. Beyond the initiating (John 14:7; 20:22; Acts 1:5; 2:38; 5:32; 1 Cor 12:13) and empowering (Acts 4:8, 31; 7:55; 13:9; 15:32) work of the Spirit, the New Testament speaks of the Spirit bringing unity (1 Cor 12:13; 2 Cor 13:14; Eph 4:3–4), sanctifying (Rom 5:5; 8:13–16; 15:16; 2 Thess 2:13), convicting (Heb 10:15; 1 John 3:24), interceding (Rom 8:26–27), freeing (Rom 8:2), and teaching (1 Cor 2:13) in the life of a Christian.

connection between Spirit Baptism and speaking in tongues to which the doctrine attests, many do not see that such a connection is best captured by the doctrine's current wording.

Conclusion

In the last three chapters, we have explored the original connection that the first generation of Pentecostals made between tongues and Spirit Baptism, the codifying of that connection in the doctrine of initial evidence, and the ensuing explications, critiques and reconsiderations of the doctrine during the past century. What we have seen is that the classical Pentecostal tradition has always placed primary importance on the inherent connection between a phase of the Christian life inaugurated by the Baptism in the Holy Spirit and the charismatic phenomenon of speaking in tongues. At times, the tradition has understood this connection as their primary contribution to the worldwide church. Yet, Pentecostals have often struggled to articulate and expound the connection in a way that could be appreciated, affirmed and promoted by those outside the tradition. While recent Pentecostal scholarship has done much to improve the respectability of the Pentecostal tradition among non-Pentecostal theologians, the doctrine of initial evidence, as it is currently worded, is still perceived as seriously flawed. Thus, the role the doctrine of initial evidence should play in the classical Pentecostal community is an important subject of debate among Pentecostal scholars. Its role has changed considerably over the last century, and it is to the task of exploring this changing role in detail that we now turn.

5

The Function of the Doctrine of Initial Evidence in the History of Classical Pentecostalism

Introduction

ALTHOUGH THE DOCTRINE OF initial evidence has been the defining doctrine of classical Pentecostals throughout much of the last century, Pentecostal scholars have recently developed some compelling new ways of conceiving of the connection between Spirit Baptism and speaking in tongues. These developments have raised some significant questions about the possibility of doctrinal reform in classical Pentecostal denominations. Has Pentecostal theology developed and progressed to the point that what is considered essential to Pentecostalism, the Baptism in the Holy Spirit, ought to be formally stated differently? If so, can one uphold the authority of the Holy Spirit's leading in the past without quenching His leading in the present?

In search of answers to these questions, developments in the field of doctrinal criticism have indicated a helpful way forward. Since the publication of George Lindbeck's *The Nature of Doctrine*, much scholarly attention has been given to how the cultural and linguistic historicity of doctrinal statements might allow for changes and developments in doctrine over time without condemning past formulations as either heretical or ignorant. Lindbeck's cultural-linguistic approach to doctrine has been

The Function of the Doctrine of Initial Evidence

criticized,[1] especially for its misrepresentation and complete abandonment of other approaches to doctrine,[2] inherent difficulties in determining how doctrines should be put into practice,[3] and its constraining the task of Christian theology to deal only within the constructs of its own received narrative tradition.[4] Yet, despite these weaknesses in Lindbeck's approach, his cultural-linguistic categories are important for Pentecostals to consider in relation to Spirit Baptism because of the relative dependence of the doctrine upon the particular language and culture imbedded within the classical Pentecostal community.[5] A cultural-linguistic approach to the doctrine of Spirit Baptism allows Pentecostal scholarship to break free from constructing apologies solely on the basis of exegetical concerns or the explanation of certain experiences (although each of these is certainly needed as well), and to understand and criticize doctrine on the basis

---

1. McGrath provides a helpful citation of early criticisms of Lindbeck and a summary of some of the difficulties in Lindbeck's approach that he seeks to resolve with his own. McGrath, *Scientific Theology*, 2:240–42.

2. Some critics see Lindbeck as misrepresenting the cognitive-propositional and experiential-expressive approaches in order to bolster the viability of his own cultural-linguistic approach. The result is that one is led to decide between the three approaches when a hybrid may be more appropriate. Wainwright, "Ecumenical Dimensions," 121–32. For specific criticisms of Lindbeck's characterization of the cognitive approach, see McGrath, *The Genesis of Doctrine*, 16–20.

3. Lee Barrett identifies a difficulty in determining what specific practices are in accordance with doctrinal rules. Lindbeck gives no paradigm for effectively dealing with conflicting practices that derive from a singular rule. In short, there is no overarching rule of practice that helps to determine normative behaviors, emotions or thoughts within a particular community. Barrett, "Theology as Grammar," 155–72. Within the Evangelical community, similar criticisms have been levied against the cultural-linguistic approach for its specific exclusion of canonical texts that may form an overarching foundation for norming practices within a particular community. Vanhoozer, *The Drama of Doctrine*, 94–97.

4. Operating within a coherence theory of truth, Lindbeck's scheme relativizes religions, making it futile to attempt to construct a meta-narrative by which doctrines and practices of different religions may be mutually criticized. Further, Lindbeck's approach assumes the doctrines that are essential to identity of a particular relgous group are "given" and "stable" so that a doctrine's intra-systematic consistency can be easily evaluated. If, however, the grounds for evaluation are called into question or changed, it creates difficulties that Lindbeck fails to adequately address. McGrath, *Scientific Theology*, 2:46–50; McGrath, *The Genesis of Doctrine*, 28.

5. Joel Shuman makes a strong case for the use of Lindbeck's cultural-linguistic categories to analyze the Pentecostal doctrine of Spirit Baptism based on the fact that defenses of the doctrine are rooted in "practices and assumptions about language, experience, and knowledge" that are culturally dependent and not absolutes. Shuman, "Toward a Cultural-Linguistic Account," 222.

of its performance of various functions within the classical Pentecostal community.

The Nature of Doctrine
George Lindbeck

George Lindbeck's seminal work, *The Nature of Doctrine*, elaborates three basic models for understanding religious doctrines in the field of doctrinal criticism: the cognitive-propositional approach, the experiential-expressive approach, and his own cultural-linguistic approach. Though his descriptions of these approaches have been heavily criticized, his basic categories provide an excellent framework for discussing the nature of doctrine in terms of its function in the religious community. In Lindbeck's analysis, the cognitive-propositional approach understands church doctrines to function as "informative propositions or truth claims about objective realities." In his view, the propositionalist sees a doctrinal statement as being either true or false based on its success or failure to correspond with objective reality, a reality that is unaffected by the historical and cultural particularities from which the doctrine arose. Thus, according to Lindbeck, a propositionalist understands a doctrine that is once true (at a specific time and in a specific culture) to always be true (at any time and in any culture). The approach to doctrine Lindbeck calls "experiential-expressive" interprets doctrine as "symbols of inner feelings, attitudes, or existential orientations." As an outward interpretation of an inward reality, the reference point for any one doctrine is entirely subjective and open to endless interpretations. Thus, assent to or denial of a doctrine becomes meaningless because neither can be a reliable indicator of what one is actually experiencing.[6] The alternative that Lindbeck proposes to the propositionalist and expressivist is his cultural-linguistic approach to doctrine. In his view, doctrines are best understood as "communally authoritative rules of discourse, attitude, and action."[7] Rather than being a claim to ontological truth or a symbol of religious experience, Lindbeck argues that doctrines make claims to "intrasystematic" truth rooted in the grammatical and religious traditions of a given context.[8] Thus, doctrines are best understood to be right or wrong (authentic) on the basis of their

---

6. Lindbeck, *The Nature of Doctrine*, 16–17.
7. Ibid., 18–19.
8. Ibid., 64, 80.

The Function of the Doctrine of Initial Evidence

coherence with the imbedded language and practices of a given religious tradition, and their own unique conception of "the Ultimate Mystery."[9]

Though the propositionalist and expressionist are in direct opposition to each other in terms of where one looks first for God's revelation and the basis for true doctrine, Lindbeck levies the same charge against both, a charge that reveals the practical investment that Lindbeck, as an ecumenist, has in his proposal. Lindbeck argues that it is difficult to envision "doctrinal reconciliation without capitulation" with either approach.[10] For the propositionalist, the nature of doctrine as ontological truth claims means the acceptance of one doctrine necessitates the denial of many other doctrines. For the expressionist, the polyvalent nature of doctrine as symbols of religious experience means the acceptance or denial of a specific doctrine is superfluous. In Lindbeck's approach, however, doctrines are accepted or denied only within the unique framework of a particular religious community on the basis of its own "grammar of faith." It proposes "no common framework." Thus, doctrines that appear to conflict at the propositional level can be reconciled as they are both understood to be faithful to the community's religious tradition.[11]

From a philosophical perspective, Lindbeck's arguments for the usefulness of his cultural-linguistic theory of doctrine stem from the fact that both propositionalism and expressivism are foundationalist. That is, both recognize a supra-empirical authority that cannot and need not be verified that acts as a source of truth: one outside the individual in Scripture and tradition, and the other inside the individual in the form of religious experience.[12] In contrast, the cultural-linguistic approach understands the locus of authority to reside in the "whole community of competent speakers of a language."[13] In this view, the historical-cultural location of a religious group need not be lamented, but rather embraced. Diversity and variance are not threatening forces, but signs of vitality and health. For the adequacy of a doctrinal statement lies not in its ability to transcend the cultural milieu and arrive at a truth statement that embodies ultimate reality, but in its ability to embrace a culture and move its adherents toward authentic praxis that is intrasystematically true and coheres with the im-

---

9. Ibid., 69.
10. Ibid., 16.
11. Ibid., 49. 98–104.
12. Nancey Murphy has provided an excellent summary of the foundational questions of philosophy that both "outside-in" and "inside-out" theologies have left unanswered in *Beyond Liberalism & Fundamentalism*, 76–82.
13. Lindbeck, *The Nature of Doctrine*, 102.

bedded language and rituals of that culture. Thus, Lindbeck argues, "It is the framework and the medium within which Christians know and experience, rather than what they experience or think they know, that retains continuity and unity down through the centuries."[14]

If Lindbeck is right, the primary question to which Christian doctrine seeks an answer becomes: "What is Christian?" Conversely, Christian doctrine does not intend (though it may unintentionally) to answer the question, "What is true?" or more specifically, "Is Christianity true?"[15] Thus, the function of doctrine in Lindbeck's understanding is strictly regulative. Doctrine is a rule or guiding principle for the community of faith. While it may be stated in the form of a proposition, the limits of the application of a doctrinal truth are dependent upon the system within which it originated and therefore unable to make first-order (ontological) truth claims.[16]

Lindbeck's cultural-linguistic approach to doctrine represents a welcome critique of the foundationalist presuppositions inherent in propositionalist and expressivist approaches to doctrine that tend to separate doctrines from the historically located community of faith that brought them into being, developed them in the past, and upon whom they exert their influence in the present. However, when one seeks to apply Lindbeck's approach to doctrine in specific situations within the Christian church, one is left with two lingering questions: "How does one define the boundaries of 'the framework and the medium with which Christians know and experience?'" and, "Who should be called on or trusted to formulate doctrinal statements that accurately represent the framework?" Lindbeck's answers to both of these questions are problematic in that they reveal underlying modern convictions about language and culture that are questionable.[17]

Lindbeck's method assumes that religious frameworks speak entirely different languages that can be taken and understood on their own terms in isolation from each other. Amos Yong has argued that real life is not so simple. "Cultural and religious grammars are never pure or homogeneous, but always exist as a complex togetherness of multiple histories, traditions, sources and experiences."[18] Lindbeck's call to test the authenticity of religious speech against the *consensus fidelium*—"a sample of

14. Ibid., 84.
15. Ibid., 101.
16. Ibid., 80.
17. Heyduck, *The Recovery of Doctrine*, 77.
18. Yong, *Spirit-Word-Community*, 302.

competent practitioners" taken from "the mainstream of the religion in question"—is a difficult, if not impossible task, when "the mainstream" and "competence" are not easily delimited or defined. Lindbeck argues that "competent practitioners" of a religion are those who have "so interiorized the grammar of their religion that they are reliable judges, not directly of the doctrinal formulations . . . but of the acceptability or unacceptability of the consequences of these formulations in ordinary religious life and language."[19] Yet, Yong reminds us, "Beliefs and practices are . . . never purely religious."[20] Thus, it is hard to imagine that Lindbeck's test could be applied to entire religious traditions with the "unshakable empirical certitude" that he claims.[21] Even at the local church level, objectivity is not easily obtained in measuring religious competency because an individual's religious practices are interpretations, not just of their religious tradition to which they belong, but of their entire stratus of interconnected frameworks of living and being in society. In the end, Lindbeck's theory becomes difficult to apply to concrete doctrinal disagreements in the church where insiders and outsiders are not easily defined and the consequences of doctrinal formulations extend far beyond the walls of the church.

The Need for "Real Reference"—Doctrine as Drama

The difficulties that one encounters when applying Lindbeck's cultural-linguistic theory to concrete situations in the church is largely due to Lindbeck having taken an "all or nothing" approach to propositional truth statements and referentiality. He implies that since propositional statements cannot speak completely and exhaustively about a concept outside their determinate context, they have no real reference.[22] Lindbeck's analysis of the propositionalist approach has been criticized by Alister McGrath and other theologians to be an oversimplification and, in some cases, misrepresentation of the propositional functionality of doctrine in Christian community.[23] At times, Lindbeck incorrectly equates a propositionalist understanding of *doctrine* to a propositionalist understanding of *revelation*—that God transmits conceptual knowledge about himself to human

19. Lindbeck, *The Nature of Doctrine*, 100.
20. Yong, *Spirit-Word-Community*, 302.
21. Lindbeck, *The Nature of Doctrine*, 100.
22. Heyduck, *The Recovery of Doctrine*, 80–81.
23. McGrath, *The Genesis of Doctrine*, 16; Heyduck, *The Recovery of Doctrine*, 83, 102n90.

beings through sets of "objectively and immutably true propositions" compiled in the church's sacred writings.[24] In Avery Dulles' five models of revelation, Lindbeck's description of the propositionalist approach most closely coincides with Dulles' first model, *revelation as doctrine*.[25] Lindbeck's narrow definition of propositionalism allows him to characterize the approach as pre-modern, in contrast to modern experiential-expressivist and postmodern cultural-linguistic theories of doctrine.[26] For Alister McGrath, Lindbeck's failure to do justice to those theologians, like himself, who hold, by virtue of the fact that God's revelation is imbedded in the historical narrative of Jesus Christ, that there is both a cognitive *and* affective dimension to God's revelation, gives his own cultural-linguistic theory of doctrine an air of superiority that is unwarranted.[27] In response, McGrath calls for a distinction to be made between the view of doctrine as "an exhaustible and unambiguous account of God that is transmitted conceptually by propositions on the one hand, and the view that there is a genuinely cognitive dimension, component or element to doctrinal statements on the other."[28]

If McGrath's criticism of Lindbeck is to be taken seriously, there must be a way of conceiving of the authority of Scripture and tradition for the church that effectively combines affective and cognitive aspects of divine revelation. Much ground has been made in this area on the basis of N. T. Wright's proposal concerning the authority of Scripture. Wright draws an analogy between the church and actors who are called on to improvise the final act of a play in which they have been given the first four acts and some hints about how it should end. In Wright's analogy, the church has, in the New Testament, the first scene of the final act, and

24. Lindbeck, *The Nature of Doctrine*, 21.

25. Dulles, 37–44.

26. Murphy, *Beyond Liberalism & Fundamentalism*, 42. Though Lindbeck initially presents a disagreeably narrow definition of propositionalism, he later acknowledges modern forms of propositionalism that make a distinction between what a doctrine affirms ontologically and the diverse forms through which it may be conceptualized and expressed (Lindbeck, *The Nature of Doctrine*, 80). Yet, even in his acknowledgment of these modern theories that allow for changes in doctrines (particularly Berhard Lonergan and Karl Rahner), Lindbeck dismisses them as too "awkward and complex" and "peculiarly complicated" to be persuasive (Lindbeck, *The Nature of Doctrine*, 17, 105). Therefore, he chooses to engage their arguments only occasionally *ad hoc*.

27. McGrath, *The Genesis of Doctrine*, 15–20.

28. Ibid. 20. McGrath's position rests on his understanding of the "event-character" of truth that "represents a strategic move away from any understanding of revelation as the disclosure of general principles." Ibid., 76.

The Function of the Doctrine of Initial Evidence

is required to live under the authority of the previous scenes and acts as it performs the final scenes. Thus, it is necessary for the church to engage in the complex process of balancing "*innovation* and *consistency*" as it lives out the rest of the drama in light of Scripture and tradition anointed by the Holy Spirit.[29] The strength of Wright's analogy for understanding doctrine and its relationship to Scripture and tradition has been taken up and extensively expanded upon by Kevin Vanhoozer and Richard Heyduck.[30] Specifically, the dramatic analogy helps explain how doctrines can retain their "real reference"—a necessary component for guiding faithful participation in the ongoing Christian narrative—as they change to address new situations.[31]

Building on Wright's analogy, both Vanhoozer and Heyduck uphold the importance of examining the cultural-linguistic influences on doctrine emphasized by Lindbeck while maintaining that there is an authoritative real reference point upon which to base doctrinal criticism in the "continuing dramatic narrative of God's action."[32] Heyduck and Vanhoozer agree with Lindbeck that doctrine is regulative, but they do not agree that it is *only* regulative. They argue that doctrine is better described as directive.[33] That is, doctrine is not solely concerned with regulating practices, but it is guiding a faithful interaction between God's authoritative actions in the past and the present. In this sense, doctrine has both a propositional and practical component to it; it makes truth claims and regulates action. For Vanhoozer, it is through doctrine that the Holy Spirit guides God's people to live out the truth of Scripture in new contexts. In short, "Doctrine gets caught up in the Spirit's ministry of the Word through the words of Scripture."[34] Thus, it is ultimately the Holy Spirit that provides the church a common point of authoritative reference between the past and the present. Whereas Lindbeck implies that discernment of the Holy

---

29. Wright, "How Can the Bible be Authoritative?" 9–32, particularly 18–19. Stanley Grenz and John Franke provide a helpful extension to Wright's analogy by likening the Christian tradition to the particular theatrical tradition in which actors are immersed. Though secondary to the script itself, the theatrical tradition plays an important role in determining appropriate and consistent improvisations to the script. In the same way, the Christian tradition provides an indispensable context for interpreting and applying the narrative of scripture. Grenz and Franke, *Beyond Foundationalism*, 128–29.

30. Vanhoozer, *The Drama of Doctrine*; Heyduck, *The Recovery of Doctrine*.

31. Heyduck, *The Recovery of Doctrine*, 82–83.

32. Ibid., 132.

33. Ibid., 84–93; Vanhoozer, *The Drama of Doctrine*, 77–114.

34. Vanhoozer, *The Drama of Doctrine*, 102.

Spirit's actions cannot be separated from discerning or being "caught up" in the spirit of the culture, Vanhoozer maintains that it is the Holy Spirit that allows the church to be "caught up" into what God is doing, and prophetically confront and challenge culture. This conception of doctrine allows for changes in doctrinal formulations without sacrificing substance because the locus of authority lies not in the community's use of Scripture on the one hand or in a singular proposition of Scripture on the other, but in the Holy Spirit's use of Scripture throughout time.[35]

Doctrinal Development

As attractive as Vanhoozer's conception of doctrine is from a theoretical perspective, it raises some difficult questions about how the theory is worked out in practical situations: How, given Vanhoozer's notion of doctrinal development as a dramatic interaction between Scripture and the community of faith directed by the Holy Spirit, should doctrines be criticized and critiqued? How does one discern when the church has correctly or incorrectly responded to the Holy Spirit in the formulation of a particular doctrine? How does one discern when it is appropriate for a doctrinal formulation to change? Answers to these questions are largely dependent upon what one understands the ultimate goal of doctrine to be. According to Vanhoozer, doctrine ought to direct us toward "fitting participation" in "the dramatic action between God and humanity to which Scripture attests."[36] Doctrine does this by "cultivating a sense of what God is doing in the world and how we should act in response."[37] In other words, doctrine should not just tell people what to do in a particular situation, but it should help people to become those who will naturally make right decisions regardless of the situation by encouraging patterns and habits of thinking and acting that are consistent with those of the inspired biblical authors.[38] How does one determine whether a particular doctrine is helping or hindering this process? Both Vanhoozer and Heyduck recog-

---

35. Ibid., 184, 354.

36. Ibid., 354; Heyduck, *The Recovery of Doctrine*, 193–209. The term, "fitting participation," is Vanhoozer's way of describing a doctrine that is received by the community as faithful to Scripture and the community. Heyduck prefers to use the term "happiness of doctrine" to refer to much the same thing: a doctrine that is rooted in the narrative of scripture and carries "illocutionary force" for the community in the present.

37. Vanhoozer, *The Drama of Doctrine*, 363

38. Ibid., 376–77.

nize that when the nature of doctrine is understood as dramatic, evaluating a doctrine's "fittingness" or "happiness" is a complicated and inexact process.[39] It is complicated because engaging in the critical evaluation of any one doctrine means one must take seriously the ongoing drama that produced the doctrine. It is inexact because the process of evaluating a doctrine takes place within an ongoing drama that is constantly developing and whose future is only vaguely defined.

Yet, despite the relative complexity and inexactness of evaluating a doctrine within the framework of an ongoing drama, such an endeavor is essential for doctrine to be able to speak forcefully to new situations and not to be reduced to the mere repetition of past formulations. If doctrines are separated from the narrative from which they arose, they lose their fixed connection to reality and, over time, their force in the community. In short, doctrines that are not tied to the narrative of the church may be seen as expendable.[40]

Bernhard Lonergan's analysis of doctrine suggests a helpful way forward in the evaluation of particular doctrines. According to Lonergan, all doctrinal developments in the church need not be seen as developments implicitly orchestrated by the Holy Spirit through Scripture. Neither is one forced to try to evaluate doctrine solely on its correspondence with the "plain meaning of Scripture," divorced from history. But there is a third option that must be employed by theologians who recognize the dramatic nature of doctrine. Lonergan is worth quoting in full,

> There can be many kinds of development and that, to know them, one has to study and analyze concrete historical process while, to know their legitimacy, one has to turn to evaluational history and assign them their place in the dialectic of the presence and absence of intellectual, moral, and religious conversion.[41]

Lonergan's "third option" says that doctrinal criticism is not just a matter of understanding Scripture (theological) or understanding the community (sociological), but it is a matter of understanding the narrative context in which a doctrine was formulated and developed (historical). Thus, as Shane Clifton has argued, it is vitally important that doctrinal criticism move beyond exegetical analysis of Scripture to deal explicitly with the experiences and texts that gave rise to a doctrine, and how the

---

39. Ibid., 110–11; Heyduck, *The Recovery of Doctrine*, 89, 94, 209. Also see McGrath, *The Genesis of Doctrine*, 165.

40. Vanhoozer, *The Drama of Doctrine*, 126–28.

41. Lonergan, *Method in Theology*, 312.

doctrine has functioned in the context of the particular community over time.[42] Amos Yong has argued that it is essential for a "hermeneutic of ecclesial traditions" to have a "thick" understanding of tradition in order to determine how the judgments of the past should be appropriated and/or corrected as directives for a tradition's present interaction with Scripture.[43] According to Yong, this "thick understanding" involves, "A bringing to explicit consciousness the given data of ecclesial reflection and laying bare the ways in which tradition norms theological activity.... [This must include moments] whereby the various socio-historical reasons why the Church has believed in just this way and not that are detailed, so far as such can be determined."[44]

In order to seriously engage in the historical work that Yong and Lonergan suggest, some categories for explicating the historical influence of a doctrine on a religious community are needed. Alister McGrath provides exactly this in his extensive analysis of the origins of Christian doctrine. McGrath convincingly argues that, regardless of what doctrine *ought* to be, Christian doctrine *has* functioned in four ways throughout the history of the church. According to McGrath, doctrine, generally speaking, demarcates groups socially, interprets narrative, interprets experience, and makes truth claims.[45] Within the relationship of any one particular doctrine to a historical community, one or more of these functions will be present in varying degrees at any given time. Any doctrine can function in all four of these ways, but within a community of interpreters, particular functions of a doctrine will be emphasized in different ways as contexts and times change. Understanding the various ways in which a particular doctrine functioned authoritatively in the past for a community helps one to evaluate the constant and changeable aspects of a doctrine. Practically, an evaluative history helps one to know what is the substance of a doctrine and what is peripheral in terms of the cognitive, affective, and cultural-linguistic functions of a doctrine. Theologically, an evaluative

---

42. Clifton has proposed this exact strategy in dealing with the Pentecostal doctrine of Spirit Baptism. Clifton, "The Spirit and Doctrinal Development," 11.

43. Yong, *Spirit-Word-Community*, 265–73. McGrath has also stressed the need for Evangelical theologians to unpack the philosophical and cultural assumptions that have governed a tradition's past engagement with Scripture, so that Scripture will be allowed to speak authoritatively to new people and situations. McGrath, "Engaging the Great Tradition," 146–51.

44. Yong, *Spirit-Word-Community*, 267.

45. McGrath, *The Genesis of Doctrine*, 37. This list is very similar to lists proposed by Benhard Lonergan and William Abraham. Lonergan, *Method in Theology*, 298; Abraham, *Waking from Doctrinal Amnesia*, 38.

history helps one to understand how the Holy Spirit has used a doctrine in the past and, therefore, how it might continue to be used in the present.

With these benefits in mind, in the work that follows I endeavor to evaluate the history of the doctrine of Spirit Baptism in classical Pentecostal tradition within the four categories that McGrath has detailed. It must be acknowledged, however, that there are limits to the benefits of evaluating the history of a doctrine by the categories suggested by McGrath. As Yong has forcefully argued, if the criteria for evaluating the plausibility of a doctrine are derived solely from the narrative of a particular community, the potency with which the conclusions of such an evaluation can speak to other communities, religious and otherwise, is severely undermined.[46] Thus, as it pertains to the present study, the ideological foundation for doctrinal criticism that I have adopted has as its horizon, Protestantism, and in particular, Evangelical Protestantism. Such a study, then, is only of value to the entire theological enterprise in conjunction with other studies and evaluations that adopt foundations for doctrinal criticism independent from the narrative of a particular religious community and accepted by a wider range of people. Given these limits, why not engage in such a broader reaching evaluation now? Because, a tradition must know its own voice, and know it well, before it engages critically in a conversation with other voices. While an evaluation conditioned by the narrative of a tradition weakens the force with which it speaks to other traditions, it strengthens the force with which it speaks to its own.

Four Functions of the Doctrine of Spirit Baptism

Interpretation of Narrative

The genesis of the Pentecostal movement in North America is varied and complex. Far from disseminating a single doctrine or theological perspective, the first generation of Pentecostals formed a conglomerate of many Revivalists and Restorationists from Holiness and Reformed traditions of Protestantism. Their point of unification was their intent to seek out and participate in a common experience of the Spirit that was most clearly manifest in the act of speaking with other tongues. As individuals found what they were looking for, an experience they called the Baptism in the Holy Spirit, the experience became the defining point of the movement. What came first, however, was not an experience, but the intent to seek out

---

46. Yong, "Review of *The Genesis of Doctrine*," 359–62.

an experience that was contiguous with the narrative of the early church in the Book of Acts.[47] Parham (unbeknownst to his students) came to see a need for such an experience by interacting with Scripture within a Restorationist interpretive framework that viewed the apostolic church as the measure of pure and authentic Christianity to which the modern church was called to return.[48] The uniqueness of Parham's hermeneutic lay not in its generally promoting the restoration of the apostolic faith (the title of his periodical), but in the more specific injunction that such a restoration should be evidenced by the duplication of the same physical manifestations that the apostles viewed as evidence, namely, speaking in tongues. In this respect, Parham's doctrine of the "Bible evidence" is a doctrine that was generated by the hermeneutical spiral between the narrative of Scripture and a Restorationist interpretive framework.[49]

Restorationism: Holy & Separate

Before Agnes Ozman ever spoke in tongues, Parham understood that the apostolic church was being restored in every detail, and was at least provisionally convinced by the Restorationist narrative of the need for Christians to seek out an experience that lined up with the apostles,' even to the extent of speaking in tongues.[50] For Parham (and other Restorationists), Acts 2 was not just an historical narrative of the church, but also a prophetic narrative for the church at the beginning of the twentieth century.[51] Thus, the initial experience of speaking in tongues that Parham encountered at Bethel was not a surprise experience that needed to find a narrative, but it was an experience that Parham expected, probably even led his students

---

47. There is evidence that Parham had heard of the speaking in tongues that took place in Frank Sandford's Shiloh movement and even maybe witnessed it when he was there. Thus, there is evidence to suggest that Parham led his students to conclude that tongues were the evidence of Spirit Baptism. For the students, it seemed as though Scripture was guiding them, but it is doubtful that Parham was surprised by his students' conclusions. Goff, *Fields White Unto Harvest*, 71–75; Blumhofer, *Restoring the Faith*, 51; Anderson, *Vision of the Disinherited*, 56.

48. For an excellent account of the Restorationist influences in Parham's life, see Blumhofer, *Restoring the Faith*, 43–70.

49. McGrath has developed the notion that doctrine is generated by and interprets narrative through a "hermeneutic spiral." McGrath, *Genesis of Doctrine*, 61.

50. Blumhofer, *Restoring the Faith*, 52.

51. While some Restorationists desired to work hard to recover biblical spirituality and holiness, others, particularly Pentecostals, believed that God's sovereign hand would intervene to restore the church. Blumhofer, *Restoring the Faith*, 13.

The Function of the Doctrine of Initial Evidence

into, based on his Restorationist hermeneutic. It was this hermeneutic that formed the basis for his doctrine of Spirit Baptism. Parham's particular insistence that the tongues speech of Ozman and his other students were known foreign languages was not generated by the experience, but by the narrative of Acts 2 interpreted within a Restorationist hermeneutic. This helps one to understand some of the reasons why Parham was so dogmatic about the need for tongues to be actual foreign languages. Parham could not find a place for tongues as a prayer language or Spirit-led praise and notions of Spirit Baptism as a special anointing in the narrative of Acts.[52] When it came to determining who had been baptized in the Holy Spirit, he needed to be sure. And the only sure thing was an experience that corresponded exactly to that of the apostles. Experience certainly played a role in the future development of Pentecostal theology as many Pentecostal leaders were willing to concede that there appeared to be a difference between the sign of tongues and the gift of tongues. Yet, it is important to recognize that Parham's doctrine originated in the dynamic interaction between the narrative of Scripture and Parham's Restorationist hermeneutic, and not as a response to an unexpected experience.[53]

Not only was Parham's doctrine of the "Bible evidence" *generated* by the Restorationist narrative context within which he interpreted the narrative of Scripture, but the doctrine also *interpreted* the Restorationist narrative of the first Pentecostals. The doctrine suggested that those who spoke in tongues were privy to the first realization of a fully restored church, the likes of which had not been witnessed for over 1800 years. In this respect, the doctrine interpreted the Pentecostal narrative as the narrative of a special group of Christians being called out from among others.[54] For the first Pentecostals, tongues were a special stamp of approval sent directly to them by Jesus, telling them that they were accepted into the Bride and ready to be sent out into the world.[55] The gift was understood as a di-

---

52. It was not until 1906 that Pentecostals began to find a place in the narrative of Acts for tongues as a means of prayer and worship. McGee has argued differently, saying that from the beginning of the movement in 1901 Pentecostals simultaneously upheld an understanding of tongues as a means of preaching on the foreign mission field and tongues as means of praising and worshipping God. McGee, "The New World of Realities," 113–14. However, I have argued that a careful look at the sources suggests that the idea of speaking in tongues as a means of praise and worship does not occur in print earlier than late 1905, and the idea likely originated with Carothers in Houston, Texas. See chapter 2.

53. Faupel, *The Everlasting Gospel*, 168.

54. Blumhofer, *Restoring the Faith*, 14; Wacker, "Playing for Keeps," 204.

55. Parham, *Kol Kare Bomidbar*, 25–27; "A Great Worker," *Apostolic Faith* [Melrose]

vine commissioning and caused many of the early Pentecostals to want to break free from the confines of denominations, so that they could be free to go wherever the Spirit might lead them.[56] Convinced that God would soon set the "true church" in order and purify it of errors in doctrine and teaching, Parham and many other early Pentecostal leaders were opposed to organizations that demanded accent to a creed or leader. Rather than by institutional means, they believed that unity would be accomplished by individuals submitting themselves to God.[57]

While many early Pentecostal leaders were opposed to creeds and formal structures of authority they found in the historic churches, they often felt that they had been given a divine license to speak authoritatively on matters of doctrine and teaching by virtue of their Spirit Baptism. As a result, they began to engage in the very acts of sectarianism and self-promotion that they condemned.[58] This sectarianism and exclusivism became well established in Pentecostal denominations throughout the next

---

1.2 (July 1905) 9. Reprinted from a newspaper article in *Lawrence Kansas World*. W. F. Carothers, "The Baptism with the Holy Ghost," *Apostolic Faith* [Baxter Springs] 1.9 (May 1906) 15–16.

56. Kay, *Pentecostalism*, 55–57.

57. Parham argued that unity could only be accomplished through a process whereby people laid all their "creeds, doctrines, and teachings at Jesus' feet, asking him to cleanse them." For Parham, this cleansing process began when a person was sanctified and culminated in the Baptism of the Holy Spirit. See the chapter on Unity in Parham, *Kol Kare Bomidbar*, 61–68. Carothers also believed that after a Christian was sanctified in their heart, they should continue to have their beliefs and doctrines purged. W. F. Carothers, "The Grace of Sanctification," *Apostolic Faith* [Houston] 1.7 (December 1905) 1–3. However, Carothers was less confident than Parham that Spirit Baptism signified that such a process was complete. At the top of a full page outline, "Full Teachings of the Apostolic Faith Movement," Carothers made it clear that such a statement was provisional, calling it "an individual view . . . not binding upon any individual whatever." W. F. Carothers, "History of Movement," *Apostolic Faith* [Houston] 2.2 (October 1908) 2; W. F. Carothers, "What the Movement Teaches," *Apostolic Faith* [Houston] 2.2 (October 1908) 6.

58. Parham labeled Pentecostals outside his organization as "fanatics," and said, "The first distinguishing signs [sic] of fanaticism is an *unteachable spirit*." Charles F. Parham, "Fanaticism: Fleshly and Familiar Spirits," *Apostolic Faith* [Baxter Springs] (December 1910) 2–4. Seymour argued that those who had been legitimately baptized in the Holy Spirit could not teach wrong doctrine, such as annihilationism. Seymour, *Doctrines and Disciplines*, 52. At the same time that Durham was critical of Pentecostals who felt that their Spirit Baptism guaranteed doctrinal purity he testified that God would not allow *him* to teach a wrong doctrine of sanctification after he was baptized in the Holy Spirit. W. H. Durham, "The Second Work of Grace People Answered," *Pentecostal Testimony* 1 (1911) 9; W. H. Durham, "An Open Letter to My Brother Ministers," *Pentecostal Testimony* 3.2 (1912) 14.

The Function of the Doctrine of Initial Evidence

three decades. When the Assemblies of God formed their Statement of Fundamental Truths in 1916, they maintained that such should not be construed as a creed for the church or a basis for fellowship among Christians.[59] Yet, six years later, their periodical discouraged Pentecostals from working together with Christians who rejected the doctrine of initial evidence.[60] In her ministry throughout the 1920s and 30s, Aimee preached relatively little on the Baptism in the Holy Spirit compared with the Restorationist narrative to which she believed the doctrine of Spirit Baptism testified. She was leading a cultural war, and for Aimee, the Baptism in the Holy Spirit was the weapon of choice, not the battleground.[61] These and other examples show how the classical doctrine of Spirit Baptism led some Pentecostals to interpret their narrative as one of separation and exclusivity.[62]

Restorationism: Holy & Unified

The doctrine of Spirit Baptism that Parham articulated in Kansas met with a different narrative in William Seymour. As a Methodist Episcopal, Seymour was certainly supportive of many aspects of Restorationist thinking such as the soon apocalyptic return of Christ and divine healing, but Seymour was not inclined to give up or undermine his black heritage by adopting Anglo-Israelism.[63] He saw the experience of the Spirit not just as power for personal holiness, but power for God to triumph over injustice and oppression in the social sphere, including racial segregation.[64] Seymour's black heritage and his promotion of racial integration were in conflict with Parham's views of history and eschatology. Jacobsen has noted that while Parham's books and articles are full of prophetic speculation concerning the specific details of future events that were soon to take

---

59. *Minutes of the General Council of the Assemblies of God in the United States of America, Canada and Foreign Lands held at Bethel Chapel, St. Louis, Mo. October 1–7th, 1916*, 10.

60. D. W. Kerr, "The Basis for Our Distinctive Testimony," *Pentecostal Evangel* 460–461 (September 2, 1922) 4.

61. Sutton, *Aimee Semple McPherson*, 49–54.

62. Nienkirchen, "Conflicting Visions of the Past," 120–25.

63. For more on the specifics of Parham's Anglo-Israelist views, see Jacobsen, *Thinking in the Spirit*, 28–46.

64. Robeck, *The Azusa Street Mission*, 50, 137–38; Irvin, "Drawing All Together," 43.

place, Seymour was virtually silent on the subject.[65] Thus, Jacobsen concludes, "At Azusa, biblical prophecy was virtually always used for pastoral purposes. In Charles Parham's theology, things were different. For him, eschatology itself had been key."[66] That Seymour disagreed with Parham not only practically, but also theologically, is evident by his public criticism and denunciation of Parham's belief in eight-day creationism.[67] Both Parham and Seymour agreed that the Book of Acts established speaking in tongues as the unmistakable sign that a person was baptized in the Holy Spirit and that such a sign was being restored to the church in the last days, but they disagreed on the implications of the sign for the future of the church. He reinterpreted Parham's doctrine of the "Bible evidence" within the framework of his own narrative that included African-American spirituality and racial reconciliation.[68]

Years before his meeting with Parham's Apostolic Faith organization in Texas, Seymour was involved in a Holiness group called the Evening Light Saints that heralded the soon return of Christ and the establishment of the one true church. Along with emphasizing personal holiness and divine healing, the group also practiced and promoted racial integration. Unlike Parham, whose Anglo-Israel eschatology was racially hierarchical, the Evening Light Saints promoted a future for the church where racial divisions were no more.[69] Thus, when Seymour came to Los Angeles, he was supportive of racial integration in prayer meetings at Bonnie Brae, and later in services at Azusa Street. He clearly believed that the Baptism in the Holy Spirit that he desired for himself and others transcended racial boundaries.[70] This caused the services at the Azusa Street Mission to become "one of the most racially inclusive, culturally diverse groups to gather in the city of Los Angeles at that time."[71] This fact utterly embarrassed and repulsed Parham. Parham clearly did not want to exclude the possibility of blacks being baptized in the Spirit, but he firmly opposed

---

65. Jacobsen, *Thinking in the Spirit*, 80–83. Only two articles in the Azusa paper go into specific details about future eschatological events, both unsigned: "The Millenium [sic]," *Apostolic Faith* [Los Angeles] 1.1 (September 1906) 3; "Full Overcomers," *Apostolic Faith* [Los Angeles] 1.12 (January 1908) 2.

66. Jacobsen, *Thinking in the Spirit*, 83.

67. *Apostolic Faith* [Los Angeles] 1.4 (December 1906) 1.

68. Faupel, *The Everlasting Gospel*, 209–12; MacRobert, *The Black Roots and White Racism*, 35.

69. MacRobert, *The Black Roots and White Racism*, 49–50.

70. Robeck, "The Social Concern of Early American Pentecostalism," 100–102.

71. Robeck, *The Azusa Street Mission & Revival*, 88.

the interracial contact that occurred at Azusa Street. Rather than seeing such occurrences as a sign of God's favor and presence as Seymour did, Parham saw them as signs of compromise and sinfulness and proof that their claims of Spirit Baptism were false.[72] Yet, for Seymour and many others that would visit the mission, the inclusivity of services at Azusa Street was a sign that God was restoring his true church. In that context, the doctrine of the "Bible evidence" interpreted the Pentecostal narrative as one in which unity and love were being restored through the Baptism in the Holy Spirit and symbolized in the act of speaking in tongues.[73]

Even more distressing to Parham than the close physical contact between races were the various physical manifestations and bodily outbursts of emotion displayed by those seeking the Baptism in the Holy Spirit at Azusa. Parham was vehemently opposed to such things. Instead of attributing the manifestations to the Spirit of God, Parham argued that they were at best, convoluted experiences reminiscent of primitive forms of "negro-worship," or at worst, demon possession.[74] In reference to the "Heavenly Anthem"—corporate expressions of melodic praise through tongues speech that occurred in meetings at Azusa Street—Parham gave the following commentary, "The so called Heavenly Choir was only a modification of the Negro chanting of the Southland, and was not the result of the Pentecostal Baptism."[75] Despite the harshness and blatant racism present in many of Parham's criticisms of Azusa, Parham was right to notice strong elements of black folk spirituality at Azusa. In fact, Walter Hollenweger has argued that Azusa Street represents "an outburst of enthusiastic religion of a kind well-known and frequent" in the history of black churches in America.[76] For many blacks at Azusa, the doctrine of tongues interpreted the narrative of African spirituality. It represented an effusion of black spirituality for the church and acted as a divinely ordered apologetic for their spirituality as a people. For others, the Azusa

72. Charles F. Parham, "Free Love," *Apostolic Faith* [Baxter Springs] 1.10 (December 1912) 4–5; "The Difference Between the Baptism in the Holy Ghost and the Annointing [sic]—Spooks," *Apostolic Faith* [Baxter Springs] 3.2 (February 1914) 9–10.

73. Irvin, "Drawing All Together," 25–53. Irvin notes that perpetual struggles over leadership led Seymour to eventually give up his fight for racial integration in his church, but not before such a vision was infused into the Pentecostal movement.

74. *Apostolic Faith* [Baxter Springs] 1.8 (October 1912) 6; *Apostolic Faith* [Baxter Springs] 1.8 (October 1912 supplement) 2; *Apostolic Faith* [Baxter Springs] 3.5 (July 1914) 8; Charles F. Parham, "Sources of Disease," *Apostolic Faith* [Baxter Springs] 1.6 (August 1912) 4.

75. *Apostolic Faith* [Baxter Springs] (January 1912) 6.

76. Hollenweger, *The Pentecostals*, 23–24.

revivals were less about the promotion of African spirituality and more about combating "dead formalism" in many sectors of the church.[77] The doctrine of Spirit Baptism—a doctrine that understood an unseemly and uncontrollable act of speaking in tongues as that which inaugurated the indwelling presence of the Holy Spirit—interpreted the Pentecostal narrative as a narrative of God's presence being restored to the church in direct opposition to the formalistic worship of the past.

The interpretation of the doctrine of Spirit Baptism given by Pentecostals at Azusa was welcomed by Alexander Boddy. It meshed well with his experience of the Welsh Revivals, it addressed the needs of the working-class that made up his congregation in Sunderland, and it led him to work for the spread of Pentecost around the world through his yearly conferences and monthly periodical. He believed that the Pentecostal movement was best understood as a restoration of unity and primitive spirituality for the entire church.[78] Though such a vision of Pentecostalism was rare in the United States in the era between the wars, Pentecostals involved in the ecumenical movement rekindled it. Many Pentecostals insisted that a quest for visible unity among churches was a prelude to the great apostasy of the church predicted in Revelation. A few, however, believed that working for ecclesial unity was an essential aspect of Spirit-baptized ministry.[79] As the Pentecostal experience later made its way into the historic churches, the classical Pentecostal doctrine was not well received by Charismatics. Yet many were eager to accept the narrative interpretation given to the doctrine by Pentecostals at Azusa Street, a narrative that established the importance of Spirit Baptism for the revitalization of spirituality and ecclesial unity in the church. Over the last three decades, Pentecostal scholarship has been gradually moving away from sectarianism toward ecumenism as the posture that faithfully represents the fundamental Pentecostal narrative.[80] Frank Macchia, in particular, has been helpful in showing how the classical Pentecostal connection between

---

77. W. H. Durham, "Manifestations Number II," *Pentecostal Testimony* 1.5 (July 1, 1910) 7–9.

78. "Sunderland International Pentecostal Congress," *Confidence* 2.6 (June 1909) 127.

79. Robeck, "Taking Stock of Pentecostalism," 39–45; Robeck, "Pentecostals and Ecumenism in a Pluralistic World," 341–44; Robeck, "The Assemblies of God and Ecumenical Cooperation," 107–50.

80. Macchia, "The Struggle for Global Witness," 24–26. Land, *Pentecostal Spirituality*. While this move away from sectarianism has taken place at a scholarly level, it has yet to receive widespread acceptance or implementation at an ecclesial level.

tongues and Spirit Baptism supports a narrative of social justice, spiritual freedom, and the in-breaking of the kingdom of God.[81]

Interpretation of Experience

When Seymour took Parham's doctrine of the "Bible evidence" to Azusa Street, he and others were convinced that they ought to seek out and receive (in God's timing) the experience that the apostles received on the Day of Pentecost. Initially, their exposition of this experience in the Azusa Street Paper was indistinguishable from Parham's. However, as was shown in chapter 2, soon there was a critical reevaluation of Parham's doctrine that took place following their shared experience of the Spirit reflected upon with the biblical text. They began to question the value of tongues for the mission field while they championed the value of tongues for prayer and worship. They also began to draw a distinction between evidential or sign tongues and the gift of tongues. Given these shifts in the way early Pentecostals understood tongues speech and its relationship to Spirit Baptism, it would seem likely that doctrinal statements would also change to accommodate these developments. The reality, however, is that early Pentecostal doctrinal statements concerning tongues and Spirit Baptism changed very little even as theological and biblical expositions of their shared experience changed dramatically. Clifton argues, "It was shared experience which led to the key elements of the Pentecostal doctrine."[82] There are certainly aspects of classical Pentecostal doctrinal statements that were derived from their experience. Striking, however, are the aspects of Pentecostal shared experience that were not formally stated in doctrinal statements. In fact, it seems to be the case that early Pentecostal organizations deliberately avoided codifying certain aspects of their experience of the Spirit even as they sought to formalize statements about their guiding beliefs and principles. They seem to have implicitly recognized that there were many aspects of their experience that could not adequately be put into words.[83] There are, however, three important ways in which the doctrine of Spirit Baptism in classical Pentecostalism has functioned as an interpretation of their collective experience.

---

81. Macchia, "The Struggle for Global Witness," 16–18; Macchia, *Baptized in the Spirit*, 212–18.

82. Clifton, "The Spirit and Doctrinal Development," 13.

83. Warrington, "Experience."

Norming the Abnormal

A Biblical Experience

Firstly, the doctrine of initial evidence interpreted the experience of Pentecostals as one that was rooted in Scripture. No matter how unusual, unseemly or off-putting the experience was for some, there was precedent for such an experience in the New Testament; the apostles had the same experience and it was given a specific name by Jesus. Alongside Pentecostals, there were critics who believed that the experience opened the door to excessive spiritualism and demonic influence. The fact that tongues was recorded in Scripture, and that Scripture validated and legitimated the experiences of Spirit Baptism recorded in Acts, gave early Pentecostals confidence and boldness to seek such an experience in the face of possible counterfeit or fleshly manifestations.[84] In his first publication on the subject, Parham called tongues the "Bible evidence," and Seymour's mission adopted this language. In the first issue of *Confidence*, Boddy called tongues the "scriptural sign" of the Baptism in the Holy Spirit. Many later Pentecostals would feel that a rigid doctrine of tongues as *the* "sign" or "evidence" of Spirit Baptism was moving beyond the clear teachings of Scripture, but all agreed that their experience of speaking in tongues was strongly supported and encouraged in Scripture.[85] As the religious and social backgrounds of those who experienced speaking in tongues became more diverse and cessationist theology began to fade in popularity, defending the scriptural veracity of the experience became less important. Instead, the strong scriptural support for the Pentecostal experience was recognized by non-Pentecostal groups and increasingly accepted as valid by groups of Evangelicals and Fundamentalists in North America.[86]

---

84. Parham, *Kol Kare Bomidbar*, 25–28. William J. Seymour, "Counterfeits," *Apostolic Faith* [Los Angeles] 1.4 (December 1906): 2. A. A. Boddy, "Seven Hallmarks of Heaven upon the Pentecostal Baptism with the Sign of Tongues," *Confidence* 2.8 (August 1909) 180–83. "Declaration : International Advisory Pentecostal Council. 3rd session at Sunderland," *Confidence* 6.7 (July 1913) 7. W. H. Durham, "The Great Crisis, Number Two," *Pentecostal Testimony* 1.5 (July 1, 1910) 1–4. E. N. Bell, "The Good of Speaking in Tongues," *Word and Witness* 8.6 (August 20, 1912) 4. "Discerning of Spirits," *Latter Rain Evangel* (December 1923) 14–16. Aimee Semple McPherson, "The Baptism of the Holy Spirit," *Bridal Call Foursquare* 9.8 (January 1926) 11.

85. McGee, "Early Pentecostal Hermeneutics," 96–118.

86. This is not to say that Evangelicals accepted Pentecostal explanations of their experience. They simply allowed that such an experience was biblical, and they formed their own explanations of the experience. Menzies, "The Challenges of Organization and Spirit," 125–28.

The Function of the Doctrine of Initial Evidence

A Gateway Experience

Secondly, the doctrine of initial evidence interpreted the experience of Pentecostals as the starting point for a new phase of relationship with Jesus marked by the power of the Holy Spirit. Though a period of circumspection, confession, worship or prayer often paved the way, Pentecostals understood Spirit Baptism as an experience that took place at a moment in time and not as a process. Pentecostals usually dated their experience of Spirit Baptism to the instance when they first began to speak in tongues.[87] Many corroborated this by testifying to a noticeable difference in their spiritual lives before and after they initially spoke in tongues. In December 1909, A. A. Boddy and many other European Pentecostal leaders made a point to specify that Spirit Baptism should be understood as a "Gate, not Goal."[88] This perspective became especially common among Pentecostals that accepted Durham's "finished-work" doctrine because it relinquished the need for an intermediary step between salvation and Spirit Baptism. Prior to Durham, sanctification had been understood as a prelude to the baptism so that speaking in tongues not only acted as evidence that one was baptized in the Holy Spirit, but it also acted, by way of implication, as an external verification that one was sanctified. Those who accepted Durham's teaching understood sanctification as a life-long process that was entered into upon conversion and which could be neither validated nor invalidated by the Baptism in the Holy Spirit.

If Pentecostals agreed that their Spirit Baptism should be understood as a gateway experience, they were not in agreement about what specifically was instituted by the experience. Speaking in tongues was only a small piece, and even about this, they disagreed whether it would stay.[89] Though speaking in tongues was understood as the *initial* evidence of the Bap-

---

87. This, however, was by no means a rule in the early Pentecostal movement. The majority of Pentecostals testified that their Spirit Baptism occurred in conjunction with speaking in tongues. But there were others who believed there was a delay between their Baptism and the first sign of tongues speech. Robeck, "An Emerging Magisterium?" 217–37.

88. "A London Declaration," *Confidence* 2.12 (December 1909) 288.

89 In the Assemblies of God, E. N. Bell, made it clear that those who were baptized in the Holy Spirit may only speak in tongues once and never again. E. N. Bell, "A Correction," *Christian Evangel* 252–253 (August 24, 1918) 7. Many years later, official position papers meant to clarify points of doctrine in the Statement of Fundamental Truths argued that tongues should be used devotionally in prayer by all Spirit-baptized Christians. *The Initial Physical Evidence of the Baptism in the Holy Spirit*, 11–12; *The Baptism in the Holy Spirit: The Initial Experience and Continuing Evidences of the Spirit Filled Life*, 6–8.

tism in the Holy Spirit, early Pentecostals argued that it was not the *only* evidence. Over time, many other results besides tongues would manifest themselves. Thus, it became common for Pentecostals to advise those who desired to be baptized in the Holy Spirit to seek the Baptism, not tongues. When describing the results of Spirit Baptism, Pentecostals were generally compelled to use some version of the language of Acts 1:8: "power for witnessing." But when it came to explaining the power, there were a lot of opinions. The Assemblies of God doctrine said that through Spirit Baptism, the gifts were bestowed for their use in ministry.[90] Foursquare and Open Bible did not make an explicit connection between gifts of the Spirit and Spirit Baptism. Rather, their doctrine attributed a wide range of results to Spirit Baptism including power for worship, power for inspired preaching, and power for evangelism.[91] Third-Wavers and Charismatics upheld the validity of Pentecostal experience, but interpreted it very differently. Their emphasis was upon the experience of the gifts themselves and the spiritual and ministerial effects that were added to their lives because of them. By and large, Charismatics did not interpret Pentecostal experience as a gateway experience that ushered in power in a variety of ways. Rather, they interpreted it as the culmination of a gradual process of spiritual growth.

A Sacramental Experience

Third, the doctrine of initial evidence has interpreted the Pentecostal experience of speaking in tongues as a sacramental experience. Though their opposition to institutionalized and liturgical forms of worship caused Pentecostals to refrain from using sacramental terminology, Macchia has shown that the doctrine of initial evidence has often retained a sacramental force in the Pentecostal community. "Pentecostals have not connected tongues to Spirit Baptism by a capricious external law, but through a theology of Spirit Baptism that includes tongues as an integral aspect of

---

90. *Minutes of the General Council of the Assemblies of God in the United States of America, Canada and Foreign Lands held at Bethel Chapel, St. Louis, Mo. October 1–7th, 1916,* 10. In 1961, the General Council provided a more specific explanation of some of the benefits of Spirit Baptism. They included: "overflowing fullness of the Spirit," "a deepened reverence for God," "an intensified consecration to God," and "a more active love for Christ, His Word and for the lost." Quoted in Robeck, "An Emerging Magisterium?" 239.

91. McPherson, *Declaration of Faith,* 16–17; *Policies and Principles of the Open Bible Standard Churches* (1940), 45.

the experience. . . . Pentecostals cannot separate tongues from one's initial experience of the Spirit in Spirit Baptism."[92] The Pentecostal doctrine is not solely based on a scriptural pattern in Acts, but also upon a unique encounter with God that is consistently signified in the act of speaking in tongues. It is, as Macchia puts it, "a visible context in which the experience of God is received and manifested."[93]

It was the increasingly sacramental understanding of tongues in early Pentecostalism that allowed tongues to remain at the center of Pentecostal experience even after the notion of tongues as a primary means of witnessing on the foreign mission field was abandoned. For early Pentecostals, the narrative of Acts not only established the precedent of tongues as evidence of Spirit Baptism, but it also told the story of individuals and communities that were radically transformed and empowered by an experience of God that was visibly signified in the act of speaking in tongues. The doctrine of initial evidence interpreted the act of speaking in tongues as the objective sign by which the believer enters into a new level of spiritual empowerment commensurate with that demonstrated by the apostles.[94]

Social Demarcation

Perhaps the most obvious function the doctrine of initial evidence has for the Pentecostal community is providing social definition. In fact, the focal point of the doctrine itself is the identification of tongues as an objective criterion for proving or validating an individual's experience of Spirit Baptism before a community.[95] Yet, such doctrinal statements were not the primary means by which Pentecostals distinguished themselves from outsiders early in the movement. While a doctrinal statement that formally connected speaking in tongues with a genuine experience of Spirit Baptism was integral to the self-definition of the majority of Pentecostal

---

92. Macchia, "Tongues as a Sign," 68.

93. Ibid., 70.

94. Simon Chan argues that a sacramental understanding of tongues is most easily recognized in the Pentecostal idea of tongues as "prayer language" rather than tongues as "initial evidence." As a prayer language, tongues functions not just as a singular theophany, but also as an "indeolect" for a new level of intimacy with God. Chan, *Pentecostal Theology*, 78.

95. In his first published writing on the subject, Parham emphasized the importance of having the Bible evidence of Spirit Baptism over against "*private* interpretations" of the Holy Spirit's "visible manifestations." Parham, *Kol Kare Bomidbar*, 27 (italics mine).

groups in North America, for outsiders it was the presence of tongues speech more than the doctrine of tongues that defined a Pentecostal venue, meeting, or worship service. Because early Pentecostals were alone in their use of tongues, they were more apt to be recognized socially as "tongue-speakers," not "initial-evidence believers." As a point of social definition, early Pentecostals tended to regret that tongues took such a prominent role. Pentecostals wanted to be marked as those who were more full of divine love, more devoted to Jesus or more fruitful in ministry, and not simply as those who spoke in tongues. Yet the uniqueness of the phenomenon of tongues speech and its ridicule by non-Pentecostal groups made it the defining characteristic of the earliest Pentecostals.

Defining Pentecostals vs. Non-Pentecostals

As more Holiness Christians began to accept glossolalia as a spiritual gift, debate concerning the availability of tongues for *all* Christians became more prominent. This debate caused the doctrine of initial evidence to begin to replace speaking in tongues as the defining characteristic of Pentecostals. In September 1907, G. F. Taylor published arguably the first book length Pentecostal treatise where, in response to those who looked favorably on tongues but had reservations about the doctrine of initial evidence, he argued that such a stance was essential for the Pentecostal movement and that if Pentecostals began to preach against the doctrine, the revival would end.[96] The Fire-Baptized Holiness Church, led by J. H. King, was the first denomination to include a doctrine of initial evidence in their articles of faith. This came in 1908 after King, who already encouraged speaking in tongues, became convinced that one could draw a distinction between the gift and sign of tongues. He further believed that his periodical would not faithfully represent the Pentecostal message without censoring articles that disagreed with the doctrine.[97] On the other hand, William H. Piper, editor of *The Latter Rain Evangel*, accepted and promoted the validity of the Pentecostal experience but said that he would not join the "[m]ultitudes in the movement with a theological chip on their shoulder" in their dogmatic stance on evidential tongues.[98] When

---

96. Taylor, *The Spirit and the Bride*, 45.

97. "Transformed by the Holy Ghost," *Apostolic Faith* [Los Angeles] 1.6 (February-March 1907) 5. See also *Constitution and General Rules of the Fire-Baptized Holiness Church, 1908*, 3.

98. "Manifestations and 'Demonstrations' of the Spirit: Evidence of the Baptism

W. H. Durham began publishing his periodical, *Pentecostal Testimony*, in 1909, the doctrine was far from unanimous among those who claimed to be Pentecostal. In 1910, Durham attacked the position of Piper's paper and all those who would hold to such a position quietly because they feared it would cause division or degrade the spirituality of past saints.[99] Durham further claimed that the doctrine had suffered incalculable consequences as a result of "those who claim to be Pentecostal people, and at the same time deny this great distinguishing truth of the movement."[100] Though the examples above represent a distinct move among some Pentecostals to move toward a doctrine of initial evidence as their defining characteristic during this time, it was by no means unanimous. It was not until the formation of the Assemblies of God in 1914 that the doctrine gained widespread recognition as the defining characteristic of Pentecostals.

Through the influence of E. N. Bell and Mack Pinson, Durham's teachings on sanctification and tongues came to be established in the Assemblies of God's Statement of Fundamental Truths in 1916. The decision by the Assemblies of God in 1918, in response to the Bosworth controversy, to identify the doctrine of initial evidence as "the distinctive testimony of the Pentecostal people" made the doctrine's function as a social boundary explicit.[101] In 1920, J. R. Flower argued that without the doctrine of initial evidence, the Assemblies of God had "no right to an existence as a body of people." He went on to contend for the doctrine as the point upon which "the very life of the Pentecostal movement" depended.[102] Such a desire for the organization, and Pentecostals in general, to be defined and validated by a single doctrine seems a far cry from the posture taken by E. N. Bell and the General Council at the formation of the organization four years earlier to join together for five practical purposes, only one of

---

in the Holy Spirit," *Latter Rain Evangel* 1.1 (October 1908) 19; "What Meaneth this Speaking in Tongues?" *Latter Rain Evangel* 1.1 (October 1908) 15. See also Blumhofer, "William Hamner Piper," 990.

99. W. H. Durham, "Criticisms Answered," *Pentecostal Testimony* 1.5 (July 1910) 11; "An Open Letter to my Brother Ministers," *Pentecostal Testimony* 2.3 (1912) 13, reprint from *Pentecostal Testimony* 1.8.

100. W. H. Durham, "Speaking in Tongues is the Evidence of the Baptism in the Holy Spirit," *Pentecostal Testimony* 2.2 (1912) 9.

101. *Minutes from the Sixth Annual Meeting of the General Council of the Assemblies of God in the United States of America, Canada, and Foreign Lands held at Springfield, Missouri Sept. 4–11, 1918*, 8.

102. J. R. Flower, "Do All Speak with Tongues?" *Pentecostal Evangel* 336–37 (April 17, 1920) 4.

which involved doctrine.[103] Although the formal declaration of the doctrine of initial evidence as their distinctive testimony was removed from the Assemblies of God's articles of faith in 1927, the doctrine was already firmly established in North America as the defining doctrine of Pentecostals, and which alone separated them from Evangelicals.[104] Pentecostal denominations that did not have an explicit doctrine of initial evidence, such as Open Bible Standard Churches and the International Church of the Foursquare Gospel, often chose to align themselves with those that did.[105] In 1927, the committee charged with reviewing, appending, and updating the bylaws of the Assemblies of God formally proposed that the organization change its name to The Pentecostal Evangelical Church.[106] Though the name change was never adopted, the proposal shows just how strong the impulse was for Pentecostals to identify themselves as "Evangelicals plus tongues."[107]

One Pentecostal organization that refused to be defined by tongues or a doctrine of initial evidence was the Christian and Missionary Alliance (CMA). The organization and its founder, A. B. Simpson, were held in high regard by first generation Pentecostal leaders, many of whom re-printed and recommended Simpson's writings in their own periodicals. Early on, the presence of Pentecostal phenomena such as healing and tongues in CMA meetings and the apologetics of such phenomena by CMA leaders caused the CMA to be understood as a Pentecostal organization. However, the CMA debated the merits of the doctrine of initial evidence and finally decided against such a doctrine, adopting instead a "seek not, forbid not" rule.[108] Their decision to uphold the validity of tongues speech without upholding a doctrine of initial evidence caused many to see the CMA as compromising the Pentecostal faith. On this basis, many left the organiza-

---

103. E. N. Bell, "General Convention of Pentecostal Saints and Churches of God in Christ," *Word and Witness* 9.12 (December 20, 1913) 1. *Minutes of the General Council of the Assemblies of God in the United States of America, Canada and Foreign Lands Held at Hot Springs, Ark. April 2–12, 1914*, 4.

104. Donald Gee, "Shall We Give Up Tongues?" *Pentecostal Evangel* 587 (March 7, 1925) 6.

105. *Policies and Principles of the Open Bible Standard Churches, Inc.* (1940), 45. McPherson, *Declaration of Faith*, 16–17.

106. *Final Report of Revision Committee on Essential Resolutions Presented at the 1927 General Council*, 4.

107. Poloma, "Charisma and Structure," 89.

108. Although this phraseology did not officially become a part of CMA doctrine until 1963, Paul King has documented that this view was common among CMA ministers by the late 1930s. King, *Genuine Gold*, 238.

tion.[109] Such reactions show how, in North America, the doctrine of initial evidence effectively replaced the phenomenon of tongues as that which demarcated Pentecostals socially. As Pentecostals formed fellowships and participated in ecumenical discussions in the decades immediately following WWII, the doctrine of initial evidence retained its status as the defining characteristic of Pentecostalism.

Defining Pentecostals vs. Charismatics

If the historic corner on tongues by Pentecostals began to be called into question by the CMA debate of the 1920s, it culminated in the Charismatic movement that swept across North America in the 1960s. Pentecostals, even in North America, could no longer be defined by their allowance and appreciation for private and public experiences of speaking in tongues. If Pentecostals were to be defined by the presence of enthusiastic charisms in their worship services, it could only be as a matter of degrees, not absolutes. In some cases, differences between Pentecostals and Charismatic worship services were difficult, if not impossible, to detect. Yet, behind the similar expressions in worship services were strikingly different ways of interpreting the expressions. These doctrinal distinctives—in particular, the doctrines of initial evidence and subsequence—increasingly came to be seen as that which defined Pentecostals. Lest they be considered outsiders, this renewed emphasis on the doctrine of initial evidence as that which socially demarcated Pentecostals led some denominations to be more forthright in their promotion of the doctrine.

As the doctrine of initial evidence became a defining point of Pentecostal denominations on paper, it became a point of contention among laity in Pentecostal churches. Where differences of opinion and belief concerning the doctrine of initial evidence had galvanized the Pentecostal movement previously, the growing Charismatic movement began to cause an identity crisis among Pentecostals in North America. Fearing that their theological distinctiveness might be compromised by some of their ministers, in 1960 and 1961 the Assemblies of God adopted a policy of annually asking credentialed ministers three questions: one concerning the minister's unequivocal belief in the Statement of Fundament Truths, another concerning the minister's commitment to publicly proclaim the Fundamental Truths from the pulpit, and a final question asking for the

---

109. Kay, *Pentecostalism*, 56; van de Walle, *The Heart of the Gospel*, 20. See also Synan, "The Role of Tongues as Initial Evidence," 72–75.

minister's commitment to six specific doctrines. The first of the six doctrines was the doctrine of initial evidence.[110] Despite the effort of Pentecostal denominations to shore up commitment to their most distinctive tenet, the criticisms Charismatics brought against the doctrine of initial evidence were theologically significant enough that they could not be dismissed without serious consideration and the development of forceful counter arguments. It took some time for Pentecostal scholars to develop their position, and in the process, the doctrine of initial evidence lost some of its force as that which socially demarcated Pentecostals.

It was not only the scholarly criticism that mainline denominations levied against the doctrine of initial evidence that caused some Pentecostals to question the doctrine's status as the defining point for Pentecostals. Rapid growth of Third-Wave and Charismatic congregations began to call into question the long-held conviction among Pentecostal leaders that where the doctrine of initial evidence is not believed and preached, people will not be baptized in the Holy Spirit. Based on this conviction, some Pentecostals have argued that a strong commitment to the doctrine of initial evidence is a necessary prerequisite for revival to breakout in their churches. Vinson Synan has shown that there is historical evidence to suggest that this has been true in the past.[111] Yet, recent empirical evidence suggests that, in North America, Charismatics are actually more likely than Pentecostals to speak in tongues on a regular basis. A 2006 survey by the Pew Forum on Religion & Public Life found that only 33 percent of individuals self-identified as Pentecostals in the United States claim to speak in tongues weekly or more while 49 percent admit they never speak in tongues.[112] In contrast, 50 percent of those self-identified as Charismatics said that they speak in tongues weekly or more.

Whereas the classical Pentecostal movement had been a bastion for revival in North America up until 1950, Margaret Poloma has observed that more recent revivals have tended to originate in environments less bureaucratic and more loosely structured, the result being that revivals such as the "Toronto Blessing" and "Pensacola Outpouring" have acted as significant sources of renewal and controversy for classical Pentecostal organizations.[113] Although speaking in tongues was common in

110. Menzies, "The Challenges of Organization and Spirit," 126–27.
111. Synan, "The Role of Tongues as Initial Evidence," 67–82.
112. *Spirit and Power: A 10-Country Survey of Penteco*stals, 14.
113. Although the "Pensacola Outpouring" originated in a classical Pentecostal congregation, Brownsville Assembly of God, the denomination was divided about how to respond to it. Poloma, "Charisma and Structure," 46.

The Function of the Doctrine of Initial Evidence

these revivals, other charismatic manifestations such as physical healing, personal prophecy, demonic deliverance, being "slain in the Spirit," and "holy laughter" were also frequent in services.[114] The relative absence of these non-glossolalic experiences among ministers and congregations in the Assemblies of God suggests that a rigid doctrine of initial evidence may actually impede revival if it causes one to place undue emphasis on tongues as an indicator of the Spirit's presence and revival at the expense of other charismatic activity that have been central to revival and renewal movements of the past.[115]

Defining Pentecostals vs. Evangelicals

Since about 1970, Pentecostals have not only experienced an identity crisis in their relationship with Charismatics, but also in their intentionally close relationship with Evangelicals. Spittler has observed that in the era following the Vietnam War, "Pentecostal beliefs and practices were increasingly absorbed into mainstream churches." The result was that it became harder to distinguish Pentecostals from mainstream Evangelicals.[116] According to McGee, this blurring of the line between Pentecostals and Evangelicals cleared the way for the emergence of "innovative 'Evangelical/ Pentecostal' models of worship and mission, . . . ones that affirm the charismatic dimension of spirituality in various ways but do not require tongues."[117] The undeniable growth that has taken place in churches that have embraced these integrated models of worship and mission have led to discussion among denominational leaders about what constitutes a legitimate Pentecostal revival.

For the leaders of the Assemblies of God, a supernatural worldview that stresses the Baptism in the Holy Spirit accompanied by speaking in tongues and other charismatic activity is foundational for revival. McGee notes that a "decline of speaking in tongues among constituents and lingering questions among ministers about the exegetical mooring of the doctrine of initial evidence" has moved denominational officials to look

---

114. Poloma, "The 'Toronto Blessing' in Postmodern Society," 369; Poloma, *Main Street Mystics*, 87–88, 123–24.

115. Poloma, "Charisma and Structure," 60–63

116. Spittler, "Are Pentecostals and Charismatics Fundamentalists?" 112–13. Spittler identifies two eras in the historical relationship between Evangelicals and Pentecostals: the "Evangelicalization of Pentecostals" (1940–70) and the "Pentecostalization of Evangelicals" (1970–95).

117. McGee, "More than Evangelical," 297.

for new ways in recent years to strengthen their position on initial evidence to gain a more enthusiastic acceptance among their ministers and congregations.[118]

Despite their efforts, it seems that things are moving in the opposite direction. Earl Creps has documented a growing group of ministers in the Assemblies of God that he classifies as "post-distinctive Pentecostals." While retaining a deep affection and love for their denomination and their Pentecostal heritage, this group is concerned about any theology that would impose a predictable template or rule on charismatic experience. As a result, they are not likely to propagate a rigid doctrine of initial evidence in their congregations either from their pulpits or in private. Mostly, this group chooses to remain silent on the issue for fear of igniting conflict with denominational officials. Far from unanimously rejecting the doctrine of initial evidence, this group is simply opposed to seeing the doctrine as essential for Pentecostal identity. They want some allowance for flexibility and conversation on the topic, so that the doctrine might be updated and articulated in community without a fear of being ostracized or dismissed.[119] Within the Assemblies of God, this flexible rather than dogmatic view of initial evidence doctrine has not reached the highest executives. Rather, they seem to view such flexibility as a "watered-down" form of Pentecostalism. Thus, the influence of post-distinctive Pentecostalism is more easily seen in worship services than in official statements or doctrinal changes.

Other classical Pentecostal denominations have moved in a different direction. Open Bible has seen doctrinal flexibility as an important attribute of a denomination that seeks to communicate clearly and reach new generations. Following this commitment, Open Bible made changes in 2003 to the way it articulates its doctrines on the Baptism in the Holy Spirit and eschatology.[120] Concerning Spirit Baptism, Open Bible changed their Articles of Faith from a classical Pentecostal statement on initial evidence to the following: "Consistent with biblical accounts, believers may anticipate Spirit-baptism to be accompanied by speaking in tongues and other biblical manifestations."[121] One of their stated purposes in doing so was to "be as inclusive as possible, without diluting who we are

---

118. Ibid., 298–300.
119. Creps, "Postmodern Pentecostals?" 33–36.
120. Cole, "Heritage and Horizons," 165.
121. Johnson, "Transformations," 4–5.

as Pentecostals."[122] Clearly, Open Bible's constituency was in agreement that a doctrine of initial evidence was not essential to their identity as Pentecostals. In 2002, Foursquare, who had previously been inclined to advocate the doctrine of initial evidence to its constituency, also decided to assess themselves regarding their "availability to the intimacy and fullness of the Holy Spirit."[123] In doing so, Foursquare assigned a six-person committee to review their Statement of Faith, particularly regarding their stance on the Baptism in the Holy Spirit. The committee concluded that the statement, first put forward by Aimee Semple McPherson in 1914 that included no explicit doctrine of initial evidence, needed no revision, and reaffirmed their commitment to the document that they felt was crafted in such a way as to be appreciated and appropriated by later generations.[124]

Recent trends in Pentecostal theology have been toward establishing a theology that is organically connected to the origins of the movement rather than a single doctrine tacked on to Evangelical theology. Donald Dayton has argued that it is only by "bracketing" tongues that one can get at the core theology of the Pentecostal movement. Dayton proposes that Pentecostalism naturally emerged out of the Holiness movement and that at its core are four interdependent emphases: Jesus Christ as Savior, Healer, Baptizer in the Holy Spirit, and Coming King.[125] The eschatology component of Dayton's gestalt has been singled out by D. William Faupel as the theological driving force behind the Pentecostal movement. Not wishing to discredit the importance of Latter-Rain eschatology for Pentecostalism that Faupel has identified in Pentecostal history, Frank Macchia has focused on the concept of Baptism in the Holy Spirit as the central component of Pentecostal theology. Other Pentecostal theologians would argue that Pentecostals miss the mark entirely when they attempt to distinguish themselves either by a single doctrine or belief system, and that their real defining point is their experience, in particular their emphasis on a personal encounter with God.[126]

---

122. *National Convention Business Meeting Minutes, June 21, 2003*, 9.

123. Risser, "79th Annual Foursquare Convention Opens in Denver, Colorado," *Foursquare News Source* 130 (April 10, 2002) 1.

124. Paul Risser, "The Year 2001 Was One of the Most Fruitful," *Fore Cast* 3.1 (2002) 1. Though not explicitly stated, it is probable that one of the questions considered by the committee was whether to revise their Statement of Faith to include a statement on initial evidence.

125. Dayton, *Theological Roots of Pentecostalism*, 173.

126. Warrington, "Experience," 5. Warrington argues that it is the expectancy "to touch and be touched by God" that stands at the core of Pentecostal experience and

Truth Claim

An important function of doctrine throughout the history of the Christian church has been that of making truth claims. Although a doctrinal statement will likely serve interpretive and social functions for the community of faith, its primary reason for existing is to identify an essential component of the faith that has implications for all people.[127] Thus, Christians have traditionally held that the doctrines to which they assent have some degree of ontological reference even if they are stated in culturally and historically conditioned language. This ontological reference point is different depending upon the particular doctrine in question. Most Christian doctrines, however, make truth claims that are either implicitly or explicitly connected to the history of Jesus Christ as communicated through the narratives of Scripture and tradition. In as far as a doctrine's cognitive force is rooted in the ontological reality of Jesus Christ, then a doctrine can be rightly said to make a first-order truth claim.

There is no question that the vast majority of Pentecostals have understood doctrine to make first-order, ontological truth claims based upon their view of Scripture as a source of inerrant propositional truth. There are, however, other kinds of truth claims that a doctrine can make. McGrath has identified three ways in which Christian doctrine functions as truth claims for the community of faith: interpreting the Christ-event, ensuring the internal consistency of the Christian faith, and evoking appropriate responses to the Christ-event.[128] The first of McGrath's categories is concerned with first-order or ontological truth claims, the other two are

---

which justifies the existence of a Pentecostal theology as much or more than their beliefs and practices. See also Warrington, *Pentecostal Theology*.

127. McGrath notes, "Doctrines are not invented to serve social functions . . . rather, their claims to truth are foundational for their social function." McGrath, *The Genesis of Doctrine*, 80.

128. In his truth claim category, McGrath assumes a correspondence theory of truth over against the coherence and pragmatic theories to which Lindbeck and Yong subscribe respectively. McGrath holds that for a doctrine to be considered true it must correspond, albeit inadequately, with "the reality of the living God, incarnate in Jesus Christ." Thus, while McGrath appreciates that coherence is an important test of the truth of a doctrine, it is not the only test. Building on the arguments developed by Thomas Torrance, McGrath argues that true doctrine must correspond *and* cohere. This philosophical presupposition is behind much of the problems that McGrath identifies in Lindbeck's cultural-lingusitic approach to doctrine. McGrath, *Theological Science*, 1:75–76, 2:19–20; *The Genesis of Doctrine*, 72–76. See also Torrance, *Theological Science*, 141–202. For an excellent summary of these three theories of truth, see Cartledge, *Practical Theology*, 42–45.

concerned with second-order or intra-systematic truth claims.[129] While Pentecostals have certainly favored the first, all three levels of truth claims may be identified in the history of the classical Pentecostal tradition.

Interpreting the Christ-Event

According to McGrath, doctrine seeks to make a truth claim about the significance of the history of Jesus Christ as transmitted in the narratives of the Christian tradition.[130] Important for the Pentecostal is the historical promise made by Jesus Christ to his disciples that he would baptize them with the Holy Spirit. Based on the fulfillment of that promise recorded in the narratives of the Book of Acts, Pentecostals have made an assertion about the present reality of the Holy Spirit. Specifically, they have claimed that *the full empowering presence of the Holy Spirit that Jesus Christ desires His Church to receive will result in the manifestation of speaking in other tongues.* The controversial implication of the Pentecostal's truth claim is that Christians who have spoken in tongues have a fuller experience of the Holy Spirit than Christians who have not spoken in tongues.[131] At times, those outside the Pentecostal movement have elucidated this truth claim better than Pentecostals have themselves.[132]

Much of the debate about the doctrine of initial evidence between Pentecostals and non-Pentecostals has centered on the Pentecostal's desire to make the above truth claim a part of the Christian credo. As Macchia puts it,

> There are many who feel that the Pentecostals have elevated tongues far beyond the teaching of scripture in granting them such doctrinal and confessional status. Some would even conclude that we have thereby elevated our own sense of self-importance as among the only bearers of the Spirit's fullness, since we are among the only ones who speak in tongues.[133]

---

129. Here, I am applying Lindbeck's categories of first and second-order truth claims to McGrath's divisions. Lindbeck, *The Nature of Doctrine*, 80.

130. McGrath, *The Genesis of Doctrine*, 76.

131. I have here used the word "fuller" to describe the Pentecostal's view that the Holy Spirit comes upon all Christians at the moment of salvation, but that there remains another dimension of the Spirit that is particularly connected to speaking in tongues that Pentecostals term the Baptism in the Holy Spirit.

132. Bruner, *Theology of the Holy Spirit*, 281–82. Donald Gee, "The Challenge of 'Tongues' Today," *Pentecostal Evangel* 1631 (August 11, 1945) 1.

133. Macchia, "Groans Too Deep For Words," 151.

Pentecostals have been heavily criticized by some theologians and biblical scholars for basing their distinctive doctrine solely on the narrative portions of Acts. Some Pentecostals would even argue that it is questionable whether such a defense "still carries cognitive force."[134] To use McGrath's terminology, the first-order propositional truth claim of the doctrine of initial evidence has been increasingly called into question as a matter of orthodoxy for Pentecostals because it is no longer seen as an adequate answer to the questions regarding a Spirit-filled life that arise from the history of Jesus of Nazareth.[135]

Yet, even Pentecostals who fully recognize the inadequacy of the doctrine of initial evidence as a first-order truth claim, have not been quick to dismiss it. Some of this resistance is surely due to the well-founded feeling that their identity as a group is wrapped up in the doctrine. As Lindbeck notes, "A religious body cannot exist as a recognizably distinctive collectivity unless it has some beliefs and/or practices by which it can be identified."[136] Another, and perhaps more common, reason for Pentecostals to have reservations about getting rid of the controversial doctrine is that they feel the doctrine gets at some important second-order truth claims about the reality of the Spirit-filled life to which they assent. These intrasystematic truth claims cannot be understood apart from the language of the Christian faith. In fact, the best way to understand them is within the cultural-linguistic tradition of the Restorationist-Holiness groups that first formulated the doctrine. As such, the truth claims have little value for those that stand outside the Christian faith. Yet, among those familiar with the language of faith, the truth claims may be quite valuable for fostering ecumenical dialogue and mutual accountability. It is to these second-order truth claims for which the doctrine of initial evidence has functioned as a support that we now turn.

Ensuring Internal Consistency

Few Pentecostals would argue that the doctrine of initial evidence is a matter of salvific importance. Pentecostals have traditionally upheld the presence of the Holy Spirit in the lives of all Christians. Thus, the Pentecostal would be more likely to label those opposed to the doctrine of initial evidence as ill-informed rather than heretical. Yet, Pentecostals

---

134. Clifton, "The Spirit and Doctrinal Development," 19.
135. McGrath, *The Genesis of Doctrine*, 74–76.
136. Lindbeck, *The Nature of Doctrine*, 74.

would argue that tongues signifies the Christian's achievement of a unique connectedness with God that is essential for vibrant worship, prayer and ministry in the world, and which could be said to be absent without tongues. To that end, the doctrine of initial evidence serves the Pentecostal community by normalizing certain aspects of the Christian's experience of the Holy Spirit. The doctrine ensures that there is internal consistency between those who claim to have the fullness of the Spirit's presence and the manifestations of that presence. According to McGrath, this kind of truth claim establishes its authority upon the basis of its logical consistency with other foundational Christian truths, rather than its isolated presence in the historical and biblical canons of the church.[137]

Simon Chan has argued that the doctrine of initial evidence may be best defended as this type of truth claim. He argues,

> The doctrine of "initial evidence" as it stands is difficult to defend as long as we try to do it on the basis of historical or biblical evidence. But I would like to argue . . . that it can be coherently understood if we could establish the logical relationship between glossolalia and Spirit-baptism.[138]

Chan admits that this logical connection can only be established on the basis of a broader conception of Spirit Baptism that moves beyond Lukan categories of empowerment to include the Pauline conception of Spirit Baptism as an intimate encounter with God. Thus, the Lukan texts do not offer a conclusive defense of the initial evidence doctrine, but point to a link between tongues and Spirit Baptism that makes logical sense within the context of the entire New Testament.[139] Within the cultural-linguistic framework of the Pentecostal tradition, Chan observes that the filling of the Holy Spirit is integrally connected with the sign of tongues in the same way that Catholic mystics would connect being filled with the presence of God with participating in a passive prayer of recollection or silence.[140] Thus, rather than being opposed to each other, the Catholic prayer of quiet and Pentecostal prayer of tongues may be said to function respectively as different "theological markers" that are logically connected to the same spiritual experience within the language of faith.

This logical connection between tongues and Spirit Baptism as a supernatural expression of an intimate encounter with God was frequently

137. McGrath, *The Genesis of Doctrine*, 78.
138. Chan, "Evidential Glossolalia," 195.
139. Ibid., 45.
140. Ibid., 199–201.

recognized in the early stages of the Pentecostal movement. Early Pentecostals were not as concerned with establishing a doctrine as they were about formally stating the integral connection between Spirit Baptism and tongues that they were experiencing. The doctrine of initial evidence was meant as a testimony to their experience and a way of maintaining and passing along that experience to others. This may explain why William Seymour, Alexander Boddy, F. F. Bosworth, A. B. Simpson and Aimee Semple McPherson all preferred to leave doctrinal statements open on the issue of evidential tongues. They felt that it was one thing to name, validate and encourage an experience and quite another to define it, require it and reproach those who did not experience it. In other words, early Pentecostals were unanimously agreed that speaking in tongues was a truthful way of validating an experience of Spirit Baptism, but they were not agreed that the doctrine of initial evidence was the only way to verbalize this truth.

Evoking Appropriate Response

McGrath's final category for understanding the truth claims of a doctrine has to do primarily with the claim doctrine makes on the individual. Doctrine should not only make truth claims to which the community of faith should passively assent, but they should also compel the individual to actively respond to the Christ-event.[141] Or, as Vanhoozer puts it, doctrine directs individuals and communities toward "fitting participation in the drama of redemption."[142] Both McGrath and Vanhoozer argue convincingly that a doctrine's truthfulness is directly related to its ability to evoke appropriate or truthful practices within the lives of the people that believe them. As discussed above, Pentecostals have historically understood Spirit Baptism to be a gateway experience into a vibrant spiritual life. Yet, ironically, Pentecostals have commonly understood the doctrine of initial evidence to only be of limited value for producing the expected results.

Much of the reason for this can be attributed to the way Pentecostals have responded to two questions: 1) How do evidential tongues relate to the gift of tongues that Paul writes about in 1 Cor 12:27–31 and 14:1–40? 2) How are the fruit of the Spirit related to Spirit Baptism? With regard to the first question, Pentecostals have traditionally responded that there is a distinct difference between "the purpose and use" of evidential tongues and the gift of tongues. The former is given to all at the moment of Spirit

---

141. McGrath, *The Genesis of Doctrine*, 78–79.
142. Vanhoozer, *The Drama of Doctrine*, 102–5.

Baptism, and the latter is only given to some. This hermeneutic led many early proponents of the doctrine of initial evidence to assert that a genuinely Spirit-baptized saint may speak in tongues once in their life and never again. With regard to the second question, Pentecostals have commonly held that tongues is the only fool-proof way to validate a genuine experience of Spirit Baptism, and that the fruit of the Spirit, though important, could be appealed to only as a secondary witness to the authenticity of the experience. This hermeneutic was commonly used by Pentecostals as an apologetic for those who claimed to be Spirit-baptized but were seen as lacking in the area of spiritual fruit. The result of Pentecostals arguing against particular gifts of the Spirit or the fruit of the Spirit as necessary responses to the doctrine of initial evidence was that the doctrine was most commonly put into practice in the form of altar calls and tarrying services.

Yet, for most early Pentecostal congregations, the claim the doctrine of initial evidence had on the practices of the individual entailed more than masses of people coming to the altar, seeking God, and tarrying until they received God's fullness and the accompanying manifestation of speaking in tongues. Truthful action entailed greater acceptance of different kinds of people, regular expressions of intimacy toward God in prayer and worship, willingness to entail hardship and personal sacrifices for the sake of ministry, and expectancy of the manifestation of all kinds of gifts of power and authority in ministry situations. Although most of these results were not explicitly referred to in the doctrine of initial evidence, early Pentecostals understood them to be an indirect result of their espousal of the doctrine. The doctrine led people to the altar and pointed the way to an experience of Spirit Baptism. Once experienced, Jesus Christ was responsible for the results and the doctrine became almost superfluous.[143] The Pentecostal's emphasis on the individual learning about Spirit Baptism through experience rather than through doctrine explains why Pentecostals have not possessed a sense of urgency about reforming their doctrine. As long as the doctrine was at least compelling enough to get people to the altar to be baptized in the Spirit, it had done its duty.

---

143. D. W. Kerr, one of the most avid proponents of a rigid doctrine of initial evidence in early Pentecostalism, suggested that the doctrine had most of its value in getting a person in contact with Jesus: "What makes us different from other folks! Talking in tongues surely does. But that is not the whole of the matter. If it were not for Him we would not have it. 'Once it was the blessing, now it is the Lord.' If it were not for the Lord we would not have the blessing. Once we were occupied with the blessing, now we are occupied with the Lord, the Blesser. This is what makes us different from other folks—that Thou goest with us." D. W. Kerr, "The Practice of the Presence of God," *Pentecostal Evangel* 584 (February 14, 1925) 2.

Norming the Abnormal

There is, however, a growing concern among Pentecostals that the doctrine of initial evidence is becoming non-operational in many of the churches and denominations that espouse the doctrine. It exists, and people assent to it, but it does not result in a significant difference in the practices or experiences it was intended to change. May Tan has rightly correlated the difficulties Pentecostals have with understanding and appropriating their doctrinal distinctive with a lack of creedal clarity. In particular, Tan focuses in on the Pentecostal's insistence on tongues as normative to Spirit Baptism as counter productive. "It produces an unnecessary psychological uptightness in the seekers. It also shifts the focus to the physical manifestation of tongues so much so that they forget the more important issue of Spirit-baptism."[144] In order to move away from a doctrine that often evokes a response that is widely accepted as theologically "untrue" (seeking a particular physical manifestation rather than Jesus Christ), Tan would like the doctrine to be expressed more as an open invitation to an experience rather than a closed invitation to an exclusive club. It is thought that adopting a "Why not?" attitude toward speaking tongues rather than "You must!" would be more apt to evoke an appropriate response in the lives of those who hear it.[145]

Conclusion

This chapter set out to evaluate the history of the classical Pentecostal doctrine of initial evidence within McGrath's four functional categories for understanding doctrine as a historical phenomenon. In doing so, it was first argued that the doctrine built on the narrative of the Restorationist-Holiness movements in two different ways: one emphasizing personal holiness by calling individuals to be separate and fully sanctified, the other emphasizing personal holiness by calling individuals to bridge racial, religious and socio-economic divides in their communities. Second, it was argued that the doctrine of initial evidence has interpreted the experience of Pentecostals as biblically founded, a gateway to a full Christian life, and a sacramental sign of an inward work of Christ. Third, the argument was made that Pentecostals have often looked to the doctrine of initial evidence as a source of identity in relation to other groups within Christendom. Prior to the Charismatic movement, the doctrine primarily served to distinguish Pentecostals from non-Pentecostals. Since the 1960s,

144. Tan, "A Response to Frank Macchia," 180.
145. Ibid., 182. Macchia and Fee also advocate such a position.

The Function of the Doctrine of Initial Evidence

the doctrine has served to demarcate classical Pentecostals socially from Charismatics and Evangelicals. Finally, the truth claims, both ontological and intra-systematic, associated with the doctrine of initial evidence in the history of Pentecostalism were examined. It was found that there is considerable disagreement among Pentecostals as to the content and meaning of the core Pentecostal doctrine. The vast majority of Pentecostal history has focused on defending the doctrine exegetically on the basis of the relevant passages in Acts. Recently, however, Pentecostal scholars have argued that a stronger defense for the connection between Spirit Baptism and tongues might be found by interacting with broad scriptural themes in the context of other Christian doctrines and traditions. It was also found that the history of Pentecostalism has seen the doctrine of initial evidence worked out in the lives of those who assent to it primarily in relation to the beginnings of a Spirit-filled life, and very little in association with its ongoing vibrancy.

The above findings, while grounded in the history of the movement, may or may not be a valid indication of how the doctrine of Spirit Baptism is currently being received and put into practice by ministers in the classical Pentecostal tradition. The classical Pentecostal community has clearly experienced a growing sense of urgency to reform its doctrine in order to meet postmodern theological and ecclesial demands, as well as to rekindle authentic manifestations of the Holy Spirit in congregations that seem to be waning. Yet, unless one is clear about the current state of affairs, it is difficult to know exactly where reform may need to take place. The Pentecostal doctrine has clearly been used to bring the fullness of His presence to many individuals and groups around the world. The doctrine has also provided the Pentecostal community with social and interpretive guidance that amounts to far more than a simple propositional truth claim. Expanding the doctrinal discussion beyond exegetical and systematic-theological concerns to include the many varied ways in which the doctrine of initial evidence has guided the Pentecostal community over the years will help individuals, denominations and organizations to make informed decisions about the value of their current doctrinal statements, and also aid them in the process of discerning appropriate changes.

6

Spirit Baptism & Speaking in Tongues
Current Beliefs and Practices

Study Overview

Conceptual Model

THE LAST FOUR CHAPTERS gave a history of the origin and development of the doctrine of initial evidence in the classical Pentecostal tradition. Chapters 2–4 comprised a descriptive history divided into three time periods: the formation (1900–1910), the establishment (1910–40), and the upholding (1940–present) of the doctrine. Chapter 5 evaluated the history of the doctrine and identified the various historical functions of the doctrine in the classical Pentecostal tradition according to McGrath's four categories: interpretation of narrative, interpretation of experience, social demarcation and truth claims. It was argued that understanding the various capacities by which the doctrine has historically been of service to the classical Pentecostal community helps one to assess the present value and efficacy of the doctrine—how the doctrine may or may not be working—and how the doctrine might be developed or improved in order to maximize its value to the community.

While the history is important for understanding the value and effectiveness of doctrinal statements for a particular community over time, one must also have a clear understanding of how the historic doctrines and practices currently function in the community in order to make proposals that are grounded in the realities of the present day. To that end, an

Spirit Baptism & Speaking in Tongues

empirical analysis of a constellation of historical beliefs and practices of classical Pentecostals in relation to speaking in tongues and Spirit Baptism was conducted among a sample of classical Pentecostal ministers across three denominations in order to test how the doctrine of Spirit Baptism currently functions in the classical Pentecostal community according to McGrath's scheme.

The goals of the study were two-fold. First, just as the historical analysis showed that certain beliefs and practices associated with Spirit Baptism and speaking in tongues correlated with certain of McGrath's four functions of a doctrine for a community, the current beliefs and practices of classical Pentecostal ministers were categorized and interpreted to test how the doctrine of Spirit Baptism is currently functioning in the classical Pentecostal community. Second, this study tested how different cultural-linguistic communities within the classical Pentecostal tradition (distinctive, non-distinctive and post-distinctive) may or may not account for differences in the specific functions the doctrine of Spirit Baptism performs for their respective communities.

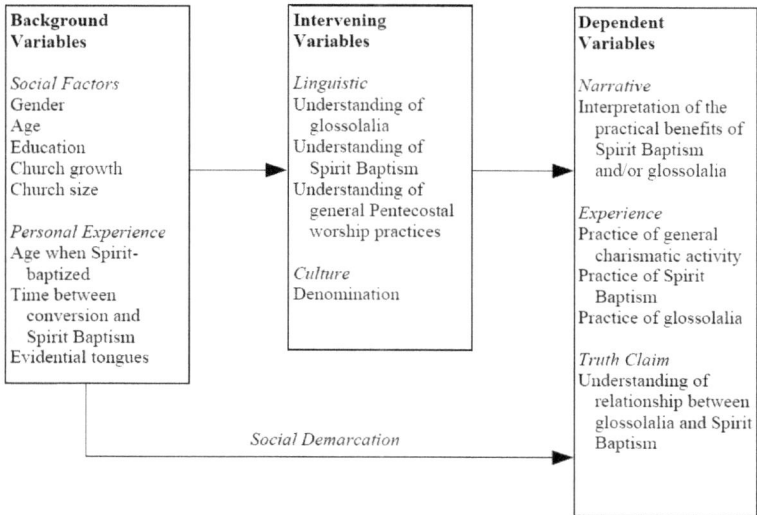

Figure 6.1 *Spirit Baptism Belief & Practice Survey: Conceptual Model*

Figure 6.1 represents the conceptual model for the study.[1] The conceptual model arose out of the above investigation of the historical

---

1. According to Van der ven, the conceptual model, rooted in the textual analysis (chapters two–five), should include three things: "concepts or variables, relationships

development and function of the doctrine of Spirit Baptism in the classical Pentecostal community. Background variables related to the social factors and personal experience of each minister were operationalized in part one of the research survey that asked ministers to report various demographic and experiential items about themselves and their congregation. The historical investigation showed that classical Pentecostals have developed a variety of theories to explain speaking tongues and Spirit Baptism as separate but closely related experiences. Both speaking in tongues and Spirit Baptism, in turn, have been understood to produce a variety of practical benefits for the Pentecostal community. The various explanations and benefits of speaking in tongues and Spirit Baptism were compiled into a list of forty-eight statements comprising part two of the research survey. These variables, along with the denomination of each minister, operationalized the cultural-linguistic tradition out of which the doctrine of Spirit Baptism is formulated and developed. Part three of the research survey listed a compilation of representative practices that Pentecostals have historically valued in association with Spirit Baptism in order to quantify the extent to which those practices are currently being experienced in Pentecostal communities.

The arrows in Figure 6.1 indicate causal relationships between the variables.[2] There is no causal relationship assumed between variables on the same plane. These relationships form the basis for the following six hypotheses that will be tested:

1. Classical Pentecostals are unified in their beliefs about what Spirit Baptism contributes to the Christian life, even if they disagree about how it is received.

2. Classical Pentecostals experience similar public and private manifestations of the Holy Spirit in their lives even if they disagree about the doctrinal explanations of such experiences.

---

between the concepts or variables, and the research units." Van der ven, *Practical Theology*, 131. Out of this model, hypotheses are formed that are the subject of the empirical-theological testing.

2. Van der ven divides the variables that comprise a theological-conceptual model into four groups: independent-dependent, intervening, moderator and experimental-control. Van der ven, *Practical Theology*, 132–33. One of the key features of this conceptual model is that the truth claims associated with the doctrine of Spirit Baptism are not intervening or moderator variables, but variables on the same plane as the narratives and experiences associated with Spirit Baptism and co-dependent on the cultural-linguistic tradition of the community.

3. The doctrine of initial evidence does not currently function significantly as an interpretation of the experience or narrative of classical Pentecostals.

4. Regular practice of speaking in tongues privately is a defining characteristic of classical Pentecostals, and the practice is not correlated to a rigid doctrine of initial evidence.

5. The doctrine of initial evidence does not function primarily as a first-order truth claim for the classical Pentecostal community, but as a second-order truth that ensures internal consistency and designates appropriate practices.

6. The dominant function of the doctrine of initial evidence in classical Pentecostalism is currently that of a social demarcation.

Procedure

The Quantitative Approach

A quantitative empirical approach has been chosen to analyze the beliefs and practices of classical Pentecostals concerning Spirit Baptism. The primary reason for choosing quantitative methods over qualitative in this study is to be able to ascertain, as much as possible, group generalizations and comparisons of denominations within the classical Pentecostal tradition. Jaco Dreyer forcefully argues that whether one uses qualitative or quantitative methods of empirical theological research, they are each subject to the same epistemological challenges and limitations.[3] This is not to say that the two methods can be used interchangeably, but that they differ, not in their reliability, but in their ability to deal with certain objects of research. Each method may be preferable depending on the subject and goals of the research questions.

Quantitative methods are particularly suited to gaining a broad, large-scale perspective on situations or groups of people that are large and diverse. While quantitative research cannot and should not attempt to avoid participation in the subject matter, it is directed toward distanciation in order to get a bird's eye view of a complicated situation on the ground. The goal of a quantitative approach is for the researcher to distance one's self from the subject of research as much as is possible in order to get an outside analysis of the subject. Thus, the quantitative approach has certain

---

3. Dreyer, "Establishing Truth," 18–19.

advantages over the qualitative approach, such as reproducibility, the ability to compare with other studies, and the ability to group respondents. For this particular study the quantitative approach allows enough responses to be gained to adequately compare the constituents from one denomination to another. This will be done in order to say something about the effect of doctrines on belief and practice in comparison to each other and in relation to the whole. A secondary reason for choosing a quantitative approach in this particular study is the assumption that the diversity and complexity of beliefs associated with Spirit Baptism across Pentecostal denominations is largely affected by demographics and leadership. It would be difficult to vary the participants in a qualitative study enough to be able to make such larger group generalizations.

A goal of doctrinal criticism (testing current doctrinal formulations) is particularly suited to a quantitative approach over qualitative because doctrines are meant to regulate (bring in to conformity) practices and beliefs of a whole group of people and not just individuals. With this goal in mind, richness is sacrificed for the sake of precision. It is entirely probable that some individuals who completed the survey felt that their beliefs and practices were not adequately captured or represented in the completed survey. At the same time, individuals were forced to make decisions about issues they may not have touched in a qualitative approach. A single empirical study cannot possibly describe the diversity and complexity of people's beliefs about Spirit Baptism. In the end, my chosen approach is not meant to be a substitute for qualitative approaches to empirical theology, but rather to place alongside and in dialogue with relevant qualitative studies.

Represented Denominations

The term "denomination" has fallen out of favor in some sectors of the church because it implies a closed posture toward outsider input and a desire for conformity at the expense of diversity within its constituency. Some groups have officially dropped the use of the term altogether in favor of terms like "association" or "consortium." A denomination, however, does not necessarily refer to a group that is closed or inflexible. Kay has pointed out that a "denomination" may be distinguished from a "sect" by its willingness to accept the validity and positive societal contribution of groups other than themselves.[4] "Socially, denominations are willing to co-exist with other groups and doctrinally[sic] they are able to reconcile themselves to having only a partial grasp on truth."[5] Thus, denominations may be characterized by a posture of openness to other groups because their very existence necessitates a situation of religious pluralism, where each ecclesial body "concedes the authenticity of other churches even as it claims its own."[6] Whether or not they officially call themselves a denomination, the three religious organizations that are the subject of this study—The Assemblies of God, Open Bible Churches, and The Foursquare Church—will be referred to as such, where the term simply refers to "a group of congregations united under a common and distinct faith, name and organization."[7]

The Assemblies of God (USA) is the largest Pentecostal denomination in the world. In 2009, they reported 12,371 churches[8] and 28,992 licensed ministers[9] in the United States. In 2011, they were ranked as the ninth largest denomination in the United States.[10] Individual churches in the Assemblies of God operate according to their own bylaws and they are able to choose their own pastor, provided he or she is licensed in the Assemblies of God. Local church doctrinal matters and minister licensing are overseen by one of the sixty-one district councils, and the General Council.

By comparison, Open Bible Churches is a much smaller Pentecostal denomination. In 2009, they reported 302 churches and 1,004 licensed ministers in the United States.[11] Oversight and governance are provided by a national board and five regional offices (Pacific, Mountain Plains, Central, Eastern and Southeast) with the highest concentration of churches being in the Pacific Northwest and Upper Midwest. Each congregation is autonomous; they own their property and call their own pastor, in most

4. Kay, *Pentecostals in Britain*, xviii.
5. Battaglia, "Sect or Denomination," 134.
6. Richey, "Denominations and Denominationalism," 75–76. Richey argues that denominationalism operates under the authority of a "branch theory" that recognizes the authenticity and importance of branches other than themselves even if those branches are not regarded as orthodox.
7. Roozen and Nieman, *Church, Identity and Change*, 5.
8. "2009 Vital Statistics Summary," 1.
9. "2009 Full Statistical Report," 57.
10. National Council of Churches, "Trends Continue in Church Membership," para. 20.
11. "National Board Statistical Report."

cases. The national board handles most doctrinal issues. Licensing and ordination of ministers is usually dealt with at the regional level and supported by the national board.

In terms of size, The Foursquare Church falls in between the Assemblies of God and Open Bible Churches. In 2009, they reported 1,866 churches and 6,894 licensed ministers in the United States.[12] The highest concentration of churches is along the west coast of the United States and in Hawaii. In most cases, the ownership of local church property is transferred to the denomination.[13] Oversight and administration of the denomination's activities are distributed between the president, board of directors and an executive council (comprised of a cabinet and supervisors from fourteen districts). The board of directors oversees doctrine and licensing with assistance and guidance from an eleven-member committee assigned by the board.

These three denominations have been chosen because they are all historically rooted in the classical Pentecostal movement in North America (see Figure 6.2). In addition to a common classical Pentecostal heritage, all three denominations subscribe to a "finished-work" doctrine of sanctification.[14] Classical Pentecostal organizations that have historically subscribed to a Holiness or "second-work" doctrine of sanctification such as the Church of God in Christ,[15] International Pentecostal Holiness Church,[16] and the Church of God, Cleveland[17] have not been directly ad-

12. "National Church Office Report," 2.

13. *Corporate Bylaws of the International Church of the Foursquare Gospel* (2009), 20.

14. The development and promulgation of the finished-work doctrine of sanctification in these classical Pentecostal denominations is described in more detail in chapter 3.

15. Although the Church of God in Christ's current doctrinal statement is process oriented, the denomination has traditionally upheld a doctrine of sanctification as a definite work of grace subsequent to salvation. Butler, "A Peculiar Synergy," 78–79; Daniels, "They Had a Dream," 19–21.

16. In 1908, the International Pentecostal Holiness Church stated their belief in sanctification as an "instantaneous, definite, second work of grace," and that all full members of the church must show satisfactory evidence of the experience. *Constitution and General Rules of the Fire Baptized Holiness Church, 1908* (n.p., 1908), 2, 4. In 2005, their statement deviated little from the original statement saying, "We believe [sanctification] includes a definite, instantaneous work of grace achieved by faith subsequent to regeneration." *International Pentecostal Holiness Church Manual 2005–2009*, 32.

17. The Church of God, Cleveland did not have an official Declaration of Faith until 1948. However, their early commitment to a doctrine of sanctification as a

dressed in this survey. This was done so that the doctrine of Spirit Baptism and its relationship to the Christian life could be examined without accounting for divergent views on sanctification between "finished-work" and "second-work" Pentecostals. However, it would be quite interesting and worthwhile for a similar survey to be conducted in "second-work" classical Pentecostal denominations to see if there are any clear differences between the two groups.

Figure 6.2 *Antecedents to Three Classical Pentecostal "Finished-Work" Denominations: Assemblies of God (USA), The Foursquare Church and Open Bible Churches*

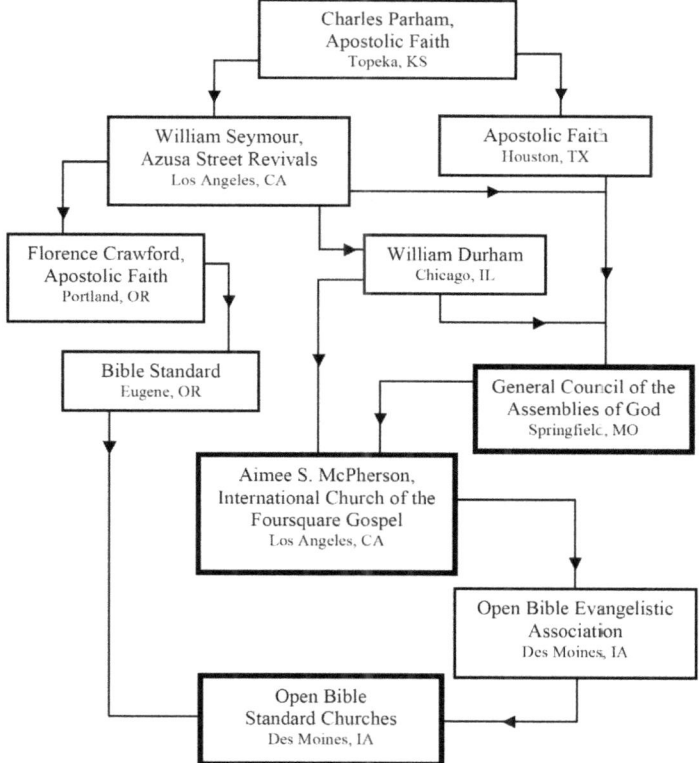

Although the three denominations that are the subject of this study have roots in the classical Pentecostal tradition, each denomination has a

definite experience, subsequent to justification is clear in earlier writings published by the denomination. Hughes, *Church of God Distinctives*, 117–35. See also *The Book of Doctrines*, 29–36; *Echoes from the General Assembly*, 30; Tomlinson, *The Last Great Conflict*, 195.

201

distinct approach to the doctrine of Spirit Baptism in their articles of faith. All three denominations have historically supported an initial evidence position, but only the Assemblies of God currently has such a statement in their articles of faith.[18] Open Bible and Foursquare have statements that may be read in support of tongues as evidence of Spirit Baptism, but which call for such an experience to be expected or anticipated rather than normative. Their current doctrinal formulations are as follows:

Assemblies of God

The baptism of believers in the Holy Spirit is witnessed by the initial physical sign of speaking with other tongues as the Spirit of God gives them utterance (Acts 2:4). The speaking in tongues in this instance is the same in essence as the gift of tongues (1 Corinthians 12:4–10, 28), but different in purpose and use.[19]

Open Bible

We believe the Holy Spirit comes to dwell in every believer at the moment of salvation. The baptism in the Holy Spirit is distinct from salvation, releasing the power of the Holy Spirit through faith. Consistent with biblical accounts, believers should anticipate Spirit baptism to be accompanied by speaking in tongues and other biblical manifestations.[20]

Foursquare

... this being still the dispensation of the Holy Spirit, the believer may have every reason to expect His incoming to be after the same manner as that in which He came upon Jew and Gentile alike in Bible days, and as recorded in the Word, that it may be truly said of us as of the house of Cornelius: the Holy Ghost fell on them as on us at the beginning.[21]

---

18. See chapters 3 and 4 for more on how the doctrine of initial evidence developed in each denomination.

19. *Minutes of the 53rd Session of the General Council of the Assemblies of God*, 93.

20. *Open Bible Churches Manual*, updated October 2009 (Des Moines: Open Bible National Office, 2009), 2.2.

21. *Corporate Bylaws of the International Church of the Foursquare Gospel* (2009), 3. McPherson, *Declaration of Faith*, 17.

The variation in doctrinal statements on Spirit Baptism between these denominations may appear slight to the causal observer. Within the classical Pentecostal tradition, however, these statements represent different perspectives on what constitutes Pentecostal definition, and also differences of opinion concerning how Pentecostal experience should be defined and defended.[22] This study will test whether or not more flexibly worded doctrines at the denominational level can be correlated with any differences in practice or belief among their constituents. In other words, this study seeks an answer to the question: Are the beliefs and practices of the licensed ministers of the three represented denominations more closely related to: a) their common heritage, or b) the doctrinal statements of their respective denominations?

Survey

Data were gathered from licensed ministers in Assemblies of God, Open Bible, and Foursquare in the form of a print and online survey questionnaire in English (see Appendix). The print survey was sent to a random sample of 500 ministers in each denomination, making a total of 1,500 print surveys. In order to retain anonymity, mailing lists for the print surveys were compiled and handled by denominational officials. Official permission was obtained for the distribution of the survey from national leaders in each denomination. To help avoid language problems, ministers living outside the United States were excluded from the random sample. Each minister was mailed the anonymous and confidential survey with a return postage-paid envelope and cover letter (see Appendix). In addition to the print survey, the same survey in an online format was made available to the ministers in Foursquare and Open Bible through follow-up email correspondence.[23] Email address lists were generated from the random sample of ministers and the email was sent anonymously as bulk email in order to retain minister confidentiality. Assemblies of God would not approve the solicitation of survey responses through electronic mail.[24]

---

22. I have categorized these three types of denominations as distinctive, post-distinctive and non-distinctive. See chapter 1 for further explanation.

23. This online version was provided to all ministers in the sample for whom the denomination had record of a valid email address at the time the survey was sent out. The web-based survey system, Survey Monkey (www.surveymonkey.com) was used for the development of the survey.

24. It is a general policy of the Assemblies of God not to utilize minister email addresses for any solicitation not directly associated with official denominational

The survey was composed of three parts. Part 1 asked for some general information about the minister and their congregation. The information gathered in this section included: denomination, age, gender, education, vocation, congregational size, congregational growth, devotional habits and some details about their personal experiences of Spirit Baptism and speaking in tongues. Part 2 was comprised of forty-two statements concerning various details related to the minister's beliefs about Spirit Baptism and/or speaking in tongues. The ministers were asked to assess their level of agreement with each statement according to the five-point Likert Scale ("Agree Strongly," "Agree," "Not Certain," "Disagree," or "Disagree Strongly"). Part 3 asked ministers to share the frequency with which they participated and/or experienced various charismatic activities in their own lives or congregational gatherings in the past three months. Respondents were asked to check one of seven boxes for each activity: "0," "1-3," "4-6," "7-12," "13-18," "19+," or "Not Sure."

The data were analyzed by means of SPSS, Version 17–19 statistical packages.

Results of Study: Description

The total number of surveys returned was 531 (327 in print, 204 online). The breakdown of denominational responses is as follows: Assemblies of God—102 (all print), Open Bible—230 (123 print, 107 online), Foursquare—199 (102 print, 97 online). The response rate for the entire sample of 1,500 ministers was 35.4 percent (Assemblies of God: 20%, Open Bible: 46%, Foursquare: 40%). The difference in size between the Assemblies of God sample and the Open Bible and Foursquare sample makes percentage measurements of the responses of the entire sample on any given item skewed toward Open Bible and Foursquare. Thus, most survey results have been reported separately with denominations divided. Whole sample reports have been given only when variance between the denominations was not shown to be significant for the item.[25]

Given the ratio of the research sample size in comparison to the size of each constituency, the results for Assemblies of God ministers are least likely to be representative of the denomination as a whole (102:28,992)

---

business. Although the survey was approved by the Assemblies of God (USA) to be administered to a select group of ministers by mail, solicitation of responses via the web would have been considered a violation of denominational policies.

25. ANOVA: $p < .000$

while the results for Open Bible ministers are most likely to be representative of the denomination as a whole (230:1,004). Although the genders and ages represented in the Assemblies of God sample were close to the known values of the denomination, the Assemblies of God results could be skewed by other factors that have not been measured. The findings indicate that the survey results coincide well with the results of other similar surveys of the Assemblies of God. However, if any results are surprising or in conflict with other surveys of the Assemblies of God that have not been considered in this study, the small sample size may be a possible explanation.

The sample of respondents was 82 percent male and 18 percent female with the highest percentage of female respondents being in Foursquare and the lowest being in the Assemblies of God (see Table 6.01). This gender response ratio is consistent with the ratios reported by these denominations as a whole.

The mean age of the sample was just under fifty-two years of age with Open Bible being the oldest at fifty-four and Foursquare being the youngest at forty-nine (see Table 6.02). The mean age of the sample was slightly younger than the known mean ages of licensed ministers in their respective denominations (AG—mean minister's age = 53 yrs.,[26] OBC—mean minister's age = 55 yrs.,[27] ICFG—mean minister's age = 52 yrs.[28]).

Table 6.01 *Gender of Sample*

Group		Male	Female
Assemblies of God	Count	92	10
	% within denomination	90.2	9.8
Open Bible	Count	189	39
	% within denomination	82.9	17.1
Foursquare	Count	153	44
	% within denomination	77.7	22.3
Total Sample	Count	434	93
	% within total sample	82.4	17.6

26. "2007 Full Statistical Report," 84.

27. Mean estimated based on age grouping data provided by Teri Beyer, Secretary of Open Bible Churches, in OBC National Board Statistical Report, October 22, 2008 (unpublished).

28. Mean estimated based on age grouping data provided by ICFG in email correspondence with Beth Mead, Sr. Administrative Assistant of Foursquare Church Health, in 2008.

Table 6.02 *Age of Sample*

Denomination	Mean Age (years)	N
Assemblies of God	52.63	99
Open Bible	54.06	216
Foursquare	49.01	189
Total Sample	51.88	504

Just under 60 percent (59.8%) of the responding ministers received formal residential training for ministry leading to a degree. None of the denominations surveyed require their licensed ministers to have a college degree.[29] Table 6.03 shows the breakdown of the education of ministers by denomination and degree.

Table 6.03 *Education of Sample*

Highest Degree Earned	AG %	OBC %	ICFG %
Associate	4.9	8.3	7.0
Bachelor's Degree	36.3	31.3	27.6
Master's Degree	15.7	13.9	15.1
ThM	2.0		0.5
DMin	5.9	4.3	
PhD	3.9	1.7	2.5
Other	2.0	3.5	2.0
Total	70.6	63.0	54.8

Ministers were asked to report their congregation's size and also assess the percentage by which their congregation had grown and/or declined in the past year. The collected responses were not significantly different depending upon denomination. The results for the entire sample are reported in Table 6.04.

---

29. The Assemblies of God bylaws state, "Any level of formal academic achievement (diploma or degree) shall not be a requirement for credentials." However, evidence of qualification should be shown to exist through minister's educational background, self-study, or ministerial experience. *Minutes of the 53rd Session of The General Council of the Assemblies of God* (Springfield, MO: General Council, 2009), 118. As of 2009, Open Bible and Foursquare do not have any formal education requirements for their ministers listed in their bylaws.

Table 6.04 *Percentage Decline and Growth of Minister's Congregation in Past Year*

Percentage Congregation Declined Last Year	AG %	OBC %	ICFG %	Total %
none that I know of	60.0	61.1	57.8	59.5
1–5%	28.8	29.4	32.2	30.5
6–10%	7.5	6.7	6.7	6.8
11–20%	2.5	1.7	2.2	2.0
21–30%	1.3	0.6	0.6	0.7
more than 30%		0.6	0.6	0.5

Percentage Congregation Grew Last Year	AG %	OBC %	ICFG %	Total %
none that I know of	12.0	12.5	8.4	10.7
1–5%	34.9	26.1	29.5	29.1
6–10%	22.9	26.1	23.2	24.3
11–20%	16.9	14.1	16.3	15.5
21–30%	7.2	8.7	6.3	7.4
more than 30%	6.0	12.5	16.3	12.9

Around 40 percent of the respondents reported that their churches had experienced a decline by at least 5 percent in the past year. About 60 percent of the respondents reported that their church had grown by at least 5 percent in the past year. Table 6.05 shows that about half (49.9%) of the ministers reported that their average weekend attendance was under 100 adults, about 20 percent reported the average weekend attendance to be between 100 and 200, and about 30 percent reported that more than 200 adults attended their congregation on an average weekend.

Table 6.05 *Average Congregational Weekend Attendance by Denomination*

Average Congregational Weekend Attendance	AG %	OBC %	ICFG %	Total %
> 50	25.0	26.3	16.2	22.0
50–100	26.1	29.4	27.2	27.9
100–200	16.3	19.1	22.0	19.7
200+	32.6	25.2	34.6	30.4
Mean Value	2.57	2.43	2.75	2.58

Results of Study: Explorations

The results of this study have been categorized according to McGrath's four historical functions of doctrine that were elaborated in chapter 5 with respect to the classical Pentecostal doctrine of initial evidence. The doctrine has, at certain periods in the last century, contributed substantively to each of these four functions in the Pentecostal community. Yet, the willingness of some Pentecostals to reformulate the doctrine may be an indication that it is currently not performing these functions effectively in sectors of the classical Pentecostal tradition. In an effort to understand how the doctrine of initial evidence is currently functioning in the classical Pentecostal tradition, answers to detailed questions concerning the nature, purpose, reception and benefits of Spirit Baptism and *charismata* (particularly glossolalia) by ministers in the three denominations were examined.

Spirit Baptism and the Pentecostal Experience

Spirit Baptism

As expected, the entire sample, with one exception, believed that they have been baptized in the Holy Spirit (Table 6.06) regardless of whether or not they theologically connected speaking in tongues with the experience.[30] The sheer rarity of Pentecostal ministers that believe they have not been baptized in the Holy Spirit is evidence that the vast majority of Pentecostals are upholding the importance of an experience of Spirit Baptism that they believe they have had themselves.

Table 6.06 *Frequency of Baptism in the Holy Spirit*

Denomination	Yes %	No %
Assemblies of God	100.0	
Open Bible	99.5	0.5
Foursquare	100.0	

---

30. The numbers here corroborate the similar findings of Kay in his study of British Pentecostal ministers across four denominations. In that study, 99.8 percent of ministers believed that they had been baptized in the Holy Spirit. Kay, *Pentecostals in Britain*, 73.

Spirit Baptism & Speaking in Tongues

Whether or not one believes that tongues is *the initial evidence* of the Baptism in the Holy Spirit, for ministers in classical Pentecostal denominations it is an empirically verifiable *consequence* that they have experienced. Table 6.07 shows that less than 4 percent of ministers in Open Bible or Foursquare have not spoken in tongues. Thus, it appears that the reservations some classical Pentecostal ministers have about making tongues the initial evidence has little to do with their own lack of glossolalic experiences and much more to do with other reasons (i.e., exegetical or pastoral concerns).[31]

Table **6.07** *Frequency of Speaking in Tongues When Baptized in the Holy Spirit*

Denomination	Yes, immediately %	Yes, within 24 hours %	Yes, within a week %	Yes, sometime later %	No %
Assemblies of God	87.0	3.0	2.0	8.0	
Open Bible	70.5	5.9	5.4	16.4	1.8
Foursquare	62.2	5.6	3.6	25.0	3.6

Table 6.08 shows the breakdown of age when ministers were baptized in the Holy Spirit. The median age when baptized in the Holy Spirit of the sample was eighteen years old. Over 40 percent of the sample were baptized in the Spirit in junior high or high school (ages twelve-eighteen) and 75 percent had experienced Spirit Baptism by the time they reached the age of twenty-six. Only 3.6 percent were not baptized in the Spirit by the time they reached the age of forty.

Table **6.08** *Age When Baptized in the Holy Spirit*

Age When Baptized in the Holy Spirit	0–11	12–14	15–18	19–25	26–40	40+
Entire Sample		10.4	15.2	25.3	24.4	21.1	3.6

31. It should be noted that none of the Pentecostal denominations has indicated in their doctrinal statements when tongues should be expected or anticipated to accompany a person's Baptism in the Holy Spirit. The term "initial evidence" may suggest that tongues comes right away, but it has also been interpreted to not necessarily carry the idea of immediacy. In 2000, the Assemblies of God issued an official position paper that addressed this issue and deemed the idea of tongues as "delayed evidence" to be inconsistent with Scripture. *The Baptism in the Holy Spirit: The Initial Experience and Continuing Evidences of the Spirit-Filled Life* (Springfield, MO: General Council, 2000), 4–5. See also Robeck, "An Emerging Magisterium?" 185, 193, 208.

Median Age = 18

Table 6.09 shows that 69 percent of the sample experienced Spirit Baptism within five years of their conversion and over a third within a year. If one compares these results with those in Table 6.08, one can imagine a common scenario for a Pentecostal minister being that of an experience of conversion some time in later elementary school or junior high followed by an experience of Baptism in the Holy Spirit some time in the next five years. This study indicates that the time in life when people will most likely be dealing with the implication of the doctrine of Spirit Baptism for their own life will be from adolescence to young adulthood. After reaching forty, ministers will likely have had the personal experiences that will interpret and be interpreted by their doctrine of Spirit Baptism.

Table 6.09 *Duration of Time Between Conversion and Baptism in the Holy Spirit*

Duration	N	Entire Sample %
Less than a day	27	5.0
Less than a month	36	6.7
Less than a year	119	22.2
1–5 years	188	35.1
6–10 years	77	14.4
More than 10 years	67	12.5

From a pastoral perspective, a denomination's doctrinal statement on Spirit Baptism would have the greatest impact on youth pastors and young adult pastors. They are the ones who would most likely be in a position to field questions from adolescents and young adults seeking such an experience and they would likely be involved in the planning and directing of "seeker" services designed to give young people an opportunity to receive the Baptism in the Holy Spirit. By the time the average congregant leaves their youth group or college group to assimilate into the adult life of their congregation, they would have already had the experience(s) by which they define their Spirit Baptism.

Glossolalia

Tongues speech is a regular part of the private devotional prayer life of 97 percent of the sample. Table 6.10 indicates that 82 percent of the sample had prayed privately in tongues more than six times in the past three months, and 66 percent more than eighteen times.[32] While speaking in tongues was shown to be a regular part of the private prayer lives of the sample, public utterances in tongues were not. Only 28 percent of the sample had given any public utterance in tongues during the past three months. Nearly 40 percent of the sample had not heard any public utterance of tongues in their church during the past three months.

Table 6.10 *Frequency of Individual Experiences of Glossolalia in the Past Three Months*

Glossolalic Experience	None %	1–6 %	7–12 %	13–18 %	19+ %	Not Sure %	Mean
Spoken in tongues while praying privately.	2.8	12.2	8.0	8.0	65.9	3.2	4.32
Spoken in tongues while praying for an individual.	8.4	30.2	16.6	8.8	32.4	3.6	3.37
Given a public utterance in tongues	71.7	21.3	2.8	0.6	2.0	1.6	1.45
Heard a public utterance in tongues.	37.8	46.5	7.6	3.2	4.0	0.8	1.92
Interpreted tongues.	73.7	21.8	1.0	1.2	1.4	0.8	1.37
Sung in tongues.	27.4	33.2	12.9	6.4	18.9	1.2	2.60

There were statistically significant differences between the three denominations concerning the frequency of every item of glossolalic experience. The cultures of the three denominations are clearly different with regard to speaking in tongues. Public utterances in tongues occur most frequently in the Assemblies of God. Table 6.11 shows that over 80 percent

---

32. Table 6.10 and other tables in the chapter that do not specify a particular denomination refer to the entire sample. The mean column represents the mean value of the entire sample returned for that particular survey question based on the following encoding ("None"=1, "1–6"=2, "7–12"=3, "13–18"=4, "19+"=5). The "Not Sure" responses were not included in calculating the mean.

of Assemblies of God ministers had heard a public utterance in tongues in their congregation in the past three months, compared with 51 percent of Open Bible ministers and 63 percent of Foursquare ministers. Conversely, Foursquare ministers are most likely to sing in tongues with 83 percent of Foursquare ministers having sung in tongues during the past three months, compared with 64 percent of Open Bible and Assemblies of God ministers. All three denominations had a high percentage of their ministers engage in glossolalic activity in private devotional prayer (>92%) and intercessory prayer (>83%).

Table 6.11 *Frequency of Individual Experiences of Glossolalia in the Last Three Months by Denomination*

Glossolalic Experience	Denomination	0 %	1–12 %	13+ %	Not Sure %
Spoken in tongues while praying privately.	AG	1.0	17.7	78.2	3.1
	OBC	5.7	26.5	64.6	3.3
	ICFG	0.5	14.7	82.2	2.6
	$F = 12.162, P < .000$				
Spoken in tongues while praying for an individual.	AG	3.1	45.8	43.7	7.3
	OBC	14.1	51.6	32	2.3
	ICFG	4.2	42.3	50.2	3.2
	$F = 14.416, P < .000$				
Given a public utterance in tongues.	AG	65.3	27.4	5.3	2.1
	OBC	77.3	18.5	2.4	1.9
	ICFG	68.4	29	1.6	1.1
	$F = 2.834, P = .060$				
Heard a public utterance in tongues in your congregation.	AG	18.1	65.9	14.8	1.1
	OBC	48.6	46.2	4.8	0.5
	ICFG	35.4	57.7	5.8	1.1
	$F = 13.056, P < .000$				
Interpreted tongues.	AG	64.2	28.4	5.3	2.1
	OBC	80.7	17	1.8	0.5
	ICFG	70.5	26.9	2.2	0.5
	$F = 7.033, P = .001$				

Sung in tongues.	AG	34.7	48.5	15.8	1.1
	OBC	34	42	22.7	1.4
	ICFG	16	49.5	33.5	1.1
	F = 12.959, P < .000				

Pentecostal Experience Scales

Three scales for charismatic experience were constructed using Part 3 of the survey. This section of the survey asked ministers to register "How often in the past three months you have . . ." and then gave them a list of various charismatic experiences. They were given seven different options for response: "0," "1–3," "4–6," "7–12," "13–18," and "Not Sure." The responses were ranked and then arranged into three scales: 1) revelatory experience, 2) visible-manifestations experience, and 3) prayer-language experience.

The construction of scales has a two-fold purpose. First, scales that return an alpha coefficient above a certain standard limit are more reliable indicators of underlying attitudes and beliefs of the sample than a single item.[33] Whereas responses to a single item may fluctuate for a variety of reasons, a number of items that fluctuate in the same way across the entire sample are likely to be an indication of a single underlying factor by which they are all related. Second, the construction of scales is intended to allow future researchers to replicate the work, so as to test the same attitudes and beliefs within other groups or measure changes in attitudes and beliefs over time.

The revelatory experience scale (see Table 6.12) was constructed using nine items that measure the frequency by which divine knowledge or instructions were recently disclosed to individuals in various capacities by supernatural means. The scale proved to be statistically reliable, returning an alpha coefficient of $\alpha = .862$.

---

33. Darren George and Paul Mallery suggest the following standards for evaluating the reliability of Cronbach's alpha coefficient: "> .9 excellent, > .8 good, > .7 acceptable, > .6 questionable, > .5 poor, < .5 unacceptable." *SPSS for Windows Step by Step*, 231.

Table 6.12 *Revelatory Experience (RevlExp) Scale*

How often in the past three months have you:	Item rest of test (r)	α If item deleted
publicly prophesied	.525	.854
given a prophecy privately to another person	.525	.854
been anointed by the Spirit	.503	.857
received divine inspiration in interpreting Scripture	.550	.854
received divine inspiration while preaching	.675	.839
received divine inspiration while evangelizing	.591	.848
felt led by God to perform a specific action	.591	.848
received a word from God	.710	.837
given a word of wisdom or word of knowledge	.695	.838

α = .862

The prayer language experience scale was constructed using three questions from Part 1 of the survey and one additional question from Part 3 that each had to do with the minister's perceived regularity of praying in tongues (see Table 6.13). The question from Part 1 was recoded to align with the questions surveying charismatic activity in Part 3 (see Table 6.14). This scale was constructed to simply measure the regularity of the individual's utilization of a personal prayer language in various capacities. The 4-item scale returned an alpha coefficient of α =.770.

Table 6.13 *Prayer Language Experience (PrLangExp) Scale*

Item	Item rest of test (r)	α If item deleted
How often in the past three months have you:		
- spoken in tongues while praying privately	.666	.671
- spoken in tongues while praying for an individual	.597	.704
- sung in tongues	.476	.786
General regularity of speaking in tongues privately	.668	.704

α = .770

Spirit Baptism & Speaking in Tongues

Table 6.14 *Frequency of Speaking in Tongues Privately*

Denomination	nearly everyday %	at least once a week %	at least once a month %	occasionally %	used to, but not now %	never %
AG	62.0	28.0	1.0	9.0		
OBC	50.7	26.9	6.7	13.0	0.4	2.2
ICFG	63.1	25.3	5.1	6.1		0.5
Total	57.6	26.5	5.0	9.6	0.2	1.2

The visible manifestations scale was constructed using eight items that measured the frequency with which individuals experienced various outward supernatural manifestation of God's presence (see Table 6.15). Each of the manifestations has outwardly observable phenomena associated with them. The scale returned an alpha coefficient of $\alpha = .818$.

Table 6.15 *Visible Manifestations Experience (VisbManExp) Scale*

How often in the past three months have you:	Item rest of test (r)	α If item deleted
given a public utterance in tongues	.558	.793
interpreted tongues	.541	.797
experienced "laughing in the Spirit"	.459	.806
experienced being "slain in the Spirit"	.565	.795
seen people baptized in the Spirit as a result of your ministry	.518	.804
seen people "slain in the Spirit" as a result of your ministry	.670	.775
seen people "laughing in the Spirit" as a result of your ministry	.620	.787
heard a public utterance in tongues in your congregation	.446	.812

$\alpha = .818$

Table 6.16 shows that the variance of the three charismatic experience scales are significantly related to denominations. Assemblies of God and Foursquare ministers are more likely than Open Bible ministers to have recently had revelatory experiences. Foursquare ministers are most likely to have recently experienced prayer language. Assemblies of God ministers are more likely to have experienced visible manifestations of the Holy Spirit. While each classical Pentecostal denomination has its own unique "flavor" of charismatic experience, revelatory experiences and prayer language activity are not directly associated with a denomination's stance on the connection between Spirit Baptism and speaking in tongues. The comparison of denominations suggests that holding fast to a rigid connection between speaking in tongues and Spirit Baptism does not necessarily lead to a vibrant Pentecostal prayer life or intimacy with God. In contrast, the visible manifestations scale was significantly related to a rigid stance on initial evidence.[34] Those ministers who subscribe to a rigid doctrine of initial evidence tend to experience visible manifestations of the Holy Spirit more frequently than those who do not. This supports the hypothesis that ministers may support a rigid doctrine of initial evidence based on a broader conviction that where the Holy Spirit is active there will be visible signs of his presence.

Table 6.16 *One-way Analysis of Variance: Denomination by Charismatic Experience Scales*

Denomination	RevlExp		PrLangExp		VisbManExp	
	Mean	SD	Mean	SD	Mean	SD
AG	31.466	11.7580	18.979	3.9166	15.247	8.1913
OBC	27.185	9.5732	17.735	5.4934	12.156	6.2281
ICFG	30.129	10.0776	20.128	3.9495	12.701	5.2835
	$F = 6.690, P = .001$		$F = 13.092, P < .000$		$F = 7.609, P = .001$	

Spirit Baptism and the Pentecostal Narrative

Pentecostal Mission

The doctrine of Spirit Baptism has functioned as an interpretation of the narrative of classical Pentecostals in the past century. One narrative classical Pentecostals have associated with Spirit Baptism has been one of

---

34. ANOVA VisManExp by BHSrigid: $F = 5.401, P < .000; r = .273$. ANOVA RevlExp by BHSrigid: $F = .878, P = NS; r = .049$. ANOVA PrLangExp by BHSrigid: $F = 1.406, P = NS; r = .114$. BHSrigid is defined later in the chapter.

restoring the church as the holy and pure Bride of Christ.[35] As one would expect, "finished-work" Pentecostals continue to associate Baptism in the Holy Spirit with the process of becoming holy, rather than something that happens after one becomes holy. While 76 percent of the respondents disagree that a stipulation for receiving Spirit Baptism is an experience of full sanctification, 62 percent agree that Spirit Baptism is essential for living a holy life. Responses to these statements did not vary significantly depending upon the denomination (See Table 6.17).

Endowment with spiritual gifts, equipping for Christian service, and enduing with power were each accepted as general results of Spirit Baptism by over 80 percent of the sample (see Table 6.18). There were not statistically significant differences between denominations on these beliefs. Almost without exception (97.8%), classical Pentecostal ministers associate power with the Baptism in the Holy Spirit. This could be attributed to "enduement with power" being directly associated with the words of Jesus recorded in Luke 24:49 in the King James Version, "And, behold, I send the promise of my Father upon you: but tarry ye in the city of Jerusalem, until ye be endued with power from on high."

Table 6.17 *Agreement with "Finished-Work" Doctrine of Sanctification*

Item	Denomination	Agree %	Not Certain %	Disagree %
I believe the Baptism in the Holy Spirit is only given to those who are fully sanctified.	AG	10.1	13.1	76.8
	OBC	12.6	15.3	72.1
	ICFG	10.4	10.4	79.3
The Baptism in the Holy Spirit is essential for living a holy life.	AG	57.6	10.1	32.3
	OBC	62.1	11.2	26.6
	ICFG	61.7	11.1	27.9

35. One question on the survey dealt with this particular wording: "The Baptism in the Holy Spirit seals the Bride of Christ." This question scored the highest percentage of uncertainty on the survey with over 27 percent of respondents reporting that they were uncertain whether they agreed of disagreed with this statement.

Table 6.18 *General Results of Spirit Baptism*

Item	Agree %	Not Certain %	Disagree %
The Baptism in the Holy Spirit endows the Christian with spiritual gifts (charismata).	81.7	5.7	12.6
The Baptism in the Holy Spirit equips the Christian for service.	91.6	3.4	5.0
The Baptism in the Holy Spirit endues the Christian with power.	97.8	1.6	0.6

While ministers tend to positively associate Spirit Baptism with these general results, what about specific results? What do classical Pentecostal ministers see as the practical benefits that Spirit Baptism gives to individuals? Ministers are quite diverse in how they perceive the practical benefits of speaking in tongues. Spirit Baptism has been associated with a variety of benefits by individuals in the classical Pentecostal community over the past century ranging from a limited aid in prayer to a broad heightened sensitivity to the Holy Spirit that significantly enhances the entirety of one's service to God.

Practical Helps Scale

Table 6.19 *Practical Helps Item Scores*

Item	Mean	SD
The Baptism in the Holy Spirit helps to foster unity among Christians.	3.62	1.084
The Baptism in the Holy Spirit helps prevent racial prejudice among Christians.	3.30	1.174
The Baptism in the Holy Spirit helps one to witness effectively.	4.28	.796
The Baptism in the Holy Spirit helps one to interpret Scripture.	3.93	.988
The Baptism in the Holy Spirit helps one to preach better.	4.05	.996
The Baptism in the Holy Spirit helps one to pray when one doesn't know how to pray.	4.73	.556
The Baptism in the Holy Spirit helps one to worship God.	4.56	.631

Table 6.19 shows that classical Pentecostal ministers positively associate Spirit Baptism with a variety of practical helps.[36] Ministers are most likely to associate Spirit Baptism with help in prayer and worship. Ministers are less likely to associate Spirit Baptism with fostering unity and preventing racial prejudice. The belief that Spirit Baptism helps in prayer and worship was not significantly dependent upon denominations.[37] The extremely high percentage of agreement among ministers that Spirit Baptism helps in prayer and worship is an indication that classical Pentecostals unanimously understand a "prayer language" to be a primary result of Spirit Baptism.[38] Practical helps that are not directly associated with a "prayer language" are less likely to be associated with Spirit Baptism, but still quite common.

The practical helps scale was constructed using the five items that were not directly connected to speaking in tongues: fostering unity, preventing racial prejudice, witnessing effectively, interpreting Scripture and preaching better. These five items were turned in to a reliable scale (Table 6.20) that measures the minister's belief that Spirit Baptism is associated with practical benefits beyond those directly connected to speaking in tongues ($\alpha = .796$).

Table 6.20 *Practical Helps (BHSpractical) Scale*

Item	Item rest of test (r)	α If item deleted	Agree %
The Baptism in the Holy Spirit helps to foster unity among Christians.	.602	.750	62.7%
The Baptism in the Holy Spirit helps prevent racial prejudice among Christians.	.608	.750	48.3%
The Baptism in the Holy Spirit helps one to witness effectively.	.488	.785	88.8%
The Baptism in the Holy Spirit helps one to interpret Scripture.	.641	.738	75.4%
The Baptism in the Holy Spirit helps one to preach better.	.567	.761	78.6%

$\alpha = .796$

36. All of these items were marked using a five point Likert Scale. Therefore, a value of 3 represents a neutral attitude toward the item and anything above 3 indicates at least a slightly positive attitude.

37. $F = 2.723$, Sig. $= .067$ (NS); $F = 2.193$, Sig. $= .113$ (NS)

38. 98.5 percent agreed with the statement: "The Baptism in the Holy Spirit helps

Despite high scores on the practical helps scale by all three denominations, Table 6.21 shows that the scores registered by the Assembles of God on the scale were significantly higher than those of Open Bible or Foursquare ministers.

Table 6.21 *One-way Analysis of Variance: BHSpractical by Denomination*

Denomination	Mean	SD
AG	20.40	3.62
OBC	18.87	3.89
ICFG	18.89	3.65
Total	19.16	3.78

$F = 6.399, P = .002$

The comparison of means in Table 6.22 reveals that Open Bible and Foursquare are not significantly different from each other while the Assemblies of God scored significantly higher on the scale than either Open Bible or Foursquare. One might have hypothesized that the Assemblies of God, a denomination that unanimously professes a belief in a rigid connection between Spirit Baptism and speaking in tongues, would be less likely to associate Spirit Baptism with practical helps that are not directly connected to speaking in tongues. This does not appear to be the case. In fact, further analysis suggests that the Assemblies of God's higher scores on the BHSpractical scale are primarily related to denomination factors beyond their rigid stance on initial evidence.[39]

Table 6.22 *Multiple Comparisons of Means (Bonferroni): BHSpractical by Denomination*

(I) denomination	(J) denomination	Mean Difference (I-J)	Std. Error
AG	OBC	1.5374*	.4623
	ICFG	1.5146*	.4694
OBC	AG	-1.5374*	.4623
	ICFG	-.02286	.3732
ICFG	AG	-1.5146*	.4694
	OBC	.02286	.3732

*. The mean difference is significant at the 0.005 level.

---

one to pray when one doesn't know how." 96.6 percent agreed with the statement: "The Baptism in the Holy Spirit helps one to worship God."

39. Table 6.26 shows that only one of seven practical helps (effective witness) is significantly related to the BHSrigid scale described later in this chapter.

The high means registered on the items by all three denominations seems to be an indication that the notion of Spirit Baptism as a gateway experience appears to be a defining characteristic of the entire classical Pentecostal community. In one article addressing the issue of "disappointing baptism" published by the Assemblies of God, the following testimony was given:

> When I got my spiritual priorities in order, I sought a closer walk with Him. And that night I received an experience that was not disappointing. Yes, I did speak in tongues, but this was merely incidental compared to the warmth of God's love that flooded my soul. . . . Praise and worship and expressions of love to my wonderful Lord became as spontaneous as breathing. Also the ministries Jesus said the Holy Spirit would perform in me have become a reality. Disappointing Baptism? Not if we seek the Baptizer, rather than just an experience. The Baptism should not be merely a one-time experience but the beginning of a life in the Spirit.[40]

Most Pentecostal ministers would seem to agree with the final sentence. Regardless of how they feel about the doctrine of initial evidence, Pentecostal ministers uphold the experience of Spirit Baptism as valuable to individuals and congregational life on a number of different levels, not just as prayer language or as evidence of Spirit Baptism.

Spirit Baptism and Pentecostal Truth Claims

Pentecostal Doctrinal Assent

Although the denominations represented in this survey have historically supported an initial evidence position, their doctrinal statements on the connection between Spirit baptism and speaking in tongues are quite different. Table 6.23 shows how licensed ministers in the three denominations agree with their own denomination's stated doctrine and with each other's. Assemblies of God and Open Bible had the high percentage of ministers who agree with their own doctrinal statement that one would expect to see (94% and 89% respectively). Surprisingly, over one quarter (26.9%) of licensed Foursquare ministers were uncertain or disagreed with their denomination's doctrinal statement. Open Bible's statement received a high percentage of agreement (>88%) from all three denominations, making it

---

40. C. L. Strom, "Are You Disappointed With Your Baptism?" 49.

Norming the Abnormal

the most inclusive classical Pentecostal doctrinal statement. In contrast, almost half the ministers in Foursquare and Open Bible disagree with the Assemblies of God's position on initial evidence.

Table 6.23 *Agreement with Denominational Doctrinal Statements on Spirit Baptism*

Item	Denom	Agree %	Not Certain %	Disagree %
Assemblies of God: I believe the Baptism in the Holy Spirit is witnessed by the initial physical sign of speaking with other tongues as the Spirit of God gives them utterance	AG	94.0	2.0	4.0
	OBC	34.7	10.6	54.7
	ICFG	42.2	12.5	45.3
Open Bible: I believe Christians should anticipate Spirit Baptism to be accompanied by speaking in tongues and other biblical manifestations	AG	94.0	4.0	2.0
	OBC	88.7	3.8	7.5
	ICFG	90.3	5.6	4.1
Foursquare: I believe Christians should expect the Spirit's incoming to be after the same manner as that in which He came upon believers in the days of the Early Church	AG	82.7	5.1	12.2
	OBC	69.6	13.1	17.3
	ICFG	73.1	11.9	15.0

In 1994, Susie Stanley presented a paper at the Society for Pentecostal Studies Meeting in which she reported the findings of a survey she conducted of charismatic clergy in Oregon within the three denominations that are the subject of this present study: Assemblies of God, Foursquare, and Open Bible. Here is what she reported concerning the ministers' beliefs concerning the doctrine of initial evidence:

> The percentage of pastors who believe that speaking in tongues is the initial evidence of the baptism of the Holy Spirit varied widely, depending on denominational affiliation. Eighty-eight percent of the Assemblies of God clergy answered "yes" decreasing to 55 percent for Open Bible pastors and 42 percent

for Foursquare pastors. This issue drew the most marginal comments in the theological section of the survey. Several wrote that speaking in tongues is not the only evidence of the baptism of the Holy Spirit. Others said that speaking in tongues is "an initial evidence" rather than "the initial evidence." Three added "physical" to describe evidence.[41]

It is interesting to note that between 1994 and 2010 the percentage of Assemblies of God and Foursquare ministers who agreed with the initial evidence doctrine remained almost unchanged, while the percentage of Open Bible ministers in agreement with the doctrine dropped from 55 percent to less that 35 percent. This dramatic change among Open Bible ministers is likely to be directly associated with the doctrinal change made by the denomination in 2002 that moved away from a rigid initial evidence doctrine to a more flexible doctrinal statement that tongues was *an anticipated* evidence, but not *the* evidence.[42] The change is also evidence that the doctrine of initial evidence may have already been non-operational among many ministers in Open Bible, so that when the doctrinal change officially occurred at the institutional level in 2002 individual ministers were quick to follow suit.[43]

Pentecostals have historically understood Baptism in the Holy Spirit to be an experience that acts as a gateway into a new phase of the Christian life lived in the power of the Holy Spirit. While classical Pentecostal denominations affirm the Holy Spirit's presence in the lives of all Christians, Pentecostals have been criticized for believing that Christians who have not been baptized in the Holy Spirit (and, by way of deduction, have not spoken in tongues) do not have the Holy Spirit. This perspective seems to be, in part, a misunderstanding of classical Pentecostal doctrine.[44] The classical Pentecostal position does not deny the Spirit to non-Pentecostals. In fact, official doctrines and/or statements of the three denominations surveyed specifically affirm the presence of the Holy Spirit in the life of the believer from the moment of conversion.[45] Yet, the survey shows that

---

41. Susie Stanley, "Pentecostal and Charismatic Clergy in Oregon," 9.

42. See chapter 5 above.

43. I use Richard Heyduck's use of the term "non-operational doctrine" to describe a doctrine that is assented to but does not change the practices of churches or individuals (operating procedure). Thus, a doctrine can be changed and/or removed at the institutional level with ease.

44. Clifton, "The Spirit and Doctrinal Development," 16–17.

45. *Open Bible Manual* (2009), 2.2. *Foursquare Licensing Process Guide* (2009), 7.3. The Foursquare website also notes, "All believers have a portion of God's Spirit within

despite their denomination's doctrinal stance on the subject a considerable number (21%) of classical Pentecostals do not believe that all Christians receive the Holy Spirit when they become a Christian (Table 6.24). Though still a minority, that number appears to be large enough among classical Pentecostal ministers to fuel a notion that Pentecostals believe you do not have the Holy Spirit unless you speak in tongues. It also is evidence that Pentecostal denominations have allowed their ministers to deviate on this doctrine and still retain their license.

Table 6.24 *Holy Spirit Reception at Conversion & Water Baptism*

Item	Denomination	Agree %	Not Certain %	Disagree %
I believe all Christians receive the Holy Spirit when they become a Christian.	AG	67.3	5.1	27.6
	OBC	74.1	1.9	24.1
	ICFG	83.3	2.6	14.1
	Total	76.3	2.8	20.9
I believe all Christians receive the Holy Spirit when they are baptized in water.	AG	4.1	2.0	93.9
	OBC	3.7	5.6	90.7
	ICFG	12.0	4.7	83.3
	Total	6.9	4.6	88.5

As one might expect, classical Pentecostals in North America mostly disagree that water baptism is connected to receiving the Holy Spirit. However, 12 percent of ICFG ministers believe that all Christians receive the Holy Spirit in water baptism. This may suggest that some Foursquare ministers are sacramentalists with regard to their understanding of water baptism. However, it may be that those ministers who associate water baptism with the reception of the Spirit believe in the possibility of multiple Spirit Baptisms so that "receiving" the Spirit at water baptism is not initiatory, but one of many special "fillings," "baptisms," or "anointings" that may be expected to occur throughout the life of a Christian.

---

them." The Foursquare Church, "What We Believe: The Spirit-Filled Life," para. 4. *AG Official Position Papers: Baptism in the Holy Spirit*, 12.

Spirit Baptism & Speaking in Tongues

All three denominations show a marked division among their ministers concerning the possibility of multiple Spirit Baptisms (Table 6.25). The doctrinal statements of all three denominations draw a distinction between Spirit Baptism as a one-time experience (an "initial infilling" or "release" of the Spirit) and subsequent fillings or anointing of the Holy Spirit that should come upon Christians subsequent to their initial experience of Spirit Baptism.[46] Yet, it is clear that this distinction is not uniformly recognized among classical Pentecostal ministers. In fact, the results seem to be an indication that there is uncertainty and disagreement among Pentecostals concerning Spirit Baptism as *a gateway experience into a new phase of the Christian life* and Spirit Baptism as *an ongoing experience of the Spirit in which one must actively participate and continually appropriate*. Pentecostals want to emphasize both aspects as essential for the "Spirit-filled life" and, as a result, neither Spirit Baptism as a one-time experience or an ongoing experience ought to be understood as the singular truth claim of Pentecostals in practice.

Table 6.25 *Multiple Spirit Baptisms*

Item	Denomination	Agree %	Not Certain %	Disagree %
It is possible to be baptized in the Holy Spirit more than once.	AG	42.1	22.1	35.8
	OBC	42.1	19.6	38.3
	ICFG	32.3	19.8	47.9
	Total	38.4	20.2	41.4

Spirit Baptism Rigidity Scale

A scale of rigidity (BHSrigid) of belief in the connection between speaking in tongues and Spirit Baptism was constructed using the following two questions in the survey:

- Speaking with tongues is necessary as the initial physical evidence of the Baptism in the Holy Spirit.

---

46. *Open Bible Manual*, 2.2. *Foursquare Licensing Process Guide*, 11.4. *AG Official Position Papers: Baptism in the Holy Spirit*, 10–11.

- I believe the Baptism in the Holy Spirit is witnessed by the initial physical sign of speaking with other tongues as the Spirit of God gives them utterance.

To each of these questions, respondents could reply: agree strongly, agree, not certain, disagree or disagree strongly. The items were tested for reliability by computing the Cronbach alpha coefficient (α = .897).

Table 6.26 *Spirit Baptism Rigidity (BHSrigid) Scale*

Item	Item rest of test (r)	α If item deleted	Agree %
Speaking with tongues is necessary as the initial physical evidence of the Baptism in the Holy Spirit.	.816	NA	50.0%
I believe the Baptism in the Holy Spirit is witnessed by the initial physical sign of speaking with other tongues as the Spirit of God gives them utterance.	.816	NA	58.8%

α = .897, NA = Not applicable due to the remainder of only a single item if the item is deleted

Two items that were originally intended to be part of the BHSrigid scale were: "I believe all Christians who have spoken in tongues have been baptized in the Holy Spirit" and "The Baptism in the Holy Spirit may be evidenced by spiritual gifts (*charismata*) besides tongues" (reverse coded). The addition of these questions to the BHSrigid scale would have resulted in a less than optimum Cronbach alpha coefficient for a three-item scale (α =.712 and α =.736, respectively). As a result, the items were not included in the BHSrigid scale. How might these lower than expected values be explained? One likely explanation is that holding to a rigid initial evidence position positively correlates to a belief that tongues is the only evidence, but it does not necessitate such a belief. This explanation would support the hypothesis that the word "initial" has real value for Pentecostal ministers in qualifying that while tongues is the *first* evidence of Spirit Baptism, it is not the *only* evidence. In other words, some "corroborating evidence" is needed to validate the authenticity of one's experience.

As indicated in Table 6.27, Assemblies of God ministers had the most rigid initial evidence position (mean = 10.950), while Foursquare was the least rigid (mean = 7.300). Using Bonforonni's coefficient to analyze individual variance between the three denominations (see Table 6.28), all three denominations surveyed are shown to have distinctly different beliefs concerning the connection between speaking in tongues and being baptized in the Holy Spirit.[47] As one would expect, the Assemblies of God scored significantly higher on the BHSrigid scale than Open Bible and Foursquare. Perhaps unexpected, Open Bible scored significantly higher than Foursquare on the scale (mean = 8.329). This finding makes more sense if one remembers that Open Bible's doctrine of Spirit Baptism was only changed to be more flexible regarding the evidence of speaking in tongues in 2002. Thus, there are likely many Open Bible ministers that continued to hold to a rigid doctrine of initial evidence even after their denomination became more inclusive.

Table 6.27 *One-way Analysis of Variance: BHSrigid by Denomination*

Denomination	Mean	SD
AG	8.918	1.47
OBC	6.607	2.68
ICFG	5.760	2.32
Total	6.733	2.61

F = 58.960, P < .000

Table 6.28 *Multiple Comparisons of Means (Bonferroni): BHSrigid by Denomination*

(I) denomination	(J) denomination	Mean Difference (I-J)	Std. Error
AG	OBC	2.312*	.287
	ICFG	3.158*	.292
OBC	AG	-2.312*	.287
	ICFG	.846*	.233
ICFG	AG	-3.158*	.292
	OBC	-.846*	.233

*. The mean difference is significant at the 0.001 level.

Table 6.29 indicates that while most ministers spoke in tongues immediately when they were baptized in the Holy Spirit, those that did not

---

47. The information in Table 6.28 gives some duplicate information as each relationship is presented twice. The information is presented in this way for ease of reference.

scored significantly lower on the BHSrigid scale. This indicates that even though a rigid doctrine of initial evidence may not necessarily carry with it the idea of immediacy, most Pentecostal ministers interpret the doctrine in that way. They do not feel comfortable believing in a rigid doctrine of initial evidence if they believe they were baptized in the Holy Spirit before they spoke in tongues.

Table 6.29 *BHSrigid Scale Score by Experience of Evidential Tongues*

Did you speak in tongues when you were baptized in the Holy Spirit?	Mean	SD
yes, immediately	7.421	2.41
yes, within 24 hours	5.593	2.68
yes, within a week	6.048	2.33
yes, sometime later	4.880	2.13
no	3.636	1.74

$F = 28.329$, $P < .000$ $r = -.421$

While almost all classical Pentecostals speak in tongues in private prayer at least occasionally, the frequency with which they do is significantly related to their score on the BHSrigid scale (see Table 6.30). Even though the doctrine only explicitly addresses one's entrance into the experience, those who speak in tongues on a daily or weekly basis are much more likely to dogmatically link Spirit Baptism with speaking in tongues than those who speak in tongues only occasionally or not at all. Thus, one's beliefs about how tongues are connected to the Spirit first coming upon a person can be correlated with how one participates in the ongoing experience.

Table 6.30 *BHSrigid Scale Score by Frequency of Speaking in Tongues Privately*

How often do you speak in tongues privately?	Mean	SD
nearly everyday	7.171	2.46
at least once a week	6.417	2.60
at least once a month	4.962	2.54
occasionally	6.122	2.80
never	4.333	2.94

$F = 6.308$, $P < .000$ $r = -.207$

Further Analysis

Ministers were overwhelmingly in favor of describing the experience of speaking in tongues as edifying (98.6% agree), holy (93.9% agree) and not uncontrollable (92.3% disagree). Most also agreed that the experience is calming (87.8% agree) and exciting (84.8% agree). Thus, classical Pentecostal ministers generally understand speaking in tongues as a positive experience that benefits the participant in a variety of ways and can be controlled by the speaker in such a way as to not cause disorder. Table 6.31 shows how various scale scores correlated to five different adjectives (edifying, calming, uncontrollable, holy and exciting) used to describe speaking in tongues. The scales do seem to account for some subtle differences among ministers in how they describe the experience of speaking in tongues. Ministers who frequently use tongues as a prayer language are more likely to describe the experience of speaking in tongues as calming and controllable. Ministers who associate Spirit Baptism with practical helps are most likely to view speaking in tongues as a holy and exciting experience. Ministers who hold a rigid doctrine of initial evidence are likely to describe speaking in tongues as edifying and exciting.

Table **6.31** *Correlation Coefficients (r): Glossolalic Experience Adjectives*

Item	To speak with tongues is an edifying experience	To speak with tongues is a calming experience	To speak with tongues is an uncontrollable experience	To speak with tongues is a holy experience	To speak with tongues is an exciting experience
BHSrigid	.194**	.005	.012	.132**	.188**
BHSpractical	.220**	.153**	.129**	.336**	.232**
RevlExp	.136**	.014	-.075	.036	-.007
PrLangExp	.287**	.230**	-.142**	.083	.075
VisbManExp	.112*	.044	.052	.006	.115*

**. Correlation is significant at the 0.01 level
*. Correlation is significant at the 0.05 level

There was no significant relationship shown between the BHSrigid scale and the BHSpractical scale.[48] Table 6.32 shows a correlation matrix for the ministers' scores on the BHSrigid scale and the individual items of practical helps associated with Spirit Baptism. Effective witnessing was the only practical help item that was significantly related to the BHSrigid scale score. Thus, it seems that a minister's belief or disbelief in a rigid doctrine of initial evidence is generally not related to the specific practical benefits that the minister perceives as originating from an experience of Spirit Baptism. In this sense, the doctrine of initial evidence functions for classical Pentecostals as a validation of whether or not one has been baptized in the Spirit, but it does little to define that experience for Pentecostals. In short, how the Spirit comes upon a person does not dictate the practical benefits that one will receive from the Spirit. Other factors seem more important in determining one's understanding of the practical benefits of Spirit Baptism. While the BHSrigid scale was only significantly correlated with one of the practical help items in the survey, the individual practical help items were positively related to each other. Classical Pentecostal ministers do not typically associate the Holy Spirit's help with one area of life but many areas at once.

---

48. $r = .020$

Spirit Baptism & Speaking in Tongues

Table 6.32 *Correlation Coefficient Matrix (r): BHS Rigid + Practical Helps*

	BHSrigid	Spirit Baptism helps . . .						
		to foster unity among Christians	prevent racial prejudice among Christians	one to witness effectively	one to interpret Scripture	one to preach better	one to pray when one doesn't know how to pray	one to worship God
BHSrigid	1	-.087	-.047	.160*	.023	.072	.013	.053
to foster unity among Christians		1	.629*	.363*	.427*	.365*	.127	.227*
prevent racial prejudice among Christians			1	.349*	.454*	.376*	.108	.178
one to witness effectively				1	.434*	.395*	.246*	.289*
one to interpret Scripture					1	.621*	.216*	.351*
one to preach better						1	.225*	.340*
one to pray when one doesn't know how to pray							1	.549*
one to worship God								1

*. Correlation is significant at the .001 level

Table 6.33 *Other Beliefs Associated with a Rigid Doctrine of Initial Evidence (BHSrigid)*

Item	Correlation Coefficient (r)	Sig.
Churches should regularly hold services devoted to seeking the Baptism in the Holy Spirit	.121	.000
Speaking with tongues in congregational meetings should be strongly encouraged	.499	.000
Speaking with tongues symbolizes the work of the Holy Spirit in the life of a Christian	.306	.000
The interpretation of tongues should be as from God to the congregation	.261	.000
There is a difference between the "gift of tongues" and "evidential tongues"	.296	.000

Table 6.33 indicates some other beliefs that are significantly correlated with a minister's espousal of a rigid doctrine of initial evidence. Those ministers who scored high on the BHSrigid scale tended to value services devoted to seeking the Baptism in the Holy Spirit and believe that speaking in tongues should be strongly encouraged in congregational meetings. Both of these beliefs are consistent with the frequent experiences of visible manifestations of the Spirit highlighted above that are associated with a high BHSrigid scale score (see above). A strong belief in the connection between Spirit Baptism and tongues by a minister directly influences the life of a congregation. "Seeker-services" and public utterances in tongues move from being optional to essential aspects of congregational life. If tongues are necessary as evidence of the fullness of the Holy Spirit coming upon a Christian, than to not encourage speaking in tongues in a congregational meeting would be to "quench the Holy Spirit."

It should be of no surprise that ministers who scored high on the BHSrigid scale were more likely to believe there is a difference between the "gift of tongues" and "evidential tongues." Historically, classical Pentecostals reconciled their belief in the doctrine with Paul's rhetorical admonition in 1 Corinthians 12 that not all have the gift of tongues by identifying such a distinction. The Assemblies of God doctrine states it this way: the gift of tongues and evidential tongues are "the same in essence, different in purpose and use."⁴⁹ Those who score higher on the BHSrigid scale were also more likely to view tongues as symbolic of the work of the Holy Spirit in the life of a Christian. Just as in the first generation of the Pentecostal movement, Pentecostals who dogmatically associate tongues with an experience of Spirit Baptism see tongues as more than just a way to connect with God in prayer, but a symbol of God at work among His people in many ways. The experience is full of meaning beyond just the benefits in prayer.

Spirit Baptism and Pentecostal Social Demarcation

While Pentecostals uniformly agree that they have been baptized in the Holy Spirit (see Table 6.06) and speak in tongues regularly in their private devotional lives (see Table 6.14), they clearly disagree about how these two experiences are connected. Pentecostals cannot be defined in relation to other groups in Christendom by their advocacy of a rigid doctrine of initial evidence. Yet, it might be said that an earlier definition of Pentecostals as simply those who believe they have been baptized in the Holy Spirit and who speak in tongues still proves today to be a valid way to define the group. If one tries to go farther than this in defining Pentecostals, one clearly treads upon shaky ground.

In fact, a rigid doctrine of initial evidence seems only to define a sub-group among Pentecostal ministers in North America. This subgroup is represented by distinctive denominations (Assemblies of God) in their entirety and indicated by the social factors associated with a rigid doctrine of initial evidence in post-distinctive (Open Bible) and non-distinctive (Foursquare) denominations. As will be shown in the following section, outside the Assemblies of God, this sub-group tends to be older, less educated and located in smaller churches.

Spirit Baptism and Social Factors

What social factors are related to holding a rigid stance on the connection between tongues and Spirit Baptism? The BHSrigid scale was tested against the variables: denomination, age and education. All three variables are significantly related to the scale. In order to calculate the analysis of variance between age and the BHSrigid scale score, the age category was divided into six sub-categories: <30, 30–39, 40–49, 50–59,

---

49. *Minutes of the 53rd Session of The General Council of the Assemblies of God*, 93.

60–69, and 70+. Table 6.34 shows that age is a significant factor in predicting a rigid stance on the connection between speaking in tongues and Spirit Baptism. The mean follows ascending age-group with the youngest having the least rigid and the oldest having the most rigid. Pearson's correlation coefficient was shown to be significant for the entire sample ($r = .369$, $p < .000$).

Table 6.34 *One-way Analysis of Variance: BHSrigid by Age Group (Entire Sample)*

Age Group	Mean	SD
<30	5.379	2.54
30–39	5.381	2.65
40–49	6.375	2.59
50–59	6.693	2.47
60–69	7.529	2.42
70+	8.569	1.54
Total	6.718	2.59

$F = 13.751$, $P < .000$

The correlation for the entire sample between age and a rigid connection between Spirit Baptism and tongues was much higher than that measured by Poloma and Green in their 2010 study.[50] This makes sense when one considers that the Assemblies of God requires their ministers (regardless of age) to assent to a doctrine of initial evidence. When one limits the cases analyzed to only Assemblies of God ministers, the correlation coefficient is only slightly higher than the finding of Poloma and Green: $r = .285$, $p < .000$. Table 6.35 shows that when Open Bible and Foursquare were considered separately (denominations that do not have a rigid initial evidence doctrine in their statement of beliefs) the F-Ratio increased ($F = 14.469$, $P < .000$) and the correlation coefficient increased ($r = .428$, $P < .000$). As indicated in Graph 6.1, BHSrigid scale scores show

50. Poloma and Green reported a Pearson's correlation coefficient of $r = .24$ between age and support of the doctrine of tongues as initial evidence of Spirit Baptism. Poloma and Green, *The Assemblies of God*, 231. This is much higher than the correlation Poloma found in her 1988 study ($r = .16$) showing that discrepancy among younger and older ministers regarding the doctrine of initial evidence is becoming more pronounced in the Assemblies of God. Poloma, *The Assemblies of God at the Crossroads*, 267.

a marked increase as the minister's age increased. The strong connection shown between age and a rigid doctrine of initial evidence among ministers in Open Bible and Foursquare is empirical evidence corroborating an increased aversion to a rigid doctrine of initial evidence among young classical Pentecostals that some Pentecostal scholars and leaders have been sensing. One may also argue there is evidence of a tension between younger and older ministers in the Assemblies of God that lies beneath the surface of doctrinal conformity in the denomination.[51] Such a tension felt by older denominational leaders may be one reason behind the denomination officially reaffirming its commitment to the doctrine at its 2009 convention.

Table 6.35 *One-way Analysis of Variance: BHSrigid by Age Group (Open Bible & Foursquare only)*

Age	Mean	SD
<30	4.429	1.83
30–39	4.982	2.57
40–49	5.667	2.36
50–59	6.205	2.37
60–69	7.174	2.50
70+	8.237	1.61
Total	6.185	2.52

$F = 14.469, P < .000$

---

[51]. This is the point argued by Poloma and Green based on the results of their 2010 study. Poloma and Green, *The Assemblies of God*, 106.

Norming the Abnormal

Graph 6.1 *Mean Age vs. BHSrigid (Open Bible & Foursquare only)*

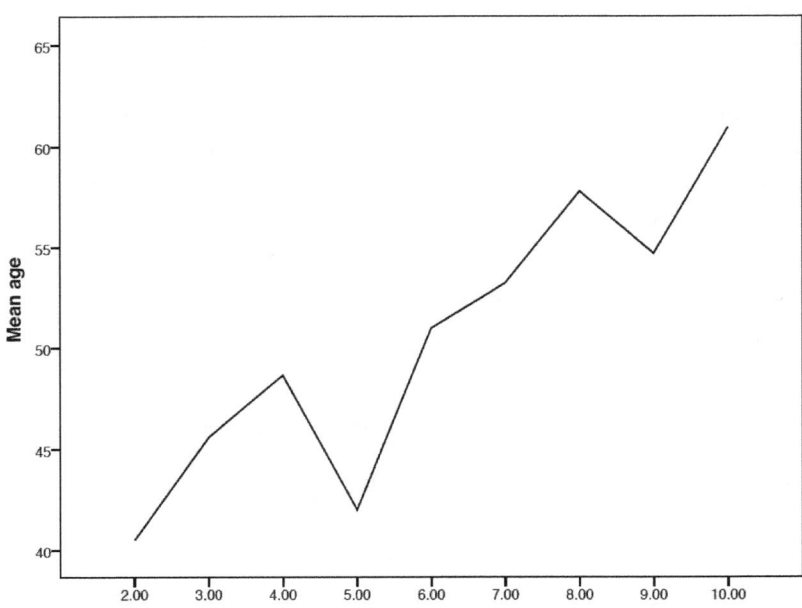

For ministers in Open Bible and Foursquare, the minister's level of education also proved to be statistically significant (though less significant than denomination or age) in predicting a belief in a rigid connection between speaking in tongues and Spirit Baptism.[52] Table 6.03 above shows that Assemblies of God ministers have an average level of education equal to or higher than ministers in Open Bible and Foursquare. However, Table 6.36 shows that as the Open Bible or Foursquare minister's level of education increases beyond the level of an Associate of Arts (A.A.) degree, the minister's beliefs regarding the connection between speaking in tongues and Spirit Baptism tends to become more flexible.[53] Ministers with a two-year A.A. degree or less who desire to be licensed in Open Bible or Foursquare would likely be required to take doctrine and polity courses directly from the denomination. These polity courses, even if they

---

52. Pearson's correlation coefficient: $r = -.156$, $P < .01$

53. The Associate of Arts degree is a two-year degree common in the United States. It is designed to give students a basic foundation of general education courses that are desirable for many entry-level jobs and which are easily transferable to other colleges. This option allows a student to complete two years at a community college or other college "close to home" and transfer to another college at a Junior status to pursue a Bachelor's degree in their chosen field of study.

do not require adherence to the doctrine, look favorably on a strong initial evidence position.[54] One would expect that these courses would lead a minister to look favorably on the doctrine as well.

As ministers seek out education beyond a basic two-year degree in a wide range of colleges and universities, one finds that the initial evidence position becomes less palatable for the average minister, though recent scholarship among members of the Society of Pentecostal Studies has demonstrated viable defenses of the doctrine of initial evidence in conversation with the latest theological disciplines. Historically, the doctrine of initial evidence has been difficult to uphold on the basis of traditional historical-critical methods of biblical interpretation.[55] Recent Pentecostal defenses of the doctrine of initial evidence are not without merit, but they have yet to be well received by the Evangelical academic community as a whole. Thus, Pentecostal ministers who go further in their theological education are confronted with the fact that to uphold the doctrine is to step outside the bounds of that which the broader Evangelical community generally accepts as a valid hermeneutic. This naturally leads to some ministers being more flexible on the connection between speaking in tongues and Spirit Baptism.

Table 6.36 *BHSrigid Mean Values by Level of Degree (Open Bible & Foursquare only)*

Degree	BHSrigid Mean	SD
None (no college, certificate/ non-degree programs)	6.538	2.45
Associate of Arts	6.500	2.60
Bachelor's Degree	6.083	2.68
Master's Degree	5.500	2.44
Doctor of Philosophy	4.875	1.25
Total	6.188	2.54

$F = 2.64, P = .034$

---

54. *We Believe*, 116–18; *Foursquare Licensing Process Guide* (2009), 10:1–2.

55. This is primarily because the historical-critical method has not usually looked favorably upon deriving theology and doctrine from narrative portions of Scripture such as Luke-Acts.

Charismatic Activity & Church Growth

Poloma and Kay have each done research showing a significant positive correlation between ministerial charismatic activity and church growth in their respective subjects of research.[56] A scale of ministerial charismatic activity was constructed using items identical or very similar to those used by Poloma and Kay.[57] The six items in the scale were based upon ministers' answers to the questions "How many times in the past three months *you* have . . ." given a public utterance in tongues, interpreted tongues, publicly prophesied, given a prophecy privately to another person, experienced being "slain in the Spirit," experienced "laughing in the Spirit"? The charismatic activity scale was broken down into four roughly equal groups. Table 6.37 shows the relationship between recent congregational church growth and ministerial charismatic activity (r = .164). Ministerial charismatic activity was shown to be a significant predictor of congregational church growth.

---

56. Poloma's book, *The Assemblies of God at the Crossroads*, published in 1989, covered an extensive survey of ministers and congregations in the Assemblies of God (USA). She found a significant correlation between congregational charismatic experience and evangelistic activity (r = .45) where a congregation's charismatic experience was linked to the minister's level of charismatic activity and individual evangelistic activity was assumed to be a significant predictor of church growth and institutional success. Kay's 2000 study surveyed ministers across four "classical" Pentecostal denominations in Britain: British Assemblies of God, the Elim Pentecostal Church, the Apostolic Church and the Church of God. Kay found a significant positive correlation between the percentage by which a minister's congregation had recently grown and the level of charismatic activity of the congregation. In 2007, Kay published key findings from a similar survey of Apostolic Network ministers in *Apostolic Networks in Britain*.

57. Kay's questions included in his scale measuring charismatic activity were as follows: "How many times in the past three months *you* have . . ." given a public utterance in tongues, interpreted tongues, sung in tongues, prophesied, danced in the Spirit, given a word of wisdom/knowledge? The alpha coefficient for this 6-item scale was α = .713. Kay, *Pentecostals in Britain*, 253. The survey items in Poloma's 7-item scale measuring charismatic experience (CharEx) were: frequency of praying in tongues, frequency of receiving definite answers to prayer requests, divinely inspired to perform some specific action, given a prophecy in a church service, given a prophecy privately to another, frequency of being slain in the Spirit, and personal confirmation of Scriptural truths. Poloma's scale returned an alpha coefficient of α = .55. Poloma, *The Assemblies of God at the Crossroads*, 12–13, 258.

Table 6.37 *Percentage Congregation Grew Last Year by Ministerial Charismatic Activity Level*

Ministerial Charismatic Activity Level	Mean	SD
Low	2.82	1.49
Low-Medium	3.02	1.36
High-Medium	3.47	1.49
High	3.52	1.55

$F = 4.168, P = .006$

The connection between church growth and ministerial charismatic activity that Kay and Poloma reported in their studies was proven to still apply to classical Pentecostals in North America. Table 6.38 indicates that ministers in congregations experiencing growth of 30 percent or more in the past year scored over four points higher on the charismatic activity scale than ministers reporting no growth in their congregation. Further analysis indicates that the revelatory experiences scale ($r = .174$) and the visible manifestations scale ($r = .173$) were significant predictors of congregational growth while the prayer language scale ($r = .084$) was not. This makes sense if one considers that the minister's prayer language is primarily concerned with their individual relationship with God and does little to involve the congregation. In contrast, the minister's revelatory experiences and visible manifestations of the Spirit are experiences that may be observed by the congregation and with which they may participate.

Table 6.38 *Ministerial Charismatic Activity (CharAct) by Percentage Congregation Grew Last Year*

Percentage Congregation Grew Last Year	Mean	SD
None that I know of	8.23	3.65
1–5%	10.94	5.59
6–10%	9.80	4.36
11–20%	10.99	5.23
21–30%	11.85	4.76
More than 30%	12.29	6.16

$F = 4.212, P = .001$

In contrast to church growth, the ministerial charismatic activity scales were not statistically linked to church size either positively or negatively. One might surmise from this that ministerial charismatic activity accounts for a short-term growth in attendance but does not necessarily lead to sustained congregational growth. When one adds to these findings those of Kay in his two studies of congregations and ministers in Britain, a clearer picture presents itself. Kay found that as a congregation's size increases a minister's example (either charismatic or evangelistic) becomes less important for growth than the life of the congregation itself. It was only in churches below 50 congregants that the charismatic activity of the minister was a significant factor related to church growth by itself.[58] If Kay's analysis of classical Pentecostals in Britain holds true for classical Pentecostal congregation in the United States, than ministerial charismatic activity would only be significantly related to size for the smallest congregations in the sample.

There was a negative correlation between the minister's score on the BHSrigid scale and size of the minister's congregation. The larger the minister's congregational size the lower the minister's BHSrigid scale score tended to be ($r = -.126$). As one would expect, when Open Bible and Foursquare ministers were surveyed by themselves, the negative correlation was more pronounced ($r = -.164$). Table 6.39 shows the mean scores on the BHSrigid scale for ministers who attended Open Bible and Foursquare congregations of varying sizes. Overall, the table seems to indicate that ministers in Open Bible and Foursquare with smaller congregations tended to have a more rigid stance on initial evidence. Analysis of variance on the sample, however, indicates that congregational size was not significantly associated with the minister's score on the BHSrigid scale.[59] Rather, a minister's BHSrigid scale score was shown to be significantly associated with the size of the minister's congregation ($F = 2.622$, $P = .005$). Foursquare and Open Bible ministers in smaller congregations may or may not have a rigid doctrine of initial evidence, but congregations with ministers who hold to a rigid doctrine of initial evidence will tend to be smaller than those with ministers who are more flexible on the doctrine. This correlation may simply be the result of an underlying factor in the personality of the minister (i.e., open-minded vs. closed-minded; legalistic vs. flexible) that either helps or hinders church growth. However, this finding suggests

---

58. Kay, *Pentecostals in Britain*, 261–64.

59. ANOVA: BHSrigid by Congregational Weekend Attendance ($F = 1.368$, $P = .201$).

that, *all other factors being equal,* a minister's decision to uphold a rigid doctrine of initial evidence may have an adverse effect on the growth of his or her church.

Table 6.39 *BHSrigid Mean by Congregational Weekend Attendance (Open Bible & Foursquare only)*

Average Congregational Weekend Attendance	Mean	SD
> 25	6.964	2.55
25–50	6.736	2.41
50–75	6.200	2.66
75–100	5.946	2.54
100–150	6.200	2.12
150–200	5.786	2.30
200–250	6.125	2.90
250–300	5.786	2.58
300–350	5.466	2.59
< 350	5.476	2.69

Hypotheses

Based upon the above findings, the hypotheses made at the beginning of the chapter can now be evaluated. First, the hypothesis that classical Pentecostals are unified in their beliefs about what Spirit Baptism contributes to the Christian life even if they disagree about how it is received is corroborated. Pentecostals are in agreement that Spirit Baptism brings a variety of practical results most commonly defined as "power for service." They also agree that help in prayer, help in understanding and proclaiming God's Word, and bringing unity are all benefits that come from Spirit Baptism. Thus, classical Pentecostals can join together in one voice in proclaiming the benefits of Spirit Baptism for the Christian life. As has been the case throughout the history of the Pentecostal movement in North America, differences in opinion about how one enters into an experience of Spirit Baptism are still prevalent, but Pentecostals seem to intuitively agree about the benefits of the experience.

Second, the hypothesis that classical Pentecostals experience similar public and private manifestations of the Holy Spirit in their lives even if they disagree about the doctrine of initial evidence is uncorroborated. Classical Pentecostal ministers who uphold a rigid doctrine of initial evidence are more likely to experience public manifestations of the Spirit in worship services and engage in glossolalic activity in private prayer more frequently. Thus, the doctrine does not only influence a person's reception of the Spirit, but it also seems to denote openness to the presence of God through visible manifestations. This means that debate about the doctrine has more at stake than simply the propositional truth claims associated with the doctrine.

Third, the hypothesis that the doctrine of initial evidence does not currently function significantly as an interpretation of the experience or narrative of classical Pentecostals is corroborated only for a certain segment of the population. Ministers outside the Assemblies of God (a distinctive denomination) who are younger, more educated, and in larger churches tend not to look at the doctrine of initial evidence as an interpretation of their experience or narrative even if they have experienced speaking in tongues in conjunction with their own Baptism in the Holy Spirit. Thus, it is likely that the reasons why the doctrine of initial evidence has fallen out of favor among some Pentecostals have to do primarily with changes in culture and intellectual concerns. This observation identifies a target group (younger and well-educated) upon which distinctive denominations should focus their attention when seeking to defend the doctrine of initial evidence, and it also may predict the communities where distinctive denominations may have the most difficulty and success in planting churches.

Fourth, the hypothesis that the regular practice of speaking in tongues privately is a defining characteristic of classical Pentecostals and does not correspond to a rigid doctrine of initial evidence is partially corroborated. It is corroborated with respect to the general practice of speaking in tongues and uncorroborated with respect to the specific regularity of the practice. Although virtually all Pentecostal ministers speak in tongues, the frequency with which they do is correlated, at least in part, with their belief in the doctrine of initial evidence. Even though the doctrine of initial evidence only formally addresses speaking in tongues in relation to receiving the Baptism in the Holy Spirit, it has implications for how Pentecostals value speaking in tongues (and other charismata) in the rest of their lives. Pentecostal ministers who believe that tongues are indispensably connected to an experience of Spirit Baptism are more likely to speak in tongues privately and experience public manifestations of tongues in their congregations.

Fifth, the hypothesis that the doctrine of initial evidence does not function primarily as a first-order truth claim for the classical Pentecostal community but as a second-order truth that ensures internal consistency and designates appropriate practices is corroborated. Most Pentecostals have some reservations about how they interpret the doctrine's exclusivity. Those ministers who affirm their belief in a rigid doctrine of initial evidence also tend to affirm other evidences besides tongues and disagree that all Christians who have spoken in tongues have been baptized in the Holy Spirit. Classical Pentecostals seem to be uncomfortable identifying tongues as the defining characteristic of those who are Spirit-baptized and more inclined to view it as an integral part of a multidimensional experience. It would seem that the doctrine functions more to designate tongues as a common practice of the classical Pentecostal community than as an *absolute truth claim*.

Sixth, the hypothesis that the dominant function of the doctrine of initial evidence in the classical Pentecostal community is currently that of a social demarcation is corroborated for post-distinctive and non-distinctive denominations. In denominations that do not enforce a belief in a rigid connection between tongues and Spirit Baptism, the more *traditional* in their community are demarcated on the basis of their beliefs and practices: belief in the doctrine of initial evidence and the practice of public charismatic manifestations. In distinctive denominations, the more *spiritual* are demarcated based upon their practices: the presence or absence of public charismatic manifestations.

Conclusion

The above study gathered survey responses from over 500 ministers across three classical Pentecostal denominations with different doctrinal statements concerning Spirit Baptism. The study reported on the specific beliefs and practices of these ministers in order to understand the current situation in the classical Pentecostal community with regard to the doctrine of initial evidence and to test some hypotheses arising out of the doctrine's historical development in relation to McGrath's four main functional categories.

The study found that there is much common ground among classical Pentecostals with regard to these four areas. There is unity among classical Pentecostals with regard to their personal narratives of Spirit Baptism and their private experiences of prayer language. Thus, whether or not classical Pentecostals agree on the doctrine, their stories of Spirit Baptism are quite similar and they uniformly value and practice speaking in tongues in private prayer. Classical Pentecostals agree that the doctrine of initial evidence should not separate Pentecostals and non-Pentecostals solely on the basis of whether or not they speak in tongues. Finally, the study found that classical Pentecostals agree that there is a logical connection between Spirit Baptism and speaking in tongues, even if they disagree about how such a connection might be articulated in a doctrinal statement.

The study also identified some important differences among classical Pentecostals regarding their doctrine of Spirit Baptism. While practical benefits and revelatory experiences were not significantly related to holding a rigid doctrine of initial evidence, visible manifestations of the Spirit stood out as experiences significantly related to the rigidity of one's doctrinal stance. Ministers with a rigid doctrinal stance were more likely to have recently experienced visible manifestations of the Spirit. In addition to this greater frequency of visible manifestations of the Spirit, ministers with a rigid stance were on average older, less educated and in smaller congregations.

These findings have important implications for the future practices of classical Pentecostals in North America. There are some important areas in which classical Pentecostal denominations have often struggled to find their way. They have struggled to pass on their story to future generations. They have struggled to articulate authentic Pentecostal experience. They have struggled to define themselves. They have struggled to develop a doctrine of Spirit Baptism that encapsulates their core beliefs. The final chapter will identify some ways forward for classical Pentecostals with regard to Spirit Baptism in these four key areas: 1) mission, 2) worship, 3) denominational identity, and 4) doctrine.

7

The Doctrine of Initial Evidence in the Future of Pentecostalism

Introduction

CHAPTERS 2–5 OF THIS study explored the origin and development of the doctrine of initial evidence in the classical Pentecostal tradition. The historical analysis shows that the doctrine of initial evidence did not originate and develop uniformly as the defining doctrine of the classical Pentecostal community. Even though the doctrine has, at times, been a point of unity and strength for the Pentecostal community, the doctrine has been a constant source of debate and criticism among classical Pentecostals. As a result, approaches to and explanations of the doctrine have been varied throughout the history of the Pentecostal movement. The doctrine was originally conceived on the basis of a Restorationist hermeneutic being applied to the Book of Acts, but the doctrine changed and developed over time as the needs of the Pentecostal community changed. The doctrine has functioned as far more than a distinctive propositional truth claim for classical Pentecostals in the last century. In addition to making a truth claim, which many Pentecostals have been uneasy of accepting, the doctrine has interpreted the narrative and experience of Pentecostals and provided social definition for the community.

Chapter 6 of this study set out to articulate the current beliefs and practices of Pentecostal ministers across three classical Pentecostal denominations with regard to speaking in tongues and Spirit Baptism. The ways in which the doctrine contributes positively or negatively to congregational life in the classical Pentecostal community has been a source of disagreement as the doctrine has been practically implemented at denominational and local church levels. While the Assemblies of God denomination has held a rigid stance on the doctrine since 1916, other classical Pentecostal denominations such as Open Bible and Foursquare are uncomfortable with a rigid doctrinal formulation, and have allowed their ministers to be more flexible. The study of 531 classical Pentecostal ministers found that the doctrine of initial evidence is still a defining doctrine for Assemblies of God ministers, but less than half of ministers in Open Bible and Foursquare agree with the doctrine. With such a divergence of opinion on the doctrine in classical Pentecostalism, this study identified points of unity that still exist among classical Pentecostals with regard to Spirit Baptism and speaking in tongues. The study also found other beliefs and practices that could be linked with the doctrine so as to find out what the doctrine currently contributes to the Pentecostal community in North America.

This final chapter will summarize the results of this study in relation to McGrath's four functions of doctrine for a community: interpretation of narrative, interpretation of experience, social demarcation, and making truth claims. Based on these findings, some implications and proposals for the future of classical Pentecostalism in North America will be given in four areas: mission, worship, identity, and doctrine. The proposals are meant to provide some helpful ways forward for classical Pentecostal influencers—ministers, denominational leaders, instructors and scholars—who deal regularly with a gap between the theory and practice of Pentecostals in relation to their doctrine of Spirit Baptism. The goal of this study, as stated in the opening chapter, is to move toward an understanding and corresponding practice of the doctrine of Spirit Baptism that is faithful to the heritage of the classical Pentecostal movement and consistent with the present experience of its members.

Summary of Findings and Implications for the Future

The Narrative of Classical Pentecostals

Findings

This study of classical Pentecostal ministers across three denominations found that there is a common narrative that classical Pentecostals share.

The Doctrine of Initial Evidence in the Future of Pentecostalism

Classical Pentecostals generally agree that their experience of Spirit Baptism provides for them power for service. This power for service is seen in a variety of practical benefits that Pentecostals associate with Spirit Baptism from help in prayer and worship to congregational witness to ecumenical mindedness. As such, Spirit Baptism for classical Pentecostals is currently less about preparing for the next life in purity and holiness and more about equipping the church with practical aids that will help the church to fulfill its God-given mission today.

The notion of Spirit Baptism as preparation for the church as the Bride of Christ has waned among classical Pentecostals. This is seen in the Pentecostal ministers' uncertain and scattered opinions about Spirit Baptism's association with holiness and sealing the Bride of Christ while being unified in associating Spirit Baptism with practical helps.[1] Classical Pentecostals have looked with favor upon William Seymour and Charles Parham as founding voices in the Pentecostal movement. However, both Seymour and Parham intimately connected the powerful benefits of Spirit Baptism for service with an imminent eschatology that upheld Spirit Baptism as necessary preparation for Christ's soon return. Pentecostals seem to have moved away from this primitivism—a desire to return to the first way of doing things—to pragmatism—a desire to do what practically works—as the dominant narrative by which they understand Spirit Baptism. For Pentecostals, God's Spirit coming upon a person as in the first generation of Christianity to give them power to serve Christ fully is more about empowering the church for today rather than restoring the church for tomorrow.[2]

Is there a common narrative that classical Pentecostals uniquely associate with the doctrine of initial evidence? This study indicates that there is not. Pentecostals appear to have the same story to tell whether or not they agree concerning the doctrine of initial evidence. The majority of Pentecostals readily associate speaking in tongues with their own initial and ongoing experience of Spirit Baptism, even if they do not uphold a rigid doctrine of initial evidence. Pentecostals also agree that speaking in tongues ought to be a point of unity for their community, not as an end in

---

1. See chapter 6 above.

2. This is not to say that Pentecostals have completely lost the restoration narrative that Archer and Faupel have emphasized (see Archer, "Pentecostal Story, 45–59; Faupel, *The Everlasting Gospel*), but it is to say that the eschatological focus of the story has shifted from the preparation of the Bride for heaven to bringing about God's kingdom on earth.

itself, but as a significant point of contact with God that is a sign of new life lived in the power of the Spirit.

This study shows that the origin of classical Pentecostalism should not be assumed to be one and the same with the origin of the doctrine of initial evidence. Pentecostal leaders have not uniformly accepted the doctrine and Pentecostal denominations have not always valued the doctrine. It has been a point of unification at times and division at other times. Approaches to the doctrine have been diverse, explained and defended in many different ways. The doctrine certainly played an important role in the formation of classical Pentecostal denominations. However, the doctrine's establishment in the Assemblies of God as the "distinctive testimony" of the organization should not be construed as simply voicing a common belief in Pentecostalism. It is best understood as an attempt to consolidate varied and diverse viewpoints among classical Pentecostals on the relationship between tongues and Spirit Baptism. Thus, the classical Pentecostal tradition must not be associated strictly with a belief in the doctrine of initial evidence. Rather, classical Pentecostalism is best defined as those groups with roots in the historical denominations that carry on a tradition of Spirit Baptism as a gateway experience that leads to a full Christian life of service empowered by the Holy Spirit.

Implications for Pentecostal Mission

Addressing some areas of convergence between postmoderns and Pentecostals, Veli-Matti Kärkkäinen points out the importance of the Pentecostal's common narrative for mission in a postmodern context:

> Observing Pentecostals, especially their mission, I discern a definite cultivation and building up of communalism. For postmodern people and Pentecostals, communities are shaped and brought about by a shared narrative, a story that is unfolding in the life of the community. "The Pentecostal community is a distinct coherent narrative tradition within Christianity. Pentecostal communities are bound together by their charismatic experiences and common story."[3]

The common story that Archer and Kärkkäinen refer to is a point that must be recognized and appreciated as Pentecostals seek to engage postmoderns who are skeptical about the authenticity and usefulness of

3. Kärkkäinen, "'The Leaning Tower of Mission," 88. The last two sentences are a quote from Archer, "Pentecostal Story," 40–42.

Pentecostal experiences. What is this common story and how does it relate to the doctrine of initial evidence?

This study has shown that there is a unified story of the origins and development of classical Pentecostalism that can be told apart from the idea that tongues evidences Spirit Baptism. This story is the history of Pentecostals being empowered for service. By focusing on their common narrative of empowerment for service, classical Pentecostal denominations may find a basis for unity that transcends divisions concerning the doctrine of initial evidence. Pentecostals uniformly tell a story of being empowered by the Holy Spirit to witness for Christ in the world. This happens through the gift of tongues, but in many other ways as well. Pentecostals have historically believed that Spirit Baptism empowers their preaching, church planting, overcoming obstacles on the mission field, ministry of social justice, and success in the political arena. In as far as glossolalia has contributed to these practical benefits directly (as a source of missionary tongues, help in worship and aid in intercessory prayer) or indirectly (as a source of intimacy with God, mark of holiness and sign of the Spirit's presence) it is viewed as an important, if not indispensable, part of the Pentecostal story. In as far as glossolalia has hindered these benefits directly (as a source of embarrassment, fanaticism and division) or indirectly (as a source of theological confusion, mark of spiritual immaturity and sign of neglecting the Spirit), it has been viewed as a problematic and superfluous part of the Pentecostal story.

Classical Pentecostals must recognize that tongues has both supported and hindered their empowerment for service in the above listed ways throughout the history of the movement. A minister's appreciation or disdain for the doctrine of initial evidence may be divided along these same lines based on their assessment of the current needs facing their own local church or denomination. Thus, Pentecostal leaders who look to empowerment for service as an overarching story of Pentecostal beginnings may find ministers who are being faithful to their heritage on both sides of the initial evidence debate.

Those who are comfortable identifying providential activity as an organizing framework for understanding Pentecostal history must also recognize that there are consistent reasons why providence may have been at work on both sides of the doctrine. At times, God may have been working for the doctrine's demise and at other times God may have been working for the doctrine's promulgation, all for the sake of empowering Pentecostals for service.[4]

All three groups in classical Pentecostalism that are the subject of this study—distinctives, post-distinctives, and non-distinctives—should be understood as significant contributors to the heritage of Pentecostalism. One group should not be viewed as orthodox and the others as compromisers. Each came into being during the same time period with common roots, experiences and problems. They each also faced similar questions related to the establishment of consistent Pentecostal doctrine. The answers they gave were different, but their own testimonies of spiritual empowerment and new life often converged where doctrinal statements may have diverged. This study shows that the testimonies of classical Pentecostals today continue to converge around the idea of spiritual empowerment for service, just as they did in the first-generation of Pentecostals.

In the same way that personal testimonies of Spirit Baptism and empowerment were the most important vehicles for passing along the full gospel message to others in early Pentecostalism, they may be the most important vehicle for engaging in successful mission to postmoderns today. If this is true, Pentecostals in North America may find that their greatest successes will happen outside traditional denominational structures. Kay has shown that the apostolic network churches in Britain "map onto post-modern society much more adequately than conventional denominational structures."[5] Although they are not without their own implicit hierarchical structures, they are seen as less sectarian and more embracing of social diversity than traditional denominations, and as such, more at home in postmodern society. In this environment, collective testimony is more easily understood as authoritative for belief rather than illustrative of belief. If the testimony of Pentecostals is to regain a central place in passing on the Pentecostal experience to younger generations, it will do this most easily outside denominational structures that tend to minimize the importance of testimonies in relation to doctrinal statements.

---

4. Kay has shown that the value of a providential understanding of history need not be completely disregarded as is common today in academia. Guided by Karl Popper's view of history and good history writing, Kay proposes that providence may be an appropriate framework for conceiving of Pentecostal history in that it is this approach that may be best suited to get at the "logic of situations" that the historian seeks to elucidate. Kay, "Karl Popper and Pentecostal Historiography," 5–15.

5. Kay, "Apostolic Networks in Britain: An Analytic Overview," 40.

The Doctrine of Initial Evidence in the Future of Pentecostalism

The Experience of Classical Pentecostals

Findings

This study found that there is a common experience of the Holy Spirit that classical Pentecostals share: prayer language. Engagement in the practice of speaking in tongues privately in prayer is a defining characteristic of classical Pentecostals. Pentecostal ministers almost unanimously speak in tongues in their private devotional lives, regardless of whether they rigidly associate speaking in tongues with an initial experience of Spirit Baptism. The fact that at least 78 percent of ministers in each of the three denominations surveyed speak in tongues privately at least once per week shows that speaking in tongues is a valuable experience for most classical Pentecostal ministers.[6] Thus, the early definition of Pentecostals as "tongues-speakers" seems to still be an accurate, albeit incomplete, definition of classical Pentecostals today. The issue of associating speaking in tongues with Spirit Baptism becomes a controversial issue in the Pentecostal community only as an absolute truth claim or requisite experience and not as an overarching characteristic of Pentecostal devotional and worship practices.

At the same time, the rigidity with which a minister holds to a doctrine of initial evidence is a key factor in predicting the frequency with which the minister speaks in tongues privately and experiences tongues publicly in their local congregation. Pentecostals who hold to a rigid doctrine of initial evidence tend to speak in tongues more than those who are flexible on the doctrine. Thus, while Pentecostals overwhelmingly describe the experience of speaking in tongues positively and as beneficial for their community, the frequency with which they experience these benefits is different. The doctrine of initial evidence also interprets visible manifestations as important indicators of God's presence among His people. This impacts the public Pentecostal experience. In congregations where the doctrine of initial evidence is espoused, visible manifestations of the Spirit are more common. As a result, those who support a rigid doctrine of initial evidence may be understood not just as guardians of a doctrine, but guardians of a particular experience that Pentecostals express in worship services through visible manifestations of the Holy Spirit.

Of the three ways in which the doctrine of initial evidence has functioned as an interpretation of experience in the history of classical Pentecostals, the third—a sacramental experience—seems to be most dominant

---

6. See chapter 6 above.

today.[7] The doctrine of initial evidence does not function to validate the scriptural basis of speaking in tongues for the classical Pentecostal community. Nor does it work to encourage speaking in tongues as a gateway experience into a full Christian life. Whether or not Pentecostals rigidly associate speaking in tongues with Spirit Baptism, they uniformly believe in the scriptural veracity of the experience and attribute many practical benefits to the experience. Yet, the doctrine of initial evidence still articulates something significant for Pentecostals, a depth of experience in the Spirit that naturally will result in speaking in tongues and other charismatic manifestations.

Implications for Pentecostal Worship

Frank Macchia has argued that the function of the doctrine of initial evidence may be more accurately described as a "sacramental sign" rather than "empirical evidence" of the Spirit's presence.[8] Although there are important differences between the Pentecostal understanding of tongues as free and unpredictable and the liturgical understanding of the sacraments as orderly and predictable, there is a common emphasis in both traditions on "a visible context in which the experience of God is received and manifested."[9] The finding in this study that there is a significant correlation between ministers that uphold a rigid doctrine of initial evidence and believe that "speaking in tongues symbolizes the work of the Holy Spirit in the life of a Christian" is evidence that Macchia's proposal may capture the heart of what Pentecostals are trying to articulate with the doctrine. Despite the original concern of the doctrine with the entrance of the Spirit in the life of a Christian, the doctrine also serves Pentecostals by making a value judgment about one's ongoing experiences of the Spirit as "contexts for a dynamic and personal divine/human encounter."[10] In communities where speaking in tongues functions sacramentally as an indispensable external indicator of an inner working of Christ in the life of a Christian, the doctrine of initial evidence will likely be supported and

---

7. It was argued in chapter 5 that the doctrine of initial evidence has functioned historically as an interpretation of the experience of the classical Pentecostal community in three ways. It has interpreted it as: 1) a scriptural experience, 2) a gateway experience, and 3) a sacramental experience.

8. Macchia, "Groans Too Deep for Words," 172–73.

9. Macchia, "Tongues as a Sign," 70.

10. Ibid., 71.

affirmed. Other visible manifestations of the Spirit besides tongues will likely be valued and affirmed in these contexts as well.

In this regard, the Assemblies of God and other distinctive denominations seem to be making an important contribution to classical Pentecostalism in North America as groups that uphold the importance of public and visible manifestations of the Spirit. It seems that distinctive denominations are cognizant of this contribution. Despite increased criticism of the doctrine by Pentecostals within and outside of their denomination, particularly by those who are younger, Assemblies of God denominational leaders have not demonstrated any desire to soften or forego the initial evidence doctrine. In fact, they have solidified and reaffirmed their stance. Concerned that some ministers were compromising the doctrine, in 2009 the General Council reaffirmed their commitment to the doctrine and called anew for the regular teaching and preaching of the doctrine in their pulpits.[11]

It must not be assumed that Assemblies of God officials reaffirmed this doctrine solely to bring conformity and unity in belief. They wanted to address specific practical concerns that ministers in the denomination were facing. In 2009, *Christianity Today* published an article about the recent resolution. Along with perceived doctrinal compromise among ministers, the practical reduction of speaking in tongues in public and praying for people to be baptized in the Holy Spirit were concerns that prompted the resolution to be raised in the Assemblies of God.[12] In 2007, the Spiritual Life Committee of the Assemblies of God reported, "Pastors lament the loss of the 'twenty-somethings'[sic] in our churches, yet fear that significant changes directed at reaching them might be considered compromise."[13] In the same report, the committee identified compromise on the doctrine of initial evidence as an area of particular concern.

---

11. The resolution was proposed by the South Texas District at the 53rd General Council of the Assemblies of God in Orlando, Florida. Initially, the Council did not even want to put the resolution to a vote because a vote to the contrary would contradict the existing bylaws of the denomination. However, since a district council passed the resolution it was automatically deemed appropriate and in accordance with AG bylaws. Officially, the General Council voted to reaffirm their commitment to the "Pentecostal Distinctive: The Initial Physical Evidence of Holy Spirit Baptism," and resolved to "continue to require our credentialed ministers to not only have the aforementioned Pentecostal experience in their own lives, but actively preach and teach this doctrine as well." *Minutes of the 53rd Session of The General Council of the Assemblies of God*, 49–52.

12. McMullen, "Holding Their Tongues," 15–18.

13. *Minutes of the 52nd Session of The General Council of the Assemblies of God*, 9.

> The distinctive doctrine that once united us has, in some circles, become a point of contention. We lament the increasing rarity of the gifts of the Spirit in our worship setting. We wonder where, in our busy church schedules, will people have the opportunity to tarry at the altars for a transforming Pentecostal experience?[14]

But, can such a resolution as was passed in 2009 succeed in bringing about the practices that the Assemblies of God desires? The Assemblies of God leaders clearly recognize that enforcing doctrinal conformity among its ministers is not enough to change practices in their churches. They know that a gap between doctrine and practice can only be addressed through preaching and teaching at the local level, which is why they called not just for doctrinal conformity but regular preaching on the doctrine of initial evidence. Yet, for preaching of a doctrine to be effective at moving people toward corresponding practices, it must move beyond simply repetition or reiteration of a doctrine. The above findings suggests that Pentecostal preaching and teaching must focus on training congregations as to how Spirit Baptism is worked out in congregational life. In particular, ministers would do well to emphasize the sacramental nature of speaking in tongues as the context in which God manifests his presence that leads to a changed life. Poloma and Green have prescribed such a response in their 2010 study:

> If it fails to provide opportunities for modeling tongues through its use in church rituals, through testimonials of frequent glossolalics, and in teachings that resonate with actual experiences, glossolalia may continue to slide into irrelevance with the increasing evangelicalization of AG congregations.[15]

Although this study shows that an observed decrease in public manifestations of tongues can be correlated with a decrease in belief in the doctrine of initial evidence, it is naive to assume that Pentecostal ministers who believe in the doctrine will inevitably create environments for the public manifestation of tongues. George Wood, General Superintendent of the Assemblies of God, has attributed decreases in speaking in tongues in worship gatherings more to "cultural influences" than a lack of confidence in the doctrine. "There's been a cultural shift in the last 30 years. Sunday morning services used to be for believers, and Sunday night services were more evangelistic," he said. "Sunday night services have declined, and now

14. Ibid., 9.
15. Poloma and Green, *The Assemblies of God*, 115.

the morning service is more for people to bring friends."[16] It is these kinds of cultural shifts that Wood says are the main cause of decreases in the practice of charismatic manifestations. If speaking in tongues functions for Pentecostals as a sacramental sign of God's presence, then ministers must ensure that there are regular times for the "sacrament" of tongues to be received corporately.

Youth and young adult pastors are at the center of the struggle to create environments for Pentecostal "sacraments" to be received. This study shows that by the time congregations assimilate into the adult life of their church they will have already had whatever experience they will consider their personal Baptism in the Holy Spirit.[17] Thus, it is the youth pastor rather than the senior pastor that is more likely to deal practically with questions about how Spirit Baptism is received and the results of such an experience. This means that denominational leaders must be particularly attuned to the needs of their youth and young adult pastors in discussions about how the doctrine relates to experience.

Classical Pentecostal denominations that have decided that a rigid doctrine of initial evidence no longer represents a faithful articulation of the Pentecostal's testimony are faced with a challenge all their own. They must discern how to uphold the integrity of the experience of the Spirit in their past while maintaining that such an experience cannot be dogmatized in the same way. Open Bible has not completely done away with the idea that tongues evidences Spirit Baptism; they have simply said their constituents "should anticipate" such a manifestation rather than guarantee it. While the change is slight, it removes the grounds for a denomination enforcing the preaching and teaching of tongues as an indispensable practice. Without a doctrine that rigidly associates speaking in tongues with Spirit Baptism, pastors and preachers are left to make the connection at a local church level and lead their congregations to anticipate such experiences.

How best to incorporate the gifts of the Spirit in services by remaining not only open to them, but also expectant and anticipatory, is an issue that non-distinctive and post-distinctive denominations must address. It is doubtful that Open Bible or Foursquare denominational officials, by having more flexible doctrinal statements, desire to de-emphasize manifestations of tongues and other charismata in public worship gatherings.

---

16. McMullen, "Holding Their Tongues," 18.
17. See chapter 6 above.

Their desire is to be more inclusive.[18] Yet, whether they intended it or not, the empirical evidence suggests that public manifestations of the Spirit are less frequent in denominations that are more flexible on the connection between speaking in tongues and Spirit Baptism. It seems that without a doctrine that explicitly connects speaking in tongues with the presence of the Spirit, non-distinctive and post-distinctive congregations may be less apt to create environments that are conducive for speaking in tongues in the public worship setting and therefore are prone to relegate tongues to the private prayer lives of their congregants. Thus, it is important for ministers in non-distinctive and post-distinctive denominations to preach and teach about the sacramental nature of speaking in tongues and other charismata as they relate to the rest of the Christian life, and to purposefully create environments where such sacraments may be received corporately.

The Social Identity of Classical Pentecostals

Findings

This study found that in classical Pentecostal denominations that allow for flexibility on the doctrine of initial evidence (Open Bible and Foursquare), ministers that affirm the doctrine tend to be older, less educated, and in smaller churches. This finding could be seen as especially problematic for the long-term health of denominations that support the doctrine. Denominations that continue a trend of aging ministers, shrinking congregations and weak education will ultimately die. Yet, this study found that ministers in the Assemblies of God are not on average significantly older or less educated than ministers in Open Bible and Foursquare, and their churches are not smaller. The Assemblies of God requirement that ministers adhere to the doctrine and also publicly affirm the doctrine regularly in congregational meetings does not seem to have led to the same kind of trends one sees among Open Bible and Foursquare ministers who espouse the same doctrine. Thus, it appears that the Assemblies of God may represent a

---

18. At the 2003 National Convention Business Meeting for Open Bible Churches, President Jeff Farmer identified the central reasons upon which they based the proposed changes to their doctrinal statement on Spirit Baptism, which was ultimately approved and adopted. "The question is: must the evidence always be speaking in tongues? The issue is, how can we be as inclusive as possible, without diluting who we are as Pentecostals?" *National Convention Business Meeting Minutes, June 21, 2003*, 9. At the same time, President Farmer has been open about his concern that the movement not lose its emphasis on Spirit Baptism and the gifts of the Holy Spirit, as doing so could be a threat to the movement. Cole, "Heritage and Horizons," 167.

The Doctrine of Initial Evidence in the Future of Pentecostalism

vibrant subgroup of classical Pentecostals for whom the doctrine of initial evidence is a point of unity and strength while it is a point of contention and weakness for other Pentecostal denominations.[19]

Yet, this study also suggests that younger and more educated ministers in Pentecostalism will tend not to uphold the doctrine of initial evidence when they are given the freedom to do so by their denomination. Outside the Assemblies of God, the doctrine demarcates a subgroup of classical Pentecostal ministers that is older and less educated and in smaller churches.[20] Based on these findings, the Assemblies of God will find its rigid doctrine of initial evidence increasingly called into question by Pentecostal ministers outside the denomination who are younger, more educated or pastors of larger churches. How will this criticism influence the Assemblies of God? If Assemblies of God ministers are truly unified in their belief in a rigid doctrine of initial evidence, increased criticism among Pentecostals will likely work to strengthen the identity and self-definition of ministers in the Assemblies of God as a unique and important subgroup of classical Pentecostals. However, if Crepe and Poloma and Green are right in their assessments that there is a growing concern about the doctrine of initial evidence among younger ministers in the Assemblies of God, this criticism may work to draw younger and more educated ministers away from the Assemblies of God to other denominations that are more flexible in their doctrinal position.[21]

Implications for Pentecostal Denominational Identity

DISTINCTIVE DENOMINATIONS: ASSEMBLIES OF GOD

Although this study did not survey the general population of Christians, the above findings among Pentecostal ministers causes one to expect

---

19. Poloma and Green argue that although a majority of Assemblies of God constituents agree with the doctrine of initial evidence it is a point of increasing concern and disunity for the denomination. Poloma and Green, *The Assemblies of God*, 104–6, 109. This is the case when comparing their findings to Poloma's 1988 study of the Assemblies of God. However, in comparison to Foursquare and Open Bible, the Assemblies of God seems to have relatively unified stance on the doctrine.

20. The only denomination with a doctrine of initial evidence in this study was the Assemblies of God. One would expect that other classical Pentecostal denominations with the doctrine (Church of God, Cleveland; Church of God in Christ) would follow a similar trend. It would be interesting to survey these groups.

21. Creps, "Postmodern Pentecostals?" 27–47; Poloma and Green, *The Assemblies of God*, 109.

that Christians outside the Pentecostal tradition will increasingly view ministers and churches who espouse the doctrine of initial evidence as traditionalists, simpleminded and out-of-touch. If this is true, Pentecostal denominations that subscribe to the doctrine of initial evidence have three options before them if they are going to continue to grow and multiply in the United States.

First, distinctive denominations can choose to shift their focus from the doctrine to other points of demarcation and distinction that are more broadly appealing. So far, the Assemblies of God has been unwilling to do this. In 2009, the denomination officially broadened its mission to include demonstrations of compassion and love to the world. But, as stated earlier, they also reaffirmed their allegiance to the doctrine of initial evidence at the same meeting.[22] The Assemblies of God clearly wants the world to know that the denomination is concerned with more than just their Pentecostal distinctives, but they do not want to do this at the expense of those distinctives.

In fact, some writers argue that de-emphasizing their distinctives is what has caused a recent slowdown in growth for the Assemblies of God. Rather than recommending that they broaden their focus, they believe the best way forward is for them to re-establish their unique identity in relation to other groups in Evangelicalism. In 2003, Gary McGee proposed, "The greatest hurdle in [the Assemblies of God's] path into the twenty-first century, therefore, stands in how successfully it recaptures what it means to be 'more than evangelical.'"[23]

Addressing McGee's concern, Ed Stetzer wrote an article for the Assemblies of God's *Enrichment Journal* in which he argued that the church has lost its influence in America because it has forgotten its mission. He observed, "I have seen churches across North America fighting over preferences and drawing battle lines over issues that do not matter, while the world and the surrounding communities are dying without Christ."[24] Stetzer called for churches to distinguish between beliefs that should be held with a "closed right-hand" (things they will contend for at all costs) and beliefs that should be held with an "open left-hand" (things they are

---

22. In 2009, the General Council voted to officially add a fourth reason for the denomination's existence to their Statement of Fundamental Truths: "to be a people who demonstrate [God's] love and compassion to all the world." *Minutes of the 53rd Session of The General Council of the Assemblies of God*, 49–52.

23. McGee, "More Than Evangelical," 300.

24. Stetzer, "Writing on the Wall," 38.

willing to contextualize). Identifying the "right-hand" tenets of the Assemblies of God, Stetzer argued,

> We must absolutely preserve [in] certain beliefs if we are to remain faithful to the Scriptures. These include tenets, such as the Virgin Birth and the authority and inerrancy of Scripture. The Assemblies of God must also maintain other certain distinctive theological beliefs—such as the Baptism in the Holy Spirit with the initial physical evidence of speaking in tongues. This is a right hand, non-negotiable issue for the Assemblies of God.[25]

Stetzer went on to say, "The answer to reaching a lost world is not to create a bland evangelicalism . . . we need movements that are deeply committed to their scripturally formed distinctives."[26] Stetzer is correct in his assertion that a denomination that ignores or smoothes over the rough edges of their "scripturally formed distinctives" will lose their ability to be a force for positive change, but one wonders whether the doctrine of initial evidence is a distinctive that may be better suited for the left hand than the right when it comes to the future success of distinctive denominations in North America.

Second, distinctive denominations may effectively deal with the demographic trends in this study by defending the doctrine of initial evidence in new and creative ways that are appealing to the younger and more educated in their constituency. Seeing a pattern in the Book of Acts is not enough for either group. Those who are younger may be appealed to by emphasizing the benefits of Spirit Baptism that are important to them and, at the same time, practically or symbolically connected to speaking in tongues. Benefits such as intimacy with God in prayer, expressions of human need and brokenness, and solidarity with people of other cultures and races are important to young people in North America, and these benefits can be directly linked to speaking in tongues. As these benefits of speaking in tongues are emphasized in the worship services of those who claim to be Spirit-baptized, the doctrine of initial evidence may naturally become more appealing to young people.

James K. A. Smith, who has engaged in some groundbreaking research on glossolalia from a philosophical perspective, agrees with Stetzer and McGee that a desire to appeal to "seekers" and align themselves with Evangelicalism has caused some congregations in the Assemblies of God to lose their charismatic emphasis in worship services.

25. Ibid., 40.
26. Ibid., 41.

Yet, Smith believes that re-emphasizing the doctrine of initial evidence at the denominational level will do little to rekindle charismatic revival in a church culture that believes that glossolalia is problematic for church growth. The solution, according to Smith, is in educating lay people in appropriate practices of tongues and other charismatic manifestations in the public worship setting.[27] This study supports Smith's conclusion.

Understanding the doctrine of initial evidence within Lindbeck's cultural-linguistic framework for doctrine may be the most important direction for Pentecostal scholars to work in appealing to those who are more educated. Lindbeck's framework, although in need of the modifications that Vanhoozer and McGrath suggest, allows for the doctrine to be understood and appreciated on the basis of the culture and language of the Pentecostal community without condemning those who do not have such a doctrine. Shuman has argued that the Pentecostal doctrine of initial evidence is best understood as an "expression of one of the practices of a particular cultural-linguistic community."[28] Thus, the doctrine is best critiqued within the boundaries of that community. Pentecostals would do well to heed Shuman's advice by admitting that the initial evidence doctrinal formulation is culturally and linguistically driven. Doing so would not relativize the truth to which Pentecostals seek to attest, but it would keep Pentecostals from contending for the inerrancy of the language and culture in which the truth has been captured and passed on.[29] Such an admission would be well received by Pentecostals who appreciate the Pentecostal experience but have reservations about dogmatizing such an experience in language that is exclusive and which lends itself to conceiving of spirituality in levels.

If things continue as they are, the doctrine of initial evidence will continue to fall out of favor with older and less educated Pentecostals. Thus, a third option available to distinctive denominations that desire growth is to recognize and embrace this trend through their church planting and growth strategies. Instead of trying to appeal to people of

---

27. McMullen, "Holding Their Tongues," 18–19. Smith was interviewed by *Christianity Today* for the article by McMullen.

28. Shuman, "Toward a Cultural-Linguistic Account," 233.

29. Ibid., 217. Shuman argues that a cultural-linguistic account of doctrine does not exclude the possibility of a doctrine's "permanence or normativeness." It simply recognizes that the truths to which doctrines attest are embedded in the practices of a particular worshipping community so that they can only be experienced within the framework of language and culture that gave rise to such practices (or possibly an overlapping framework with shared suppositions).

all different demographics in the United States, distinctive denominations may find that their efforts are best directed to those demographics that are older and less educated. This option need not be seen as a capitulation to critics of the doctrine or an admission that the doctrine is not robust; such a move simply recognizes that some mission fields are more fruitful than others and that certain groups more readily accept some teachings than others. While this cannot be seen as good for the long-term health of a denomination, it may possibly lead to short-term growth.

Post-Distinctive Denominations: Open Bible

Post-distinctive denominations must articulate why they have changed their doctrine and what such a change is meant to accomplish. Lest the past be thought of as simply an example of poor judgment and/or Pentecostal excesses, the denominations must work to give their constituents a sense of identity and an interpretation of their experience that they can embrace. They must also show how such a tenet is not essential to their identity as a denomination or as Pentecostals. Those denominations that choose to move from distinctive to post-distinctive orientations must show how the change is not a retreat or capitulation but a move forward and an embracing of values important for the group.

The seeds of constructing such a defense are certainly present in Open Bible. From the beginning, the association of churches desired to show its inclusive orientation to others by refraining from printing a rigorous statement of faith. While maintaining a Pentecostal orientation, they desired to keep most matters of doctrinal debate in the local church. Just as in the Assemblies of God, Open Bible moved away from advocating an extreme pacifist stance toward military service. Instead, they upheld the "authority of conscience" as the final guide in such matters.[30] Paul Alexander has proposed that such a stance may be effectively applied to other doctrines such as initial evidence.[31] In many ways, Open Bible was a forerunner of the approach advocated by Alexander.

---

30. For the move away from pacifism in Open Bible compare the 1940 *Policies and Principles of Open Bible Standard Churches* with subsequent editions.

31. Alexander, *Peace to War*, 340.

Non-Distinctive Denominations: Foursquare

Non-distinctive denominations have not officially held a doctrine of initial evidence. As a result, they have relied upon their roots, leadership, congregational experience, or other doctrines to define themselves as classically Pentecostal. Thus, there have been a variety of ways in which their tradition has been articulated and passed down to future generations. This diversity brings its own challenges. If non-distinctive denominations believe that charismatic manifestations are important for the life of their congregations, then they must work to establish compelling reasons as to why they are important besides their connection to Spirit Baptism. They must also work to define how one receives an experience of Spirit Baptism, and how one can know that such an experience has occurred apart from tongues. If it is simply assumed that all Christians have already been baptized in the Holy Spirit, than the denomination has lost its Pentecostal heritage entirely. Thus, a post-distinctive denomination must establish some practical ways in which those who desire to be baptized in the Holy Spirit can do so and what, if any, are the indicators of such an experience.

The Truth Claim of Classical Pentecostals

Findings

This study has shown that the first-order truth claim made by the doctrine of initial evidence has always been controversial and the subject of debate both within and outside of Pentecostalism since its inception. As such, the doctrine of initial evidence represents a first-order truth claim (a statement of fact rooted in the Christ-event) for only a portion of classical Pentecostal ministers. For those ministers who do hold to a rigid doctrine of initial evidence, there seems to be disagreement among them about exactly what claim is being made with the doctrine. For example, this study found that many Pentecostals that uphold the doctrine do not believe they can separate those who are Spirit-baptized from those who are not solely on the basis of whether they have spoken in tongues.[32]

One of the two second-order truth claims, outlined in chapter 5, made by the doctrine of initial evidence—ensuring internal consistency—is well

---

32. 69.7 percent of those who subscribe to the doctrine of initial evidence believe that all Christians who have spoken in tongues have been baptized in the Holy Spirit. 81.7 percent of those who subscribe to the doctrine of initial evidence believe that Spirit Baptism may be evidenced by spiritual gifts (*charismata*) besides tongues.

received by a majority of ministers in all three denominations surveyed. Even if they do not believe it should be a rule, classical Pentecostal ministers uniformly associate tongues with their entrance into the Spirit-filled life, reinforcing their belief in the logical connection between the two experiences. Those who claim to be baptized in the Holy Spirit regularly speak in tongues in private prayer, and they believe that speaking in tongues is beneficial for the ecclesial body to experience. Further, at least 75 percent of ministers in all three denominations surveyed dated their initial experience of Spirit Baptism within a week of when they first spoke in tongues.[33] Despite strong disagreement about the first-order truth claims of the doctrine of initial evidence, they agree that there is a logical connection between speaking in tongues and Spirit Baptism. As a result, some classical Pentecostals who are unsure about the doctrine of initial evidence are still predictably sympathetic to those who believe in the doctrine because they realize that the doctrine articulates a connection between tongues and Spirit Baptism that they believe is important.

The other second-order truth claim made by the doctrine of initial evidence—evoking appropriate response—is a point of disagreement for classical Pentecostal ministers. The actions and responses of Pentecostals who believe in a rigid doctrine of initial evidence are markedly different than those who do not. While Pentecostals agree concerning the practical benefits that one experiences through Spirit Baptism, these benefits are expressed in very different ways. Thus, the hypothesis that classical Pentecostals are unified in their beliefs about what Spirit Baptism contributes to the Christian life even if they disagree about how it is received is uncorroborated.

Another way of putting this finding is that the primary way in which the doctrine of initial evidence functions as a truth claim for the Pentecostal community is as a second-order truth claim in evoking appropriate response. In performing the function of evoking appropriate response, the doctrine of initial evidence validates two specific responses for classical Pentecostals. First, the doctrine of initial evidence validates the importance of visible manifestations of the presence of God in a worship service. Belief in the doctrine of initial evidence is significantly related to a belief that speaking in tongues symbolizes the work of the Holy Spirit in the life of the Christian.[34] Ministers who scored high on the Spirit Baptism Rigidity scale also scored high on the scale that measured their experi-

---

33. See chapter 6 above, Table 6.07.
34. $r = .306$

ence of visible manifestations of the Spirit.[35] Second, the doctrine of initial evidence validates the need for congregations to allow opportunities for speaking in tongues in their worship services (a sign of the Spirit's presence among his people). Those ministers who scored high on the Spirit Baptism Rigidity scale were much more likely to advocate such opportunities.[36] It is logical that if one believes speaking in tongue is a necessary physical manifestation for everyone who is baptized in the Holy Spirit, than one must allow for opportunities for members of the congregation to speak in tongues. To do otherwise would be to surely "quench the Spirit." In the same vein, the doctrine of initial evidence also validates the need for designated services in which Christians can seek to be baptized in the Holy Spirit. If a uniform evidence of Spirit Baptism can be expected, then one ought to create an environment in which that particular evidence is welcomed and encouraged.

Implications for Pentecostal Doctrine

Frank Macchia's emphasis on the scriptural *metaphors* of Spirit Baptism is a significant step toward emphasizing the second-order truth claims of Pentecostals to which the doctrine of initial evidence attests. Macchia shows that the metaphor of Spirit Baptism is used in the New Testament to describe judgment, cleansing, empowerment, incorporation into the life of the church and the final new creation.[37] Macchia's use of metaphor is an excellent method for dealing with the diversity of voices in Scripture on the subject of Spirit Baptism, but it also gives Pentecostals a much-needed method for dealing with the diversity present in their movement. As Macchia puts it,

> This diversity of viewpoints concerning Spirit Baptism opens up the question as to what purpose it serves to speak of Spirit Baptism as the dominant Pentecostal theological distinctive if there has been little agreement as to what the doctrine might mean within the broader context of the Christian life.[38]

---

35. $r = .279$
36. $r = .499$
37. Macchia, "Baptized in the Spirit: Toward a Global Theology of Spirit Baptism," 17.
38. Ibid., 10.

The Doctrine of Initial Evidence in the Future of Pentecostalism

By focusing on the scriptural metaphor of Spirit Baptism rather than a particular doctrine of Spirit Baptism to describe the theological distinctive of global Pentecostalism, Macchia allows for new flexibility in terminology. The concept of Spirit Baptism is not confined to function solely as a propositional truth (first-order truth claim), but can effectively function as a verbal picture that describes a spiritual reality (second-order truth claim).

When the doctrine of Spirit Baptism is understood as a metaphor, it becomes less important for the Pentecostal community to assent to a specific wording of the doctrine and more important that the doctrine ensures internal consistency (the presence and interrelationship of the various dimensions of new life in the power of the Spirit) and evokes appropriate response (the specific practices associated with new life in the power of the Spirit) within the community. On the other hand, just because a doctrine encapsulates the propositional truth claim of a group does not mean that it is effective. If it is ineffective at bringing internal consistency and evoking appropriate response then it likely needs to change.

In addition to understanding Spirit Baptism as a metaphor for the various dimensions of new life in the Spirit, a revitalization of Pentecostal doctrine may occur in distinctive denominations only in conjunction with a realization that a doctrinal statement can never fully encapsulate a testimony. When a doctrine is understood as the "distinctive testimony" of a group, doctrinal change becomes almost impossible without calling into question the identity of the group. However, if a doctrine is referred to as that which brings internal consistency and evokes appropriate response, than doctrinal changes can take place based on results in these areas while affirming the identity of the group. It is this shift in understanding the relationship of doctrine to testimony that must take place if Pentecostals are to appreciate changes in doctrine as opportunities for the Spirit to renew and revive the movement without undermining the experiences and beliefs of those who have gone before them.

Based on the result of this study, distinctive denominations should not "get rid" of their doctrine of initial evidence, or simply reword it to make it more inclusive of other charismatic experiences. Such an action would likely not be helpful in producing the desired results. Rather, doctrinal explanations that emphasize the scriptural metaphors of Spirit Baptism could better lead others into practices that are appropriate for and consistent with such an experience.

If the above findings are correct, changes to the doctrine of initial evidence will be well received by classical Pentecostal ministers when they can be shown to generate appropriate responses better than the community's current doctrinal formulation. A desire to place a renewed emphasis on the responses and practices that result from the doctrine of initial evidence is clear in the concluding statement of the Assemblies of God's updated official position paper on the doctrine in 2010.

> Baptism in the Holy Spirit must be more than a safeguarded and cherished doctrine; it must be a vital, productive and ongoing experience in the life of believers and their personal relationship with the Lord, their interaction with other believers, and their witness to the world. The vitality and vibrancy of the Church can be realized only when believers personally and corporately manifest the power of the Holy Spirit that was experienced by Jesus himself and that He promised to His followers.[39]

Shane Clifton has rightly suggested that despite the sincere desire of Pentecostals to have their doctrine lead to an authentic and transformative encounter with God (as indicated in the quote above), the doctrine's focus on an empirically verifiable explanation of tongues diminishes its potential to move people toward such an encounter.[40]

Classical Pentecostal denominations would do well to focus on articulating and explaining how speaking in tongues is related to a vibrant and ongoing experience of the Spirit. Most Pentecostal denominations include little in their doctrinal statements specifically about how speaking in tongues is logically or symbolically connected to the benefits of Spirit Baptism in the life of the individual or the local church. The result is that ministers and local churches are left to define the importance and significance of glossolalic experiences for themselves. Pentecostal ministers mostly agree that Spirit Baptism inaugurates a more intimate relationship with God, establishes a greater unity in the church, and empowers the community for their mission in the world. If such an experience is normally instituted in the act of speaking in tongues, than a doctrinal explanation that articulates such a relationship is critical. The scholarship of Macchia, Yong, Chan, Fee, Clifton, and others has provided the theological basis upon which such doctrinal explanations can be made, but it remains for Pentecostal denominations to make use of such scholarship in their formal doctrinal statements.

39. *AG Official Position Papers: Baptism in the Holy Spirit*, 13.
40. Clifton, "The Spirit and Doctrinal Development," 18.

Conclusion

Throughout the last century, Pentecostals have consistently drawn a connection between speaking in tongues and Spirit Baptism. At the same time, Pentecostals have often disagreed about how best to articulate that relationship. The doctrine of initial evidence emerged among classical Pentecostals as the normative way to define the relationship. Yet, people both within and outside of Pentecostalism have often questioned the exegetical, pastoral, and theological veracity of the doctrine. Over time, an impasse has developed between those who support the doctrine as an indispensable element of Pentecostal spirituality and worship and those who oppose the doctrine as unnecessarily divisive and legalistic.

The first step in moving beyond this impasse is the establishment of the doctrine's history. Chapters 2–4 of this study addressed the need for a thorough history of the origin and development of the doctrine of initial evidence in the classical Pentecostal tradition.[41] Such a history laid the necessary foundation for accurately assessing how the doctrine relates to other Pentecostal beliefs and how the doctrine has functioned to support or hinder the Pentecostal community's activities in chapter 5.

In chapter 2, representative approaches to the connection between speaking in tongues and Spirit Baptism in early Pentecostalism were expounded to show the varied ways in which the doctrine was first formulated and put into practice. Parham's doctrine of "the Bible evidence" emerged in the early twentieth century as a result of Parham's Restorationist hermeneutic being applied to the Book of Acts, in addition to the glossolalic experience of his students. Parham's functional approach to Spirit Baptism led him to believe that the doctrine was significant for the church in what it could directly offer a preacher or missionary: 1) the ability to speak the unfiltered Word of God at home or abroad by bypassing the human intellect, and 2) the ability to know definitively whom Christ had called out and separated from among other Christians as his Bride. At Azusa Street, Parham's doctrine was reinterpreted to include symbolic benefits of tongues in prayer and intimacy with Christ that were believed to help unify the church in its witness to the world. In contrast to the divisions that characterized the Pentecostal movement in the United States, when the Pentecostal experience made its way to Great Britain, Alexander Boddy's pastoral approach to Spirit Baptism allowed the Pentecostal

---

41. See chapter 1 above.

movement to be maintained for a short time within the established church structures.

Chapter 3 examined the individuals, organizations, and social factors that led to the emergence of a classical Pentecostal tradition in North America. William Durham's "finished-work" doctrine of sanctification coupled with his adamant stance on initial evidence led to a simplification of the stages of the Christian life that was appealing to the masses. Although Durham's "finished-work" doctrine was modified after his death, his rigid doctrine of initial evidence became established in the Assemblies of God through the influence of E. N. Bell and others. The initial evidence doctrine was an immediate source of controversy in the denomination through harsh criticism of the doctrine by one of the group's leaders, F. F. Bosworth. The denomination's response led to the gradual establishment of the doctrine as the "distinctive testimony" of classical Pentecostals in North America. Yet, not all classical Pentecostals upheld such a belief. Aimee Semple McPherson, while upholding the doctrine of initial evidence, did not refer to the doctrine as the distinctive testimony of Pentecostals but preferred to focus on an experience of Spirit Baptism. When constructing the Foursquare Declaration of Faith, she preferred to stay away from initial evidence language. Open Bible, despite roots in the Assemblies of God and Apostolic Faith organizations, also chose not to include a rigid doctrine of initial evidence in their articles of faith.

Chapter 4 detailed the growth and development of the classical Pentecostal tradition in North America after WWII. The rise of ecumenical associations and groups after WWII and the growth of the Charismatic movement in mainline churches in the 1950s and 60s caused Open Bible and Foursquare to be more explicit in defining themselves as Pentecostals in their doctrine. Thus, both groups took steps to establish the doctrine of initial evidence as a matter of orthodoxy for their respective organizations: Open Bible by revising their statement of faith in 1958, Foursquare by issuing an official statement in support of the doctrine in 1975. While Pentecostal groups felt the pressure to define themselves over against Charismatics during this time, they also felt increasing pressure to align themselves with Evangelicals. Both of these moves caused Pentecostal and non-Pentecostal scholars to focus in on the doctrine of initial evidence, the one doctrine that separated classical Pentecostals from both Evangelicals and Charismatics. The result was twofold. On the one hand, a much more robust Pentecostal theology emerged in response to criticism from Evangelicals and Charismatics that could withstand attacks from both Roman

The Doctrine of Initial Evidence in the Future of Pentecostalism

Catholic and Protestant scholars. On the other hand, the increasing occurrence of Pentecostal manifestations in non-Pentecostal congregations caused the implicit link between classical Pentecostal theology and classical Pentecostal experience to be severed. These changes raised questions for classical Pentecostals about the veracity and importance of the initial evidence position.

Classical Pentecostal denominations answered those questions in different ways. Distinctive denominations (represented by the Assemblies of God) have held fast to the doctrine of initial evidence and sought to re-emphasize the doctrine for new generations and contexts without reformulating it. Post-distinctive denominations (represented by Open Bible) that have historically upheld the classic doctrine of initial evidence have updated the wording of the doctrine so as to remove the most controversial elements and incorporate exegetical methods favored by their constituents. Non-distinctive denominations (represented by Foursquare), while historically aligning themselves with distinctive denominations, have never explicitly had a rigid doctrine of initial evidence in their tenets of faith. These denominations affirmed the openness and flexibility in their position and looked to other aspects of their heritage to define themselves as classically Pentecostal.

Having established the origin and development of the doctrine of initial evidence in classical "finished-work" Pentecostalism, chapter 5 evaluated the history of the doctrine in order to understand the various functions the doctrine has had for the community. Evaluating the history of Pentecostalism from a doctrinal perspective, it is clear that the doctrine of initial evidence has functioned in the classical Pentecostal community in all four of the ways that Alister McGrath has identified. The doctrine has functioned as both a first-order propositional truth claim and a second-order intra-systematic truth claim. In addition to formalizing a truth claim of classical Pentecostals, the doctrine has interpreted their narrative, interpreted their experiences, and demarcated the group socially. As the doctrine has performed these various functions for the community, different aspects of the doctrine have been emphasized at different times. In recent years, Open Bible and Foursquare have taken steps to change or de-emphasize the doctrine because it is no longer performing these functions for the community effectively. The Assemblies of God has taken steps to re-emphasize and re-appropriate the doctrine for the same reason.

Chapter 6 endeavored to measure how the doctrine of initial evidence was currently serving the classical Pentecostal community in relation to the history. The empirical theological method proposed by van der Ven was used to develop a quantitative empirical study of the beliefs and practices of classical Pentecostal ministers regarding Spirit Baptism and speaking in tongues.[42]

A survey of over 500 classical Pentecostal ministers in Assemblies of God, Open Bible and Foursquare found that there are some important areas of disagreement and convergence among classical Pentecostals related to McGrath's four functions of doctrine. There is a unity of story among classical Pentecostals. Regardless of their stance on the doctrine of initial evidence, they associate Spirit Baptism with empowerment for service in the world. There is also a partial unity of experience among classical Pentecostals. Classical Pentecostal ministers generally associate Spirit Baptism with speaking in tongues in their own lives and in the lives of others. However, the regularity and frequency of experiencing speaking in tongues and other visible charismatic manifestations is an area of divergence and at least partially correlated with how rigidly a minister upholds a doctrine of initial evidence. Those ministers who do uphold a doctrine of initial evidence tend to be older, less educated and in smaller churches. This phenomenon has significant implications for all three types of denominations. There does not seem to be agreement among classical Pentecostal ministers about the propositional truth claim to which the doctrine of initial evidence calls one to assent. The dominant truth claim made by the doctrine is the second-order truth claim of evoking appropriate response; classical Pentecostal ministers that uphold the doctrine look to it primarily as a means to bring about the responses and actions that the community values and affirms.

The implications of this research for the future of Pentecostalism were summarized in chapter 7. In the final analysis, there is no question that the doctrine of initial evidence has played a significant role throughout the history of the classical Pentecostal tradition. Vinson Synan's assessment, "It is unthinkable that the Pentecostal movement could have developed as it did without the initial evidence position,"[43] is not an overstatement. Throughout the last century, the doctrine has provided the Pentecostal community with various functions that have been crucial for the movement's establishment and growth, and the spread of Pentecostal experience. Yet, there are clear signs that the doctrine is not performing these functions in the classical Pentecostal community as well as it has in

---

42. See chapter 1 above.
43. Synan, "The Role of Tongues," 82.

the past. Rather than simply forego the doctrine or repeat the doctrine, classical Pentecostals must work carefully and concertedly to institute doctrinal changes that can better lead Pentecostals into the practices that their community has historically appreciated as essential for the fulfillment of their God-given mission. This study will hopefully be a useful guide for Pentecostal influencers who have been called to take part in such a work under the guidance and direction of the Holy Spirit.

Appendix

Spirit Baptism Belief
& Practice Survey

PART 1

> **INSTRUCTIONS: This part of the questionnaire asks for some information about yourself and your church. Please check the appropriate box(es).**

Of which denomination are you a minister?	Assemblies of God	1	
	Open Bible Churches	2	
	International Church of the Foursquare Gospel	3	
	other (please specify below):	4	

What is your gender?	male	1	
	female	2	

How long have you been engaged in ministry recognized by the denomination to which you belong (in years)?			

Is your current ministry	paid	1	
	unpaid	2	

Do you currently have paid secular employment as well as having a position within the church?	no	1	
	yes, part-time	2	
	yes, full-time	3	

Have you ever undertaken distance learning training for ministry?	no	1	
	yes	2	

If yes, where?		

Have you ever undertaken formal residential training for ministry leading to a degree?	no	1	
	yes	2	

If yes, from where did you receive your highest degree?		

If yes, which degree(s) do you hold? (mark more than one if necessary)	Associate	1	
	Bachelor's Degree	2	
	Master's Degree	3	
	ThM	4	
	Dmin	5	
	PhD	6	
	other (please specify below):	7	

How many different adults attend your congregation on a weekend?	less than 25	1	
	25-50	2	
	50-75	3	
	75-100	4	
	100-150	5	
	150-200	6	
	200-250	7	
	250-300	8	
	300-350	9	
	more than 350	10	

By what percentage would you judge the number of people in your ministerial care has grown in the past 12 months?	none that I know of	1	
	1-5%	2	
	6-10%	3	
	11-20%	4	
	21-30%	5	
	more than 30%	6	

By what percentage would you judge the number of people in your ministerial care has declined in the past 12 months?	none that I know of	1	
	1-5%	2	
	6-10%	3	
	11-20%	4	
	21-30%	5	
	more than 30%	6	
Are you in charge of your current congregation?	no	1	
	yes, in sole charge	2	
	yes, as senior minister	3	
	yes, as part of a team	4	
How often do you preach in your congregation?	more than once a week	1	
	once a week	2	
	once a month	3	
	less than once a month	4	
	never	5	
How often do you pray by yourself?	nearly everyday	1	
	at least once a week	2	
	at least once a month	3	
	occasionally	4	
	used to, but not now	5	
	never	6	
How often do you read your Bible by yourself?	nearly everyday	1	
	at least once a week	2	
	at least once a month	3	
	occasionally	4	
	used to, but not now	5	
	never	6	
Have you been baptized in the Holy Spirit?	yes	1	
	no	2	
If yes, did you speak in tongues when you were baptized in the Holy Spirit?	yes, immediately	1	
	yes, within 24 hours	2	
	yes, within a week	3	
	yes, sometime later	4	
	no	5	
If yes, how old were you when you were baptized in the Spirit (in years)?			
If yes, how long after your conversion were you baptized in the Holy Spirit?	less than a day	1	
	less than a month	2	
	less than a year	3	
	1-5 years	4	
	6-10 years	5	
	more than 10 years	6	
How often do you speak in tongues privately?	nearly everyday	1	
	at least once a week	2	
	at least once a month	3	
	occasionally	4	
	used to, but not now	5	
	never	6	

How many times have you publicly spoken a message in tongues that was publicly interpreted?	never	1	
	1-5	2	
	6-10	3	
	11-20	4	
	more than 20	5	
What percentage of your congregation has been baptized in the Holy Spirit?	Don't Know	1	
	0-20%	2	
	20-40%	3	
	40-60%	4	
	60-80%	5	
	80-100%	6	
In what position do you currently serve in your congregation?	Senior/Lead Pastor	1	
	Assistant Pastor	2	
	Co-Pastor	3	
	Executive Director	4	
	Youth Pastor	5	
	Children's Pastor	6	
	Worship Pastor	7	
	College/Young Adult Pastor	8	
	other (please specify below):	9	
	Not Applicable	10	
What is your age (in years)?			

PART 2

INSTRUCTIONS. This section is concerned with some of your attitudes and beliefs concerning Spirit baptism and spiritual gifts (*charismata*). Read the sentence carefully and think, 'Do I agree with it?'

If you *Agree Strongly*, put a circle around	AS
If you *Agree*, put a circle around	A
If you are *Not Certain*, put a circle around	NC
If you *Disagree*, put a circle around	D
If you *Disagree Strongly*, put a circle around	DS

Speaking with tongues in congregational meetings should be strongly	AS A NC D DS
Speaking with tongues symbolizes the work of the Holy Spirit in the life of a Christian	AS A NC D DS
Speaking with tongues has no practical use	AS A NC D DS
Speaking with tongues is a form of private prayer	AS A NC D DS
Speaking with tongues is necessary as the initial physical evidence of the baptism in the Holy Spirit	AS A NC D DS
To speak with tongues is an edifying experience	AS A NC D DS
To speak with tongues is a calming experience	AS A NC D DS
To speak with tongues is an uncontrollable experience	AS A NC D DS
To speak with tongues is a holy experience	AS A NC D DS
To speak with tongues is an exciting experience	AS A NC D DS
The baptism in the Holy Spirit is a powerful experience	AS A NC D DS
The baptism in the Holy Spirit is a sign to unbelievers	AS A NC D DS
The baptism in the Holy Spriit is a sign to believers	AS A NC D DS
The baptism in the Holy Spirit is evidenced by signs following	AS A NC D DS
The baptism in the Holy Spirit is essential for living a holy life	AS A NC D DS
The baptism in the Holy Spirit seals the Bride of Christ	AS A NC D DS
The baptism in the Holy Spirit endows the Christian with spiritual gifts (*charismata*)	AS A NC D DS
The baptism in the Holy Spirit equips the Christian for service	AS A NC D DS
The baptism in the Holy Spirit endues the Christian with power	AS A NC D DS
The baptism in the Holy Spirit may be evidenced by spiritual gifts (*charismata*) besides tongues	AS A NC D DS
The baptism in the Holy Spirit helps to foster unity among Christians	AS A NC D DS
The baptism in the Holy Spirit helps prevent racial predjudice among Christians	AS A NC D DS
The baptism in the Holy Spirit helps one to witness effectively	AS A NC D DS
The baptism in the Holy Spirit helps one to interpret Scripture	AS A NC D DS
The baptism in the Holy Spirit helps one to preach better	AS A NC D DS
The baptism in the Holy Spirit helps one to pray when one doesn't know how to pray	AS A NC D DS
The baptism in the Holy Spirit helps one to worship God	AS A NC D DS
I believe the baptism in the Holy Spirit is always accompanied by speaking in a known foreign language	AS A NC D DS
I believe the baptism in the Holy Spirit is only given to those who are fully sanctified	AS A NC D DS
I believe the baptism in the Holy Spirit is witnessed by the initial physical sign of speaking with other tongues as the Spirit of God gives them utterance	AS A NC D DS
I believe the baptism in the Holy Spirit is enjoyed by all Christians	AS A NC D DS

I believe the baptism in the Holy Spirit is a special blessing only given to some Christians	AS	A	NC	D	DS
I believe Christians should anticipate Spirit baptism to be accompanied by speaking in tongues and other biblical manifestations	AS	A	NC	D	DS
I believe Christians should expect the Spirit's incoming to be after the same manner as that in which He came upon believers in the days of the Early Church	AS	A	NC	D	DS
I believe all Christians receive the Holy Spirit when they are baptized in water	AS	A	NC	D	DS
I believe all Christians receive the Holy Spirit when they become a Christian	AS	A	NC	D	DS
I believe all Christians who have spoken in tongues have been baptized in the Holy Spirit	AS	A	NC	D	DS
I believe all Spirit baptized Christians have the gift of tongues	AS	A	NC	D	DS
I believe the Holy Spirit is at work in the ecumenical movement	AS	A	NC	D	DS
Pentecostal churches should cooperate more with each other	AS	A	NC	D	DS
Pentecostal churches should cooperate more with other denominations	AS	A	NC	D	DS
Churches should regularly hold services devoted to seeking the baptism in the Holy Spirit	AS	A	NC	D	DS
Churches should regularly hold services devoted to seeking spiritual gifts	AS	A	NC	D	DS
The interpretation of tongues should be as from God to the congregation	AS	A	NC	D	DS
The interpretation of tongues should be as from the congregation to God	AS	A	NC	D	DS
It is possible to be baptized in the Holy Spirit more than once	AS	A	NC	D	DS
Tarrying is important for receiving the baptism in the Holy Spirit	AS	A	NC	D	DS
There is a difference between the 'gift of tongues' and 'evidential tongues'	AS	A	NC	D	DS

PART 3

INSTRUCTIONS: Please check one box in the each row to indicate how often in the past three months *you* have:

0	1-3	4-6	7-12	13-18	19+	Not Sure	
							spoken in tongues while praying privately
							spoken in tongues while praying for an individual
							given a public utterance in tongues
							interpreted tongues
							sung in tongues
							publicly prophesied
							given a prophecy privately to another person
							prayed for someone to be baptized in the Spirit
							been annointed by the Spirit
							experienced 'laughing in the Spirit'
							experienced being 'slain in the Spirit'
							heard God speak through a dream or vision
							received divine inspiration in interpreting Scripture
							received divine inspiration while preaching
							received divine inspiration while evangelizing
							seen people baptized in the Spirit as a result of your ministry
							seen people 'slain in the Spirit' as a result of your ministry
							seen people 'laughing in the Spirit' as a result of your ministry
							heard a public utterance in tongues in your congregation
							felt led by God to perform a specific action
							received a word from God
							given a word of wisdom or word of knowledge

PART 4 (optional)

Please list two publications excluding the Bible that have influenced your understanding of Spirit baptism:

Were your beliefs about Spirit baptism influenced by any of your formal academic training?

PLEASE USE THE SPACE BELOW TO WRITE ANY POINTS THAT NEED TO
BE CLARIFIED OR COMMENTS YOU HAVE ABOUT THIS QUESTIONNAIRE.

Thank you for your help.

Bibliography

Archived Periodicals

Apostolic Faith [Baxter Springs, KS], 1906–12. Flower Pentecostal Heritage Center, Springfield, MO.
Apostolic Faith [Baxter Springs, KS], May 1913–July 1914. IPHC Archives & Research Center, Oklahoma City.
Apostolic Faith [Fort Worth, TX], 1914. Flower Pentecostal Heritage Center, Springfield, MO.
Apostolic Faith [Houston, TX], 1908. Flower Pentecostal Heritage Center, Springfield, MO.
Apostolic Faith [Houston, TX], December 1905. Flower Pentecostal Heritage Center, Springfield, MO.
Apostolic Faith [Los Angeles, CA], 1906–8. Flower Pentecostal Heritage Center, Springfield, MO.
Apostolic Faith [Melrose, KS], August–October/November 1905. Flower Pentecostal Heritage Center, Springfield, MO.
Apostolic Faith [Melrose, KS], July 1905. IPHC Archives & Research Center, Oklahoma City.
Apostolic Faith [Topeka, KS], 1899–1900. Flower Pentecostal Heritage Center, Springfield, MO.
Bible Standard Overcomer, 1932–35. Open Bible Heritage Center, Eugene, OR.
Bible Standard, 1920–28. Open Bible Heritage Center, Eugene, OR.
Bridal Call Foursquare, 1924–34. Foursquare Church Archives, Los Angeles.
Bridal Call, 1917–23. Foursquare Church Archives, Los Angeles.
Confidence, 1908–26. Flower Pentecostal Heritage Center, Springfield, MO.
Foursquare Crusader, 1936. Foursquare Church Archives, Los Angeles.
Foursquare World Advance, 1975. Foursquare Church Archives, Los Angeles.
Full Gospel Men's Voice, 1953. Fuller Theological Seminary Archives, Pasadena.
Latter Rain Evangel, 1908–39. Flower Pentecostal Heritage Center, Springfield, MO.
Live Coals [Royston], 1907. Flower Pentecostal Heritage Center, Springfield, MO.
Live Coals of Fire, 1899–1900. IPHC Archives & Research Center, Oklahoma City.
Living Truths, 1906. Flower Pentecostal Heritage Center, Springfield, MO.

Bibliography

Message of the Open Bible, 1944–present. Open Bible National Office, Des Moines, IA.
Open Bible Messenger, 1932–35. Open Bible Heritage Center, Eugene, OR.
Overcomer, 1926–32. Open Bible Heritage Center, Eugene, OR.
Pentecost, 1948–60. Fuller Theological Seminary Archives, Pasadena.
Pentecostal Evangel (also *Weekly Evangel* and *Christian Evangel*), 1916–69. Flower Pentecostal Heritage Center, Springfield, MO.
Pentecostal Holiness Advocate, 1971. Fuller Theological Seminary Archives, Pasadena.
Pentecostal Testimony, 1909–11. Flower Pentecostal Heritage Center, Springfield, MO.
Redemption Tidings, 1924–39. Donald Gee Research Center, Mattersey, UK.
Tongues of Fire, 1907–8. Arizona State University, Tempe, AZ.
Word and Witness, 1912–15. Flower Pentecostal Heritage Center, Springfield, MO.

Regular Sources

"2007 Full Statistical Report." Springfield, MO: General Council, 2008.
"2009 Full Statistical Report." Springfield, MO: General Council, 2010.
"2009 Vital Statistics Summary." Springfield, MO: General Council, 2010.
Abraham, William. *Waking from Doctrinal Amnesia*. Nashville: Abingdon, 1996.
AG Official Position Papers: Baptism in the Holy Spirit. Adopted by the General Presbytery: August 9–11, 2010.
Alexander, Kimberly Ervin. "Boundless Love Divine: A Re-Evaluation of Early Understandings of the Experience of Spirit Baptism." Draft copy of unpublished article, July 2009.
Alexander, Paul. *Peace to War: Shifting Allegiances in the Assemblies of God*. Telford, PA: Cascadia, 2009.
Anderson, Allan. "Diversity in the Definition of 'Pentecostal/Charismatic' and its Ecumenical Implications." *Mission Studies* 19 (2002) 40–55.
———. "The Dubious Legacy of Charles Parham: Racism and Cultural Insensitivities among Pentecostals." *Pneuma* 27 (2005) 52–55.
———. "Introduction: The Charismatic Face of Christianity in Asia." In *Asian and Pentecostal: The Charismatic Face of Christianity in Asia*, edited by Allan Anderson and Edmond Tang, 1–12. Oxford: Regnum, 2005.
———. *An Introduction to Pentecostalism: Global Charismatic Christianity*. Cambridge: Cambridge University Press, 2004.
———. "Introduction: World Pentecostalism at a Crossroads." In *Pentecostals after a Century: Global Perspectives on a Movement in Transition*, edited by Allan Anderson and Walter J. Hollenweger, 19–31. Sheffield, UK: Sheffield Academic Press, 1999.
———. "Revising Pentecostal History in Global Perspective." In *Asian and Pentecostal: The Charismatic Face of Christianity in Asia*, edited by Allan Anderson and Edmond Tang, 147–73. Oxford: Regnum, 2005.
———. *Spreading Fires: The Missionary Nature of Early Pentecostalism*. Maryknoll, NY: Orbis, 2007.
Anderson, Ray S. *The Shape of Practical Theology: Empowering Ministry with Theological Praxis*. Downer's Grove, IL: InterVarsity, 2001.
Anderson, Robert Mapes. *Vision of the Disinherited: The Making of American Pentecostalism*. Oxford: Oxford University Press, 1979.

Archer, Ken. "Pentecostal Story: The Hermeneutical Filter for the Making of Meaning." *Pneuma* 26 (2004) 36–59.
Atkinson, William P. *Baptism in the Spirit: Luke-Acts and the Dunn Debate*. Eugene, OR: Pickwick, 2011.
The Baptism in the Holy Spirit: The Initial Experience and Continuing Evidences of the Spirit-Filled Life. Springfield, MO: General Council, 2000.
Barfoot, Chas H. *Aimee Semple McPherson and the Making of Modern Pentecostalism (1890–1926)*. London: Equinox, 2011.
Barratt, David. "Global Statistics." In *The New International Dictionary of Pentecostal and Charismatic Movements*, edited by Stanley M. Burgess, 284–302. Grand Rapids: Zondervan, 2002.
Barratt, T. B. *The Baptism of the Holy Ghost and Fire: What is the Scriptural Evidence?* Springfield, MO: Gospel, n.d.
Bartleman, Frank. *Azusa Street: The Roots of Modern-day Pentecost*. Plainfield, NJ: Logos, 1980.
———. *How Pentecost Came to Los Angeles*. 2d ed. Los Angeles: self-published, 1925. Facsimile reprint in *Witness to Pentecost: The Life of Frank Bartleman*. New York: Garland, 1985.
Battaglia, Anthony. "'Sect' or 'Denomination': The Place of Religious Ethics in a Post-Churchly Culture." *Journal of Religious Ethics* 16 (1988) 128–42.
Bennett, Dennis, and Rita Bennett. *The Holy Spirit and You: A Study-Guide to the Spirit-Filled Life*. Plainfield, NJ: Logos, 1971.
Beverley, James. *Holy Laughter and the Toronto Blessing: An Investigative Report*. Grand Rapids: Zondervan, 1995.
Blumhofer, Edith L. *Aimee Semple McPherson: Everybody's Sister*. Grand Rapids: Eerdmans, 1991.
———. "Alexander Boddy and the Rise of Pentecostalism in Great Britain." *Pneuma* 8 (1986) 31–40.
———. *The Assemblies of God: A Chapter in the Story of American Pentecostalism, Vol. 1*. Springfield, MO: Gospel, 1989.
———. "Restoration as Revival: Early American Pentecostalism." In *Modern Christian Revivals*, edited by Edith L. Blumhofer and Randall Balmer, 145–60. Urbana, IL: University of Illinois Press, 1993.
———. *Restoring the Faith: The Assemblies of God, Pentecostalism, and American Culture*. Urbana, IL: University of Illinois Press, 1993.
———. "William Hamner Piper." In *The New International Dictionary of Pentecostal and Charismatic Movements*, edited by Stanley M. Burgess, 989–90. Grand Rapids: Zondervan, 2002.
———. "William H. Durham: Years of Creativity; Years of Dissent." In *Portraits of a Generation: Early Pentecostal Leaders*, edited by James R. Goff, Jr. and Grant A. Wacker, 123–42. Fayetteville, AR: University of Arkansas Press, 2002.
Boddy, A. A. *The Pentecostal Baptism: Counsel to Leaders and Others*. Sunderland, UK: All Saints Vicarage, n.d. [1908?].
The Book of Doctrines, Issued in the Interest of The Church of God. Cleveland, TN: Church of God, 1922.
Bosworth, F. F. *Do All Speak with Tongues?* New York: Christian Alliance, n.d.
———. Letter of Resignation from the Assemblies of God, July 24, 1918. Personal Papers of F. F. Bosworth.

Bibliography

Breshears, Gerry. "Encountering the Vineyard." Paper presented at the Northwest Regional Evangelical Theological Society Meeting, Tacoma, WA, 21 April 1990.

Brumback, Carl. *Suddenly . . . from Heaven*. Springfield, MO: Gospel, 1961.

Bruner, Frederick Dale. *A Theology of the Holy Spirit: The Pentecostal Experience and the New Testament Witness*. Grand Rapids: Eerdmans, 1970.

Bundy, David. "Donald Gee." In *The New International Dictionary of Pentecostal and Charismatic Movements*, edited by Stanley M. Burgess, 662–63. Grand Rapids: Zondervan, 2002.

———. "Donald Gee: The Pentecostal Leader Who Grew in Wisdom and Stature." *Assemblies of God Heritage* 12 (Fall 1992) 9–11.

———. "An Early Pentecostal Theological Treatise: Thomas Ball Barratt on Pentecostalism and Glossolalia." Paper presented at the 22nd Annual Meeting of the Society for Pentecostal Studies, Springfield, MO, 12–14 November 1992.

———. "Spiritual Advice to a Shaker: Letters to T. B. Barratt from Azusa Street, 1906." *Pneuma* 14 (1992) 159–70.

———. "Welsh Revival." In *The New International Dictionary of Pentecostal and Charismatic Movements*, edited by Stanley M. Burgess, 1187–88. Grand Rapids: Zondervan, 2002.

Burgess, Stanley, editor. *The New International Dictionary of Pentecostal and Charismatic Movements*. Grand Rapids: Zondervan, 2002.

Butler, Anthea. "A Peculiar Synergy: Matriarchy and the Church of God in Christ." Ph.D. diss., Vanguard University, 2002.

Callahan, Leslie. "Redeemed or Destroyed: Re-evaluating the Social Dimensions of Bodily Destiny in the Thought of Charles Parham." *Pneuma* 28 (2006) 203–27.

———. "A Sanctified Body: Reassessing Sanctification in the Thought of Charles Parham." Paper presented at the 33rd Annual Meeting of the Society for Pentecostal Studies, Milwaukee, WI, March, 2004.

Carothers, W. F. *The Baptism with the Holy Ghost and the Speaking in Tongues*. Houston, TX: s.p., 1906–7.

Cartledge, Mark J. *Charismatic Glossolalia: An Empirical-Theological Study*. Burlington, VT: Ashgate, 2002.

———. "The Early Pentecostal Theology of *Confidence* Magazine (1908–1926) A Version of the Five-Fold Gospel?" Paper presented at the Pentecost at Sunderland: Centenary Conference on Pentecostal Origins in Britain, St John's College, Durham, 19–21 September 2007.

———. *Practical Theology: Charismatic and Empirical Perspectives*. Carlisle, UK: Paternoster, 2003.

———, editor. *Speaking in Tongues: Multi-Disciplinary Perspectives*. Milton Keynes, UK: Paternoster, 2006.

Catechism of the Catholic Church. Chicago: Loyola University Press, 1994.

Cerillo, Augustus. "The Beginnings of American Pentecostalism: A Historiographical Overview." In *Pentecostal Currents in American Protestantism*, edited by Edith L. Blumhofer, Russell P. Spittler, and Grant A. Wacker, 229–59. Urbana, IL: University of Illinois Press, 1999.

———. "Interpretive Approaches to the History of American Pentecostal Origins." *Pneuma* 19 (Spring 1997) 29–52.

Chan, Simon. "Evidential Glossolalia and the Doctrine of Subsequence." *Asian Journal of Pentecostal Studies* 2 (1999) 195–211.

———. "The Language Game of Glossolalia, or Making Sense of the 'Initial Evidence.'" In *Pentecostalism in Context: Essays in Honor of William W. Menzies*, edited by Wonsuk Ma and Robert Menzies, 80–95. Sheffield, UK: Sheffield Academic Press, 1997.

———. *Pentecostal Theology and the Christian Spiritual Tradition*. Sheffield, UK: Sheffield Academic Press, 2000.

Christenson, Larry. "Dennis Joseph and Rita Bennett." In *The New International Dictionary of Pentecostal and Charismatic Movements*, edited by Stanley M. Burgess, 369–70. Grand Rapids: Zondervan, 2002.

Clayton, Allen. "The Significance of William H. Durham for Pentecostal Historiography." *Pneuma* 1 (Fall 1979) 27–42.

Clifton, Shane. "The Spirit and Doctrinal Development: A Functional Analysis of the Traditional Pentecostal Doctrine of the Baptism in the Holy Spirit," *Pneuma* 29 (Fall 2007) 5–23.

Coggins, James and Paul Hiebert, editors. "The Man, the Message and the Movement." In *Wonders and the Word: An Examination of Issues Raised by John Wimber and the Vineyard Movement*, 15–22. Winnipeg, Canada: Kindred, 1989.

Cole, David. "Heritage and Horizons: The Derivation and Destiny of Open Bible Churches." In *The Future of Pentecostalism in the United States*, edited by Eric Patterson and Edmund Rybarczyk, 157–76. Lenham, MD: Lexington, 2008.

Constitution and General Rules of the Fire Baptized Holiness Church 1908. Royston, GA: n.p., 1908.

Constitution and General Rules of the Pentecostal Holiness Church 1911. Falcon, NC: n.p., 1911.

Cox, Raymond. "Was Amy Semple McPherson Pentecostal?" Paper presented at the 26th Annual Meeting of the Society for Pentecostal Studies, Oakland, CA, 13–15 March 1997.

Creech, Joe. "Visions of Glory: The Place of the Azusa Street Revival in Pentecostal History." *Church History* 65 (1996) 405–24.

Creps, Earl. "Postmodern Pentecostals? Emerging Subcultures Among Young Pentecostal Leaders." In *The Future of Pentecostalism in the United States*, edited by Eric Patterson and Edmund Rybarczyk, 27–47. Lenham, MD: Lexington, 2008.

Cullmann, Oscar. *Baptism in the New Testament*. Philadelphia: Westminster, 1950.

Daniels, David. "They Had a Dream." *Christian History* 17 (1998) 19–21.

Dayton, Donald W. *Theological Roots of Pentecostalism*. Metuchen, NJ: Scarecrow, 1987.

Dorries, David. "Edward Irving and the 'Standing Sign.'" In *Initial Evidence: Historical and Biblical Perspectives on the Pentecostal Doctrine of Spirit Baptism*, edited by Gary B. McGee, 41–56. Peabody, MA: Hendrickson, 1991.

Dreyer, Jaco. "Establishing Truth from Participation and Distanciation in Empirical Theology." In *Empirical Theology in Texts and Tables: Qualitative, Quantitative and Comparative Perspectives*, edited by Leslie Francis, Mandy Robbins, and Jeff Astley, 3–25. Leiden: Brill, 2009.

Du Plessis, David. "'Born Of' and 'Baptized In' the Holy Spirit." Unpublished paper. Fuller Seminary Archives, Pasadena, CA.

———. "Golden Jubilees of Twentieth-Century Pentecostal Movements." *International Review of Missions* 47 (1958) 193–201.

———. "Jesus is the Baptizer." *Message of the Open Bible* 54 (February 1971) 5.

Bibliography

———. Private correspondence to Donald Gee, March 8, 1961. Fuller Theological Seminary Archives, Pasadena, CA.

Duffield, Guy P. "The Pentecostal Baptism with the Holy Spirit." *Foursquare Magazine* 33, March 1960, 14.

Dulles, Avery. *Models of Revelation*. Garden City, NY: Doubleday, 1983.

Dunn, James D. G. *Baptism in the Holy Spirit: A Re-examination of the New Testament Teaching on the Gift of the Spirit in Relation to Pentecostalism Today*. London: SCM Press, 1970.

———. "Born Again: Baptism and the Spirit—A Protestant Response." In *Pentecostal Movements as an Ecumenical Challenge*, edited by Jürgen Moltmann and Karl-Josef Kuschel, 109–15. London: SCM, 1996.

Echoes from the General Assembly held at Cleveland, Tennessee January 9-14, 1912. Cleveland, TN: s.p., 1912.

Ervin, Howard. *Conversion-Initiation and the Baptism in the Holy Spirit*. Peabody, MA: Hendrickson, 1984.

Farkas, Thomas. "William H. Durham and the Sanctification Controversy in Early American Pentecostalism, 1906-1916." Ph.D. diss., Southern Baptist Theological Seminary, 1993.

Faupel, D. William. *The Everlasting Gospel: The Significance of Eschatology in the Development of Pentecostal Thought*. Sheffield, UK: Sheffield Academic Press, 1996.

———. "Theological Influences on the Teachings and Practices of John Alexander Dowie." *Pneuma* 29 (2007) 226–253.

———. "William H. Durham and the Finished Work of Calvary." In *Pentecost, Mission and Ecumenism, Essays on Intercultural Theology: Fetschrift in Honour of Professor Walter J. Hollenweger*, edited by J. A. B. Jongeneel, 85–95. Frankfurt: Lang, 1992.

Fee, Gordon. "Baptism in the Holy Spirit: The Issue of Separability and Subsequence." *Pneuma* 7 (Fall 1985) 87–99.

———. *Gospel and Spirit: Issues in New Testament Hermeneutics*. Peabody, MA: Hendrickson, 1991.

———. "Hermeneutics and Historical Precedent: A Major Problem in Pentecostal Hermeneutics." In *Perspectives on the New Pentecostalism*, edited by Russell P. Spittler, 118–32. Grand Rapids: Baker, 1976.

Finney, Charles. *Systematic Theology*. 1878. Reprint. South Gate, CA: Kemp, 1944.

Flokstra, Gerald J., III. "Sources for the Initial Evidence Discussion: A Bibliographic Essay." *Asian Journal of Pentecostal Studies* 2 (1999) 241–59.

Forrester, Duncan. *Truthful Action: Explorations in Practical Theology*. Edinburgh: T. & T. Clark, 2000.

The Foursquare Church. "What We Believe: Spirit-Filled Life." No pages. Accessed October 2, 2010. Online: http://www.foursquare.org/about/what_we_believe/spirit_filled_life.

Foursquare Licensing Process Guide. Los Angeles: International Church of the Foursquare Gospel, 2009.

Frodsham, Stanley Howard. *With Signs Following: The Story of the Pentecostal Revival in the Twentieth Century*. Rev. ed. Springfield, MO: Gospel, 1946.

Fudge, Thomas. "Did E. N. Bell Convert to the 'New Issue' in 1915?" *Journal of Pentecostal Theology* 18 (2001) 122–40.

Gee, Donald. *The Pentecostal Movement Including the Story of the War Years (1940–1947)*. London: Victory, 1949.

———. *Wind and Flame: Incorporating the Former Book The Pentecostal Movement with Additional Chapters*. Croydon, UK: Assemblies of God, 1967.
Gelpi, Donald "Ecumenical Problems and Possibilities." In *The Holy Spirit and Power: The Catholic Charismatic Renewal*, edited by Kilian McDonnell, 173–86. Garden City, NY: Doubleday, 1975.
The General Council of the Assemblies of God. *The Initial Physical Evidence of the Baptism in the Holy Spirit*. Springfield, MO: Gospel, 1981.
George, Darren, and Paul Mallery. *SPSS for Windows Step by Step: A Simple Guide and Reference. 11.0 update*, 4th ed. Boston: Allyn & Bacon, 2003.
Gitre, Edward. "The 1904–05 Welsh Revival: Modernization, Technologies, and Techniques of the Self." *Church History* 73 (2004) 792–827.
Goff, James R., Jr. "Apostolic Faith (Baxter Springs, KS)." In *The New International Dictionary of Pentecostal Charismatic Movements*, edited by Stanley M. Burgess, 326–27. Grand Rapids: Zondervan, 2002.
———. "Charles Parham and the Problem of History: A Response to Cecil M. Robeck." In *All Together in One Place: Theological Papers from the Brighton Conference on World Evangelzation*, edited by Harold Hunter and Peter Hocken, 186–91. Sheffield, UK: Sheffield Academic Press, 1993.
———. *Fields White Unto Harvest: Charles F. Parham and The Missionary Origins of Pentecostalism*. Fayetteville, AR: University of Arkansas Press, 1988.
———. "The Theology of Charles Fox Parham." In *Initial Evidence: Historical and Biblical Perspectives on the Pentecostal Doctrine of Spirit Baptism*, edited by Gary B. McGee, 57–71. Peabody, MA: Hendrickson, 1991.
Gohr, G. W. "Kansas City Prophets." In *The New International Dictionary of Pentecostal and Charismatic Movements*, edited by Stanley M. Burgess, 816–17. Grand Rapids: Zondervan, 2002.
Goss, Ethel E. *The Winds of God: The Story of the Early Pentecostal Days (1901–1914) in the Life of Howard A. Goss*. New York: Comet, 1958.
Gregory, Brad S. *Salvation at Stake; Christian Martyrdom in Early Modern Europe*. Cambridge: Harvard University Press, 1999.
Grenz, Stanley, and John Franke. *Beyond Foundationalism: Shaping Theology in a Postmodern Context*. Louisville, KY: Westminster John Knox, 2001.
Hayford, Jack. *The Beauty of Spiritual Language: My Journey toward the Heart of God*. Dallas, TX: Word, 1992,
Heimbrock, Hans-Günter. "From Data to Theory: Elements of Methodology in Empirical Phenomenological Research in Practical Theology." *International Journal of Practical Theology* 9 (2005) 273–99.
Heyduck, Richard. *The Recovery of Doctrine in the Contemporary Church*. Waco, TX: Baylor University Press, 2002.
Hocken, Peter. "Cecil H. Polhill—Pentecostal Layman." *Pneuma* 10 (Fall 1988) 116–40.
Hollenweger, Walter J. "After Twenty Years' Research on Pentecostalism." *International Review of Mission* 75 (1986) 3–12.
———. "The Black Roots of Pentecostalism." In *Pentecostals after a Century: Global Perspectives on a Movement in Transition*, edited by Allan Anderson and Walter J. Hollenweger, 33–44. Sheffield, UK: Sheffield Academic Press, 1999.
———. "Crucial Issues for Pentecostals." In *Pentecostals after a Century: Global Perspectives on a Movement in Transition*, edited by Allan Anderson and Walter J. Hollenweger, 176–91. Sheffield, UK: Sheffield Academic Press, 1999.

Bibliography

———. "From Azusa Street to the Toronto Phenomenon." In *Pentecostal Movements as an Ecumenical Challenge*, edited by Jürgen Moltmann and Karl Josef Kuschel, 3–14. Concilium 3. London: SCM, 1996.

———. *Pentecostalism: Origins and Developments Worldwide*. Peabody, MA: Hendrickson, 1997.

———. "Pentecostal Research in Europe: Problems, Promises, and People." *EPTA Bulletin* 4 (1985) 124–53.

———. *The Pentecostals: The Charismatic Movement in the Churches*. Minneapolis: Augsburg, 1972.

———. "Two Extraordinary Pentecostal Ecumenists: The Letters of Donald Gee and David Du Plessis." *Ecumenical Review* 52 (2000) 391–402.

Holm, Randall. "A Paradigmatic Analysis of Authority within Pentecostalism." Ph.D. diss., Laval University, 1995.

———. "Varieties of Pentecostal Experience: Pragmatism and the Doctrinal Development of Pentecostalism." *Eastern Journal of Practical Theology* 8 (Spring 1994) 26–41.

Hornshuh, Fred. *Historical Sketches of the Bible Standard Churches which Merged with the Open Bible in 1935*. Eugene, OR: Eugene Bible College, 1976.

Hudson, Neil. "Strange Words and Their Impact on Early Pentecostals: A Historical Perspective." In *Speaking in Tongues: Multi-Disciplinary Perspectives*, edited by Mark J. Cartledge, 52–80. Milton Keynes, UK: Paternoster, 2006.

Hughes, Ray. *Church of God Distinctives*. Cleveland, TN: Pathway, 1968.

Hunter, Harold. "Aspects of Initial Evidence Dogma: A European-American Holiness Pentecostal Perspective." *Asian Journal of Pentecostal Studies* 1 (1998) 185–202.

———. *Spirit Baptism: A Pentecostal Alternative*. Eugene, OR: Wipf & Stock, 2009.

International Pentecostal Holiness Church Manual 2005–2009. Franklin Springs, GA: LifeSprings Resources, 2005.

The Interpretation of the Constitutional Agreements and Essential Resolutions Recommended by the Executive Presbytery of the General Council of the Assemblies of God, 1925. Springfield, MO: General Council, n.d.

Irwin, Dale. "Pentecostal Historiography and Global Christianity: Rethinking the Question of Origins." *Pneuma* 27 (2005) 34–50.

Jacobsen, Douglas. "Knowing the Doctrines of Pentecostals: The Scholastic Theology of the Assemblies of God, 1930–55." In *Pentecostal Currents in American Protestantism*, edited by Edith L. Blumhofer, Russell P. Spittler, and Grant A. Wacker, 90–107. Urbana, IL: University of Illinois Press, 1999.

———. *Thinking in the Spirit: Theologies of the Early Pentecostal Movement*. Bloomington, IN: Indiana University Press, 2003.

Jones, Charles Edwin. *The Charismatic Movement: A Guide to the Study of Neo-Pentecostalism*. Philadelphia: Scarecrow, 1995.

Johnston, Robin. "Howard A. Goss: A Pentecostal Life." Ph.D. diss., Regent University, 2010.

Kärkkäinen, Veli-Matti. "Anonymous Ecumenists? Pentecostals and Christian Identity." *Journal of Ecumenical Studies* 37 (Winter 2000) 13–27.

———. "'The Leaning Tower of Mission in a Postmodern Land': Ecumenical Reflections on Pentecostal Mission in the After-Edinburgh World." *The Journal of the European Pentecostal Theological Association* 30 (2010) 82–93.

———. "The Pentecostal Movement in Finland." *Journal of the European Pentecostal Theological Association* 23 (2003) 102–28.

———, *Spiritus Ubi Vult Spirat: Pneumatology in Roman Catholic-Pentecostal Dialogue (1972–1989)*. Helsinki: Luther Agricola Society, 1998.

Kay, William K. "Apostolic Networks in Britain: An Analytic Overview." *Transformation* 25 (2008) 32–42.

———. "Assemblies of God: Distinctive Continuity and Distinctive Change." In *Pentecostal Perspectives*, edited by Keith Warrington, 40–63. Carlisle, UK: Paternoster, 1998.

———. "Donald Gee: An Important Voice of the Pentecostal Movement." *Journal of Pentecostal Theology* 16 (2007) 133–53.

———. "Empirical Theology: A Natural Development?" *Heythrop Journal* 55 (2003) 167–81.

———. "The 'Initial Evidence': Implications of an Empirical Perspective in a British Context." *The Journal of the European Pentecostal Theological Association* 20 (2000) 25–31.

———. *Inside Story: A History of British Assemblies of God*. Mattersey, UK: Mattersey Hall, 1990.

———. "Karl Popper and Pentecostal Historiography." *Pneuma* 32 (2010) 5–15.

———. *Pentecostals in Britain*. Carlisle, UK: Paternoster, 2000.

———. *Pentecostalism*. London: SCM, 2009.

———. "Sunderland's Legacy in New Denominations." Paper presented at the Pentecost at Sunderland: Centenary Conference on Pentecostal Origins in Britain, St John's College, Durham, 19–21 September 2007.

———. "Three Generations On: The Methodology of Pentecostal History." *EPTA Bulletin* 11 (1992) 58–70.

Kendrick, Klaude. *The Promise Fulfilled: A History of the Modern Pentecostal Movement*. Springfield, MO: Gospel, 1961.

King, Paul. *Genuine Gold: The Cautiously Charismatic Story of the Early Christian and Missionary Alliance*. Tulsa, OK: Word & Spirit, 2006.

Koch, Gunter. "Sacraments of Initiation." In *Handbook of Catholic Theology*, edited by Wolfgang Beinert and Francis Fiorenza, 634–36. New York: Crossroad, 1995.

Land, Steven. *Pentecostal Spirituality: A Passion for the Kingdom*. Sheffield, UK: Sheffield Academic Press, 1993.

Lawrence, B. F. *The Apostolic Faith Restored*. St. Louis: Gospel, 1916.

Lederle, Henry. "Initial Evidence and the Charismatic Movement: An Ecumenical Appraisal." In *Initial Evidence: Historical and Biblical Perspectives on the Pentecostal Doctrine of Spirit Baptism*, edited by Gary McGee, 131–41. Peabody, MA: Hendrickson, 1991.

———. *Treasures New and Old: Interpretations of "Spirit-Baptism" in the Charismatic Renewal Movement*. Peabody, MA: Hendrickson, 1988.

Lee, Paul. "Pneumatological Ecclesiology in the Roman Catholic–Pentecostal Dialogue: A Catholic Reading of the Third Quinquennium (1985–1989)." Ph.D., Rome: Pontificia Studiorum Universitas, 1994.

Lindbeck, George. *The Nature of Doctrine: Religion and Theology in a Postliberal Age*. Louisville, KY: Westminster John Knox, 1984.

Lonergan, Bernard. *Method in Theology*. New York: Herder & Herder, 1972.

Bibliography

Manwaring, Randle. *From Controversy to Co-existence: Evangelicals in the Church of England 1914-1980*. Cambridge: Cambridge University Press, 1985.

Macchia, Frank D. *Baptized in the Spirit: A Global Pentecostal Theology*. Grand Rapids: Zondervan, 2006.

———. "Baptized in the Spirit: Toward a Global Theology of Spirit Baptism." In *The Spirit in the World: Emerging Pentecostal Theologies in Global Contexts*, edited by Veli-Matti Kärkkäinen, 3–20. Grand Rapids: Eerdmans, 2009.

———. "Groans Too Deep for Words: Toward a Theology of Tongues as Initial Evidence." *Asian Journal of Pentecostal Studies* 1 (1998) 149–73.

———. "Sighs Too Deep for Words: Towards a Theology of Glossolalia." *Journal of Pentecostal Theology* 1 (October 1992) 47–73.

———. "The Struggle for Global Witness: Shifting Paradigms in Pentecostal Theology." In *The Globalization of Pentecostalism: A Religion Made to Travel*, edited by Murray Dempster, Byron Klaus, and Douglas Peterson, 8–29. Oxford: Regnum, 1999.

———. "Tongues as a Sign: Towards a Sacramental Understanding of Pentecostal Experience." *Pneuma* 15 (1993) 61–76.

MacRobert, Iain. *The Black Roots and White Racism of Early Pentecostalism in the USA*. London: MacMillan, 1988.

McDonnell, Kilian. "Classical Pentecostal/Roman Catholic Dialogue: Hopes and Possibilities." In *Perspectives on the New Pentecostalism*, edited by Russell Spittler, 246–68. Grand Rapids: Baker, 1976.

———. "The Function of Tongues in Pentecostalism." In *Roman Catholic/Pentecostal Dialogue [1977–1982]: A Study in Developing Ecumenism*, vol. 2, edited by Jerry Sandidge, 20–56. Frankfurt: Lang, 1987.

———. "Holy Spirit and Pentecostalism." *Commonweal* 89 (November 8, 1968) 198–204.

———. "Statement of the Theological Basis of the Catholic Charismatic Renewal." *Worship* 47 (1973) 610–20.

McDonnell, Kilian, editor. *Presence, Power, and Praise*. Collegeville, MN: Liturgical, 1980.

McDonnell, Kilian, and Arnold Bittlinger. *The Baptism in the Holy Spirit as an Ecumenical Problem*. Notre Dame: Charismatic Renewal Services, 1972.

McDonnell, Kilian, and George Montague. *Christian Initiation and Baptism in the Holy Spirit: Evidence from the First Eight Centuries*. Collegeville, MN: Liturgical, 1991.

McGee, Gary B. "The Calcutta Revival of 1907 and the Reformulation of Charles F. Parham's 'Bible Evidence' Doctrine." *Asian Journal of Pentecostal Studies* 6 (2003) 123–143.

———. "Early Pentecostal Hermeneutics: Tongues as Evidence in the Book of Acts." In *Initial Evidence: Historical and Biblical Perspectives on the Pentecostal Doctrine of Spirit Baptism*, edited by Gary B. McGee, 96–118. Peabody, MA: Hendrickson, 1991.

———. "'Latter Rain' Falling in the East: Early-Twentieth-Century Pentecostalism in India and the Debate over Speaking in Tongues." *Church History* 68 (1999) 648–65.

———. "More than Evangelical: The Challenge of the Evolving Theological Identity of the Assemblies of God." *Pneuma* 25 (2003) 289–300.

———. "'The New World of Realities in Which We Live:' How Speaking in Tongues Empowered Early Pentecostals." *Pneuma* 30 (2008) 108–35.

———. "Pentecostal Missiology: Moving beyond Triumphalism to Face the Issues." *Pneuma* 16 (1994) 275–281.
McGrath, Alister. "Engaging the Great Tradition: Evangelical Theology and the Role of Tradition." In *Evangelical Futures: A Conversation on Theological Method*, edited by John Stackhouse, 139–58. Grand Rapids: Baker, 2000.
———. *The Genesis of Doctrine: A Study in the Foundation of Doctrinal Criticism.* Grand Rapids: Eerdmans, 1997.
———. *Scientific Theology.* 3 Vols. Grand Rapids: Eerdmans, 2002.
McMullen, Carl. "Holding Their Tongues." *Christianity Today* 53, October 2009, 15–19.
McPherson, Aimee Semple. *Declaration of Faith.* Los Angeles: Echo Park Evangelistic Association, n.d. [1923?].
———. *The Foursquare Gospel.* Compiled by Georgia Stiffler. Los Angeles: Echo Park Evangelistic Association, 1946.
———. *The Holy Spirit.* Los Angeles: Challpin, 1931.
Menzies, Robert. *Empowered for Witness.* Sheffield, UK: Sheffield Academic Press, 1994.
———. "The Essence of Pentecostalism." *Paraclete* 26 (Summer 1992) 1–9.
Menzies, William. "The Challenges of Organization and Spirit in the Implementation of Theology in the Assemblies of God." In *Church, Identity, and Change*, edited by David Roozen and James Nieman, 97–131. Grand Rapids: Eerdmans, 2005.
Menzies, William and Robert Menzies. *Spirit and Power: Foundations of Pentecostal Experience.* Grand Rapids: Zondervan, 2000.
Miller, Donald. *Reinventing American Protestantism.* Berkley: University of California Press, 1997.
Minutes of the Annual Business Meeting for the Society for Pentecostal Studies, Pasadena, California, November 20, 1982. Fuller Seminary Archives, Pasadena, CA.
Minutes of the Constitutional Convention of the Pentecostal Fellowship of North America, Des Moines, Iowa, October 26–28, 1948. Fuller Seminary Archives, Pasadena, CA.
Minutes of the Executive Committee, National Convention and Board of Directors of Open Bible Standard Churches, 1956–1960. Open Bible National Office, Des Moines, IA.
Minutes of the General Council of the Assemblies of God, 1914–2009. Flower Pentecostal Heritage Center, Springfield, MO.
Minutes of the Open Bible Standard Churches, 1932–1945. Open Bible National Office, Des Moines, IA.
Mitchell, R. Bryant. *Heritage & Horizons: The History of Open Bible Standard Churches.* Des Moines, IA: Open Bible, 1982.
Moon, Tony. "J. H. King on Initial Evidence: Did He Change?" *Journal of Pentecostal Theology* 14 (2006) 261–86.
Murphy, Nancey. *Beyond Liberalism & Fundamentalism.* Valley Forge, PA: Trinity, 1996.
Nathan, Rich, and Ken Wilson. *Empowered Evangelicals: Bringing Together the Best of the Evangelical and Charismatic Worlds.* Ann Arbor, MI: Servant, 1995.
"National Board Statistical Report." Unpublished report obtained through email correspondence with the Secretary/Treasurer of Open Bible Churches, Teri Beyer.
"National Church Office Report." Los Angeles: Foursquare Cabinet, 2011.
National Convention Business Meeting Minutes, June 21, 2003. Open Bible National Office, Des Moines, IA.
National Council of Churches. "Trends Continue in Church Membership Growth or Decline, Reports 2011 Yearbook of American & Canadian Churches." No pages. Online: http://www.ncccusa.org/news/110210yearbook2011.html.

Bibliography

Nienkirchen, Charles. "Conflicting Visions of the Past: The Prophetic Use of History in the Early American Pentecostal-Charismatic Movements." In *Charismatic Christianity as a Global Culture*, edited by Karla Poewe, 119–33. Columbia: University of South Carolina Press, 1994.

Oliphant, M. O. W. *The Life of Edward Irving*. New York: Harper, 1862.

Open Bible Manual. Des Moines, IA: Open Bible Churches, 2009.

Parham, Charles F. *The Everlasting Gospel*. 1920. Reprint. New York: Garland, 1985.

———. *Kol Kare Bomidbar: A Voice Crying in the Wilderness*. 1902. Reprint. Baxter Springs, KS: Apostolic Faith Bible College, 1910.

Parham, Sarah E. *The Life of Charles F. Parham*. Baxter Springs, KS: Sarah E. Parham, 1930.

Pinnock, Clark. *Flame of Love: A Theology of the Holy Spirit*. Downer's Grove, IL: InterVarsity, 1996.

Plüss, Jean-Daniel. "Azusa and Other Myths: The Long and Winding Road from Experience to Stated Belief and Back Again." *Pneuma* 15 (1993) 189–201.

———. "Initial Evidence or Evident Initials? A European Point of View on a Pentecostal Distinctive." *Asian Journal of Pentecostal Studies* 1 (1998) 213–22.

Policies and Principles of the Open Bible Standard Churches, Inc. Des Moines, IA: Open Bible, 1940. Open Bible National Office, Des Moines, IA.

Poloma, Margaret. *The Assemblies of God at the Crossroads: Charisma and Institutional Dilemmas*. Knoxville: University of Tennessee Press, 1989.

———. "Charisma and Structure in the Assemblies of God: Revisiting O'Dea's Five Dilemmas." In *Church, Identity, and Change*, edited by David Roozen and James Nieman, 45–96. Grand Rapids: Eerdmans, 2005.

———. *Main Street Mystics: The Toronto Blessing and Reviving Pentecostalism*. Walnut Creek, CA: AltaMira, 2003.

———. "Toronto Blessing." In *The New International Dictionary of Pentecostal and Charismatic Movements*, edited by Stanley Burgess, 1149–52. Grand Rapids: Zondervan, 2002.

———. "The 'Toronto Blessing': Charisma, Institutionalization, and Revival." *Journal for the Scientific Study of Religion* 36 (1997) 257–71.

———. "The Toronto Blessing: A Holistic Model of Healing." *Journal for the Scientific Study of Religion* 37 (1998) 257–72.

———. "The 'Toronto Blessing' in Postmodern Society." In *The Globalization of Pentecostalism: A Religion Made to Travel*, edited by Murray Dempster, Byron Klaus, and Douglas Peterson, 363–385. Oxford: Regnum, 1999.

Poloma, Margaret, and John Green. *The Assemblies of God: Godly Love and the Revitalization of American Pentecostalism*. New York: New York University Press, 2010.

Purves, J. "The Interaction of Christology and Pneumatology in the Soteriology of Edward Irving." *Pneuma* 14 (1992) 81–90.

Quebedeaux, Richard. "Charismatic Renewal: The Origins, Development, and Significance of Neo-Pentecostalism as a Religious Movement in the United States and Great Britain, 1901–74." Ph.D. diss., University of Oxford, 1975.

———. *The New Charismatics: The Origins, Development, and Significance of Neo-Pentecostalism*. New York: Doubleday, 1976.

———. *The New Charismatics II: How a Christian Renewal Movement Became Part of the American Religious Mainstream*. San Francisco: Harper & Row, 1983.

Quesnel, Michel. "Discerning Who Builds the Church: A Catholic Response." In *Pentecostal Movements as an Ecumenical Challenge*, edited by Jürgen Moltmann and Karl-Josef Kuschel, 115–20. London: SCM, 1996.

Reed, David. "Origins and Development of the Theology of Oneness Pentecostalism in the United States." Ph.D. diss., Boston University, 1978.

Richey, Russell. "Denominations and Denominationalism: An American Morphology." In *Reimagining Denominationalism: Interpretive Essays*, edited by Robert Bruce Mullin and Russell Richey, 74–98. New York: Oxford University Press, 1994.

Risser, Paul. "79th Annual Foursquare Convention Opens in Denver, Colorado." *Foursquare News Source* 130, 10 April 2002, 1.

———. "The Year 2001 Was One of the Most Fruitful." *Fore Cast* 3, 2002, 1.

Robeck, Cecil M., Jr. "The Assemblies of God and Ecumenical Cooperation: 1925–1965." In *Pentecostalism in Context: Essays in Honor of William W. Menzies*, edited by Wonsuk Ma and Robert Menzies, 107–50. Sheffield, UK: Sheffield Academic Press, 1997.

———. *The Azusa Street Mission & Revival: The Birth of the Global Pentecostal Movement*. Nashville: Nelson, 2006.

———. "An Emerging Magisterium? The Case of the Assemblies of God." *Pneuma* 25 (2003) 212–52.

———. "Forward" In *Asian and Pentecostal: The Charismatic Face of Christianity in Asia*, edited by Allan Anderson and Edmond Tang, xi–xii. Oxford: Regnum, 2005.

———. "International Church of the Foursquare Gospel." In *The New International Dictionary of Pentecostal Charismatic Movements*, edited by Stanley M. Burgess, 793–94. Grand Rapids: Zondervan, 2002.

———. "The International Significance of Azusa Street." *Pneuma* 8 (1986) 1–4.

———. "Kilian McDonnell." In *The New International Dictionary of Pentecostal and Charismatic Movements*, edited by Stanley M. Burgess, 853. Grand Rapids: Zondervan, 2002.

———. "Making Sense of Pentecostalism in a Global Context." In *Papers of the Twenty-Eighth Annual Meeting of the Society for Pentecostal Studies*. Springfield, MO: Society for Pentecostal Studies, 1999.

———. "National Association of Evangelicals." In *The New International Dictionary of Pentecostal and Charismatic Movements*, edited by Stanley M. Burgess, 922–25. Grand Rapids: Zondervan, 2002.

———. "The Past: Historical Roots of Racial Unity and Division in American Pentecostalism." *Cyberjournal for Pentecostal/Charismatic Research* 14 (May 2005). No pages. Online: http://www.pctii.org/cyberj/cyberj14/robeck.html.

———. "Pentecostals and the Apostolic Faith: Implications for Ecumenism." *Pneuma* 9 (1987) 61–84.

———. "Pentecostals and Christian Unity: Facing the Challenge." *Pneuma* 25 (2004) 307–38.

———. "Pentecostals and Ecumenism in a Pluralistic World." In *The Globalization of Pentecostalism: A Religion Made to Travel*, edited by Murray Dempster, Byron Klaus, and Douglas Peterson, 338–62. Oxford: Regnum, 1999.

———. "Pentecostal Origins from a Global Perspective." In *All Together in One Place: Theological Papers from the Brighton Conference on World Evangelization*, edited by Harold Hunter and Peter Hocken, 166–80. Sheffield, UK: Sheffield Academic Press, 1993.

Bibliography

———. "Pentecostal World Conference." In *The New International Dictionary of Pentecostal and Charismatic Movements*, edited by Stanley M. Burgess, 971–74. Grand Rapids: Zondervan, 2002.

———. "The Social Concern of Early American Pentecostalism." In *Pentecost, Mission and Ecumenism: Essays on Intercultural Theology: Festschrift in Honour of Professor Walter J. Hollenweger*, edited by Jan A. B. Jongeneel, 97–106. Frankfurt: Lang, 1992.

———. "Taking Stock of Pentecostalism: The Personal Reflections of a Retiring Editor." *Pneuma* 15 (1993) 35–60.

———. "William J. Seymour and the 'Bible Evidence.'" In *Initial Evidence: Historical and Biblical Perspectives on the Pentecostal Doctrine of Spirit Baptism*, edited by Gary B. McGee, 72–95. Peabody, MA: Hendrickson, 1991.

Robeck, Cecil M., Jr., editor. "CH 547–847 History of Pentecostal-Charismatic Movements Syllabus." Unpublished, 2003.

Robeck, Cecil M., Jr., and Jerry Sandidge. "World Council of Churches." In *The New International Dictionary of Pentecostal and Charismatic Movements*, edited by Stanley M. Burgess, 1213–17. Grand Rapids: Zondervan, 2002.

Römer, Jürgen. *The Toronto Blessing*. ÅBO, Finland: Åbo Akademi University Press, 2002.

Roozen, David, and James Nieman. *Church, Identity and Change: Theology and Denominational Structures in Unsettled Times*. Grand Rapids, Eerdmans, 2005.

Sandidge, Jerry. *Roman Catholic / Pentecostal Dialogue (1977–1982): A Study in Developing Ecumenism*. Frankfurt: Lang, 1987.

Sarles, Ken. "An Appraisal of the Signs and Wonders Movement." *Bibliotheca Sacra* 146 (1988) 57–82.

Schrag, Martin. "The Spiritual Pilgrimage of the Reverend Benjamin Hardin Irwin." *Refleks* 7 (2008) 22–33.

Sepulveda, Juan. "Born Again: Baptism and the Spirit: A Pentecostal Perspective." In *Pentecostal Movements as an Ecumenical Challenge*, edited by Jürgen Moltmann and Karl-Josef Kuschel, 104–9. London: SCM, 1996.

———. "Future Perspectives for Latin American Pentecostalism." *International Review of Mission* 87 (1998) 189–95.

———. "Pentecostalism and the Chilean Experience." In *Pentecostals after a Century: Global Perspectives on a Movement in Transition*, edited by Allan Anderson and Walter J. Hollenweger, 111–34. Sheffield, UK: Sheffield Academic Press, 1999.

Serra, Dominic. "Baptism and Confirmation: Distinct Sacraments, One Liturgy." *Liturgical Ministry* 9 (Spring 2000) 63–71.

Seymour, William J. *The Doctrines and Discipline of the Azusa Street Apostolic Faith Mission of Los Angeles, California*. Los Angeles: Apostolic Faith Mission, 1915.

Shuman, Joel. "Toward a Cultural-Linguistic Account of the Pentecostal Doctrine of the Baptism of the Holy Spirit." *Pneuma* 19 (1997) 207–23.

Smedes, Lewis B., editor. *Ministry and the Miraculous: A Case Study at Fuller Theological Seminary*. Pasadena: Fuller Theological Seminary, 1987.

Spirit and Power: A 10-Country Survey of Pentecostals. Washington, DC: The Pew Forum on Religion & Public Life, 2006.

Spittler, Russell P. "Are Pentecostals and Charismatics Fundamentalists? A Review of American Uses of These Categories." In *Charismatic Christianity as Global*

Culture, edited by Karla Poewe, 103–16. Columbia: University of South Carolina Press, 1994.

———. "David du Plessis." In *The New International Dictionary of Pentecostal and Charismatic Movements*, edited by Stanley M. Burgess, 589–93. Grand Rapids: Zondervan, 2002.

———. "Preface." In *Perspectives on the New Pentecostalism*, edited by Russell P. Spittler, 7–10. Grand Rapids: Baker, 1976.

Stanley, Susie. "Pentecostal and Charismatic Clergy in Oregon." Paper presented at the 24th Annual Meeting of the Society for Pentecostal Studies, Wheaton, IL, 10–12 November 1994.

Stetzer, Ed. "Writing on the Wall: The Future of the Church and its Mission." *Enrichment* 13 (Spring 2008) 36–41.

Strom, C. L. "Are You Disappointed With Your Baptism?" In *Questions and Answers about the Holy Spirit*, edited by Hal Donaldson, Ken Horn, & Ann Floyd, 47–49. Springfield, MO: Pentecostal Evangel, 2001.

Stronstad, Roger. "The Biblical Precedent for Historical Precedent." *Paraclete* 27 (Summer 1993) 1–10.

———. *The Charismatic Theology of St. Luke*. Peabody, MA: Hendrickson, 1984.

———. "The Hermeneutics of Lucan Historiography." *Paraclete* 22 (Fall 1988) 5–17.

———. "Pentecostal Hermeneutics: A Review Essay of Gordon Fee's *Gospel and Spirit*." *Pneuma* 15 (1993) 215–22.

———. "Trends in Pentecostal Hermeneutics." *Paraclete* 22 (Summer 1988) 1–12.

Sutton, Matthew A. *Aimee Semple McPherson and the Resurrection of Christian America*. Cambridge: Harvard University Press, 2007.

———. "'Between the Refrigerator and the Wildfire': Aimee Semple McPherson, Pentecostalism, and the Fundamentalist-Modernist Controversy." *Church History* 72 (2003) 159–88.

Synan, Vinson. "Fifteen Years of the Society for Pentecostal Studies." Paper presented at the 15th Annual Meeting of the Society for Pentecostal Studies, Gathersburg, MD, 14–16 November 1985.

———. *The Holiness-Pentecostal Movement in the United States*. Grand Rapids: Eerdmans, 1971.

———. *The Holiness-Pentecostal Tradition: Charismatic Movements in the Twentieth Century*. 2d ed. Grand Rapids: Eerdmans, 1997.

———. "The Role of Tongues as Initial Evidence." In *Spirit and Renewal: Essays in Honor of J. Rodman Williams*, edited by Mark Wilson, 67–82. Sheffield, UK: Sheffield Academic Press, 1994.

———. *Under His Banner: History of Full Gospel Business Men's Fellowship International*. Costa Mesa, CA: Gift, 1992.

Tan, May Ling. "A Response to Frank Macchia's 'Groans Too Deep for Words: Towards a Theology of Tongues as Initial Evidence.'" *Asian Journal of Pentecostal Studies* 1 (1998) 175–83.

Taylor, G. F. *The Spirit and the Bride*. 1907. In *A Reader in Pentecostal Theology: Voices from the First Generation*, edited by Douglas Jacobsen, 58–69. Bloomington, IN: Indiana University Press, 2006.

Thomas, John Christopher. "Pentecostal Theology in the Twenty-First Century." *Pneuma* 20 (1998) 3–19.

Torrance, Thomas F. *Theological Science*. Oxford: Oxford University Press, 1969.

Bibliography

Tomlinson, A. J. *The Last Great Conflict*. Cleveland, TN: Rodgers, 1913.

Underwood, B. E. *Christ—God's Love Gift: Selected Writings of Joseph Hillary King*, Vol. 1. Franklin Springs, GA: Advocate Press, 1969.

Van Cleave, Nathaniel. *Foursquare Sunday School Lessons: The Declaration of Faith*. Los Angeles: ICFG, 1949.

———. *The Vine and the Branches*. Los Angeles: International Church of the Foursquare Gospel, 1992.

van der Ven, Johannes. *Practical Theology: An Empirical Approach*. Translated by Barbara Schultz. Leuven: Peeters, 1998.

———. "An Empirical or a Normative Approach to Practical-Theological Research? A False Dilemma." *Journal of Empirical Theology* 15 (2002) 5–33.

van de Walle, Bernie. *The Heart of the Gospel: A. B. Simpson, the Fourfold Gospel, and Late Nineteenth-Century Evangelical Theology*. Eugene, OR: Pickwick, 2009.

Vanhoozer, Kevin J. *The Drama of Doctrine: A Canonical-Linguistic Approach to Christian Theology*. Louisville, KY: Westminster John Knox, 2005.

Visser't Hooft, W. A. *The Genesis and Formation of the World Council of Churches*. Geneva: World Council of Churches, 1982.

Wacker, Grant A. *Heaven Below: Early Pentecostals and American Culture*. Cambridge: Harvard University Press, 2001.

———. "Playing for Keeps: The Primitivist Impulse in Early Pentecostalism." In *The American Quest for the Primitive Church*, edited by Richard Hughes, 196–219. Urbana, IL: University of Illinois Press, 1988.

———. "Wimber and Wonders: What About Today?" *The Reformed Journal* 37 (April 1987) 16–19.

Wagner, C. Peter. "Healing Without Hassle." *Leadership* 6 (Spring 1985) 114–15.

———. "A Third Wave?" *Pastoral Renewal* 8 (July-August 1983) 1–5.

———. "Third Wave." In *The New International Dictionary of Pentecostal and Charismatic Movements*, edited by Stanley M. Burgess, 1141. Grand Rapids: Zondervan, 2002.

Wainwright, Geoffrey. "Ecumenical Dimensions of Lindbeck's 'Nature of Doctrine.'" *Modern Theology* 4 (1988) 121–32.

Waldvogel [Blumhofer], Edith. "The 'Overcoming Life': A Study in the Reformed Evangelical Origins of Pentecostalism." Ph.D. diss., Harvard University, 1977.

Wakefield, Gavin. *Alexander Boddy: Pentecostal Anglican Pioneer*. Milton Keynes, UK: Paternoster, 2007.

———. *The First Pentecostal Anglican: The Life and Legacy of Alexander Boddy*. Cambridge: Grove, 2001.

Walsh, Tim. "'Signs and Wonders that Lie': Unlikely Polemical Outbursts against the Early Pentecostal Movement in Britain." In *Signs, Wonders, Miracles: Representations of Divine Power in the Life of the Church*, edited by Kate Cooper and Jeremy Gregory, 410–22. Woodbridge, UK: Boydell, 2005.

Warner, Wayne. "Pentecostal Fellowship of North America." In *The New International Dictionary of Pentecostal and Charismatic Movements*, edited by Stanley M. Burgess, 968–69. Grand Rapids: Zondervan, 2002.

Warrington, Keith. "Experience: The *sina qua non* of Pentecostalism." Paper presented at the 36th Annual Meeting of the Society for Pentecostal Studies, Cleveland, TN, 8–10 March 2007.

———. *Pentecostal Theology: A Theology of Encounter*. London: T. & T. Clark, 2008.

We Believe. Des Moines, IA: Open Bible Churches, 2003.
Wesley, John. "A Plain Account of Christian Perfection." In *The Works of John Wesley*, vol. 12, edited by Thomas Jackson, 366–446. 1872. Reprint. Grand Rapids: Baker, 2002.
White, Allen. "Pentecost with Signs: The Pneumatology of European Pentecostalism as Recorded in *Confidence* Magazine." *Assemblies of God Heritage* 12 (Fall 1992) 12–15.
Williams, Rodman. "Presidential Address: A Pentecostal Theology." Paper presented at the 15th Annual Meeting of the Society for Pentecostal Studies, Gaithersburg, MD, 14–16 November 1985.
———. *Renewal Theology*. Grand Rapids: Academie, 1990.
Wilson, Everett. "They Crossed the Red Sea Didn't They? Critical History and Pentecostal Beginnings." *The Globalization of Pentecostalism: A Religion Made to Travel*, edited by Murray Dempster, Byron Klaus, and Douglas Peterson, 85–115. Oxford: Regnum, 1999.
Wright, N. T. "How Can the Bible be Authoritative?" *Vox Evangelica* 21 (1991) 9–32.
Yearbook: Report of the Twenty-First Annual Foursquare Convention and War Council. Los Angeles: ICFG, 1943.
Yong, Amos. "Review of *The Genesis of Doctrine* by Alister McGrath." *Pneuma* 21 (1999) 359–62.
———. *The Spirit Poured Out on All Flesh: Pentecostalism and the Possibility of Global Theology*. Grand Rapids: Baker Academic, 2005.
———. *Spirit-Word-Community: Theological Hermeneutics in Trinitarian Perspective*. 2002. Reprint. Eugene, OR: Wipf and Stock, 2006.
———. "'Tongues of Fire' in the Pentecostal Imagination: The Truth of Glossolalia in Light of R. C. Neville's Theory of Religious Symbolism." *Journal of Pentecostal Theology* 12 (1998) 39–65.
Yun, Koo Dong. *Baptism in the Holy Spirit: An Ecumenical Theology of Spirit Baptism*. Lanham, MD: University Press of America, 2003.